THE WORKS

of

JOHN HALES

Volumes 1 & 2

AMS PRESS
NEW YORK

THE
WORKS
OF THE
EVER MEMORABLE
Mr. JOHN HALES
OF
EATON.

NOW FIRST COLLECTED TOGETHER,

IN THREE VOLUMES.

The wifdom that is from above, is firft pure, then peaceable, gentle, and eafy to be intreated, full of mercy and good fruits, without partiality, and without hypocrify, and the fruit of righteoufnefs is fown in peace of them that make peace. James iii. 17, 18.

VOL. I.

GLASGOW:

PRINTED BY ROBERT AND ANDREW FOULIS.

SOLD BY J. TONSON, A. MILLAR, AND D. WILSON, LONDON; J. BALFOUR, EDINBURGH; AND R. AND A. FOULIS, GLASGOW.
M.DCC.LXV.

Reprinted fromt he edition of 1765, Glasgow
First AMS EDITION published 1971
Manufactured in the United States of America

International Standard Book Number
Complete Set 0-404-03050-5
Volume One 0-404-03051-3
Volume Two 0-404-03052-1

Library of Congress Number: 77-131037

AMS PRESS INC.
NEW YORK, N. Y. 10003

TO THE

RIGHT REVEREND

WILLIAM,

BISHOP OF GLOUCESTER,

THIS EDITION

OF THE

WORKS

OF

MR. JOHN HALES,

UNDERTAKEN WITH HIS APPROBATION,

IS INSCRIBED

BY

THE EDITOR.

THE
PREFACE.

A Complete edition of the works of Mr. JOHN HALES of Eaton, is now for the firſt time offered to the public. Hitherto his pieces have been ſeparately printed, at various times, and in volumes of different ſize : ſome of them are become exceedingly rare.

This, it is hoped, will be found preferable, on many accounts, to the former editions : the quotations, from a multitude of authors, are removed from the text, and placed in notes ; the original paſſages, ſo far as they can be diſcovered, are pointed out ; and ſuch of them as the author had quoted in their original language, are now tranſlated.

Some few obſolete words have been occaſionally altered for others now in more general uſe : the correƈtions in ſpelling and punƈtuation are too minute to require any apology : but ſome apology may be neceſſary for the ſuppreſſion of two paſſages in the ſermons of Hales.

The author, in enforcing his arguments
againft intemperance, quotes the concluding words of the Sympofium of Xenophon;
this, as improper in a popular difcourfe, is
omitted. For a like reafon another fhort
fentence is omitted, where the author, according to the manner of his times, fpeaks
of the Divinity in a ftrain which would
now be thought too familiar.

It remains only to obferve, that the author, in his citations from fcripture, fometimes follows the old verfion, and fometimes fpeaks from memory. The editor
has not thought fit to make any alteration
in either of thofe particulars, but has marked the places where there appears any material variation from the verfion generally
ufed.

It would be high prefumption in the
editor to endeavour to juftify every pofition which is contained in thefe volumes. He
has neither inclination nor right to fet up
the opinions of any fallible man as a perfect ftandard of juft opinions;—in the writings of this worthy perfon, he doubts not,
there will be found crude and erroneous,

and, perhaps, inconfiftent notions, together with fome marks of human paffions and prejudice.

That the author, with all his errors, was efteemed a good man by thofe who knew him, and an able writer by thofe who could judge of his works, is manifeft from the *Teftimonies* fubjoined. They who are acquainted with the literary and political hiftory of England, will perceive, that the leading men of all parties, however different and difcordant, have, with a wonderful unanimity, concurred in praife of the virtues and the abilities of the *ever memorable Mr. John Hales of Eaton.*

TESTIMONIES

CONCERNING

Mr. JOHN HALES.

EARL of CLARENDON.

Mr. JOHN HALES had been Greek profeſſor in the univerſity of Oxford; and had born the greateſt part of the labour of that excellent edition and impreſſion of St. Chryſoſtom's works, ſet out by Sir Harry Savile; who was then warden of Merton-college, when the other was fellow of that houſe. He was chaplain in the houſe with Sir Dudley Carleton, ambaſſador at the Hague in Holland, at the time when the ſynod of Dort was held, and ſo had liberty to be preſent at the conſultations in that aſſembly; and hath left the beſt memorial behind him, of the ignorance, and paſſion, and animoſity, and injuſtice of that convention; of which he often made very pleaſant relations; though, at that time, it received too much countenance from England. Being a perſon of the greateſt eminency for learning, and other abilities, from which he might have promifed himfelf any preferment in the church, he withdrew himfelf from all purfuits of that kind, into a private fellowfhip in the college of Eaton, where his friend Sir Harry Savile was provoft; where he lived amongft his books, and the moft feparated from the world of any man then living; though he was not in the leaft degree inclined to melancholy, but, on the contrary, of a very open and pleafant converfation; and therefore was very well pleafed with the refort of his friends to him, who were fuch as he had chofen, and in whofe company he delighted, and for whofe fake he would fometimes, once in a year, refort to London, only to enjoy their chearful converfation.

He would never take any cure of fouls; and was fo great a contemner of money, that he was wont to fay, That his fellowfhip, and the burfar's place (which, for the good of the college, he held many years) was worth to him fifty pounds a year more than he could fpend; and yet, befides his being very charitable to all poor people, even to liberality, he had made a greater and better collection of books, than were to be found in any other private library that I have seen; as he had sure read more, and carried more about him, in his excellent memory, than any man I ever knew; my Lord Falkland only excepted, who I think sided him. He had, whether from his natural temper and constitution, or from his long retirement from all crowds, or from his profound judgment, and discerning spirit, contracted some opinions, which were not received, nor by him published, except in private discourses; and then rather upon occasion of dispute, than of positive opinion; and he would often say, his opinions he was sure did him no harm, but he was far from being confident, that they might not do others harm, who entertained them, and might entertain other results from them than he did; and therefore he was very reserved in communicating what he thought himself in those points, in which he differed from what was received.

Nothing troubled him more than the

brawls which were grown from religion;
and he therefore exceedingly detested the
tyranny of the church of Rome, more for
their impofing uncharitably upon the confciences of other men, than for the errors
in their own opinions; and would often
fay, that he would renounce the religion
of the church of England to-morrow, if it
obliged him to believe that any other Chriftians fhould be damned; and that no body
would conclude another man to be damned,
who did not wifh him fo. No man more
ftrict and fevere to himfelf; to other men
fo charitable as to their opinions, that he
thought that other men were more in fault
for their carriage towards them, than the
men themfelves were, who erred; and he
thought that pride, and paffion, more than
confcience, were the caufe of all feparation from each others communion; and he
frequently faid, that that only kept the
world from agreeing upon fuch a liturgy,
as might bring them into one communion;
all doctrinal points upon which men differed in their opinions being to have no
place in any liturgy. Upon an occafional

discourse with a friend, of the frequent,
and uncharitable reproaches of heretic and
schismatic, too lightly thrown at each o-
ther, amongst men who differ in their judgment, he writ a little discourse of Schism,
contained in less than two sheets of paper;
which being transmitted from friend to
friend in writing, was, at last, without any
malice, brought to the view of the Archbishop of Canterbury, Dr. Laud, who was
a very rigid surveyer of all things which
never so little bordered upon schism; and
thought the church could not be too vigi-
lant against, and jealous of such incursions.

He sent for Mr. Hales, whom, when
they had both lived in the university of
Oxford, he had known well, and told him,
that he had in truth believed him to be
long since dead; and chid him very kindly
for having never come to him, having been
of his old acquaintance; then asked him,
whether he had lately writ a short discourse
of Schism, and whether he was of that o-
pinion which that discourse implied. He
told him, that he had, for the satisfaction
of a private friend (who was not of his

mind) a year or two before, writ such a small tract, without any imagination that it would be communicated; and that he believed it did not contain any thing that was not agreeable to the judgment of the primitive fathers; upon which the Archbishop debated with him upon some expressions of Irenaeus, and the most antient fathers; and concluded with saying, that the time was very apt to set new doctrines on foot, of which the wits of the age were too susceptible; and that there could not be too much care taken to preserve the peace and unity of the church; and from thence asked him of his condition, and whether he wanted any thing, and the other answering that he had enough, and wanted, or desired no addition, so dismissed him with great courtesy; and shortly after sent for him again, when there was a prebendary of Windsor fallen, and told him, the King had given him the preferment, because it lay so convenient to his fellowship of Eaton; (which, though indeed the most convenient preferment that could be thought of for him) the Archbishop could

not, without great difficulty, perſuade him
to accept; and he did accept it rather to
pleaſe him than himſelf; becauſe he really
believed he had enough before:——*Life
of the Earl of Clarendon. vol.* i. *p.* 27, 28.

LORD SAY and SEAL.

I SHALL ſay of this word *ſeparatiſt*, as
that learned man Mr. Hales of Eaton ſaith
in a little manuſcript of his which I have
ſeen, ' That where it may be rightly fix-
' ed, and deſervedly charged, it is certain-
' ly a great offence; but in common uſe
' now among us, it is no other than a theo-
' logical ſcarecrow.'——*Speech in the houſe
of Lords. Troubles and Trial of Archbiſhop Laud. p.* 494, 495.

PEARSON, BISHOP of CHESTER

I SHALL ſpeak no more than my own
long experience, intimate acquaintance,
and high veneration, grounded upon both,
ſhall freely and ſincerely prompt me to.
Mr. John Hales, ſometime Greek profeſ-

for of the univerſity of Oxford, long fellow of Eaton-college, and, at laſt, alſo prebendary of Windſor, was a man, I think,
of as great a ſharpneſs, quickneſs, and ſub-
tility of wit, as ever this or perhaps any
nation bred. His induſtry did ſtrive, if it
were poſſible, to equal the largeneſs of his
capacity, whereby he became as great a
maſter of polite, various, and univerſal
learning, as ever yet converſed with books.
Proportionate to his reading was his meditation, which furniſhed him with a judgment beyond the vulgar reach of man, built
upon unordinary notions, raiſed out of
ſtrange obſervations, and comprehenſive
thoughts within himſelf. So that he really was a moſt prodigious example of an a-
cute and piercing wit, of a vaſt and illimited knowledge, of a ſevere and profound
judgment.

Although this may ſeem, as in itſelf it
truly is, a grand elogium; yet I cannot e-
ſteem him leſs in any thing which belongs
to a good man, than in thoſe intellectual
perfections: and had he never underſtood
a letter, he had other ornaments ſufficient

to indear him. For he was of a nature (as we ordinarily speak) so kind, so sweet, so courting all mankind, of an affability so prompt, so ready to receive all conditions of men, that I conceive it near as easy a task for any one to become so knowing, as so obliging.

As a Christian, none more ever acquainted with the nature of the gospel, because none more studious of the knowledge of it, or more curious in the search, which being strengthened by those great advantages before-mentioned, could not prove otherwise than highly effectual. He took, indeed, to himself a liberty of judging, not of others, but for himself; and if ever any man might be allowed in these matters to judge, it was he, who had so long, so much, so advantageously considered; and which is more, never could be said to have had the least worldly design in his determinations. He was not only most truly and strictly just in his secular transactions, most exemplary meek and humble, notwithstanding his perfections, but beyond all example charitable, giving unto all, preserving nothing

b

but his books, to continue his learning and himſelf.

This teſtimony may be truly given of his perſon, and nothing in it liable to the leaſt exception, but this alone, that it comes far ſhort of him. Which intimation I conceive more neceſſary for ſuch as knew him not, than all which hath been ſaid.—*Preface to the Golden Remains of Mr. John Hales.*

Dr. H E Y L I N.

H A L E S of Eaton, a man of infinite reading, and no leſs ingenuity, free of diſcourſe, and as communicative of his knowledge as the celeſtial bodies of their light and influences. —— *Life of Archbiſhop Laud. p.* 361.

A N D R E W M A R V E L.

A MOST learned divine, and one of the church of England, and moſt remarkable for his ſufferings in the late times, and his Chriſtian patience under them. And I reckon it not one of the leaſt ignominies of that age, that ſo eminent a perſon ſhould have been, by the iniquity of the times, reduced to those neceffities under which he lived, as I account it no fmall honour to have grown up into fome part of his acquaintance, and converfed a while with the living remains of one of the cleareft heads and beft prepared breafts in Chriftendom. *The Rehearfal tranfpofed. p.* 175.

ANTHONY A' WOOD.

THIS moft incomparable perfon, whom I may juftly ftile a walking library.—*Athen. Oxon. vol.* xi. *col.* 124.

STILLINGFLEET, BISHOP of WORCESTER.

A VERY learned and judicious divine. *Irenicum. p.* 108.   To this I fhall fubjoin the judgment of as learned and judicious a divine as moft our nation hath bred, in his excellent, though little, tract concerning Schifm; 'In thefe fchifms,' faith he, 'which 'concern fact,' &c. Thus far that excellent perfon, whofe words I have taken the pains to tranfcribe, becaufe of that great wifdom, judgment, and moderation contained in them; and the feafonableness of his counfel and advice to the prefent pofture of affairs among us. *Irenicum. p.* 120, 121. That incomparable man, Mr. Hales, in his often cited tract of Schifm, whofe words are thefe; ' But that other head of ' epifcopal ambition,' &c. Thus that grave and wife perfon, whofe words favour of a more than ordinary tincture of a true fpirit of Chriftianity, that fcorns to make religion a footftool to pride and ambition.— *Irenicum. p.* 395, 396.

HOADLEY, BISHOP of WINCHESTER.

THE ever memorable Mr. Hales, who, if he ever defpifed any of the antient writing of the fathers, certainly did it not out of ignorance, but out of knowledge; whofe uncommon learning will, I hope, fet him above difdain; and whofe more uncommon happinefs it was to have a judgment equal to his great reading, and an heart freely to make ufe of it.— *Anfwer to the Dean of Worcefter's Sermon. p.* 98.

A

PARAPHRASE

ON THE

TWELFTH CHAPTER

OF

St. MATTHEW'S GOSPEL.

A

A
PARAPHRASE

ON THE

TWELFTH CHAPTER

OF

St. MATTHEW'S GOSPEL.

SCHOLAR.

I THANK you for the pains you have taken in facilitating to my underſtanding the ſcope and purpoſe of the eleventh of St. Matthew: if I might not be too troubleſome to you, I would alſo deſire you to take the like pains with me in the twelfth.

MASTER. I ſhall, with all my heart; provided that you will make your objections, as they riſe within you; for peradventure, I may think you underſtand that which you do not, and not underſtand that which you do, and ſo loſe my labour.

S. I ſhall obey you readily; and therefore to begin with the beginning of the chapter; I pray, Sir, how is it ſaid, 1. That 'at that time Jeſus 'went through the corn, with his diſciples;' when in the very next chapter before, it is ſaid, ' That ' he ſent all his diſciples away from him?'

M. By thefe words, ' at that time,' is not meant the very next immediate inftant of time to that, when he fpake the laft words going before; but fuch a convenient portion of time, wherein the twelve difciples might have gone about thofe parts, whereunto they were fent, and returned back again. So St. Matthew having fpoken newly of Chrift's dwelling in Nazareth, when he was a child of about two years old, immediately fub- joins; ' In thofe days came John the Baptift;' iii. 5. as if John had come within fome few days after his coming into Nazareth; when we know there paffed eight and twenty years between.

S. I believe it as you fay, and therefore fhall pafs to that which doth more trouble me; and that is, What that was, which the difciples did, ' which was not lawful on the Sabbath-day.'

M. How come you to be troubled at that? Is it not faid in plain terms, ' They plucked the ' ears of corn, and did eat them?' Why fhould not you think that this was their fault?

S. I fhall tell you why: to my thinking, there are three things faid; 1. ' That they went through ' the corn. 2. That they plucked the ears. ' 3. That they eat them.' Now whether all thefe, or one of thefe, was their fault, I cannot tell; and I fhall tell you the reafon of my doubt.

Firft, It is true that their very walking might have been their fault, becaufe it was not lawful on the Sabbath to walk above the fpace of two thousand cubits, and we not know how far Christ and the disciples might have come that day: but yet methinks, if that had been it, they should have reproved Christ as well as his disciples, because it is very likely they walked the one as much and as far as the other.

Secondly, It is true, that their plucking the ears of corn might have been their fault, but yet methinks it should not, in regard the law is so clear, in Deut. xxiii. 25. ' When thou comest into the ' standing corn of thy neighbour, then thou mayst ' pluck the ears with thine hand, but thou shalt ' not move a sickle unto thy neighbour's standing ' corn.' And truly why that which is so plainly lawful at another time, should be unlawful on the Sabbath (being it is so far from being any kind of labour or servile work) I cannot imagine.

Thirdly, It is true, that they did eat them; and I cannot see what fault there is in that, unless you can shew me.

M. And peradventure I shall shew you more in that than you thought on. It is true that the general consent of expositors runs on their plucking the ears upon the Sabbath-day, as being the thing condemned by the Pharisees for an unlawful thing: but I think they would be much troubled to prove it. The custom and manner of the Jews (especially since the times of the Maccabees) being to allow acts of greater labour and pain, than the plucking of an ear, namely, waging war againſt their enemies, the travelling of carriers and merchants, with ſuch others, even on the Sabbath-day. I ſhould rather incline to think, that their fault was eating; eſpecially if that be true, which the very Heathen poets tax and ſcoff them ſo with; namely, their Sabbath-faſts. For if all things be well conſidered, I believe there will more be ſaid for this, than for the other crime. And if a man will go no further than that anſwer which our Saviour makes for them, he ſhall find ground enough to be of this opinion. For, if the pretended fault had been working or labouring, our Saviour Chriſt might have eaſily laid his anſwer upon Joſhua, or upon many others, who did greater work than this upon the Sabbath. But laying it as he doth upon David, and upon his eating that which was forbidden; he ſeems to anſwer one unlawful eating with another, when neceſſity was a ſufficient diſpenſation for both. I do not oblige you to believe this as a poſitive truth, but only tell you that as much may be ſaid for the one as the other; but if you would be ſure to know what their fault was, you had beſt put them both together, and you will not miſs.

S. I thank you for this light; I wiſh you could give me as good in my next objection.

M. I ſhall do my beſt; what is that I pray?

S. Our Saviour ſaith, in the third verſe of this chapter, that ' David did eat of the ſhew-bread, ' and they that were with him;' and the Holy Ghoſt

faith, 1 Sam. xxi. 1. where this history is recorded, That there was no man with him: for it is
said there, that ' Ahimelech the priest was afraid
' at the meeting of David, and said unto him,
' Why art thou alone, and why is no man with
' thee?' How shall I reconcile this contradiction
to my thinking?

M. The truth is, the words of our Saviour in
St. Matthew, are too plain and evident, to admit
of any other construction, but that there were
some other men with David; and if they could
admit of it, yet St. Mark would put all out of
doubt, for he saith expresly, ' that David did eat
' the shew-bread, and gave it to them that were
' with him,' Mark ii. 26. And therefore, when
the priest saith, that there was no man with him,
in Samuel, it is best to understand that, of no man
in sight; because, peradventure, David might have
caused them to withdraw for the present, till he
had got relief from the priest, both for himself
and them. And this I conceive the best satisfaction unto that doubt.

S. I think it not improbable; but before I
leave this story of David, I pray tell me how it
comes to pass that our Saviour saith, ' David en-
' tred into the house of God,' in ver. 4. of this
chapter, when as yet the house of God was not
built, (i. e.) when as yet there was no temple.

M. It was well objected, and the answer to be
given is this; that our Saviour calls that place

A 4

where the tabernacle then was, ' the houſe of ' God,' which afterwards became the proper appellation of the temple.

S. It is very likely: now, if you pleaſe, let us paſs from this anſwer concerning David, to that concerning the prieſts, in the 5th verſe; where Chriſt ſaith ' That the prieſts on the Sabbath-day ' profane the Sabbath, and are blameleſs : ' What doth he mean by that ?

M. In thoſe words, our Saviour uſeth another argument, in behalf of his diſciples ; which they call an argument from the leſs to the greater; to juſtify their plucking and their eating on the Sabbath-day. Amongſt the Jews, the law of the Sabbath was ever ſo to be interpreted, as that it hindered not the works of the temple; and therefore it was a kind of rule in the Jewiſh law, that in the temple there was no Sabbath. From this ſubmiſſion of the law of the Sabbath to the works of the temple, our Saviour argueth to that which is greater than it, the works of a prophet, who was above a prieſt. His anſwer is in brief this : the prieſts, by their work in the temple upon the Sabbath, were not thought to profane the Sabbath ; and therefore there is leſs reaſon that my diſciples, who are prophets, ſhould be thought to profane it, in doing of that which is a leſs work than theirs. And that this is the ſcope of his reply, will appear by that which follows, when he ſaith, ' That in this place, there is one greater

' than the temple,' in the 6th verse: for, the truth is, every prophet was greater than the temple, that is, he was obliged in no case to the laws and customs of the temple, but might sacrifice out of it, when he pleased, as appears in the practice of Elijah. And whereas it may be objected, that the priestly function, on the Sabbath, could not be performed without the labour of offering, but the prophetical function of the disciples might be performed on the Sabbath without plucking ears and eating: the answer is, that both our Saviour and his disciples were so intent upon their prophetical employment, that, as elsewhere, ' They forgat to take bread,' Matth. xvi. 5. so here, they either forgat, or had no time for the provision of victuals before the Sabbath, whereon to feed on the Sabbath.

S. I apprehend your meaning, and desire you to make the force of Christ's third argument as evident unto me, which follows in the 7th verse; where he saith, ' But if ye had known what this ' meaneth, I will have mercy and not sacrifice, ye ' would not have condemned the guiltless.'

M. His meaning is no more but this, That when two laws seem to clash so against one another, that both cannot be kept; the better is to be observed, and the worse omitted. The law which willeth us ' to do good to all men,' and to further them in the means of their salvation, which to a Christian is a law moral, never to be omitted;

is better than the law which willeth us 'not to
' work or eat upon the Sabbath,' which is only a
law ritual. Chrift could not intend to teach, and
the difciples intend to prepare and fit the minds of
the people to be taught, and withal intend the
preparing of fuch things, as were requifite to the
ftrict obfervation of the Sabbath; and therefore
in equity, the law of the Sabbath ought to give
place to the law of inftructing the world in the
ways of happinefs, and not to have juftled with it.

S. I conceive this argument; but yet, methinks, there follows fomewhat like a reafon,
which I do not yet conceive, in the next verfe ;
' For the Son of man is Lord even of the Sab-
' bath.' Pray fhew me what the meaning is of
that ?

M. They that by ' the Son of man' here underftand Chrift, or the Meffias, do miftake; for
in that acceptation of the words, the reafon doth
not hold: for if Chrift had meant only, that he,
as the Meffias, was Lord of the Sabbath, and fo
could abrogate it at his pleafure, then what needed all the three other arguments that went before? By ' the Son of man' therefore is to be underftood every common ordinary man, as appears
moft evidently by that of St. Mark ii. 27. ' The
' Sabbath was made for man, and not man for the
' Sabbath.' Befides, at this time, Chrift neither
had preached, nor would have others to preach
that he was the Meffiah: and a good while after

this, as you may see in Matth. xvi. 20. ' Then
' charged he his difciples that they fhould tell no
' man that he was Jefus the Chrift.' The fenfe
therefore of the words is this; That which is ordained for another thing, ought to give place to
that thing for which it is ordained: but the Sabbath was ordained for man, every man; therefore it ought to give place unto him: namely,
when a thing fo nearly concerning man as his falvation fteppeth in between. For to be ' Lord of
' the Sabbath' is to difpofe and order the Sabbath unto his own ufe, and to have a right fo to
order and difpofe it.

S. I thank you for this pains; and becaufe I
have put you to fo much already, I fhall trouble
you with nothing concerning the next ftory of the
man which had the withered hand, becaufe I
think I do well enough underftand it: only let
me defire you to give me your opinion, why, when
our Saviour Chrift had healed him and divers o-
ther men of their difeafes, it is added in the 16th
verfe of this chapter, ' And he charged them, that
' they fhould not make him known.'

M. Truly, that which was the caufe of his fe-
cefs, or his withdrawing himfelf from them, in
the verfe before, may very well be conceived tho
caufe alfo of this enjoined filence; namely, that
he might be fafer from all violence and force:
but they which fay, that he did it out of charity
to thofe Pharifees who did feek his life, fay not

amifs; as Origen reports of Ariftotle, that he
withdrew himfelf from Athens, not for his own
fake, but for the Athenians fake, left he fhould
give them an occafion of committing another murder, after the murder of Socrates. Hitherto, as
yet, this zeal and endeavours of the Pharifees to
maintain the traditions of their elders, and the religion of their fathers, might feem fomewhat ex-
cufable; and therefore Chrift, adding miracle to
miracle, did wait for their repentance and amendment; in the mean time preventing them by e-
fcapes, and concealing of himfelf, from doing him
any violence or mifchief, till fuch time as that, refifting the light and teftimony of their own confcience (as fome of them did very fhortly after,
as we fhall fee anon) they had more defervedly
drawn upon themfelves the guilt of that innocent
blood, which afterwards fell upon their heads. So
that when Chrift charged them, that they fhould
not make him known, he meant only, that they
fhould not difcover where he was, that fo with the
more filence, and lefs oppofition, he might do the
bufinefs of his Father. And this fenfe is agreeable
to that which follows out of the prophet Ifaiah, in
the 17th, 18th, 19th, 20th, and 21ft verfes.

S. I take it to be fo indeed; but in thefe
words out of Ifaiah, there is fomewhat which does
much trouble me how to underftand; and that is
the latter part of the 20th verfe, where it is faid,
‘ Till he fend forth judgment unto victory.’ Pray

what do you take to be the meaning of thofe words?

M. I fhall run through the whole words of the prophet, and by that you will better underftand that part. Thefe words of the prophet Ifaiah are produced by St. Matthew, for a confirmation of that meeknefs, humility, quietnefs, and filence, with which the great bufinefs of our falvation was to be difpatched: for by thefe words ' I will ' put my fpirit on him ' is underftood the fpirit of meeknefs, gentlenefs, and humility, which was emblemed in the dove, when it came upon him; and by thofe words ' and he fhall fhew judgment unto the Gentiles' is underftood the preaching of the Chriftian law; and therefore if you mark it, in the xliid of Ifaiah, and the 4th verfe, it is ad- ded as an explication of the word ' judgment' go- ing before; ' and the ifles fhall wait for his law.' When he comes to preach this law, or to fhew forth this judgment, faith the prophet, ' he fhall ' not ftrive nor cry;' that is, he fhall difcover no fign of anger or difcompofure in his mind: ' nei- ' ther fhall any man hear his voice in the ftreets,' faith the prophet; that is, he fhall caufe no tu- mult or popular hubbub, he fhall not expofe the vices of men to the knowledge and cenfure of the world, of whom he hath but the leaft hope that they will amend. ' A bruifed reed fhall he not break,' faith the prophet; that is, the mind which is afflicted, he fhall not afflict more: ' And the

'smoaking flax shall he not quench;' that is,
where he does but see a little smoke, he will look
for some fire; he will so comply with the weak-
nesses and infirmities of all mankind, that he will
not be out of hope to cherish them up into virtues. And all this he will do, saith the prophet,
'Till he send out judgment unto victory;' of
which words, whatsoever the sense or meaning be,
this is plain, that they contain the success or e-
vent of that meekness, gentleness, and quietness
which went before. Now, taking it for granted,
that there is nothing left out in these words, as
St. Jerom does suspect, I can imagine but two
senses that can be put upon them; and those two
senses arise out of the two several acceptations of
the word 'judgment.' For (1.) If by 'judgment' in
this place be meant the same which was meant
by 'judgment' in the 18th verse going before, then
the sense of the words is this; He shall preach
the Christian law with all meekness and mildness,
maugre all the opposition and malice of those that
do oppugn it, till that law have prevailed, or gotten the victory; that is, till the greatest part of
all the world embrace it: and this sense is no improper sense, if we look no further. But then,
(2.) If by 'judgment' be meant the disceptation or
discussion of a cause (in which sense it is often
taken in the scriptures) then the meaning of the
words is this; He shall use so much meekness and
gentleness in working upon the minds of all men

in the world, that let any man fit in judgment
upon that which he hath done; he shall carry the
cause, or bear away the victory. To this purpose faith the psalmist of God, that ' he is clear
' when he is judged,' Psal. li. 6. And in this sense
God faith of himself, ' O ye men of Judah! judge
' ye, I pray you, between my vineyard and me;'
Isa. v. 3. And in this judgment Christ got the
victory; when with all patience and long-suffe-
rance, with all gentleness and meekness, he endured the perverse and crooked dispositions of the
people of the Jews, and spared no time or labour
to reform them, if they would have hearkned unto him.

S. Sir, I confess there is much reason in what
you say; but, methinks, it seems a little strained
sense to be put upon those words, as you read
them, ' Till he shall send forth judgment:' for,
according to your sense, we should read them
thus, at least, ' Till he shall carry away the judg-
' ment with victory, or to victory.'

M. You have judged very right, and so indeed
should we read them: for the word ἐκϐάλλειν,
which we render ' shall send forth,' is of the same
signification with ἐκφέρειν, which doth signify ' to
' carry away.' But you must bear with more faults
in the translation of your Testament than this;
and I hope you will bear with me, if I tell you
plainly of them when I meet with them.

S. I beseech you do; for though I have a very

great opinion of those' men who did translate the Testament, yet I would be loth to be a loser by my reverence. But if you' please, I will proceed in framing my objections.

M. You shall not need, for I foresee whither you are driving, even towards the great scruple that affrights the world, the sin against the Holy Ghost; of which there is mention in this chapter, upon the occasion of Christ's healing of the blind and dumb man possessed of the devil, in the 22d verse of this chapter.

S. I was indeed; and therefore, if you please, let us come unto that story.

M. With all my heart: and, first, I must let you know, that so soon as the Pharisees saw that great miracle which Christ had done, they said, ' That he casteth out devils by Beelzebub, the ' prince of the devils,' in the 24th verse of this chapter. And truly this was no unusual practice amongst the sorcerers and magicians, as is evident by many of the ancient poets, when they could not prevail any other way, to use the help of the great and chiefest devil (whose name they would threaten him to publish, if he did not help them) to expel or cast out other less devils that possessed men. In Jamblichus there is mention of that form, in which they threatened him; and Porphyry says, that his name was Serapis. But our Saviour sufficiently refuted that calumny several ways: 1st, By a common and known axiom a-

mongft themfelves,' Every kingdom divided againft
' itfelf, is brought to defolation : and every city
' or houfe divided againft itfelf, fhall not ftand.'
and the meaning thereof is this, That the devils are
wife, there is no queftion ; but they that are wife,
will rather feek to eftablifh themfelves and their
own power, which is done by concord and agreement, than to diftract and diflocate it, which is
done by faction and divifion : therefore it is not
likely that the devils will fo differ and difagree,
as the one to expel the other, as they would perfuade the world. 2ly, By retortion, in thefe
words ; ' If I by Beelzebub do caft out devils, by
' whom do your children caft them out ?' ver. 27.
And the force of Chrift's argument is this : In a
like caufe, equity wills that men give a like judgment ; when your difciples do caft out devils, do
not you think that they caft them out by a divine power ? Therefore fo fhould you even think
of me, if you thought aright. But I fhould take
this to be an irony rather.

S. I confefs I did partly conceive the fcope
of thefe two arguments before, but that which
follows I do not underftand : ' But if I caft out
' devils by the Spirit of God, then is the king-
' dom of God come unto you.' Pray make me underftand it, that is, (1) What is meant by the
' kingdom of God ?' (2.) What is the meaning
of this confequence, ' If I by the Spirit of God
' caft out devils, then is the kingdom of God

' come unto you?' For I fee not how it follows.

M. By the kingdom of God is meant the time of the Meffiah's being in the world, as in Dan. iv. 29. and Dan. vii. 14. and the confequence there inferred, is this; that as God by fundry works and miracles, gave his people of Ifrael a fign of their inftant deliverance out of Egypt; fo the great miracles of Chrift were ordained by him, to be a fign unto the world of a greater deliverance, which was now working for them: and therefore where they faw the one, they fhould expect the other.

S. I believe you have gueffed right; but what fay you to the verfe which follows, ' Or elfe how ' can one enter into a ftrong man's houfe, and ' fpoil his goods, except he firft bind the ftrong ' man? and then he will fpoil his houfe.' It looks like another argument which Chrift ufeth in his own defence againft this calumny of the Pharifees; but I confefs I do not yet apprehend it.

M. It is not unlikely, but anon you will. This is indeed a third argument of Chrift's, and it toucheth to the quick: for whereas his other two ferved only to convince certain men, this comes to the very thing itfelf, and quite overthrows it. There have been, faith Chrift, who have caft out devils through Beelzebub; it may be fo, but this hath been without any harm or lofs from the one unto the other; it hath not come to fpoiling of goods, to extirpate out of the minds of men any of their fins, but rather to increafe them; this hath been nothing but a mere collufion and cheat: but when I caft out devils, you may fee I fpoil them to the purpofe, I rob them of their power; for I plant in the minds of men fuch doctrine, as will admit of no vice and wickednefs to be near it (wherein the power of the devil does confift) and therefore you may well imagine that I am in good earneft; for I bind him and fpoil him, which no one devil ever yet did unto another, or ever will.

S. I fhall defire to put you to no more trouble in this verfe; if you pleafe, let us pafs unto the next.

M. As I take it, that is this; ' He that is not ' with me, is againft me; and he that gathereth ' not with me, fcattereth abroad.'

S. Truly, as the words ftand alone, I fhould not trouble you at all with them, for to my think-ing they are eafy enough; but as they follow upon what went before, I fee not what our Sa-viour Chrift might intend by them.

M. Having declared himfelf to be fo far from cafting out devils in the name of Beelzebub, that he laboured to bind even Beelzebub himfelf, and to fpoil him of all his power which he exercifed in the hearts of wicked men, he carries the con-fideration of this enmity between the devil and himfelf to fuch a height, as that he will not ad-

mit of any neutrality in any other man; profeffing, that whofoever is not the devil's enemy, is
his; according to that axiom of the wars, *Medii
habentur pro hoftibus*, ' All indifferent men are ene-
' mies.' And if all this be not enough to fhew
how far he was from operating by the help of
Satan, furely nothing can be. And therefore having faid this, conceiving he had faid as much as
man could fay, he adds, ' Wherefore I fay un-
' to you,' (ver. 31.) that is, feeing it is evident by thefe reafons and arguments, that all the
figns and miracles which I do, I do by the
power of God, and not by the help of the devil;
confider what a wretched punifhment you draw
upon yourfelves, that thus do flander and belie
me. This connexion St. Mark does teach us plainly, chap. iii. 30. where he fays, ' Becaufe they
' faid he hath an unclean fpirit.' And yet it is to
be confidered, that our Saviour Chrift proceeds
not merely upon the ftrength of his own arguments, but as knowing their thoughts, as St.
Matthew tells us in the 25th verfe of this chapter: that is, he faw in unto them, and he knew
that they verily believed that the miracle which he
wrought, was wrought by the power of God;
but yet he faw, that they would rather invent any
lye, or afperfe him with any flander (though they
knew it well enough to be a lye and flander) than
to fuffer the people to forfake their chair, and to
follow Chrift.

S. I thank you, Sir, for this pains which you have taken, to prepare me for the underſtanding of my great doubt, which now, methinks, I begin to have a little glimpſe of, but deſire you to give me better light.

M. I ſhall: but firſt I would gladly know what you conceive of thoſe words in the 31ſt verſe, ‘ All manner of ſin and blaſphemy ſhall be ‘ forgiven unto men;’ bccauſe by underſtanding of what ſin ſhall be forgiven, you will the more eaſily underſtand me, when I tell you what manner of ſin ſhall not.

S. Why, Sir, I underſtand any manner of ſin whatſoever; and I underſtand the ſin of the Holy Ghoſt to be the only ſin which ſhall never be forgiven.

M. I did fear as much, and therefore I did aſk you: but you muſt know that you are much miſtaken, both in the one and in the other opinion. For, 1. It is to be conſidered, that Chriſt ſpeaks not of all ſin, but of that ſin which is blaſphemy or calumny (for there are many other ſins which will never be forgiven, as well as the ſin againſt the Holy Ghoſt:) and therefore in the next verſe he ſaith, ‘ Whoſoever ſpeaketh a word a‘ gainſt the ſon of man; that is, whoſoever ſlandereth or calumniateth any other man, ‘ it ſhall be ‘ forgiven him:’ and in thoſe words he expoundeth what he means by ſin and blaſphemy. 2. It is to be conſidered, that when he ſaith, ‘ All man-

' ner of fin and blafphemy fhall be forgiven,' there
is an Hebraifm in thofe words, which is often
met withal in Scripture; as in the fifth chapter of
St. Matthew, ' Heaven and earth fhall pafs away,
' but my words fhall not pafs away: ' that is,
Heaven and earth fhall fooner pafs away, than my
words fhall pafs away; (and fo St. Luke reads
them, xxi. 33.) not that heaven and earth fhall
ever pafs away, but that, if it were poffible, they
fhould fooner pafs away than his word fhall. The
meaning therefore of the words is only this; all
manner of calumnies and flanders are heavy fins,
and fhall hardly be forgiven to thofe that do commit them; but they will be more eafily forgiven
than that calumny, which he knows to be a calumny who doth commit it: and this Chrift calls
blafpheming of the Holy Ghoft, which was the cafe
of thefe Pharifees, who calumniated the miracle
which our Saviour wrought, as proceeding from
the devil, which their own confcience told them
iffued from the Holy Spirit of God.

S. I confefs, Sir, this is very plain and eafy;
and I pray proceed to the 33d verfe: ' Either
' make the tree good, and his fruit good; or elfe
' make the tree corrupt, and his fruit corrupt:
' for the tree is known by his fruit,' faith Chrift.

M. The dependance of thofe words is this: You
fay, I work by the devil, faith Chrift; but you
do not fee any other work of mine befides this
miracle, which looks like a work of the devil.

You fee I go about doing good, I exhort people to repentance, I fhew them the way to heaven; thefe are no works which the devils ufe to do: therefore either fay that I do all this in the name of Beelzebub too, or elfe acknowledge that I do my miracles by the power of God: for men judge of the quality of the mind by the common actions or habits of their life, as they do of trees by the fruits which they produce, be they good or evil. And that this is true, faith Chrift, you may judge by your own felves; for ' how can ye, being evil, ' fpeak good things ?' faith he, ver. 34. that is, you can never do it. A diffembled and forced mind will quickly fhew itfelf fome way or other, and will return unto its wonted habit: and therefore, as you may judge by yourfelves, that becaufe you fpeak and do nothing but that which is evil, therefore you yourfelves are evil; fo you fhould judge of me, that becaufe you fee I fay and do nothing but that which is good, therefore I am good; and therefore that fpirit which works in me is good.

S. I apprehend all this; and therefore fhall fave you the labour of expounding that which follows, for I fee, it all tends to the fame end and fcope: only, methinks I am much ftraitned in my mind, about the 36th verfe, which forbids ' all ' idle words;' for, if we muft give account of every one fuch, God be merciful unto me, and to many thoufand more. Pray make me to underftand the full latitude of this commination of Chrift.

M. Whatfoever is meant by this ' idle word ' here, you may be fure it hath reference to that word which the Pharifees had fpoke of Chrift, when they faid, ' He caft out devils in the name ' of Beelzebub ;' for Chrift hath not done with this calumny of theirs yet, but continues his dif-courfe upon it, till the 3 8th verfe of this chapter. Now confidering this ' idle word' in that reference, it is moft reafonable to expound it, not of every word which a man fpeaks, of which there is no profit, or which is good for nought, (for if that expofition fhould be true, which God forbid, yet it were not pertinent) but of fuch a word, wherein there is no truth; for by *idle* and *vain*, in holy Scripture, is often underftood that which is falfe: and fo ' to take the name of God ' in vain,' in the commandments, is to fwear falfe-ly. So that the fcope of Chrift in thofe words is this; Do you think that you fhall efcape for this horrid calumny which you have caft upon me, knowing it to be a calumny in your own hearts ? I tell you, nay; for no man fhall efcape in the day of judgment, for calumniating another man falfly, though he do not know that that calumny is falfe ; and therefore much lefs fhall you. By which we may learn, if not to avoid all idle words (which to the nature and education of man is almoft quite impoffible) yet to beware of calumniating perfons, not only when we know that calumny is falſe (which doubtleſs is a very grievous ſin) but when we are not evidently aſcertained that the thing is true. And therefore it is the ſpecial office of a good Chriſtian, to refrain his tongue altogether in that point; for it is a rare thing for a man to give himſelf the liberty, to repeat that of another which is falſe, and not to wiſh it true.

S. I thank you for this ſatisfaction, and, by God's help, ſhall endeavour to frame my life and converſation accordingly: for I perceive it is a ſin, which the world taketh little notice of; though indeed it be the deſtruction of charity, without which no man is a Chriſtian: for ſo they avoid doing that which is notoriouſly evil, they care not what they ſay of any man. Now if you pleaſe, we will proceed to that which follows: I pray, what do the Scribes and Phariſees mean to deſire a ſign from Chriſt, in the 38th verſe of this chapter, who had ſeen ſo many before? for methinks it ſeems a very impertinent requeſt.

M. Some interpreters are of opinion that theſe Scribes and Phariſees were not the ſame, who ſaw thoſe late miracles which our Saviour did; and they ground their opinion upon Luke xi. 16. where it is ſaid, 'That others tempted him, ſeek-' ing a ſign from heaven:' but upon examination, that opinion will not hold. The better anſwer is, That they did not deſire a bare ſign or a miracle, of which they had ſeen enough already; but they

defired a fign from heaven (as St. Luke fpeaks)
that is, that God by fome ftrange prodigy there,
fhould declare him to be a prophet fent from him,
if fo be he were fo indeed: for, as for thofe miracles which he did on earth, they were not fatisfied with them, as apprehending them pendulous
between two feveral powers; for as they might
come from God, fo they might come from the
devil: but in heaven they thought the devil had
no power.

S. I like your reafon well; but, I pray what
doth Chrift mean by that anfwer which he gives
to their requeft in the 39th, 40th, 41ft, and
42d verfes; for I do not underftand it perfectly?

M. The meaning of his anfwer is this: you
would have a fign from heaven, and then you
will believe me; God, that will omit no occafion
to leave you unexcufable, hath given you figns e-
nough, here upon earth; but he is not bound to
fatisfy your humours, and give them where and
when you would have them: he knows thefe
which you have feen are fufficient to perfuade belief, if that your avarice, and profit, and places
which you hold in the prefent Jewifh ftate, did
not make you feek all occafions and cloaks for
your incredulity: and therefore, if thofe figns
which I have done on earth, will not ferve you,
you fhall have none from heaven; but if you
will, you fhall have one from under the earth,
even the fign of the prophet Jonas: and that fign

not a fign to convert you, who after fo many figns
and miracles will not be converted; but a fign of
my innocence, and your malice, which will per-
fecute me even unto the death, for all that good
which I have done amongft you.

S. By this which you have faid, I do not only
perceive the fcope and purport of Chrift's anfwer,
which he gives them; but the drift of the 41ft
and 42d verfes alfo; wherein he complains, that
they who had fo many figns done amongft them,
never would believe; whereas thofe of Nineveh,
and the Queen of the South, without any fign or
miracle wrought either by Jonas or Solomon, believed all that was told them. But, I pray, how
comes the next difcourfe in, concerning the unclean fpirit going out of a man, in the 43d verfe?
And what is the fcope and purport of that difcourfe?

M. It is not improbable, that our Saviour
Chrift, being much afflicted with the evil and in-
credulous hearts of the people of the Jews, taketh a kind of furvey of that whole nation, even
from the time wherein they were firft led away
captive into Babylon, to the time when they were
utterly deftroyed by Titus. Before their captivity, they were full of all manner of wickednefs, as
appeareth by the prophets; under their captivity,
they were a little reclaimed, and, upon that a-
mendment, were brought back again: but then
after their return, in the times not long before

our Saviour's coming, they fell into such vices, as were abominable, even in the Heathens themselves, as is manifest in story; and to shut up all, added thereunto the contempt of their own Messiah, sent amongst them with so much power, and yet with so much meekness, as man never came. Whereupon, being justly forsaken of God, whom they had thus forsook, they became the most wretched and vicious people in the world, as Josephus doth describe them to be about their latter times. And this contemplation of their miserable condition, our Saviour seems to insinuate, even unto themselves, in this kind of parable of the unclean spirit going out of a man, and returning back again. Of which, if that which I have said be not the occasion (as I do not avow, but only offer it unto you) yet certainly this is the sense; That those men, who have once left and forsaken the vicious courses of their carnal life, if they ever relapse, and fall back again into them; all their latter sins are far more sinful than their former: Almighty God justly revenging the contempt of that grace, which he hath offered to them, by giving them up to all manner of wickedness and uncleanness.

S. I think you have guessed right, and to the purpose; but there are some terms and phrases in this parable or story, or whatsoever you will call it, which I do not understand: as, *First*, I pray what do you think Christ means by ' walking

' through dry places, and feeking reft, and find-
' ing none?'

M. Dry and fandy grounds are no fit places of
Habitation; and fuch kind of places are all thofe
places where the devil doth abide when he is out
of man, who is only capable of vice and fin, wherein the devil taketh pleafure. And the meaning of
Chrift is this, That as a man that travels, is wea-
ried with heavy, fandy, and dry way, more than
with green, foft, and pleafant fields; fo the devil
is not half fo well fatisfied, when he enters into
any other creature, as when he enters into man.

S. It may be fo indeed; but then, why taketh
he feven fpirits, more wicked than himfelf? Why
is the number of feven here pitched on, more than
any other?

M. The number of feven is the number of perfection, or the fignification of that which, in its
own kind, is grown to full maturity, whether it
be good or evil. So St. John calleth the Holy Spirit of God the ' Seven Spirits,' Rev. i. 4. So the
barren is faid to have ' born feven,' 1 Sam. ii. 5.
that is, to have been as fruitful as any other woman is, or can be. And therefore when the unclean fpirit is faid to take feven other fpirits with
him, the meaning only is, That that man becomes
perfectly wicked, when that fpirit once returns a-
gain, whom before he had caft out.

S. I approve your expofition of the word, and
think it likely. But I pray can you guefs what

bufineſs the virgin, and the brethren of Chriſt might have with him, becauſe the Scripture ſaith, ' They ſtaid without, to ſpeak with him, ' in the 47th verſe of this chapter? Peradventure you may think me curious, and therefore if expoſitors have made no conjecture thereupon, I will not urge you.

M. Truly they have, and I ſhall not conceal it from you: they do imagine, that his mother and his kindred, having had ſome inkling of the Phariſees confpiring againſt him to do him miſchief, deſired to ſpeak with him in private, and to contrive ſome way to withdraw him out of danger. This will ſeem the more probable, if we conſider that which St. Mark ſaith, chap. iii. 21. ' That ' his friends would fain have laid hold on him, ' ſaying, that he was beſide himſelf;' which, in all likelihood, they ſaid to make the Phariſees the leſs active in contriving any miſchief to him, as conceiving him a fitter ſubject for their pity, than their hate; but it ſeems Chriſt would not hearken unto them, nay would not know them, as appears by the three laſt verſes of this chapter, which are ſo plain and eaſy, that I dare not ſuſpect your ſenſe and apprehenſion of them.

A

T R A C T

CONCERNING THE

S I N

AGAINST THE

H O L Y   G H O S T.

MANY have written of the fin againſt the Holy Ghoſt, and in defining or deſcribing of it, follow their own zealous conceits, and not the canon of Holy Scriptures. The more dreadful the fin is, the more fearful we muſt be, in charging it upon any ſpecial crime or particular perſon. In defining a fin of ſo heinous a nature, direct and evident proof from Scripture is requiſite: it is not enough to conſider (as many do) what fins are moſt deſperate and deadly, and therefore to conclude ſuch fins are againſt the Holy Ghoſt. Thus indeed the School-men have done, who

have made fix differences of this fin *, without
ground or warrant from Scripture for fo doing.
And Bellarmine is fo liberal in beftowing on fuch
as he calls hereticks, that his opinion is, that a
man can fcarce be a learned Proteftant, without
committing the fin againft the Holy Ghoft. Neither are the Papifts the only men that are miftaken about this fin; but too many divines of the
reformed churches have ftarted afide from the
Scripture, and have given us fuch intricate and
contradictory definitions of this fin, as tend only
to the perplexing the tender confciences of weak
Chriftians. To make good this cenfure, I will
briefly fet down fo much touching this fin, as I
conceive is warranted by the word of God, and
humbly fubmit to the judgment of the learned.

The blafphemy againft the Holy Ghoft, was
an evil fpeaking of, or flandering of the miracles
which our Saviour did, by thofe, who though
they were convinced by the miracles, to believe
that fuch works could not be done but by the
power of God, yet they did malicioufly fay, they
were wrought by the power of the devil.

In this definition thefe points are obfervable.

1. I forbear to call it the fin againft the Holy

---

* The fix differences the School-men make of the fin a-
gainft the Holy Ghoft, are thefe:

1. Envying of our brother's graces. 2. Impugning of the
known truth. 3. Defperation. 4. Obftinacy. 5 Prefumption.
6. Final impenitency.

Ghoſt, but the blaſphemy; for though every blaſphemy be a ſin in general, yet our Saviour Chriſt terms it the blaſphemy. And the evangeliſts do all agree, to give it the ſame term; and it is now here in holy Scripture called the ſin againſt the Holy Ghoſt, and yet it appears both in St. Matthew and St. Mark, that there was juſt occaſion offered to our Saviour to call it ſo: where he compares it with the ſin againſt the Son of Man, but he forbears to call it any thing but ' the blaſ- ' phemy;' thereby, no doubt, to teach us, it conſiſteth only in curſed ſpeaking and blaſpheming. A ſerious conſideration of this point, may teach us ſo much moderation, as to confine ourſelves to that term which our Saviour in the thrée evangeliſts hath preſcribed unto us. I cannot find that any man that hath writ upon this argument, hath made any obſervation, or noted this phraſe and term uſed by the evangeliſts, in pronouncing the dreadful ſentence of our Saviour againſt the blaſphemy of the Holy Ghoſt: I will cite theſe texts where it is named; Matt. xii. 31. Mark iii. 29. Luke xii. 10.

2. A ſecond obſervation is, That blaſphemy is a ſpeaking againſt another, as both St. Matthew and St. Luke expound the word; for in the original, it is a blaſting the fame, or *blaming* of another; for from the Greek word Βλασφημέω, both the French nation and our Engliſh by contraction have made the word ' blame.'

C

To pafs from the name to the thing itfelf, we may obferve by the coherence of the texts, that blafphemy againft the Holy Ghoft was fpoken of by our Saviour, concerning the Scribes and Pharifees. It was (faith St. Mark) becaufe the Pharifees faid, he had an unclean fpirit, and that he caft out devils by Beelzebub, &c. This fpeech of the Pharifees, whereby they flandered his miracles wrought by the power of the Holy Ghoft, is properly the blafphemy againft the Holy Ghoft. How tranfcendent a crime it was, to traduce that power by which our Saviour wrought his miracles, may appear, from the end for which thefe miracles were wrought; which was, to prove to the people which faw them, that he was the Meffias; which is evident from the places of Scripture, wherein he appealed to his works; John x. 37, 38. John xiv. 11. Matt. xi. 4. John v. 36. Thefe and other places fhew, that the working of miracles was an act of the moft glorious manifeftation of the power of God; by which at the firft view, the fimpleft people were led by their outward fenfe, to the great myftery of inward faith in Chrift, their Redeemer.

Therefore, for thofe men that were eye-witneffes of thofe miracles which did make them know that Chrift was a teacher come from God, to blafpheme that power by which thefe miracles were wrought, and to fay they were done by the help of the devil, was the moft fpightful and ma-

licious flander that could be invented; for thereby they attempted, as much as in them lay, to deftroy the very principles of faith, and to prevent
the very firft propagation of the gofpel, to the
univerfal mifchief of all mankind. And though
thefe Pharifees were no Chriftians, and therefore
could not fall away from faith, which they never
had, yet they did know and believe that Chrift
was a teacher come from God; for fo our Saviour tells them, John vii. 28. ' Ye both know me,
' and whence I am.' They did not believe him
as a faviour, but as a great prophet from God;
(as the Mahometans do at this very day) they
trufted to be faved by their law; and becaufe he
taught fuch things as did abrogate their law, in
which they fo much gloried, they were fo malicious to his doctrine, which they did not believe,
that they fpoke evil of his miracles which they did
believe; left the people by approving his miracles, fhould believe his doctrine.

4. Obferve that it is faid to be blafphemy a-
gainft the Holy Ghoft; becaufe, by the Holy
Ghoft the miracles were wrought, Matt. xii. 28.
1 Cor. xii. 10.

5. The blafphemy againft the Son of Man
was, when men confidered Chrift as a mere man,
and did difgracefully tax his converfation, by faying, ' Behold a glutton, a wine bibber, a friend to
' publicans and finners.' Matt. xi. 19. But the
blafphemy againft the Holy Ghoft was, when men

beholding Chrift's miracles, did envioufly afcribe them to the devil, which they knew and believed to be done by God's power.*

6. The text formerly cited out of the three Evangelifts, being all the places wherein the blafphemy againft the Holy Ghoft is named; we cannot find by them, that we have any fafe rule to conclude, that any but the Scribes and Pharifees, and their confederates, committed that fin. I dare not fay, that Judas, Julian the Apoftate, or Simon Magus, or thofe who ftoned Stephen, were guilty thereof.

7. The apoftles have not in any of their epiftles once mentioned this blafphemy, and yet they were moft careful and frequent in exhortations from all forts of fin : it were much therefore if they fhould omit or forget fuch a fearful crime, without often and precife admonifhing to beware of it. And though negative proofs from fcripture are not demonftrative, yet the general filence of the apoftles may at leaft help to infer a probability, that the blafphemy againft the Holy Ghoft is not committable by any Chriftian, which lived not in the time of our Saviour. As for thofe texts in the fixth and tenth chapter to the Hebrews, and in 1 John v. 16. (which by late divines are expounded of the fin againft the Holy Ghoft) I do not find that the antient fathers did fo underftand them, excepting only St. Auftin, who fo interprets that one place in St. John, that all men con-

fefs him to be in an error. There be three texts in the epiftles, wherein although the blafphemy againft the Holy Ghoft be not named, yet moft think it is intended and meant. And Bellarmine confuting St. Auftin's opinion, (who held that final impenitency was the fin againft the Holy Ghoft) affirms that it feems the three texts in the epiftles, are fpoken of that fin; and yet this great Cardinal, forgetting what he had faid, in the fame chapter contradicts himfelf, and fhews how that thofe three places are not to be interpreted of that fin. I will cite the texts, and then his interpretation of them, according to the expofition of St. Ambrofe, Chryfoftom, Jerom, and other fathers, as he faith.

The firft is Heb. vi. 4, 5, 6. ' For it is im-
' poffible for thofe who were once enlightened, and
' have tafted of the heavenly gift, and were made
' partakers of the Holy Ghoft, and have tafted of
' the good word of God, and the powers of the
' world to come ; if they fhall fall away, to re-
' new them again unto repentance : feeing they
' crucify to themfelves the Son of God afrefh, and
' put him to an open fhame.' The apoftle here fpeaks only of repentance, which did go before baptifm; for fo Chryfoftom and Ambrofe, &c. expound it: which the apoftle intimates in thefe words; ' Which were once enlightened,' that is baptized; for antiently to be illuminated, fignified to be baptized. Secondly, in thefe words, ' to

'renew again;' for we are properly renewed in
baptifm. Thirdly, in thefe; 'Crucifying the Son
'of God afrefh:' for when we are baptized, we
are conformed to the likenefs of his death, Rom.
vi. 5. And as Chrift was only once crucified, fo
alfo we are only once baptized; and he that will
be again baptized, fhould again crucify to himfelf
Chrift. Let me add this, that in the verfes next
before this text, the apoftle fpeaks of the foundation of repentance, and the doctrine of baptifm.
And in this text, our new tranflation followeth
Beza (who hath varied from the original, by putting the conditional *fi*, 'if,' inftead of the copula-
tive *et*, 'and,' and by adding the caufal *ut*) fo that
whereas Beza and our tranflation is, *fi prolabantur
ut crucifigant;* the Greek and Vulgar Latin is,
παραπεσόνἼας ἀνασαυρϖνἼας, *prolapfi funt crucifigen-
tes;* for the word doth not fignify to fall away,
but to fall cafually or negligently: fo παράπἼωμα,
Gal. vi. 1. is tranflated 'fault,' but not 'falling
'away.'

The fecond text is Hebrews x. 26. 'For if
'we fin wilfully,' or willingly,' 'after we have re-
'ceived the knowledge of the truth, there re-
'maineth no more facrifice for fin.' *Anfw.* I fay
with Chryfoftom, Ambrofe, and other fathers,
The fenfe is, we muft not expect another Chrift
to die for us, or that he that died once, fhould
come again to die for us.

The third text, 1 John v. 16. 'There is a fin

' unto death : I do not fay ye fhall pray for it.' St.
Jerom faith, that nothing elfe is here meant, but
that a prayer for a fin unto death, is very hardly
or difficultly heard; and this feems to be the trueft
fenfe of this place: for St. John faith, in the verfe
immediately before, ' We know we have the peti-
' tions we defire of him :' therefore left we fhould
think this to hold true in all petitions even for o-
thers, he adds, ' If any man fee his brother fin a
' fin, which is not unto death, he fhall afk, and
' he fhall give him life for them that fin not unto
' death. He fhall afk;' that is, let him afk with
confidence, for he fhall obtain : but if it be a fin
unto death; that is a great fin, fuch an one as is
not ordinarily pardoned, but punifhed with death;
' I do not fay, ye fhall pray for it :' that is, I dare
not promife that you fhall eafily obtain, and therefore I do not fay that you fhall pray for it; that
is, with that confidence of obtaining: for often
in fuch cafes, God doth not hear the prayers of
his faints; as God faith, Jer. vii. 16. If thefe expofitions upon the former text be found, the definition of the fin againft the Holy Ghoft cannot
be grounded upon all, or any of them; for as it
is not named, fo it is not meant in any of them :
but if they feem to any to be unfound, let him
bring better and more agreeable to the literal
meaning and fenfe, coherence and fcope of the
text; and I fhall gladly learn. It feems a probable expofition of the firft place, Heb. vi. 4. 5. 6.

that a learned divine, who produceth this text for
proof of his definition of the fin againſt the Holy
Ghoſt, doth confeſs againſt himſelf, that the a-
poſtle in this place denieth a ſecond baptiſm, where
he ſpeaketh of repentance, becauſe they are mentioned together in the ſame place, and have ſome
affinity and correſpondence. As for the ſecond
text, Heb. x. 26. I muſt ſay, that if St. Paul in
this place meant the ſin againſt the Ghoſt, that
then this were the only deſperate text in the
whole Bible: for what man is there that ſins not
willingly? for ſo the word ἑκουσίως properly ſignifies. Beza tranſlates it *ultro,* the Vulgar Latin,
voluntarie, or ' willingly,' not ' wilfully,' or ' ob-
' ſtinately.' It is but a miſerable ſhift, when
St. Paul ſaith, ' If we ſin willingly,' for Mr. Calvin to tell us, that the text doth not mean every
willing ſin, but only a malicious reſiſting of the
truth. Could not St. Paul, as eaſily as Mr. Calvin, have ſaid, If we ſin maliciouſly, as ſay, If we
ſin willingly? My comfort is, that if the text be
adviſedly conſidered, there is no ſuch thing as the
ſin againſt the Holy Ghoſt, or any other deſperate
concluſion, to be found in the text. The ſcope of
the precedent verſes does evidently expound the
apoſtle's meaning to be this; to let the Jews know,
that the caſe was not now with them, as it was
under the law: for under the law they had daily
ſacrifice for ſin; but now under the goſpel they had
but one ſacrifice, once for all: ' every prieſt ſtand-

' eth daily miniftring and offering oftentimes the
' fame facrifice,—but this man after he had of-
' fered one facrifice, for ever fat down at the right
' hand of God,' as it is, verfe 11, 12. of that
chapter, which may ferve for a comment upon the
verfe now in queftion. And it is worth our noting; that the text doth not fay, If we fin wilfully, there is no facrifice for fin; this had been an
hard faying indeed: but the words are, 'There re-
' mains no more facrifice for fin.' There is fome
comfortable difference, I hope, between thefe two
propofitions; 'There is no facrifice,' and ' there re-
' mains no more facrifice for fin.' So that if we do
not believe in that one facrifice as fufficient, but
look every day for fome new facrifice for every
new fin, we muft expect nothing but judgment.

As to the third place, 1 John v. 16. many
would conclude, there is a fin, for which we may
not pray: Firft, becaufe it is irremiffible; and
this they think muft needs be the fin againft the
Holy Ghoft, meant by St. John. Their beft argument is, John's not faying we fhould pray, is a
faying we fhould not pray; his filence to them is
prohibition: this is bad grammar and worfe logic. For we find, that St. Stephen prayed for
them that ftoned him, and yet told them, they refifted the Holy Ghoft, Acts vii. 51 and 60. And
St. Peter exhorted Simon Magus to repentance,
Acts viii. 22. and yet both he and thofe that ftoned Stephen, are commonly reputed finners a-

gainft the Holy Ghoft. St. Ambrofe is of that
charitable opinion, that he thinks the fin againft the
Holy Ghoft may be pardoned by repentance, becaufe the people of the Jews, that had faid of Chrift,
that he caft out devils by Beelzebub, afterwards at
the preaching of St. Peter, are faid to be converted, Acts ii. St. Auftin in a retract concludes, we
muft defpair of no man, no not of the wickedeft,
as long as he liveth; and we fafely pray for him,
of whom we do not defpair. For though it be
exprefly faid, ' That the blafphemy againft the
' Holy Ghoft fhall not be forgiven;' yet thefe
words may juftly receive a qualification, if we will
but allow the fame mitigation of thefe words,
which all men confefs we muft needs allow to the
precedent words in the fame verfe, to which thefe
have relation: where it is faid generally, ' all fins
' and all blafphemies fhall be forgiven;' it cannot be meant of all fins always, and to all men,
for then no fin could be damnable, but the fin a-
gainft the Holy Ghoft, which is moft falfe. And
therefore the meaning muft be, all fins fhall be
forgiven ordinarily, and for the moft part; fo on
the contrary, blafphemy againft the Holy Ghoft
fhall not ordinarily, but hardly be forgiven. Even
thofe who are moft ftrict to maintain the fin a-
gainft the Holy Ghoft to be unpardonable, will
yet acknowledge, that fometimes, in fcripture, impoffibility is ufed to note a difficulty; and thofe
things are fpoken indefinitely to all, which belong

but to a part only. Thus the difficulty of a rich man's entring into the kingdom of heaven, is presented to us by our Saviour under the similitude of an impossibility.

Having dispatched these texts of scripture, which do either name, or are thought to concern, the sin against the Holy Ghost; it remains to examine those common definitions of this sin, which are now current, though different in the terms by which they define it. Some call it a total or final falling away from faith, or a wilful apostacy, or a malicious resisting of the truth; yet when they come to explain their meaning, the difference among them is not considerable. J shall chiefly apply myself to Mr. Calvin's definition, because his judgment hath gained the greatest reputation among the multitude; as also, for that he himself promises such a true definition, as shall easily, by itself, overthrow all the rest. In his *Institut. lib.* iii. *cap.* 3. he saith, They sin against the Holy Ghost, *qui divinae veritati (cujus fulgore sic perstringuntur, ut ignorantium causari nequeant) tamen destinata malitia resistunt, in hoc tantum, ut resistant.* Arminius also useth Mr. Calvin's words. The rhetorical parenthesis, which might well have been spared in a definition, being reduced to plain and brief terms; this definition of Calvin may be thus englished: 'They sin against the Holy Ghost, ' who of determined malice resist the known truth ' of God, to the end only to resist.' In this

Mr. Calvin doth not define what the fin is; but who they are that commit it; whereas by the rules of logic *concretes* admit of no definition, but only *abstracts*. But taking the definition as it is, it confifts principally of thefe three terms. *Firft*, Truth; *Secondly*, Known; *Thirdly*, Refifted: or a refifting of the known truth. The words being general and doubtful, we will confider them fingly.

FIRST, If by the truth Mr. Calvin underftands the word of God, or the whole doctrine revealed in the fcriptures, then the fenfe of this term will be too large: for even the Pharifees, which fpoke againft the Holy Ghoft, did not refift the whole truth of God in the fcripture, for they believed in the law of Mofes, and had confidence to be faved by the keeping of it; and in defence of that law (as they thought) they did blafpheme the Holy Ghoft. Therefore properly, by ' the truth of ' God,' Mr. Calvin muft confine his meaning to the truth of the gofpel or doctrine of faith; for fo both he himfelf and others expound themfelves, by terming the fin againft the Holy Ghoft, a falling away, or turning away from faith, or apoftacy.

SECONDLY, By this word ' known,' Mr. Calvin muft mean belief; for faith is properly by believing, not knowing the truth.

THIRDLY, The word ' refifting' muft mean unbelieving: for if receiving of the truth be by

belief, then resisting of the truth must be by unbelief. And indeed Mr. Calvin explains himself in
the same chapter, saying, ' There is no place for
' pardon where knowledge is joined with unbe-
' lief;' *Non esse veniae locum ubi scientia ad incre-
dulitatem accessit.* So then by this definition, to resist the known truth, is all one, as if Mr. Calvin
had said in proper terms, for a man at once to un-
believe that which he doth believe : which two
things it is impossible to do together; and if
they be not together, there can be no resistance.
It is true, that for some reasons a man may be
brought, not to believe that which he formerly
believed : this cannot be in an instant, but succes-
sively unbelief comes in the place of belief. And
this may not be called a resisting, for that all resistance consists in a violence between two at the
least; but where two succeed one another, and
are never together, it cannot possibly be. I confess a man may resist the truth, when it is a truth
in itself only, or in the understanding of some o-
ther; but to resist the truth which is known, and
believed by the resister himself, is a direct contradiction : for the nature of truth is such, that if
the understanding apprehend it for truth, it cannot but assent unto it. No man can force himself
to believe what he lists, or when he lists. Sometimes a man knows not what to believe, but finds
a suspension of his faith, or trepidation of his understanding, not knowing which way to turn. This

cannot be called a refifting of the truth, when the truth is not known, but doubted of. Again, fome truths there be, though they be affented to by the underftanding for truths, yet they are not defired as good; for truth is one degree nearer the foul of man than goodnefs. The Pharifees did apprehend the miracles of our Saviour as true, but not as good; becaufe they tended to the derogation of their law, which they efteemed a better truth. And for this caufe they blafphemed that truth, which in their hearts they believed for truth: for the truth of words, or fpeech, is (as the fchools fay) nothing elfe but the fign of truth, not truth itfelf; for truth itfelf is feated in the underftanding, and not in the fpeech. That truth which the underftanding affents to, the fpeech may affirm to be falfe; there are many things believed in deed, which are denied in word: but fuch a denial is not refifting, but only making fhew of refifting the truth; for refiftance muft be in the fame place where truth is: truth being feated in the underftanding, refiftance muft be placed there alfo; the underftanding can refift no truth, but by unbelieving of it. If Mr. Calvin had intended of the truth only in word, he had come one ftep nearer to the truth of fcripture, but he was not fo happy in the expreffion of his meaning; nay his terms of incredulity, apoftacy, falling away, &c. relate to a real, not verbal apoftacy, and unbelief. It remains then to my underftanding, that Mr. Calvin makes the resistance of the truth to be a not believing of what we do believe; which being a contradiction, he defines the sin against the Holy Ghost, to be such a sin, as no man possibly can commit. And yet in the other extreme, in expounding his own definition, he makes it such a sin, as no man living but commits; for by his doctrine, (as I take it) any sin may be the sin against the Holy Ghost. His words are these, *Quorum convicta est conscientia verbum Dei esse quod repudiant et impugnant, impugnare tamen non desistant, illi in spiritum blasphemari dicuntur.* What man is there that doth not daily, in some point or other, forsake the word of God, and ceases not to impugn it, and is convinced thereof in his conscience? I know Mr. Calvin was far from thinking, that St. Paul did sin against the Holy Ghost; and yet St. Paul, it seems, was convinced in his conscience, that it was the word of God he fought against, and yet ceased not to fight against it, when he saith, He delighted in the law of God, yet another law warring against the law of his mind, brought him into captivity of the law of sin. Rom. vii. 22, 23. What dangerous consequences weak consciences may draw to themselves, out of this unbridled, unlimited proposition of Mr. Calvin's, let others judge. There is a just cause, I presume, to except against Mr. Calvin and all others, who in this concur with him, to omit the term of 'blasphemy' in their definitions; for this is perpetually observed by our Saviour in his speech concerning this sin, by the evangelists with one consent. But instead of the word 'blasphemy,' he hath brought in the word 're-sist,' for a genus of this sin; but by what authority I know not: I cannot find it, or the equivalent to it, in any of those places, which are thought to touch this sin. I find only 'falling away' mentioned, Heb. vi. 6. which phrase is used by Mr. Calvin for 'resisting;' whereas 'falling away,' and 'resisting,' are no more alike, than fighting and running away, which are little less than contraries. The last point I shall touch in Mr. Calvin's definition, is, where he saith, the sinners against the Holy Ghost resist, to the end only that they may resist; and yet withal he tells, they resist out of a determined malice: if they resist out of malice, then the end for which they resist, is for the satisfaction of their malice. The Pharisees here condemned by our Saviour, had another end than bare resisting. The defence of the law of Moses, was the end for which they blasphemed, and not any pleasure they could have in the bare and simple act of resistance.

We find three old opinions concerning the sin against the Holy Ghost, but they were long since exploded: I will but only name them. Origen thought, all sins committed after baptism, were sins against the Holy Ghost; his reason was only a witless conceit of his own, That God the Father was in all things, the Son only in all reasonable creatures, the Holy Ghost in all regenerate men: therefore when men sin against the Divine Person which is in them, if they be Heathen, they sin against God the Father, or Son; if they be Christians, they sin against God the Holy Ghost: but this opinion is false. The Novatian heretics agreed with Origen in opinion, for they denied remission of sins to any that fell; thinking all falls of Christians to be sins against the Holy Ghost: but this opinion is false, else all sins were unpardonable to Christians. Yet we find St. Paul to remit the sins of the incestuous Corinthian. Our Saviour also chargeth the Pharisees with this, who were no Christians.

St. Austin thought final impenitency to be the sin against the Holy Ghost; but final impenitency is no blasphemy, but only a general circumstance, that may accompany any sin: besides, our Saviour intends, that this sin may be found in this life; and the Pharisees were alive, when they were accused of it.

Pet. Lombard, and Tho. Aquinas thought sins of malice to be sins against the Holy Ghost, and sins of infirmity against the Father, and sins of ignorance against the Son. This opinion is false, because the sin against the Holy Ghost, must be a sin of some certain blasphemy; but malice is no certain sin, but a general, and it is not always a blasphemy.

D

In this determination of the point of blafphe-my againſt the Holy Ghoſt, and the enquiry made into Mr. Calvin's and others new definition; I hope I have delivered nothing contrary to the articles of the church of England.

A
TRACT

ON THE

SACRAMENT

OF THE

LORD'S SUPPER;

AND

CONCERNING THE CHURCH'S MISTAKING
ITSELF ABOUT FUNDAMENTALS.

KIND SIR,

IN perufal of your letters, together with the
schedule inclofed, no circumftance did fo much
move me, as this, That fo ordinary points as are
difcuft there, and *that* in a bare and ordinary manner, fhould amufe either yourfelf or any man elfe,
that pretends to ordinary knowledge in controverfies in the Chriftian religion. For the points therein difcuffed are no other than the fubject of every
common pamphlet, and fufficiently known (that I
may fo fay) in every barber's fhop. Yet becaufe

you require my opinion of matters there in question, I willingly afford it you; though I fear I shall
more amuse you with telling you the truth, than
the disputants there did, by abusing you with error. For the plain and necessary (though perhaps
unwelcome) truth is, that in the greater part of
the dispute, both parties much mistook themselves, and that fell out which is in the common
proverb / ' Whilst the one milks the ram, the other
' holds under the sieve.' † That you may see this
truth with your eyes, I divide your whole dispute
into two heads; the one concerning the ' eucha-
' rist,' the other concerning ' the church's mistak-
' ing itself about fundamentals.'

For the *First*, It consisteth of two parts; of a
proposition, and of a reply. The proposition expresses (at least he that made it, intended it so to
do, though he mistakes) the doctrine of the reformed churches, concerning the presence of Christ
in the eucharist. The reply doth the like for the
church of Rome, in the same argument. Now that
you may see how indifferently I walk, I will open
the mistakes of both parties, that so the truth of
the thing itself (being unclouded of errors) may
the more clearly shine forth.

The *first* mistake common to both is, that they
ground themselves much upon the words of con-

† Οὐ δοκᾶ ὁ μὲν ἕτερος, τύτων, τράγον ἀμέλγειν, ὁ δὲ αὐτῷ
κόσκινον ὑποτιθέναι.

Lucian. in vit. Demonact.

fecration, as they are called; and fuppofe, that
upon the pronouncing of thofe words, fomething
befals that action, which otherways would not;
and that without thofe words the action were
lame. Sir, I muft confefs my ignorance unto you.
I find no ground for the neceffity of this doing.
Our Saviour inftituting that holy ceremony, commands us to do what he did, leaves us no precept
of faying any words; neither will it be made appear, that either the bleffed apoftles or primitive
Chriftians had any fuch cuftom : nay the contrary
will be made probably to appear, out of fome of
the antienteft writings of the church's ceremoni-
als.   Our Saviour indeed ufed the words, but it
was to exprefs what his meaning was : had he
barely acted the thing, without expreffing himfelf
by fome fuch form of words, we could never have
known what it was he did. But what neceffity is
there now of fo doing? for when the congregation is met together, to the breaking of bread and
prayer, and fee bread and wine upon the commu-
nion-table, is there any man can doubt of the
meaning of it, although the canon be not read?
it was the farther folemnizing, and beautifying that
holy action, which brought the canon in; and not
an opinion of adding any thing to the fubftance
of the action.   For that the words were ufed by
our Saviour to work any thing upon the bread
and wine, can never out of fcripture or reafon be
deduced; and beyond thefe two, I have no ground

for my religion, neither in fubftance nor in ceremony.

The main foundation that upholds the neceffity of this form of action now in ufe, is church-
cuftom, and church-error.

Now for that topic-place of church-cuftom, it is
generally too much abufed: for whereas naturally the neceffity of the thing ought to give warrant
to the practice of the church, I know not by what
device matters are turned about, and the cufto-
mary practice of the church is alledged to prove
the neceffity of the thing; as if things had received their original from the church-authority, and
not, as the truth is, from an higher hand.

As for the church's error, on which I told you
this form of action is founded, it confifts in the
uncautelous taking up an unfound ungrounded
conclufion of the fathers for a religious maxim.
St. Ambrofe, I trow, was he that faid it, and pofterity hath too generally applauded it; *Accedat
verbum ad elementum, et fiat facramentum.* By
which they would perfuade us, againft all experience, that to make up a facrament, there muft be
fomething faid and fomething done; whereas indeed, to the perfection of a facrament, or holy
myftery (for both thefe are one) it is fufficient that
one thing be done whereby another is fignified,
though nothing be faid at all. When Tarquinius
was walking in his garden, a meffenger came and
afked him, What he would have done unto the

town of Gabii, then newly taken? He anſwered
nothing, but with his wand ſtruck off the tops of
the higheſt poppies: and the meſſenger underſtanding his meaning, cut off the heads of the chief
of the city. Had this been done *in ſacris*, it had
been forthwith truly a ſacrament, or holy myſtery: *Cum in omnibus ſcientiis voces ſignificent res, hoc
habet proprium theologia, quod ipſae res ſignificatae
per voces, etiam ſignificent aliquid*, ſaith Aquinas †:
and upon the ſecond ſignification are all ſpiritual
and myſtical ſenſes founded. So that *in ſacris*, a
myſtery or ſacrament is then acted, when one thing
is done, and another is ſignified; as it is in the
holy communion, though nothing be ſaid at all.
The ancient ſacrifices of the Jews, whether week-
ly, monthly, or yearly, their paſſover, their ſitting
in booths, &c. theſe were all ſacraments; yet we
find not any ſacred forms of words uſed by the
prieſts or people in the execution of them.

To ſum up that which we have to ſay in this
point: the calling upon the words of conſecration
in the euchariſt, is too weakly founded to be made
argumentative; for the action is perfect, whether
thoſe words be uſed or forborn: and in truth, to
ſpeak my opinion, I ſee no great harm could enſue, were they quite omitted. Certainly thus
much good would follow, that ſome part (though

† ' Whereas in all ſciences words ſignify certain things,
' theology has this peculiar in it, that the things ſignified by
' thoſe words have alſo a ſecondary ſignification.'

not a little one) of the superstition that adheres to
that action, by reason of an ungrounded conceit
of the necessity and force of the words in it, would
forthwith peel off and fall away. I would not have
you understand me so, as if I would prescribe for,
or desire the disuse of the words; only two things
I would commend to you: 1. That the use of the
canon is a thing indifferent. And, 2. That in this
knack of making sacraments, Christians have taken
a greater liberty than they can well justify. (1.)
In forging sacraments more than God (for ought
doth or can appear) did ever intend. And, (2.) In
adding to the sacraments, instituted of God, many formalities and ceremonial circumstances, upon
no warrant but their own; which circumstances,
by long use, begat in the minds of men a conceit,
that they were essential parts of that, to which
indeed they were but appendant; and *that* only
by the device of some who practised a power in
the church more than was convenient.

Thus much for the first common mistake.

The *second* is worse than it. You see that both
parts agreed in the acknowledgment of the real presence of the body of Christ in the eucharist, though
they differ in the manner of his presence, and application of himself to the receiver: though the Protestant disputant seems to have gone a little beyond his leader. Had he expressed himself in the
point of bread and wine, what became of it, whether it remained in its proper nature, yea or no;

I could the better have fathomed him. Now these words of his, that the bread and wine, after consecration, are truly and really the body of Christ, howsoever they are supplied and allayed with that clause, ' not after a carnal, but after a spiritual manner,' yet still remain too crude and raw, and betray the speaker for a Lutheran at least, if not for a favourer of the church of Rome: for as for that phrase of ' a spiritual manner,' which seems to give season and moderation to his conclusion, it can yield him but small relief. For *first*, to say the flesh of Christ is in the bread, but ' *not after a carnal manner*,' is but the same nonsense which the divines of Rome put upon us on the like occasion; when telling us, that the blood of Christ is really sacrificed and shed in the sacrament, they add by way of gloss, that it is done *incruentè*, ' unbloodi-
' ly.' By the like analogy they may tell us, if they please, that the body of Christ is there incor-. porated unbodily; flesh not carnally, may pass the press jointly the next edition of the book of bulls. *Again*, in another respect, that clause of ' a spiri-
' tual manner,' doth your Protestant disputer but little service, if any at all; for the Catholic disputant contriving with himself how to seat the body of God in the eucharist, as may be most for his ease, tells us, that he is there as spirits and glorified bodies (which St. Paul calls ' spiritual' 1 Cor. xv. 44.) are in the places they possess. So then, the one tells you the body of Christ is there

really, but spiritually; the other, that he is there really, but as a spirit in a place. And what now, I pray you, is the difference between them? By the way, in the passage you may see what account to make of your Catholic disputer. Aristotle, and with him common sense, tells us thus much; ' That he that compares two bodies together, must ' know them both.' Doth this gentleman know any thing concerning the site and locality of spirits, and bodies glorified? If he doth, let him do us the courtesy as to shew us, at what price he purchased that degree of knowledge, that so we may try our credit, and see if we can buy it at the same rate: *Tertius è coelo cecidit Cato?* Is he like a second Paul, lately descended out of the third heavens, and there hath made us the discovery? for by what other means he could attain to that knowledge, my dulness cannot suggest. But if he doth not know (as indeed he neither doth nor can, for there is no means left to make discovery that way) then with what congruity can he tell us, that the body of Christ is in the bread, as spirits and glorified bodies are in their places; if he know not what manner of location and site, spirits and glorified bodies have? I shall not need to prompt your discretion thus far, as that you ought not to make dainties of such fruitless and desperate disputers; who, as the apostle notes, thrust themselves into things they have not seen, and upon a false shew of knowledge, abuse easy hearers; and of things they know not, adventure to speak they know not what.

To return then, and consider a little more of this *second* mistake common to both your disputants, I will deal as favourably as I can with your Protestant disputer: for though I think he mistakes himself, (for I know no Protestant that teacheth, that the common bread, after the word spoken, is really made the body of Christ) yet he might well take occasion thus to err out of some Protestant writings; for generally the reformed divines do falsly report that holy action, whether you regard the essence or use thereof.

For *first*, if in regard of the essence, some Protestants, and that of chief note, stick not to say, That the words of consecration are not a mere trope; and from hence it must needs follow, that in some sense they must needs be taken literally, which is enough to plead authority for the gentleman's error. But that which they preach concerning a real presence and participation of Christ's body in the sacrament, they expound not by a supposal that the bread becomes God's body, but that, together with the sacramental elements, there is conveyed into the soul of the worthy receiver the very body and blood of God; but after a secret, ineffable, and wonderful manner. From hence, as I take it, have proceeded these crude speeches of the learned of the reformed parts, some dead, some living; wherein they take upon them to as-

sure the divines of Rome, that we acknowledge a
real prefence as well as they; but for the manner
how, *con*, or *trans*, or *sub*, or *in*, ἐπέχομεν, we play
the Sceptics, and ' determine not.' This conceit,
befides the falfhood of it, is a mere novelty, neither is it to be found in the books of any of the
antients, till Martin Bucer arofe. He, out of an
unfeafonable bafhfulnefs and fear to feem to recede too far from the church of Rome, taught to
the purpofe now related, concerning the doctrine
of Chrift's prefence in the facrament; and from
him it defcended into the writings of Calvin and
Beza, whofe authority have well-near fpread it o-
ver the face of the reformed churches. This is an
error which, as I faid, touches the effence of that
holy action; but there are many now which touch
the end and ufe of it, which are practifed by the
reformed parts: for out of an extravagant fancy
they have of it, they abufe it to many ends, of
which we may think the firft inftitutor (fave that
he was God, and knew all things) never thought
of. For we make it an arbitrator of civil bufineffes, and imploy it in ending controverfies; and
for confirmation of what we fay or do, we commonly promife to take the facrament upon it. We
teach, that it confirms our faith in Chrift; whereas indeed the receiving of it is a fign of faith confirmed, and men come to it to teftify that they do
believe, not to procure that they may believe: for
if a man doubt of the truth of Chriftianity, think

you that his fcruples would be removed upon the
receiving of the facrament? I would it were fo;
we fhould not have fo many doubting Chriftians,
who yet receive the facrament oft enough. We
teach it to be *viaticum morientium*, whereby we a-
bufe many diftreffed confciences and fick bodies,
who feek for comfort there, and finding it not,
conclude from thence (I fpeak what I know) fome
defect in their faith. The participation of this facrament to fick and weak perfons, what unfeemly
events hath it occafioned? the vomiting up of the
elements anon, upon the receipt of them; the re-
furging the wine into the cup, before the minifter
could remove his hand, to the interruption of the
action. Now all thefe miftakes and errors have
rifen upon fome ungrounded and fond practices,
crept long fince (God knows how) into the church,
and as yet not fufficiently purged out. I will be
bold to inform you what it is, which is $\pi\rho\tilde{\omega}\tau o\nu$
$\psi\epsilon\tilde{\upsilon}\delta o\varsigma$, the main fundamental fallacy whence all
thefe abufes have fprung. There hath been a fan-
cy of long fubfiftence in the churches, that in the
communion there is fomething given befides bread
and wine, of which the numerality given, men
have not yet agreed. Some fay it is the body of
God, into which the bread is tranfubftantiated;
fome fay it is the fame body with which the bread
is confubftantiated; fome, that the bread remaining what it was, there paffes with it to the foul
the real body of God, in a fecret unknown man-

ner; fome, that a further degree of faith is fupplied us; others, that fome degree of God's grace,
whatever it be, is exhibited, which otherwife
would be wanting: all which variety of conceits
muft needs fall out, as having no other ground
but conjecture weakly founded. To fettle you
therefore in your judgment, both of the thing itfelf, and of the true ufe of it, I will commend to
your confideration thefe few propofitions.

1*ft*, In the communion there is nothing given
but bread and wine.

2*dly*, The bread and wine are figns indeed, but
not of any thing there exhibited, but of fomewhat
given long fince, even of Chrift given for us upon
the crofs, fixteen hundred years ago, and more.

3*dly*, Jefus Chrift is eaten at the communion-
table in no fenfe, neither fpiritually, by virtue of
any thing done there, nor really; neither metaphorically, nor literally. Indeed that which is
eaten (I mean the bread) is called Chrift by a metaphor; but it is eaten truly and properly.

4*ly*, The fpiritual eating of Chrift is common
to all places, as well as the Lord's table.

Laft of all, The ufes and ends of the Lord's
fupper can be no more than fuch as are mentioned
in the fcriptures, and they are but two.

1. The commemoration of the death and paffion of the Son of God, fpecified by himfelf at
the inftitution of the ceremony.

2. To teftify our union with Chrift, and com-

munion one with another; which end St. Paul hath taught us.

In thefe few conclufions the whole doctrine and ufe of the Lord's fupper is fully fet down; and whofo leadeth you beyond this, doth but abufe you : *Quicquid ultra quaeritur, non intelligitur.* The proof of thefe propofitions would require more than the limits of a letter will admit of; and I fee myfelf already to have exceeded thefe bounds. I will therefore pafs away to confider the fecond part of your letter.

In this *fecond* part, I would you had pleafed to have done as in the *firft* you did; that is, not only fet down the propofition of the Catholic, but fome anfwer of the Proteftant, by which we might have difcovered his judgment. I might perchance have ufed the fame liberty as I have done before, namely, difcovered the miftakes of both parties; for I fufpect that as there they did, fo here they would have given me caufe enough. Now I content myfelf barely to fpeak to the queftion : The queftion is, ' Whether the church may err in fun-' damentals ? ' By the ' church' I will not trifle as your Catholic doth, and mean only the Proteftant party, as he profeffeth he doth only the Roman faction. But I fhall underftand all factions in Chriftianity, all that entitle themfelves to Chrift, wherefoever difperfed all the world over.

1*ft*, I anfwer, That every Chriftian may err that will : for if men might not err wilfully, then there

could be no herefy; herefy being nothing elfe but
wilful error. For if we account miftakes befalling
us through human frailties to be herefies, then it
will follow, that every man fince the apoftles time
was an heretic; for never yet was there any
Chriftian, the apoftles only excepted, which did
not in fomething concerning the Chriftian faith
miftake himfelf, either by addition or omiffion, or
mifinterpretation of fomething. An evident fign
of this truth you may fee in this: by the providence of God, the writings of many learned Chriftians, from the fpring of Chriftianity, have been
left unto pofterity; and amongft all thofe, fcarcely any is to be found who is not confeft on all
hands to have miftaken fome things, and thofe
miftakes for the moft part ftand upon record by
fome who purpofely obferved them. Neither let
this (I befeech you) beget in you a conceit, as if
I meant to difgrace thofe whofe labours have been
and are of infinite benefit in the church. For if
Ariftotle, and Aphrodifeus, and Galen, and the
reft of thofe excellent men whom God hath in-
dued with extraordinary portions of natural knowledge, have with all thankful and ingenuous men
throughout all generations retained their credit
entire, notwithftanding it is acknowledged that
they have all of them in many things fwerved from
the truth; then why fhould not Chriftians exprefs
the fame ingenuity to thofe who have laboured
before us in the expofition of the Chriftian faith,

and highly efteem them for their works fake, their many infirmities notwithftanding?

You will fay, That for private perfons, it is confeft, they may and daily do err: but can Chriftians err by whole fhoals, by armies meeting for defence of the truth in fynods and councils, efpecially general; which are countenanced by the great fable of all the world, the Bifhop of Rome?

I anfwer, To fay that councils may not err, though private perfons may, at firft fight is a merry fpeech; as if a man fhould fay, That every fingle foldier indeed may run away, but a whole army cannot, efpecially having Hannibal for their captain. And fince it is confeft, that all fingle perfons not only may, but do err, it will prove a very hard matter to gather out of thefe a multitude, of whom being gathered together, we may be fecured they cannot err. I muft for mine own part confefs, that councils and fynods not only may and have erred, but confidering the means how they are managed, it were a great marvel if they did not err: for what men are they of whom thofe great meetings do confift? Are they the beft, the moft learned, the moft virtuous, the moft likely to walk uprighly? No, the greateft, the moft ambitious, and many times men neither of judgment nor learning; fuch are they of whom thefe bodies do confift. And are thefe men in common equity likely to determine for truth? *Sicut in vita, ita in caufis quoque fpes inprobas habent,* as Quintilian speaks *. Again, when such persons are thus met, their way to proceed to conclusion, is not by weight of reason, but by multitude of votes and suffrages, as if it were a maxim in nature, that the greater part must needs be the better; whereas our common experience shews, that, *Nunquam ita bene agitur cum rebus humanis, ut plures sint meliores.* It was never heard in any profession, that conclusion of truth went by plurality of voices, the Christian profession only excepted: and I have often mused how it comes to pass, that the way which in all other sciences is not able to warrant the poorest conclusion, should be thought sufficient to give authority to conclusions in divinity, the supreme empress of sciences. But I see what it is that is usually pleaded, and with your leave I will a little consider of it.

It is given out, that Christian meetings have such an assistance of God and his blessed Spirit, that let their persons be what they will, they may assure themselves against all possibility of mistaking; and this is that they say, which to this way of ending controversies, which in all other sciences is so contemptible, gives a determining to theological disputes of so great authority. And this music of the Spirit is so pleasing, that it hath taken the reformed party too; for with them likewise

* Instit. Orat. l. xii. c. 1. —— This is elsewhere thus translated by the author. ' Who, as in their lives, so in the ' causes they undertake, nourish hopes full of improbity.'

all things at length end in the Spirit, but with this difference, that thofe of Rome confine the Spirit to the bifhops and councils of Rome ; but the Proteftant enlargeth this working of the Spirit, and makes it the director of private meditations. I fhould doubtlefs do great injury to the goodnefs of God, if I fhould deny the fufficient affiftance of God to the whole world, to preferve them both from fin in their actions, and damnable errors in their opinions ; much more fhould I do it, if I denied it to the church of God: but this affiftance of God may very well be, and yet men may fall into fin and errors. St. Paul preaching to the Gentiles, tells them, that God was with them in fo palpable a manner, that even by groping they might have found him†; yet both he and we know, what the Gentiles did. Chrift hath promifed his perpetual affiftance to his church; but hath he left any prophecy, that the church fhould perpetually adhere to him? If any man think he hath, it is his part to inform us where this prophecy is to be found. That matters may go well with men, two things muft concur, the affiftance of God to men, and the adherence of men to God: if either of thefe be deficient, there will be little good done. Now the firft of thefe is never deficient, but the fecond is very often: fo that the promife of Chrift's

† Εἰ ἄρα γε ψηλαφήσειαν αὐτὸν καὶ εὕροιεν.

Act. Apoft. xvii. 27.

E 2

perpetual prefence made unto the church, infers
not at all any prefumption of infallibility. As for
that term of ' Spirit,' which is fo much taken up,
to open the danger that lurks under it, we muft a
little diftinguifh upon the word. This term ' Spi-
' rit of God' either fignifies the third perfon in the
bleffed Trinity, or elfe the wonderful power of
miracles, of tongues, of healing, &c. which was
given to the Apoftles, and other of the primitive
Chriftians, at the firft preaching of the gofpel ;
but both thefe meanings are ftrangers to our
purpofe. The Spirit of God, as it concerns the
queftion here in hand, fignifies either fomething
within us, or fomething without us: without us,
it fignifies the written word, recorded in the books
of the prophets, apoftles, and evangelifts, which
are metonymically called the Spirit, becaufe the
Holy Ghoft fpake thofe things by their mouths
when they lived, and now fpeaks unto us by their
pens when they are dead. If you pleafe to receive
it, this alone is left as Chrift's vicar in his abfence,
to give us directions both in our actions and opinions: he that tells you of another fpirit in the
church to direct you in your way, may as well tell
you a tale of a puck, or a walking fpirit in the
church-yard. But that this Spirit fpeaking without us may be beneficial to us, there muft be
fomething within us, which alfo we call the Spirit; and this is twofold: for either it fignifies a
fecret illapfe, or fupernatural influence of God up-

on the hearts of men, by which he is suppofed inwardly to incline, inform and direct men in their ways and wills, and to preferve them from fin and miftake; or elfe it fignifies that in us, which is oppofed againft the flefh, and which denominates us fpiritual men, and by which we are faid ' to ' walk according to the Spirit:' that which St. Paul means, when he tells us, ' The flefh lufteth ' againft the Spirit, and the Spirit againft the ' flefh, fo that we may not do what we lift.' Gal. v. 17. Now of thefe two, the former it is which the church feems to appeal unto, in determining controverfies by way of council. But to this I have little to fay; (1.) Becaufe I know not whether there be any fuch thing yea or no. (2.) Becaufe experience fhews, that the pretence of the Spirit in this fenfe is very dangerous, as being next at hand to give countenance to impofture and abufe: which is a thing fufficiently feen, and acknowledged both by the Papift and Proteftant party; as it appears by this, That though both pretend unto it, yet both upbraid each other with the pretence of it. But the Spirit, in the fecond fenfe, is that I contend for; and this is nothing but reafon illuminated by revelation out of the written word. For when the mind and fpirit humbly conform and fubmit to the written will of God, then you are properly faid to have the Spirit of God, and to walk according to the Spirit, not according to the flefh. This alone is that Spirit which preferves us from ſtraying from the truth: for he indeed that hath the Spirit, errs not all; or if he do, it is with as little hazard and danger as may be: which is the higheſt point of infallibility, which either private perſons or churches can arrive to.   Yet would I not have you to conceive that I deny, that at this day the Holy Ghoſt communicates himſelf to any in this ſecret and ſupernatural manner, as in foregoing times he had been wont to do; indeed my own many uncleanneſſes are ſufficient reaſons to hinder that good Spirit to participate himſelf unto me after that manner. The Holy Ghoſt was pleaſed to come down like a dove:

———*Veniunt ad candida teĉta columbae ;*
Accipiet nullas ſordida turris aves.

Ovid. Triſt. l. i. el. 9.

Now it is no reaſon to conclude the Holy Ghoſt imparts himſelf in this manner to none, becauſe he hath not done that favour unto me. But thus much I will ſay, that the benefit of that ſacred influence is confined to thoſe happy ſouls in whom it is, and cannot extend itſelf to the church in public. And if any Catholic except againſt you for ſaying ſo, warrant yourſelf and me out of Aquinas, whoſe words are theſe; *Innititur fidei naturæ revelationi apoſtolis et prophetis faĉtae, qui canonicos libros ſcripſerunt ; non autem revelationi, ſiqua fuit, aliis doĉtoribus faĉtae.*

It being granted then that churches can err, it

remains then, in the second place, to consider how far they may err. I answer for churches, as I did before for private persons, churches may err in fundamentals if they list, for they may be heretical; for churches may be wicked, they may be idolaters, and why then not heretical? Is heresy a more dangerous thing than idolatry? For whereas it is pleaded that churches cannot fall into heresy, because of that promise of our Saviour,' That ' the gates of hell shall not prevail against the ' church,' Matt. xvi. 18. it is but out of mistake of the meaning of that place: and indeed I have often mused how so plain a place could so long and so generally be misconstrued. To secure you therefore, that you be not abused with these words hereafter (for they are often quoted to prove the church's infallibility) I shall endeavour to give you the natural meaning of them : for πύλαι Ἅδȣ, ' the gates of Hell,' is an Hebraism ; for in the Hebrew expression, the gates of a thing signifies the thing itself, as the gates of Sion, Sion itself; and by the same proportion, the gates of hell signifies hell itself. Now Ἅδης, which we english ' hell,' as in no place of scripture it signifies heresy, so very frequently in scripture it signifies death, or rather the state of the dead, and is indifferently applied to good and bad. Let us then take the word in that meaning; for what greater means can we have to warrant the signification of a scripture-word, than the general meaning of it

E 4

in scripture? So that when our Saviour spake these words, he made no promise to the church of persevering in the truth; but to those that did persevere in the truth, he made a promise of victory against death and hell. And what he there says, sounds to no other purpose but this; That those who shall continue his, although they die, yet death shall not have the dominion over them; but the time shall come, that the bands of death shall be broken; and as Christ is risen, so shall they that are his rise again to immortality. For any help therefore that this text affords, churches may err in fundamentals. But to speak the truth, I much wonder, not only how any churches, but how any private man, that is careful to know and follow the truth, can err in fundamentals: for since it is most certain, that the scripture contains at least the fundamental parts of Christian faith, how is it possible that any man, that is careful to study and believe the scripture, should be ignorant of any necessary part of his faith? Now whether the church of Rome err in fundamentals, yea or no; to answer this, I must crave leave to use this distinction: To err in fundamentals, is either to be ignorant of, or deny something to be fundamental that is, or to entertain something for fundamental which is not. In the first sense, the church of Rome entertaining the scriptures as she doth, cannot possibly be ignorant of any principal part of the Christian faith; all her error is, in en-

tertaining in herself, and obtruding upon others a
multitude of things for fundamentals, which no
way concern our faith at all. Now how dangerous it is thus to do, except I know whether she
did this willingly or wittingly, yea or no, is not
eafy to define: if willingly she doth it, it is certainly high and damnable prefumption; if igno-
rantly, I know not what mercies God hath in store
for them that sin not out of malicious wickednefs. Now concerning the merriment newly start-
ed, I mean the requiring of a catalogue of fundamentals, I need to anfwer no more, but what
Abraham tells the rich man in hell, ' they have
' Mofes and the prophets, * ' the apostles and
the evangelists, let them feek them there; for if
they find them not there, in vain shall they feek
them in all the world befides. But yet to come a
little nearer to the particulars: if the church of
Rome would needs know what is fundamental in
our conceit, and what not; the anfwer, as far as
myfelf in perfon am concerned in the bufinefs,
shall be no other than this: Let her obferve what
points they are wherein we agree with her, and
let her think, if she pleafe, that we account of
them as fundamentals, efpecially if they be in the
fcriptures; and on the other hand, let her mark
in what points we refufe communion with her,
and let her affure herfelf we efteem thofe as no
fundamentals. If she defire a lift and catalogue

* Luke xvi. 29.

made of all thofe, fhe is at leifure enough, for ought I know, to do it herfelf.

Laft of all, Concerning the imputation of rebellion and fchifm againft church-authority, with which your Catholic difputant meant to affright you, all that is but merely powder without fhot, and can never hurt you : for fince it hath been fufficiently evidenced unto us, that the church of Rome hath adulterated the truth of God, by mixing with it fundry inventions of her own, it was the confcience of our duty to God that made us to feparate; for where the truth of God doth once fuffer, their union is confpiracy, authority is but tyranny, and churches are but routs. And fuppofe we, that we miftook, and made our feparation upon error, the church of Rome being right in all her ways, though we think otherwife, yet could not this much prejudice us; for it is fchifm upon wilfulnefs that brings danger with it; fchifm upon miftake, and fchifm upon juft occafion, hath in itfelf little hurt, if any at all.

S I R, I return you more than I thought, or you expected, yet lefs than the argument required : if you fhall favour me fo much as to carefully read what I have carefully written, you fhall find (at leaft in thofe points you occafioned me to touch upon) fufficient ground to plant yourfelf ftrongly againft all difcourfe of the Romifh

corner-creepers, which they ufe for the feducing
of unftable fouls. Be it much or little that I have
done, I require no other reward than the continuance of your good affection to

Your Servant,

whom you know.

MR. HALES'S

CONFESSION

OF THE

TRINITY.

THE sum of whatsoever either the scriptures teach, or the schools conclude, concerning the doctrine of the Trinity, is comprised in these few lines.

God is one; numerically one; more one, than any single man is one, if unity could *suscipere magis et minus*: yet, God is so one, that he admits of distinction; and so admits of distinction, that he still retains unity.

As he is one, so we call him God, the Deity, the Divine Nature, and other names of the same signification: as he is distinguished, so we call him Trinity; persons, Father, Son, and Holy Ghost.

In this Trinity there is one essence; two emanations; three persons, or relations; four properties; five notions.

[" A notion is that by which any person is known " or signified."]

The one essence is God, which with this relation, that it doth generate, or beget, makes the person of the Father: the same essence, with this relation that it is begotten, maketh the person of the Son: the same essence, with this relation, that it proceedeth, maketh the person of the Holy Ghost.

The two emanations are, to be begotten; and to proceed, or to be breathed out: The three persons are, Father, Son, and Holy Spirit. The three relations are, to beget; to be begotten; and, to proceed, or to be breathed out: The four properties are; the first, innascibility, and inemanability; the second, is to generate; these belong to the Father: The third is to be begotten, and this belongs unto the Son: The fourth is to proceed, or to be breathed out; and this belongs unto the Holy Spirit. The five notions are; first, innascibility; the second, is to beget; the third, to be begotten; the fourth, *spiratio passiva*, to be breathed out; the fifth, *spiratio activa*, or to breathe; and this notion belongs to the Father and the Son alike; for *Pater et Filius spirant Spiritum Sanctum.*

Hence it evidently follows, that he who acknowledgeth thus much, can never possibly scruple the Eternal Deity of the Son of God.

If any man think this Confession to be defective, (for I can conceive no more in this point necessary to be known) let him supply what he conceives be deficient, and I shall thank him for his favour.

How we come to know the SCRIPTURES *to be the* WORD *of* GOD ?

HOW come I to know that the works which we calls Livy's, are indeed his whofe name they bear ? Hath God left means to know the prophane writings of men ? hath he left no certain means to know his own records ?

The firft and outward means that brings us to the knowledge of thefe books, is the voice of the church, notified to us by our teachers and inftructors, who firft unclafped and opened them unto us, and that common duty which is exacted at the hand of every learner : *Oportet difcentem credere,* ' A learner muft believe.' And this remaining in us, peradventure is all the outward means, that the ordinary and plainer fort of Chriftians know.

To thofe who are converfant among the records of antiquity, farther light appear : to find the ancient copies of books, bearing thefe titles, to find in all ages fince their being written, the univerfal confent of all the church, ftill refolving itfelf upon thefe writings, as facred and uncontrolable ; thefe cannot chufe but be ftrong monitors unto us, to pafs our confent unto them, and to conclude, that either thefe writings are that which they are taken for, or nothing left us from

antiquity is true. For whatſoever is that gives
any ſtrength or credit to any thing of antiquity
left to poſterity, whether it be writings and records, or tradition from hand to hand, or what
things elſe ſoever, they all concur to the autho-
riſing of holy Scriptures, as amply as they do to
any other thing left unto the world.

Yea, but will ſome man reply, this proves indeed ſtrongly that Moſes and the prophets, that
St. Matthew and St. Paul, &c. writ thoſe books,
and about thoſe times which they bear ſhew of,
but this comes not home ; for how proves this
that they are of God ? If I heard St. Paul himſelf
preaching, what makes me believe him that his
doctrine is from God, and his words, the words
of the Holy Ghoſt ? For anſwer. There was no
outward means to perſuade the world at the firſt
riſing of Chriſtianity that it is infallibly from God,
but only miracles, ſuch as impoſſibly were naturally to be done. ' Had I not done theſe things'
(ſaith our Saviour) ' which no man elſe could do,
' you had had no ſin:' had not the world ſeen thoſe
miracles, which did unavoidably prove the aſſiſ-
tance and preſence of a divine power with thoſe
who firſt taught the will of Chriſt, it had not had
ſin, if it had rejected them : for though the world
by the light of natural diſcretion, might eaſily
have diſcovered, that that was not the right way,
wherein it uſually walked ; yet, that that was the
true path, which the apoſtles themſelves began to

tread, there was no means undoubtedly to prove, but miracles: and if the building were at this day to be raifed, it could not be founded without miracles. To our fore-fathers therefore, whofe ears firft entertained the word of life, miracles were neceffary; and fo they are to us, but after another order: for as the fight of thefe miracles did confirm the doctrine unto them, fo unto us the infallible records of them: for whatfoever evidence there is, that the word once began to be preached, the very fame confirms unto us that it was accompanied with miracles and wonders; fo that as thofe miracles by being feen, did prove unanfwerably unto our fore-fathers the truth of the doctrine, for the confirmation of which they were intended; fo do they unto us never a whit lefs effectually approve it, by being left unto us upon thefe records; which if they fail us, then by antiquity there can be nothing left unto pofterity which can have certain and undoubted credit. The certain and uncontroulable records of miracles, are the fame to us the miracles are.

The church of Rome, when fhe commends unto us the authority of the church in dijudicating of Scriptures, feems only to fpeak of herfelf, and that, of that part of herfelf which is at fome time exiftent; whereas we, when we appeal to the church's teftimony, content not ourfelves with any part of the church actually exiftent, but add unto it the perpetual fucceffive teftimony of the church

in all ages, fince the apoftles time, viz. fince its
firft beginning; and out of both thefe draw an
argument in this queftion of that force, as that
from it not the fubtileft difputer can find an e-
fcape; for who is it that can think to gain acceptance and credit with reafonable men, by oppo-
fing not only the prefent church converfing in
earth, but to the uniform confent of the church in
all ages.

So that in effect, to us of after ages, the greateft, if not the fole outward mean of our confent
to the holy Scripture, is the voice of the church,
(excepting always the copies of the books themfelves, bearing from their birth fuch or fuch names)
of the church, I fay, and that not only of that
part of it, which is actually exiftent at any time,
but fucceffively of the church ever fince the time
of our bleffed Saviour : for all thefe teftimonies
which from time to time are left in the writings
of our fore-fathers (as almoft every age, ever fince
the firft birth of the gofpel, hath by God's providence left us ftore) are the continued voice of the
church, witneffing unto us the truth of thefe
books, and their authority well : but this is only
fides humano judicio et teftimonio acquifita ; what
fhall we think of *fides infufa ?* of the inward working of the Holy Ghoft, in the confciences of every
believer ? How far it is a perfuader unto us of the
authority of thefe books, I have not much to fay :
only thus much in general, that doubtlefs the Holy

F

Ghoſt doth ſo work in the heart of every true believer, that it leaves a farther aſſurance, ſtrong and
ſufficient, to ground and ſtay itſelf upon : but
this, becauſe it is private to every one, and no way
ſubject to ſenſe, is unfit to yield argument by way
of diſpute, to ſtop the captious curioſities of wits
diſpoſed to wrangle ; and by ſo much the more
unfit it is, by how much by experience we have
learned, that men are very apt to call, their own
private conceit, the Spirit. To oppoſe unto theſe
men, to reform them, our own private conceits,
under the name likewiſe of the Spirit, were madneſs ; ſo that to judge upon preſumption of the
Spirit in private, can be no way to bring either
this, or any other controverſy, to an end.

If it ſhould pleaſe God, at this day, to add any
thing more unto the canon of faith, it were necef-
ſary it ſhould be confirmed by miracles.

A
T R A C T

CONCERNING THE

P O W E R

OF THE

K E Y S,

AND

AURICULAR CONFESSION.

IN opening the point concerning the doctrine of the Keys of the Kingdom of Heaven, I will follow thofe lines, that tract, which yourfelf hath been pleafed to fet me. Yet firft, e'er I come to your particulars, I will difcover, as far as generality will give me leave, what it is which we intend, when we ufe this phrafe of fpeech. At the firft appearance, it is plain, the form of words is not proper, but metaphorical. Now fome truth there is in that which you learned in the books of

your minority, from your Ariſtotle, ' Every thing
' ſpoken metaphorically is ambiguous and ob-
' ſcure.*' And indeed could we but once agree
what it is which that metaphor doth intimate, the
greateſt part of the diſpute were at an end. The
natural way to diſcover this, is to ſee what the uſe
of keys, properly taken, is; and after that, what
means they are, which in our endeavours to attain
to the kingdom of heaven, have ſomething proportionable to the uſe of keys : and this being
once diſcovered, there can remain no queſtion,
what are the keys.

Now nothing is more known, than that the only uſe of keys is to open and ſhut, to admit us
into, or exclude us from the poſſeſſion of what we
ſeek. Now ſince the kingdom of heaven is com-
pared to a houſe, from which all the ſons of Adam
by nature are excluded; whatſoever then it is that
gives us way, that removes all obſtacles which
hinder us from entrance of that houſe, that certainly muſt be underſtood by the name of keys.
Now all theſe means, or whatſoever elſe it is which
doth further us towards the poſſeſſing ourſelves
of eternal life, they were all laid down in the goſpel of our Lord Jeſus Chriſt, committed by him
fully and firſt of all to the diſpenſation of the bleſſed Apoſtles, to be reported by them, or their
means, all the world over. So that, I think, I may
ſafely lay thus much for the firſt ground of the

* Πᾶν ἀσαφὲς; τὸ κατὰ μεταφορὰν λεγόμενον.

queſtion betwixt yourſelf and me; *Claves regni coelorum ſunt doctrina evangelii.*

Now ſince keys are nothing without ſome hand to manage them, we muſt, in the ſecond place, diſcover into whoſe hands they are committed. And for this purpoſe, firſt of all, it muſt not be denied, that principally and properly (I might well enough add only, if I liſted, but that I ſpare you) the hand of God it is, that manages and applies theſe keys; for of God and Chriſt it is written, ' He hath the key, he opens, and no man ſhuts; ' he ſhuts, and no man opens.' Revel. iii. 7. Yet ſince it hath pleaſed God to uſe the miniſtry of men, to the ſaving of men, and bringing them into the kingdom of heaven; in a ſecondary ſenſe the keys of that kingdom are ſaid to be put into the hands of men: inaſmuch as it hath pleaſed the wiſdom of God, not to uſe theſe keys, at leaſt as far as concerns the beneficial and opening part, ſome act of man not firſt premiſed. For ſince that faith in Jeſus Chriſt is the ſum of the doctrine of the goſpel, and faith cometh not but by hearing, and hearing cometh not but by preaching, and preaching is the act of men alone (for God employs not angels in that behalf;) it appears that this preaching, or manifeſtation of the doctrine of the goſpel not performed, the keys muſt needs be unprofitable. By the manifeſtation of the goſpel of God, I mean not only the labour of the lip, in

F 3

expounding, praying, reproving, or the like; but
the adminiftration of facraments, the acting (if
any thing beyond this is to be acted) whatfoever
the manifeftation of the gofpel requireth. So that I
think I may fet down for a fecond ground towards
the fettling of the point in queftion, thus much;
that the managing or application of the keys, fo
far forth as men are intrufted with them, is, The
manifeftation of the doctrine of the gofpel. Thus
far have we opened in general the fubftance of
the keys, and the ufe of them. I come now to
your queries.

1*ft*, You afk of the quality of the Apoftles receiving this power, whether they had it as judges,
authoritativè; or as meffengers, *declarativè,* only
to propound, or denounce? You manifeft yourfelf
for the former, and reafons you bring, fuch as
they be. Your reafons I fhall confider in their
place, but I muft firft tell you that you afk amifs;
for your queftion is concerning the whole power
of the keys, but you anfwer only of a part, that is,
of facramental abfolution only, as if all the power
of the keys refided there. So that here you ufe the
fallacy *plurium interrogationum;* and I might well
grant you, that indeed that part were *judicativè,*
but yet contend that all the reft were only *declarativè.* To reduce you therefore, I muft do with
you, as phyficians, in fome cafes, deal with their
patients; e'er I can come to purge the humour

you are sick of, I must a little prepare you. The power of the keys is expressed by the learned in three yokes, or pairs of words.

1. To remit, and to retain.
2. To loose, and to bind.
3. To open, and to shut.

On the one side, to remit, to loose, to open, which is the one half of the power, agree in one, and signify the same thing; so do the other three, to retain, to bind, to shut, which contain the other half. To your question then, whether the power of the keys be declarative only, I answer first; For this latter part or half, it is merely declarative, neither can it be otherwise: which that you may see with your eyes, I must request you to observe, that all shutting of the kingdom of heaven, is either common to all, or casual, befalling only some The common exclusion is that state of nature, wherein we all are involved, as we spring from the first Adam: the second exclusion is that which befals Christians relapsing into sin. The first shutting was at the fall, and was then prefigured unto us, by the barring up of the way unto the tree of life. What active, what judiciary part can any minister of the gospel have here? All that the Apostles could do here, was but to open to men this their misery; a thing, before the death of our Saviour, either very sparingly, or not at all revealed. Of this therefore you must needs quit your hands, and so you must of the other, I mean exclusion upon casuality and relapse. For when a man, converted to Christianity, falleth eftsoons into some mortal sin, doth the gate of heaven stand open to him, till he fall upon some cursed priest, that used his key to shut it?

There are in the world a kind of deceitful locks with sliding bolts; I have seen myself and others much deceived by them, when the doors have fallen at our heels, and locked us out when we intended no such thing. Sir, Heaven-door hath a sliding lock, upon occasion of mortal sin; it will shut without any use of a key.

Perchance I do not well, παίζειν ἐν μὴ παικτοῖς*; yet the sober meaning of what I have spoke merrily, is but this; That either you must make the ministry of the gospel only declarative, or else it will follow that every impenitent relapser, that hath the good fortune to escape the priests being privy to his sin, is like to find heaven open at the last. So then it is apparent, that notwithstanding your heaping up of interrogatories, and your pressing of *ligaveritis et vos*, and telling me what I ever knew, that *solvere* and *ligare* be actives; yet in this part of our power, all your activity is lost, and there remains nothing for you but to report upon good evidence, what you find done by your betters to your hand.

Half your jurisdiction then is fallen: and if I had no other *medium* but this, I might with good

* ' To sport in serious matters.'

probability conclude againſt you for the other part. For if the one half made in the ſame form in the like phraſe and garb of ſpeech, yet enforceth no more but declaration and denouncing ; then why ſhould you think the other half (which in all likelihood is homogeneal to the former) to be more? Nay, there is far more natural equity that you ſhould be here only declarative, than iŋ the other. Politicians tell us, that it is wiſdom for princes, who deſire to gain the love of their ſub-jects, to adminiſter themſelves all favours and gra-ces, but to leave actions of juſtice and harſhneſs to be performed by others.

Sir, No prince can be ſo ambitious of the love of his ſubjects, as God is of the love of mankind ; why then ſhould I think him ſo ill a politician, as to make himſelf the adminiſtrator of the rough, unpleaſing, love-killing offices of binding, ſhut-ting, retaining ; and then paſs over to the prieſt, the diſpenſation of the fair, well-ſpoken, ingrati-ating offices of remitting, looſing, and opening? But I will leave this kind of topic and dialectical arguing, becauſe you are a pretender to convin-cing reaſons : I will directly enter even upon that part of your power of opening and remitting, be-ing the other part of your territory; and by main ſtrength, take all activity from you there too. Give me leave to aſk you one queſtion; you may very well favour me ſo far, for you have aſked me very many :

The converfion of a finner, is it an act of the keys, yea or no?

By your principles it is not; for you make the power of the keys to be judiciary, and therefore the converfion of an infidel pertains not to them: the church of Rome will help you with a *medium* to make this argument good. ' Do we not judge ' thofe that are within? for thofe that are with-' out, God fhall judge,' faith St. Paul, 1 Cor. v. 12. Whence fhe infers, that a converted infidel, not yet admitted to the church, is a ftranger to the judiciary power of the keys; but being once admitted into the church, he is now become the church's fubject, and fo fit matter for the prieft to work on, upon his next relapfe. What think you of this reafon? Do you take it to be good? Take heed, or elfe it will give you a deadly ftripe: for the converfion of an infidel, out of queftion, is a moft proper act of the keys. For, fince the open-ing of the kingdom of heaven is confeffed to be-long unto the keys; and heaven, which was fhut a-gainft the infidel in time of his infidelity, upon his converfion is acknowledged to be opened unto him: certainly whofoever converted him, ufed the keys; or elfe he muft pretend to have either a picklock, or the herb Lunaria, which, they fay, makes locks fall off from doors, and the fetters from horfes heels. If then the converfion of a fin-ner be an act of the keys, and by the argument of the church of Rome it be not judiciary; it follows then, that all acts of the keys are not judiciary; and if not judiciary, then declarative only: for betwixt these two I know no mean.

But because to dispute against a man out of his own principles, which perchance are false (for this we know oft falls out, that by the power of syllogisms, men may and do draw true conclusions from false premises) because, I say, thus to do, in the judgment of Aristotle, leaves a man ' per- ' suaded, but not bettered: † ' and I am willing not only to persuade you, but to better you: I will draw the little, which remains to be said in this point, from other places.

1*st*, In all the Apostles practice in converting Jews and Gentiles, find you any thing like unto the act of any judiciary power? They neither did nor could use any such thing. That they did not, appears by Philip, who having catechized the Eunuch, and finding him desirous of baptism, immediately upon profession of his faith, admitted him into the church. That they neither did nor could, appears by Peter and the rest of the Apostles in the Acts ii. 41. who could never in the space of an afternoon, being none but themselves, have converted three thousand souls, had they taken any such way, as you seem to misfancy. Again, imagine with yourself all circumstances you can, which are of force to make a power judiciary, apply them

† Πεπεισμενον μεν, ωφελημενον δε ου.

all to the practice of the Apostles, in the conversion of infidels; and if you find any one of them
agree to that action, let me be challenged upon
it, and be thought to have abused you with a fallacy.

To conclude then, since your *ligaveritis*, which
is the one half of your pretended jurisdiction, pretends to nothing above declarative; and since your
solveritis, in so great an act as is the conversion of
infidels, lays claim to no more: what act of the
power of the keys is it, wherein we may conceive
hope of finding any thing active or judiciary? I
see what you will say; there yet remains a part,
you think, wherein you have hope to speed, and
that is the reconciling of relapsing Christians. As
you fancy that in every sinning Christian, there is
a duty binding him to repair, and lay his sin open
to the minister of the gospel; and in him a power
to consider of the sins of such as repair unto him,
to weigh particulars, to consider circumstances
and occasions, and according to true judgment, either upon penance imposed to absolve sin (which
you call remitting of the sin) or to withhold him
for a time from participation of holy duties with
catholic Christians, which you call retaining of
sins; supposing that God doth the like in heaven,
as it is written, ' What you bind in earth, is bound
' in heaven, and what you loose in earth, is loosed
' in heaven,' Matth. xvi. 19. Now the rock on
which you labour to found so extravagant a con-

ccit, is no other than the words which I have quoted out of scripture; you press earnestly the *ligaveritis et vos*, all which can yield you small relief:
for if they help you not at all in those weighty
parts of the power of the keys, which but now
were laid before you; by what analogy can you
expect they should afford you any assistance here?
As is *ligare*, so is *solvere*; as is the conversion of
an infidel, so is the reconciling of a relapsing Christian, for any thing you can make appear: either
all is declarative, which is very possible, and in
many cases necessary; or all judicative, which in
some cases is impossible, and in none necessary: so
that to fit the scripture to your fancy, you are
constrained to distract and rend it without any
warrant at all. But you have found out in the
text a stronger argument against the declarative
power I contend for : you espy an *insufflavit*, a
great, a solemn, and unwonted ceremony, undoubtedly concluding some greater matter than a
poor power declarative: ' What! did our serious
' master thus spend his breath to no purpose, and,
' like a *hocus pocus*, with so much shew act us a
' solemn nothing?' I pray whose words are these?
I should have thought them to have been Porphyry's, or Julian's (but that I know your hand) for
you subscribed not your name to your letters;

Αφίσαμαι. ἀκέρδεια λέλογχεν
Θαμινὰ κακαγόρως.*   Olymp. i. 84.

* ' Vengeance awaits th' unhallowed tongue.'   West.

they are the words of your Pindarus, upon an occafion not much unlike unto this.

Sir, you have no fkill to judge, or fet a price
upon fo divine an act; he loft not his breath, when
he fpent his *infufflavit;* he opened their wits, that
they might underftand the fcripture; he revealed
to them the myfteries of Jefus Chrift, dying and
rifing again for the world's falvation, the greateft
news that ever was reported in the world, and till
then concealed : he commanded them to be the
firft bringers of this good news ; and that they
might the more undauntedly perform their charge,
he endowed them with infallibility, with infinite
conftancy and fortitude, with power of working
fuch wonders as none could do, unlefs God were
with them. *Appello confcientiam tuam:* were thofe
things fuch nothings, that they deferve to be thus
jeered? But that befals you which befals the
ftares that dwell in the fteeple, who fear not the
bells, becaufe they hear them every day. Thefe
wonderful benefits of God have every day founded in your ears, and the frequency of them hath
taught you to forget your reverence to them. Yet
all this *infufflavit,* this ceremony was for no other
end but to further a declarative power; their un-
daunted fortitude, their power of miracling, their
infallibility did but add countenance and ftrength
to their declarative power, by which they went up
and down the world, to manifeft the good tidings of
falvation. So that even thefe which ferved thus to

set off the gospel, were nothing else but means of
the better manifestation of it; therefore may they
very well pass, if not amongst the keys, yet amongst
the necessary wards. Whereas your fancy of an
active or judicative power in the priest, concurring
with God in reconciling relapsing Christians, is neither one nor other, but is indeed like unto the work
of some deceitful smith, who the better to countenance and grace his work, adds to his key super-
fluous and idle wards, which, in the opening of
the lock, are of no use at all.

To your second query, Whether the keys were
confined to the Apostles only? The answer is in
no case hard to give, it may perchance in some
case be dangerous; for there is a generation of
men in the world, (the clergy they call them) who
impropriate the keys unto themselves, and would
be very angry to understand, that others from
themselves should claim a right unto them. To
your question then, no doubt but originally none
received the keys from the mouth of our Saviour,
but the Apostles only; none did, nor ever could
manage them with that authority and splendour as
the Apostles did, who were above all most amply
furnished with all things fitting so great a work.
For whereas you seem to intimate, that the preaching mission was communicated to others, as the
seventy-two disciples, as well as the Apostles; you
do but mistake yourself, if you conceive that the
keys of the gospel were any way committed to

them: for concerning the mysteries of Jesus Christ,
and him crucified for the sins of the world (wherein indeed the opening of the kingdom of heaven
did consist) they received it not, they knew it not.
To be the prime reporters of this, was an honour
imparted only to the Apostles: yet were they not
so imparted, as that they should be confined to
them. Every one that heard and received the light
of the saving doctrine from them, so far forth as
he had understanding in the ways of life, had now
the keys of the kingdom of heaven committed to
his power, both for his own and others use. Every one, of what state or condition soever, that
hath any occasion offered him, to serve another in
the ways of life, clergy or lay, male or female,
whatever he be, hath these keys, not only for
himself, but for the benefit of others. For if natural goodness teach every man, *Lumen de lumi-
ne, erranti comiter monstrare viam*, &c. then how
much more doth Christian goodness require of e-
very one, to his ability to be a light to those who
sit in darkness, and direct their steps, who most
dangerously mistake their way? To save a soul,
every man is a priest. To whom, I pray you, is
that said in Leviticus, ' Thou shalt not see thy
' brother sin, but thou shalt reprove, and save thy
' brother?' And if the law binds a man, when
he saw his enemies cattle to stray, to put them into their way; how much more doth it oblige him
to do the like for the man himself? See you not

how the whole world confpires with me in the
fame opinion? Doth not every father teach his fon,
every mafter his fervant, every man his friend?
How many of the laity in this age, and from time
to time in all ages, have by writing for the public
good, propagated the gofpel of Chrift, as if fome
fecret inftinct of nature had put into mens minds
thus to do? I fhame to dwell fo long upon fo
plain a theme; yet becaufe I feel your pulfe, and
perceive what it is that troubles you, I muft fay
fomething to an objection, which I know you
make. You conceive that forthwith upon this
which I have faid, muft needs follow fome great
confufion of eftates, and degrees; the laity will
ftraitway get up into our pulpits, we fhall lofe our
credit, and the adoration which the fimple fort do
yield us is in danger to be loft.

Sir, Fear you not, the fufficient and able of
the clergy will reap no difcountenance, but honour by this: for he that knows how to do well
himfelf, will moft willingly approve what is well
done by another. It is extreme poverty of mind
to ground your reputation upon another man's
ignorance; and to fecure yourfelf, you do well,
becaufe you perceive perchance, that none can
judge how ill you do. Be not angry then to
fee others join with you in part of your charge.
' I would all the Lord's people did preach,' and
that every man did think himfelf bound to difcharge a part of the common good ; and make

G

account that the care of other mens souls concerned him as well as of his own. When the Apostles
took order to ordain some, upon whom the public
burden of preaching the gospel should lie, it was
not their purpose to impropriate the thing to those
persons alone; but knowing that what was left to
the care of all, was commonly worse looked unto,
in wise and most Christian care, they designed
some, whose duty it should be to wait upon the
gospel alone, the better to preserve the profession
to the world's end. It hath been the wisdom of
those, who have taken care of the propagation of
arts and sciences, not only to appoint means, that
multitudes should study and make profession privately, but that some should be constituted public
professors to teach *è cathedra*, that so all might
know to whom to repair, in the doubts incident
to their faculties; and this hath been thought a
sovereign way to preserve sciences. Sir, we are
the public professors of Christianity, we speak *è
cathedra*, which none can do, but such as are ordained. Let the private profession and practice of
Christianity improve itself never so much, yet the
honour of the public professor, so he deserve his
place, can never impair. It grieves me to stand so
long upon so plain, so unwelcome a lesson; I will
ease myself and you, and reflect upon your third
query.

In the *third* place, you require to know, What
necessity, or what convenience there is of confes-

fion: You mean, I think, that confeſſion, which is as fooliſhly as commonly called facramental, for it hath nothing of a facrament in it. Did I know your mind a little more in particular, what form of confeſſion you ſpeak of, whether as it is uſed in the church of Rome, or in ſome refined guiſe, as it ſeems ſome would, who have of late called for it in the church of England; I ſhould ſpeak peradventure more appoſitely to what you defire. But ſince you have propoſed confeſſion only in a generality, my anſwer ſhall be in like manner. And,

First of all, Confeſſion of ſins is a thing, not only convenient, but unavoidably neceſſary to ſalvation; without which none ſhall ever ſee God: and thus far, I ſuppoſe, all Chriſtians do agree. The main difference is in the manner of practiſing it; the queſtion being, What parties are to be intereſted in it?

Natural equity informeth us, that unto every party, juſtly offended, ſatisfaction ſome way or other is due. The firſt party wronged in every offence is God, againſt whoſe honour and expreſs command every ſin is committed. To him therefore, in the firſt place, ſatisfaction is due, by ſubmiſſion and acknowledgment; ſince there remains no other way of compoſition with God. But there are ſome ſins committed againſt God, ſome committed againſt God and men: in the former it is ſufficient if we pacify God alone; in the latter our neighbour, againſt whom we have treſpaſſed, muſt receive ſatisfaction for the wrong done him at leaſt, if it be in the power of the treſpaſſer. Your Primmer of Sarum will tell you, ' That not ' to make reſtitution, if you be able, and not to ' pardon, unavoidably exclude from the kingdom ' of heaven.' Now might the doctrine of confeſ-ſion and acknowledgment in caſe of offence given, have been permitted to run fair and clear, as it de-ſcends from God and good reaſon, the firſt foun-tains of it; there needed no more to be ſaid in this argument, than I have already told you. But I know not what intempeſtive fooliſh ambition hath troubled the ſtream, and it hath paſt now for a long time (till the reformation altered it) for a general doctrine in the church, That in all kind of ſins, whether againſt God or our neighbour, there can be no reconciliation betwixt the parties of-fending and offended, but by interpoſition of a prieſt; a thing utterly beſides all reaſon and com-mon ſenſe, that you ſhould open your private imperfections to one whom they concern not (for it is granted, that all parties concerned in an of-fence, muſt have reaſon at the hands of the offen-der) and who can no ways help you: for he that is conſcientious of his ſin (and without trouble of conſcience I think none would ever repair to his confeſſor) knows very well, that there is no ſin ſo great, but upon ſubmiſſion God both can and will pardon it; and none ſo ſmall, but pardon for it

must be sought, or else he hath been ill catechized.
And more than this what can any priest tell him?
Your Pliny somewhere tells you, ' That he that
' is stricken by a scorpion, if he go immediately
' and whisper it into the ear of an ass, shall find
' himself immediately eased*.' That sin is a scorpion, and bites deadly, I have always believed ;
but that to cure the bite of it, it was a sovereign
remedy to whisper it into the ear of a priest, I do
as well believe as I do that of Pliny. The patrons
of this fancy, for defect of reason and common
congruity, are fain to betake themselves to scripture; and the mischief is, there is no direct text
for it, and therefore they are constrained to help
themselves with a mere conjectural consequence :
for since it is taken for certain, that there is a
power to remit and to retain sins, how shall they,
who have this power given them, know how fit
it is to remit or to retain a sin, except they know
the sin; and know it they cannot, but by confession ? For answer to this,

1*st*, We have found and proved, that the words
of scripture must receive such a sense, as from
whence no such consequence can be inferred.

2*ly*, We have endeavoured to prove, that the
dispensation or application of the keys of the kingdom of heaven (being nothing else but the duty of
saving of souls) is a duty, which, *pro occasione ob-*

---

* ' Si quis asino in aurem percussum a scorpione se dicat,
' transire malum protinus tradunt.' Hist. Nat. l. 28. c. 10.

latâ, lies upon every Chriſtian; which if it be true (as in good faith I think it) and the clergy per- ceive it, I think they would never go about to urge that text, although we ſhould yield it them in their own meaning. For they muſt needs ſee that it follows, that you may as well make your muleteer (if you have one) your confeſſor, as your pariſh-prieſt. Tell me in good earneſt, if you can, out of what good intent can this deſire to know another man's ſin, which concerns you not, pro- ceed ? Is it to teach him that it is a ſin ? He knew that, or elſe he had never repaired to you to confeſs it. Is it to tell him that he is to repent, to reſtore, to pray, to give alms ? &c. All this he knew, or elſe he hath had his breeding under an evil clergy. Yea, but how ſhall the phyſician cure the diſeaſe, if he know it not ? Suppoſe all diſeaſes had one remedy (as all ſpiritual diſeaſes have) and what matters it, if the patient be ſick, to know whether it be an ague, or the meazles, or the pleuriſy, ſince one potion cures them all ? Yea, but if you know not the particulars, how ſhall he judge of the quantity of the doſes ? for the ſame diſeaſe, upon ſundry circumſtances, may require *majus* or *minus* in the phyſic. This is the pooreſt ſcruple of a thou- ſand ; for in the regimen of patients ſpiritually ſick, there can be but one miſtake, that is, if you give too little. Be ſure you give enough, and teach your patients to think no ſin to be little (which in men ſpiritually ſick is *error ſaluberrimus*) and you can never err : for natural phyſic is only phyſic, but spiritual physic is both physic and diet, and may be indifferently administered both to the sick and the sound; repentance perchance only excepted, of which, upon occasion, assure yourself you can hardly take too much. What reason now can you give me, why you should desire to dive into any man's breast, *et scire secreta domus* * ? except it be that which follows in the next words, *inde timeri*, as I must confess I suspect it is. The truth is, some mistaken customs of the antient church, the craft and power of the clergy, the simplicity and ignorance of the laity, these begat the Τραγέλαφος †, of which we now speak. It may be you take the practice of the antient church, and the point of excommunication, to make somewhat for you : when those cards shall come to be played (though that of church-custom is not greatly material, which way soever it looks) I believe you will not find the game you look for. Indeed I was once minded to have considered something of that ; but I think you look for a letter, not for a book, and I perceive myself already to have gone beyond the compass of a letter. Another parley therefore, if you please, shall put an end to those and other scruples, if any do arise : and for the present give, I pray you, a little respite unto

Yours,

From my study, this 8th
  day of March, 1637.   J. H.

* Juvenal. sat. iii.
† Hircocervus, a monster composed of discordant parts.

G 4

MISCELLANIES,

SECTION I.

How to know the church.

MARKS and notes to know the church, there are none, except we will make true profes-
fion, which is the form and effence of the church,
to be a mark. And as there are none, fo it is not
neceffary there fhould be: for to what purpofe
fhould they ferve? that I might go feek and find
out fome company to mark. This is no way neceffary, for glorious things are in the fcriptures
fpoken of the church; not that I fhould run up
and down the world to find the perfons of the
profeffors, but that I fhould make myfelf of it.
This I do by taking upon me the profeffion of
Chriftianity, and fubmitting myfelf to the rules of
belief and practice delivered in the gofpel; though,
befides myfelf, I knew no other profeffor in the
world. If this were not the author's end in propofal of the title, it is but a mere vanity.

SECT. II.

The description of the church.

THE church, as it imports a visible company in earth, is nothing else but the company of professors of Christianity, wheresoever dispersed in the earth. To define it thus by monarchy, under one visible head, is a novelty crept up, since men began to change the spiritual kingdom of Christ to secular pride and tyranny; and a thing never heard of, either in the scriptures, or in the writings of the antients. Government, whether by one or many, or howsoever, if it be one of the church's contingent attributes, it is all; certainly it is no necessary property, much less comes it into the definition and essence of it. I mean outward government; for as for inward government, by which Christ reigns in the hearts of his elect, and vindicates them from spiritual enemies, I have no occasion to speak, neither see I any reference to it in all your author's animadversions.

SECT. III.

How Christ is the head of the church.

FROM the world's beginning, till the last hour of it, the church is essentially one and the same, howsoever perchance in garment, and outward ceremony, it admits of difference. And as it was from the beginning of the world, so was it

Chriftian; there being no other difference betwixt the fathers before Chrift and us, but this: as we believe in Chrift that ' is come,' fo they believed in Chrift that ' was to come;' ' Jefus Chrift yefter-' day, and to day, and the fame for ever,' Heb. xiii. 8. Reference unto Chrift is the very effence of the church, and there neither is, nor ever was any church but Chrift's; and therefore the church amongft the Jews was properly and truly Chrifti-an, *quoad rem*, as we are. Now as this church at all times is Chrift's body, fo is Chrift the head of it: for it is as impoffible for the church, as for the body to be without its head; it is not there-fore as your author dreams; Chrift came not to found a new church, or to profefs a vifible head-fhip of it. That relation to this church, which we exprefs when we call him the head of it, is one and the fame, from the beginning to all eterni-ty; neither receives it any alteration in this re-fpeɛt, becaufe the perfon, in whom this relation is founded, is fometimes vifible, fometimes not. It is true indeed, the head of the church fome-times became vifible, but this is but contingent and by concomitancy: for Chrift, the fecond per-fon in the Trinity, becoming man to redeem this church, and manifeft the way of truth unto it, it fo fell out that the head of the church became vi-fible. Of this vifibility he left no fucceffor, no doɛtrine, no ufe, as being a thing merely acciden-tal. I afk, Had the church before Chrift any vifi-

ble head? If it had, then was not Chrift the firft,
as here our teacher teacher tells us. If it had
none, why then fhould the church more require
a vifible head, than it did from the beginning?
To fpeak the truth at once: all thefe queftions
concerning the notes, the vifibility, the government of the church, if we look upon the fubftance
and nature of the church, they are merely idle
and impertinent; if upon the end why learned men
do handle them, it is nothing elfe but faction.

SECT. IV.

Of Peter's minifterial headfhip of the church.

IN your author's paragraphs concerning the vifible increafe, or fucceffion of the church,
there is no difference betwixt us. As for the
proofs of Peter's minifterial headfhip, this firft
concerning his being the rock of the church, that
cannot prove it: for Peter was the rock then,
when our Saviour fpake; but then could he not
be the vifible head, for Chrift himfelf was then
living, and by our teacher's doctrine, fupplied that
room himfelf. Peter therefore, howfoever, or in
what fenfe foever he were the rock, yet could he
not be the vifible head, except we will grant the
church to have had two vifible heads at once.

2*ly*, The keys of heaven committed to Peter,
and command to feed his fheep, import no more
than that common duty laid upon all the difciples,

' To teach all nations;' Matth. xxviii. 19. for this
duty, in feveral refpects, is expreffed by feveral
metaphors. Teaching, as it fignifies the opening
of the way to life, fo it is called by the name of
keys; but as it fignifies the ftrengthning of the
foul of man by the word, which is the foul's fpiritual food, fo it is called feeding. Thus much is
feen by the defenders of the church of Rome, and
therefore they fly for refuge to a circumftance. It
is obferved, that our Saviour delivered this doctrine to Peter alone (as indeed fometimes he did)
in this it is fuppofed that fome great myftery refts:
for why fhould our Saviour thus fingle out Peter,
and commend a common duty to him, if there
were not fomething extraordinary in it, which concerned him above the reft ? This they interpret a
pre-eminence that Peter had in his bufinefs of
teaching, which they fay is a primacy and head-
fhip; inforcing thus much, that all the reft were
to depend from him, and from him receive what
they were to preach. For anfwer, Grant me there
were fome great myftery in it, yet whence is it
proved that this is that myftery? For if our Saviour did not manifeft it, then might there be a
thoufand caufes, which man's conjecture may eafily mifs. It is great boldnefs, out of caufes concealed, to pick fo great confequences, and to found
matters of fo great weight upon mere conjectures.

3ly, The prayer for confirmation of Peter's
faith, whence it came, the courfe of the ftory fet

down in the text doth shew: it was our Saviour's
prevision of Peter's danger to relapse, which danger he had certainly run into, had not our Saviour extraordinarily prayed for confirmation of his
faith. And the precept of confirming his brethren,
is but that charitable office which is exacted at e-
very Christian's hand, that when himself had e-
scaped so great a wreck, to be careful in warning and reclaiming others, whom common frailty
drives into the like distress.

These circumstances, that Peter is first named
among the disciples, that he made the first sermon,
and the like, are too weak grounds to build the
sovereignty over the world upon; and that he spake
Ananias and Sapphira dead, argues spiritual power,
but not temporal. But that Peter called the first
council in the Acts, is a circumstance beyond the
text; for concerning the calling of the council,
there is no word: all that is said, is but this,
' That the apostles and elders met;' Acts xv. 6.
no syllable of Peter's calling them together.

That Peter was twenty-five years bishop of
Rome, is not to be proved out of antiquity, before
St. Jerom, who shuffled it into Eusebius's chro-
nicle, there being no such thing extant in his story; yea, that he was bishop at all (as now the
name of bishop is taken) may be very question-
able: for the antients, that reckon up the bishops
of Rome until their times, as Eusebius, and before
him Tertullian, and before them both Irenaeus,

never account Peter as bishop of that see; and E-
piphanius tells us, that Peter and Paul were both
bishops of Rome at once: by which it is plain he
took the title of bishop in another sense than now
it is used; for now, and so for a long time upward, two bishops can no more possess one see, than
two hedge sparrows dwell in one bush. St. Peter's time was a little too early for bishops to rise.

SECT. V.

Answer to the bishop of Rome's practice of supremacy.

TO the *first*, that so many of the bishops of
Rome were martyrs, what makes that to
the purpose? Is martyrdom an argument of the
supremacy?

To the *second*, That Victor endeavoured to ex-
communicate the Asiatic bishops, is true; but
withal it is as true, that he was withstood for his
labour: for the bishops of Asia themselves did
' sharply reprove him,' the words of Eusebius*;
and Irenaeus wrote against him for it.

To the *third*, That the first four councils were
called by the popes, is an open falshood; for in
the two first, the bishops of Rome are not so much
as mentioned, save only as persons cited. In the
two last they are mentioned only as petitioners to

* Φέρονται δὲ καὶ αἱ τύτων φωναὶ, πληκτικώτερον καθαπτομένων
τῦ Βίκτορος.

Ecclef. Hift. lib. 5. c. 24.

the emperor. There are extant the ftories of Eufebius, Socrates, Ruffinus, Theodoret, Sozome-
nus, the acts of the councils themfelves, at leaft
fome of them, the writings and epiftles of Leo
bifhop of Rome : in all thefe there is not one
word of the Pope, farther than a fupplicant, and
the whole calling of the bifhops together is attri-
buted to the emperor: take for example but the
laft of them. Leo bifhop of Rome was defirous
that fome things done in a meeting of divines at
Ephefus, fhould be difannulled ; for this he becomes a fuitor to Theodofius the junior, to have a
general council, but could never procure it of him.
After his death he continues his fuit to Marcianus,
fucceffor to Theodofius, who granted his requeft:
but whereas Leo had requefted the council might
be held in Italy, the emperor would not hear him;
nay which is more, the pope, upon good reafon,
had befought the emperor to put off the day de-
figned for the holding of the council, but the emperor would not hear him : fo that Leo could do
nothing, neither for the calling the council, nor for
the place, nor for the time. And all this appears
by Leo's own epiftles †. If the popes could do fo
little well near 500 years after Chrift, how little
could they do before, when their horns were not
yet fo long ?

The plea of the Proteftants concerning the corruption of the church of Rome, which by them

† Vid. Epift. 9. 12. 24. 25. 33. 35. 43.

is confeffed fometimes to have been pure, is no more prejudicial to Chrift's promife to his church, ' That the gates of hell fhall not prevail againft ' her,' Matth. xvi. 18. than the known corruption of the churches in Afia in St. John's time, or of other churches after.

The clofe of all is a demonftration. A word unfortunately ufed by your author, to bewray his logic: for indeed a reafon drawn from fo poor and empty a fign, falls many bows wide of demonftrative proof. Firft it is falfe that all the reft of patriarchal fees are extinct. The fee of Conftantinople yet ftands, and fhews her fucceffion of bifhops from St. Andrew till this day, as well as the church of Rome can from St. Peter: the fee of Alexandria yet fubfifts, and the bifhop of that place calls himfelf ' judge of the world*,' (as myfelf have feen in fome of his letters) a title to which he hath as good right, as the bifhop of Rome hath to be the world's fovereign. If any reply they are poor, in mifery, in perfecution and affliction: this can make no difference, fince with Chrift there is neither rich nor poor, ' but a new creature.' Galat. vi. 15. And again, their cafe now is as good as was the bifhops of Rome, under the Ethnic emperors; for their lot then was no other than thofe bifhops is now. But grant that it had lafted longeft, what then? fome of them muft needs have confifted longer than the other, except we would

* Κρίτην τῆς οἰκυμένης.

fuppofe that they fhould have fallen altogether.
Peradventure the reafon of her fo long lafting is
no other but that which the Cyclops gives Ulyffes
in Homer, ' Ulyffes fhould be eaten laft of all. †'
However it be, this vaunt feems but like that of
the wicked fervant in the gofpel, ' My Lord de-
' layeth his coming,' Matth. xxiv. 48. and we doubt
not but a day of the Lord fhall overtake him who
now eats and drinks, and revels with the world,
and beats his fellow-fervants.

† Οὖτιν ἐγὼ πύματον ἔδομαι.

Odyff. i. v. 369.

H

A

T R A C T

CONCERNING

S C H I S M

AND

SCHISMATICS:

Wherein is briefly difcovered the original
Caufes of all SCHISM.

HERESY and fchifm, as they are in common ufe, are two theological Μορμῶς, or
fcarecrows, which they, who uphold a party in
religion, ufe to fright away fuch, as making inquiry into it, are ready to relinquifh and oppofe it,
if it appear either erroneous or fufpicious. For as
Plutarch reports of a painter, who having unfkilfully painted a cock, chafed away all cocks and
hens, that fo the imperfection of his art might not
appear by comparifon with nature; fo men willing for ends to admit of no fancy but their own,
endeavour to hinder an inquiry into it by way of

comparifon of fomewhat with it, peradventure truer, that fo the deformity of their own might not appear. But howfoever in the common manage, herefy and fchifm are but ridiculous terms, yet the things in themfelves are of very confiderable moment; the one offending againft truth, the other againft charity; and therefore both deadly, where they are not by imputation, but in deed.

It is then a matter of no fmall importance truly to defcry the nature of them, that fo they may fear who are guilty of them, and they, on the contrary, ftrengthen themfelves, who through the iniquity of men and times are injurioufly charged with them.

Schifm (for of herefy we fhall not now treat, except it be by accident, and that by occafion of a general miftake, fpread throughout all the writings of the antients, in which their names are familiarly confounded;) Schifm, I fay, upon the very found of the word, imports divifion; divifion is not, but where communion is, or ought to be. Now communion is the ftrength and ground of all fociety, whether facred or civil: whofoever therefore they be that offend againft this common fociety and friendlinefs of men, and caufe feparation and breach among them; if it be in civil occafions, are guilty of fedition or rebellion; if it be by occafion of ecclefiaftical difference, they are guilty of fchifm. So that fchifm is an ecclefiaftical fedition, as fedition is a lay fchifm. Yet the

great benefit of communion notwithstanding, in
regard of divers distempers men are subject to,
dissension and disunion are often necessary: for
when either false or uncertain conclusions are ob-
truded for truth, and acts either unlawful, or mi-
nistring just scruple, are required of us to be performed: in these cases consent were conspiracy,
and open contestation is not faction or schism, but
due Christian animosity.

For the further opening therefore of the nature of schism, something must be added by way
of difference, to distinguish it from necessary separation; and that is, that the causes, upon which
division is attempted, proceed not from passion or
distemper, or from ambition or avarice, or such o-
ther ends as human folly is apt to pursue; but
from well weighed and necessary reasons, and
that, when all other means having been tryed, nothing will serve to save us from guilt of conscience, but open separation. So that schism, if
we would define it, is nothing else but an unnecessary separation of Christians from that part of
the visible church, of which they were once members. Now as in mutinies and civil dissensions there
are two attendants in ordinary belonging unto
them; one the choice of one elector or guide in
place of the general or ordinary governor, to rule
and guide; the other the appointing of some public place or rendezvous, where public meetings
must be celebrated: so in church dissensions and

quarrels, two appurtenances there are which serve to make a schism compleat.

1*st*, The choice of a bishop, in opposition to the former; (a thing very frequent amongst the antients, and which many times was both the cause and effect of schism.)

2*ly*, The erecting of a new church and oratory, for the dividing party to meet in publicly; for till this be done, the schism is but yet in the womb.

In that late famous controversy in Holland, *De praedestinatione et auxiliis*, as long as the disagreeing parties went no further than disputes and pen-combats, the schism was all that while unhatched: but as soon as one party swept an old cloyster, and by a pretty art suddenly made it a church, by putting a new pulpit in it, for the separating party there to meet; now what before was a controversy, became a formal schism. To know no more than this, if you take it to be true, had been enough to direct how you are to judge, and what to think of schism and schismatics; yet because in the ancients (by whom many men are more affrighted than hurt) much is said, and many fearful dooms are pronounced in this case; will we descend a little to consider of schisms, as it were by way of story, and that partly further to open that which we have said in general, by instancing in particulars; and partly to disabuse those, who reverencing antiquity more than needs, have suffered themselves to be scared with imputation of schism, above due measure : for what the antients spake by way of censure of schism in general, is most true; for they saw (and it is no great matter to see so much) that unadvisedly, and upon fancy, to break the knot of union betwixt man and man (especially amongst Christians, upon whom, above all other kind of men, the tie of love and communion doth most especially rest) was a crime hardly pardonable; and that nothing absolves a man from the guilt of it, but true and unpretended conscience: yet when they came to pronounce of schisms in particular (whether it were because of their own interests, or that they saw not the truth, or for what other cause God only doth know) their judgments many times (to speak most gently) are justly to be suspected. Which that you may see, we will range all schism into two ranks.

1. For there is a schism, in which only one party is the schismatic: for where cause of schism is necessary, there not he that separates, but he that occasions the separation, is the schismatic.

2. There is a schism, in which both parts are the schismatics: for where the occasion of separation is unnecessary, neither side can be excused from the guilt of schism.

But you will ask, who shall be the judge what is necessary? Indeed that is a question which hath been often made, but I think scarcely ever truly an-

fwered : not becaufe it is a point of great depth
or difficulty truly to affoil it, but becaufe the true
folution carries fire in the tail of it; for it bringeth with it a piece of doctrine which is feldom
pleafing to fuperiours. To you for the prefent this
fhall fuffice: if fo be you be *animo defoecato*, if you
have cleared yourfelf from froth and grounds; if
neither floth, nor fears, nor ambition, nor any
tempting fpirits of that nature abufe you, (for
thefe, and fuch as thefe, are the true impediments,
why both that and other queftions of the like danger are not truly anfwered) if all this be, and yet
you fee not how to frame your refolution, and
fettle yourfelf for that doubt; I will fay no more
of you than was faid of Papias, St. John's own
fcholar, you are ' of fmall judgment,*' your abilities are not fo good as I prefumed.

But to go on with what I intended, and from
which that interloping queftion diverted me : that
you may the better judge of the nature of fchifms
by their occafions, you fhall find that all fchifms
have crept into the church by one of thefe three
ways; either upon matter of fact, or matter of
opinion, or point of ambition. For the *firft*; I call
that matter of fact, when fomething is required
to be done by us, which we either know or ftrongly fufpect to be unlawful. So the firft notable
fchifm, of which we read in the church, contained

---

* Σφόδρα γάρ τοι σμικρὸς ὤν τὸν νῦν.

Eufeb. Ecclef. Hift. l. 3. c. 39.

H 4

in it matter of fact:) for it being upon error taken
for neceſſary, that an Eaſter muſt be kept; and
upon worſe than error, if I may ſo ſpeak (for it
was no leſs than a point of Judaiſm forced upon
the church) upon worſe than error, I ſay, thought
further neceſſary, that the ground for the time of
our keeping that feaſt, muſt be the rule left by
Moſes to the Jews; there aroſe a ſtout queſtion,
Whether we were to celebrate with the Jews on
the fourteenth moon, or the Sunday following?
This matter, though moſt unneceſſary, moſt vain,
yet cauſed as great a combuſtion as ever was in
the church; the Weſt ſeparating and refuſing
communion with the Eaſt for many years together. In this fantaſtical hurry, I cannot ſee but all
the world were ſchiſmatics; neither can any thing
excuſe them from that imputation, excepting only
this, that we charitably ſuppoſe that all parties
out of conſcience did what they did. A thing
which befel them through the ignorance of their
guides (for I will not ſay their malice) and that
through the juſt judgment of God, becauſe through
ſloth and blind obedience men examined not the
things which they were taught, but, like beaſts of
burden, patiently couched down, and indifferently underwent whatſoever their ſuperiours laid upon them. By the way, by this you may plainly ſee
the danger of our appeal to antiquity, for reſolution in controverted points of faith, and how ſmall
relief we are to expect from thence: for if the

difcretion of the chiefeft guides and directors of the church, did in a point fo trivial, fo inconfiderable, fo mainly fail them, as not to fee the truth in a fubject, wherein it is the greateft marvel how they could avoid the fight of it; can we, without imputation of extreme groffnefs and folly, think fo poor-fpirited perfons competent judges of the queftions now on foot betwixt the churches? Pardon me, I know not what temptation drew that note from me.

The next fchifm, which had in it matter of fact, is that of the Donatift; who was perfuaded (at leaft fo he pretended) that it was unlawful to converfe or communicate in holy duties with men ftained with any notorious fin: (For howfoever Auftin and others do fpecify only the *Thurificati et Traditores*, and *Libellatici*, and the like, as if he feparated only from thofe whom he found to be fuch; yet by neceffary proportion, he muft refer to all notorious finners.) Upon this he taught, that in all places where good and bad were mixed together, there could be no church, by reafon of pollution, evaporating as it were from finners, which blafted righteous perfons who converfed with them, and made all unclean. On this ground feparating himfelf from all whom he lift to fufpect, he gave out that the church was no where to be found but in him and his affociates, as being the only men among whom wicked perfons found no fhelter; and by confequence the only clean

and unpolluted company, and therefore the only
church. Againſt this St. Auguſtine laid down this
concluſion, *Unitatem ecclesiae per totum orbem di-*
ſperſae propter nonnullorum peccata non eſſe deſeren-
dam† : which is indeed the whole ſum of that
father's diſputation againſt the Donatiſt. Now in
one part of this controverſy betwixt St. Auguſtine
and the Donatiſt, there is one thing very remarkable : the truth was there, where it was by mere
chance, and might have been on either ſide, any
reaſons brought by either party notwithſtanding ;
for though it were *de facto* falſe, that *pars Donati*,
ſhut up in Afric, was the only orthodox party,
yet it might have been true, notwithſtanding any
thing St. Auſtin brings to confute it : and on the
contrary, though it were *de facto* true, that the
part of Chriſtians diſperſed over the earth were orthodox ; yet it might have been falſe, notwithſtanding any thing St. Auſtin brings to confirm it.
For where, or amongſt whom, or amongſt how
many the church ſhall be, or is, is a thing indifferent : it may be in any number, more or leſs ;
it may be in any place, country, or nation ; it may
be in all, and (for ought I know) it may be in
none, without any prejudice to the definition of
the church, or the truth of the goſpel. North or
South, many or few, diſperſed in many places, or

---

† The ſubſtance, though not the words, of this ſentence,
is to be found in various paſſages of the Epiſtles of Auguſtine.

confined to one; none of these either prove or disprove a church.

Now this schism, and likewise the former, to a wise man that well understands the matter in controversy, may afford perchance matter of pity, to see men so strangely distracted upon fancy; but of doubt or trouble what to do, it can yield none. For though in this schism the Donatist be the schismatic, and in the former both parties be equally engaged in the schism; yet you may safely upon your occasions communicate with either, so be you flatter neither in their schism. For why might it not be lawful to go to church with the Donatist, or to celebrate Easter with the Quartodeciman, if occasion so require? Since neither nature, nor religion, nor reason doth suggest any thing to the contrary: for in all public meetings pretending holiness, so there be nothing done, but what true devotion and piety brook, why may not I be present in them, and use communication with them? Nay what if those, to whose care the execution of the public service is committed, do something either unseemly or suspicious, or peradventure unlawful? What if the garments they wear be censured as, nay indeed be, superstitious? What if the gesture of adoration be used at the altar, as now we have learned to speak? What if the Homilist, or preacher, deliver any doctrine, of the truth of which we are not well persuaded (a thing which very often falls out) yet for all this we

may not separate, except we be conftrained per-
fonally to bear a part in them ourfelves. The
priefts under Eli had fo ill demeaned themfelves
about the daily facrifice, that the fcriptures tell
us, they made it to ftink ; yet the people refufed
not to come to the tabernacle, nor to bring their
facrifice to the prieft. For in thefe fchifms, which
concern fact, nothing can be a juft caufe of refufal of communion, but only to require the execution of fome unlawful or fufpected act : for not
only in reafon, but in religion too, that maxim admits of no releafe ; *Cautiffimi cujufque praeceptum
quod dubitas, ne feceris.* Long it was ere the church
fell upon fchifm upon this occafion, though of late
it hath had very many ; for until the fecond council of Nice (in which conciliabule fuperftition and
ignorance did confpire) I fay, until that rout did
fet up image-worfhip, there was not any remarkable fchifm, upon juft occafion of fact : all the
reft of fchifms of that kind were but wantonnefs,
this was truly ferious. In this the fchifmatical party was the fynod itfelf, and fuch as confpired with
it. For concerning the ufe of images *in facris,
firft,* it is acknowledged by all, that it is not a
thing neceffary : *fecondly,* it is by moft fufpected :
thirdly, it is by many held utterly unlawful. Can
then the enjoining of the practice of fuch a thing
be ought elfe but abufe? Or can the refufal of communion here, be thought any other thing than duty? Here, or upon the like occafion, to feparate,

may peradventure bring perfonal trouble and danger (againſt which it concerns every honeſt man
to have *pectus bene praeparatum*) further harm it
cannot do. So that in theſe caſes, you cannot be
to ſeek what to think, or what you have to do.

Come we then to confider a little of the *ſecond*
fort of ſchifm, ariſing upon occaſion of variety of
opinion. It hath been the common diſeaſe of Chriftians from the beginning, not to content themſelves with that meaſure of faith, which God and
the ſcriptures have expreſly afforded us; but out
of a vain deſire to know more than is revealed,
they have attempted to diſcuſs things, of which
we can have no light, neither from reaſon nor revelation : neither have they reſted here, but upon
pretence of church-authority, which is none, or
tradition, which for the moſt part is but figment ;
they have peremptorily concluded, and confidently impoſed upon others, a neceſſity of entertaining
concluſions of that nature : and to ſtrengthen
themſelves, have broken out into diviſions and
factions, oppoſing man to man, ſynod to ſynod, till
the peace of the church vaniſhed, without all poſſibility of recall. Hence aroſe thoſe antient and
many ſeparations amongſt Chriſtians occaſioned by
Arianiſm, Eutychianiſm, Neſtorianiſm, Photinia-
niſm, Sabellianiſm, and many more both antient,
and in our time; all which indeed are but names
of ſchifm, howſoever in the common language of
the fathers, they were called hereſies. For hereſy

is an act of the will, not of reason; and is indeed
a lie, not a mistake: else how could that known
speech of Austin go for true; *Errare possum, hae-
reticus esse nolo?*' Indeed, Manichaeism, Valenti-
nianism, Marcionism, Mahometanism, are truly
and properly heresies; for we know that the authors of them received them not, but minted them
themselves, and so knew that which they taught
to be a lie. But can any man avouch that Arius
and Nestorius, and others that taught erroneously
concerning the Trinity, or the person of our Saviour, did maliciously invent what they taught,
and not rather fall upon it by error and mistake?
Till that be done, and that upon good evidence,
we will think no worse of all parties than needs
we must, and take these rents in the church to be
at the worst but schisms upon matter of opinion.
In which case what we are to do, is not a point of
any great depth of understanding to discover, so
be distemper and partiality do not intervene. I do
not yet see, that *opinionum varietas, et opinantium
unitas,* are ἀσύςαῖα; or that men of different opinions in Christian religion, may not hold communion *in sacris,* and both go to one church. Why
may I not go, if occasion require, to an Arian
church, so there be no Arianism expressed in their
liturgy? And were liturgies and public forms of
service so framed, as that they admitted not of
particular and private fancies, but contained only
such things, as in which all Christians do agree,

fchifms on opinion were utterly vanifhed. For confider of all the liturgies that are or ever have been,
and remove from them whatfoever is fcandalôus to
any party, and leave nothing but what all agree on;
and the event fhall be, that the public fervice and
honour of God fhall no ways fuffer: whereas to
load our public forms with the private fancies upon which we differ, is the moft fovereign way to.
perpetuate fchifm unto the world's end. Prayer,
confeffion, thankfgiving, reading of fcriptures, expofition of fcripture, adminiftration of facraments
in the plaineft and fimpleft manner, were matter e-
nough to furnifh out a fufficient liturgy, though
nothing either of private opinion, or of church-
pomp, of garments, of prefcribed geftures, of ima-
gery, of mufic, of matter concerning the dead, of
many fuperfluities, which creep into the churches
under the name of order and decency, did interpofe
itfelf. For to charge churches and liturgies with
things unneceffary, was the firft beginning of all
fuperftition; and when fcruples of confcience began to be made or pretended, then fchifms began
to break in. If the fpiritual guides and fathers of
the church would be a little fparing of incumbring
churches with fuperfluities, and not over rigid,
either in reviving obfolete cuftoms, or impofing
new, there were far lefs danger of fchifm or fuperftition; and all the inconvenience were likely
to enfue, would be but this, they fhould in fo doing yield a little to the imbecillities of inferiors, a

thing which St. Paul would never have refufed to
do. Mean while, wherefoever falfe or fufpected
opinions are made a piece of the church-liturgy,
he that feparates is not the fchifmatic; for it is a-
like unlawful to make profeffion of known or fufpected falfhoods, as to put in practice unlawful
or fufpected actions.

The *third* thing I noted for matter of fchifm
was ambition: I mean epifcopal ambition: fhewing itfelf efpecially in two heads; one concerning
plurality of bifhops in the fame fee; another the
fuperiority of bifhops in divers fees. Ariftotle tells
us, That neceffity caufeth but fmall faults, but a-
varice and ambition were the mothers of great
crimes. Epifcopal ambition hath made this true;
for no occafion hath produced more frequent, more
continuing, more fanguinary fchifms, than this hath
done. The fees of Alexandria, of Conftantinople,
of Antioch, and above all of Rome, do abundantly fhew thus much; and our ecclefiaftical ftories
witnefs no lefs, of which the greateft part confifts
in the factionating and tumultuating of great and
potent bifhops. Socrates apologizing for himfelf,
that profeffing to write an ecclefiaftical ftory, he
did oftentimes interlace the actions of fecular princes and other civil bufineffes, tells us that he did
thus to refrefh his readers, who otherwife were in
danger to be cloyed by reading fo much of the
acts of unquiet and unruly bifhops, ἐν οἷς κατ᾽ ἀλ-
λήλων ἐτύρευσαν, in which as a man might fay, they

made butter and cheese one of another; for τυρευειν (that I may shew you a cast out of my old office, and open you a mystery in grammar) properly signifieth to make butter and cheese: now because these are not made without much agitation
of the milk, hence τυρευειν, by a borrowed and
tranflated fignification, fignifies to do things with
much agitation and tumult.

But that I may a little confider of the two heads,
which I but now fpecified; the *firft* I mentioned
was the plurality of bifhops in one fee. For the
general practice of the church from the beginning,
at leaft fince the original of epifcopacy, as now it
is, was never to admit at once more than one bifhop in one fee: and fo far in this point have they
been careful to preferve unity, that they would
not fuffer a bifhop in his fee to have two cathedral
churches: which thing lately brought us a book
out of France, *De Monogamia Epifcoporum*, written by occafion of the bifhop of Langres, who, I
know not upon what fancy, could not be content
with one cathedral church in his diocefs, but
would needs have two; which to the author of
that work feems to be a kind of fpiritual polyga-
my. It fell out amongft the antients very often ;
fometimes upon occafion of difference in opinion,
fometimes becaufe of difference amongft thofe who
were interefted in the choice of bifhops, that two
bifhops and fometimes more were fet up; and all
parties ftriving to maintain their own bifhop, made

I

themfelves feveral churches, feveral congregations, each refufing to participate with others, and many times proceeding to mutual excommunication. This is that which Cyprian calls *Erigere altare contra altare*, ' to rear altar againft altar:' to this doth he impute the original of all church-diforders: and if you read him, you would think he thought no other church-tumult to be a fchifm but this. This perchance might plead fome excufe; for though in regard of religion itfelf, it matters not whether there be one or more bifhops in the fame diocefs, and fometimes two are known to have fat at once, (for Epiphanius reckoning up the bifhops of Rome, makes Peter and Paul the firft; and St. Auftin acknowledgeth, that for a time he fat fellow-bifhop with his predeceffor, though he excufeth it, that he did fo by being ignorant that the contrary had been decreed by the council of Nice *) yet it being a thing very convenient for the peace of the church to have it fo; neither doth it any way favour of vice or mifdemeanour; their punifhment fleeps not, who unneceffarily and wantonly go about to infringe it.

But that *other* head of epifcopal ambition, concerning fupremacy of bifhops in divers fees, one claiming fuperiority over another, as it hath been, from time to time, a great trefpaffer againft the church's peace, fo it is now the final ruin of it; the Eaft and the Weft, through the fury of

* Epift. ccxiii. §. 4.

the two prime bishops, being irremediably sepa-
rated without all hope of reconcilement. And besides all this mischief, it is founded in a vice contrary to all Christian humility, without which no
man shall see his Saviour: for they do but abuse
themselves and others, that would persuade us,
that bishops, by Christ's institution, have any superiority over other men, further than of reverence; or that any bishop is superior to another,
further than positive order agreed upon amongst
Christians, hath prescribed. For we have believed
him that hath told us, ' That in Jesus Christ there
' is neither high nor low; and that in giving ho-
' nour, every man should be ready to prefer ano-
' ther before himself.' Rom. xii. 1 0. which saying
cut off all claim most certainly to superiority, by
title of Christianity; except men can think that
these things were spoken only to poor and private
men. Nature and religion agree in this, that neither of them hath a hand in this heraldry of *se-
cundum, sub et supra;* all this comes from composition and agreement of men among themselves.
Wherefore this abuse of Christianity, to make it
lacquey to ambition, is a vice for which I have no
extraordinary name of ignominy, and an ordinary
I will not give it, lest you should take so transcen-
dent a vice to be but trivial.

Now concerning schisms arising upon these
heads, you cannot be for behaviour much to seek;
for you may safely communicate with all parties,

as occasion shall call you; and the schismatics here
are all those who are heads of the faction, together with all those who foment it: for private and
indifferent persons, they may be spectators of these
contentions as securely in regard of any peril of
conscience (for of danger in purse or person, I
keep no account) as at a cock-fight. Where serpents fight, who cares who hath the better? the
best wish is, that both may perish in the fight.

Now for conventicles, of the nature of which
you desire to be informed; thus much in general.
It evidently appears, that all meetings upon unnecessary occasions of separation are to be so stiled;
so that in this sense, a conventicle is nothing else
but a congregation of schismatics: yet time hath
taken leave sometimes to fix this name upon good
and honest meetings, and that perchance not altogether without good reason; for with public
religious meetings thus it fares: First, it hath been
at all times confessed necessary, that God requires
not only inward and private devotion, when men
either in their hearts and closets, or within their
private walls, pray, praise, confess and acknowledge; but he further requires all those things to
be done in public, by troops and shoals of men:
and from hence have proceeded public temples, al-
tars, forms of service, appointed times, and the
like, which are required for open assemblies. Yet
while men were truly pious, all meetings of men for
mutual help of piety and devotion, wheresoever

and by whomsoever celebrated, were permitted without exception.

But when it was espied that ill-affected persons abused private meetings, whether religious or civil, to evil ends, religiousness to gross impiety, (as appears in the Ethnic Eleusinia, and Bacchanalia; and Christian meetings under the Pagan princes, when for fear they durst not come together in open view, were charged with foul imputations, as by the report of Christians themselves plainly appears; and civil meetings many times, under pretence of friendly and neighbourly visits, sheltered treasonable attempts against princes and commonweals:) hence both church and state joined, and jointly gave order for forms, times, places of public concourse, whether for religious or civil ends; and all other meetings whatsoever, besides those of which both time and place were limited, they censured for routs and riots, and unlawful assemblies in the state, and in the church for conventicles.

So that it is not lawful, no not for prayer, for hearing, for conference, for any other religious office whatsoever, for people to assemble otherwise, than by public order is allowed. Neither may we complain of this in times of incorruption; for why should men desire to do that suspiciously in private, which warrantably may be performed in public? But in times of manifest corruptions and persecutions, wherein religious assembling is

I 3

dangerous, private meetings, howsoever besides
public order, are not only lawful, but they are of
necessity and duty; else how shall we excuse the
meetings of Christians for public service, in time
of danger and persecutions, and of ourselves in
Queen Mary's days? and how will those of the
Roman church amongst us, put off the imputation
of conventicling, who are known amongst us privately to assemble for religious exercise, against all
established order, both in state and church? For
indeed all pious assemblies in times of persecution
and corruption, howsoever practised, are indeed,
or rather alone the lawful congregations; and public assemblies, though according to form of law,
are indeed nothing else but riots and conventicles,
if they be stained with corruption and superfti-
tion.

A

LETTER

TO

ARCHBISHOP LAUD,

Upon occasion of the TRACT
concerning SCHISM.

MAY IT PLEASE YOUR GRACE,

WHEREAS of late an abortive difcourfe
indited by me for the ufe of a private
friend, hath without lawful pafs, wandred abroad;
and miftaking its way, is arrived at your Grace's
hands: I have taken the boldnefs to prefent myfelf before you, in behalf of it, with this either
apology or excufe indifferently, being refolved *in
utramvis aleam*, to beg either your approbation, or
your pardon. For myfelf, I have much marvel-
led, whence a fcribled paper, dropt from fo worth-
lefs and inconfiderable a hand as mine, fhould recover fo much ftrength, as to be able to give offence. But I confefs it to be moft true, that *Bellum inchoant inertes, fortes finiunt;* and a weak
hand often kindles that fire, which the concourfe

I 4

of the whole vicinity cannot quench. If therefore any fire can arife out of fo poor a fpark, (which I can hardly conceive) I am myfelf here at hand to pour on water, to prevent a farther mifchief.

Whatfoever there is in that fchedule, which may feem apt to give offence, confifts either in phrafe and manner of expreffion, or in the conceits and things themfelves, there preffed and infifted upon. For the *firft*, Whofoever hath the misfortune to read it, fhall find in it, for ftile, fome things over-familiar, and fubruftic; fome things more pleafant than needed; fome things more four and fatirical. For thefe, my apology is but this, That your Grace would be pleafed to take in confideration, *Firft*, What the liberty of a letter might entice me to. *Secondly*, I am by genius open and uncautelous; and therefore fome pardon might be afforded to harmlefs freedom, and gaiety of fpirit, utterly devoid of all diftemper and malignity. *Thirdly*, Some part of the theme I was to touch upon, was (or at leaft feemed to me) of fo fmall and inconfiderable a moment, and yet hath raifed that noife and tumult in the church, that I confefs it drew from me that indignation which is there expreffed. When Auguftus the Emperor was afked what was become of his Ajax; (for he made a tragedy upon the life and fortunes of that man) he anfwered, *Incubuit in fpongiam.** For all thefe things which I have above touched upon,

* Sueton. Aug. c. 85.

my anſwer is, *Incumbant in ſpongiam*. And I could heartily wiſh (for in the caſe I am, I have nothing but good wiſhes to help me) that they into whoſe hands that paper is unluckily fallen, would favour me ſo much as to ſpunge them out.

Now concerning the things diſcuſt in the pamphlet, I humbly beg leave, before I come to particulars, to ſpeak for myſelf thus much in gene-ral. If they be errors which I have here vented (as perchance they are) yet my will hath no part in them, and they are but the iſſues of unfortunate inquiry. Galen, that great phyſician, ſpeaks thus of himſelf, * ' I know not how (ſays that worthy ' perſon) even from my youth up, in a wonderful ' manner, whether by divine inſpiration, or by fu-' ry and poſſeſſion, or however you may pleaſe to ' ſtile it, I have much contemned the opinion of ' the many; but truth and knowledge, I have above ' meaſure affected: verily perſuading myſelf, that ' a fairer, more divine fortune could never befal a ' man.' Some title, ſome claim I may juſtly lay to the words of this excellent perſon ; for the purſuit of truth hath been my only care, ever ſince I firſt underſtood the meaning of the word. For

---

* Εγὼ δὲ ὐκ οἶδ᾽ ὅπως εὐθὺς ἐκ μειρακίν θαυμαςῶς, ἢ ἐνθίως, ἢ μανικῶς, ἢ ὅπως ἄν τις ὀνομάζειν ἐθίλῃ, κατεφρόνησα μὲν ΤΩ̃Ν ΠΌΛΛΩΝ ΑΝΘΡΏΠΩΝ δόξης, ἐπεθύμησα δὲ ΑΛΗΘΕΊ-ΑΣ ̔ ̩ ΕΠΙΣΤΉΜΗΣ, ὐδὲν ἔναι νομίσας ὔτε κάλλιον ἀνθρώ-ποις, ὔτε θειότερον κτῆμα.

Method. Medendi lib. 7. c. 1.

this, I have forsaken all hopes, all friends, all desires, which might bias me, and hinder me from
driving right at what I aimed. For this, I have
spent my money, my means, my youth, my age,
and all I have; that I might remove from myself
that censure of Tertullian,——*Suo vitio quis quid ig-
norat?* If with all this cost and pains, my purchase is but error; I may safely say, to err hath
cost me more, than it has many to find the truth:
and truth itself shall give me this testimony at last,
that if I have missed of her, it is not my fault, but
my misfortune.

Having begged your Grace's pardon for this
περιαυτολογία †, (peradventure unseasonable) I
will take liberty to consider of the things themselves discust in the pamphlet.

And *first*, howsoever I have miscast some par-
cels of my account, yet I am most certain that the
total sum is right; for it amounts to no more than
that precept of the Apostle,——' As far as it is pos-
' sible, have peace with all men.' For this purpose, having summoned up sundry occasions of
schism, and valuing them with the best judgment
I could; I still ended with advice to all possible
accommodation and communion, one only excepted. Now certainly there could be no great harm
in the premises, where the conclusion was nothing
else but peace.

One of the antient Grammarians, delivering the

† Egotism.

laws of a comedy fomewhat fcrupuloufly, thought, *non poffe ferrum nominari in comoedia, ne tranfeat in tragoediam;* that to name a fword in a comedy, was enough to fright it into a tragedy. The very theme I handled, caufed me to fall on words of diffenfion, and noife, and tumult, and ftir: yet I hope it is but an unneceffary fear, that the laft fcene being peace, the difcourfe will prove any other than comical.

To touch upon every jarring ftring in it, were too much to abufe your Grace's patience, of which once already you have been fo extraordinary liberal unto me. All that may feem to lie open to exception, I will comprife under two heads; within compafs of which all other petty and inferior matters will eafily fall. The *firft* concerns my carriage towards antiquity; the *fecond* towards authority: againft both which, I may be fuppofed to trefpafs. For the *firft*, I am thought to have been too fharp in cenfuring antiquity, beyond that good refpect which is due unto it. In this point, my error, if any be, fprang from this; that taking actions to be the fruit by which men are to be judged, I judged of the perfons by their actions, and not of actions by the perfons from whom they proceeded: for to judge of actions by perfons and times, I have always taken it to be moft unnatural. Hence it is, that having no good conceit (for I will fpeak the truth) of our rule by which we celebrate the feaft of Eafter; (*Firft*, becaufe it is

borrowed of Moses, without any warrant, for
ought I know: *Secondly*, becaufe it is of no ufe ;
for which way is the fervice of God or man any
jot more advanced by making that feaft wander
betwixt day and day, than by fixing it on one
known day? *Thirdly*, becaufe it is obfcure and intricate, few fcholars acquainting themfelves there-
with, and there being nothing more ridiculous
than *difficiles nugae*, ufelefs intricacies and obfcu-
rities:) I could not with patience fpeak gently of
thofe, who ufed fo fmall and contemptible an occafion, to the great difturbance and rending of the
churches; and in maintenance of a toy and fimple ceremony, which it is no way beneficial to preferve, to fall into that error, than which, themfelves every where tell us, there can fcarcely any
be more dangerous.

Whereas in one point, fpeaking of church-
authority, I bluntly added [which is none;] I
muft acknowledge it was uncautioufly fpoken,
and, being taken in a generality, is falfe; though
as it refers to the occafion which there I fell upon,
it is (as I think I may fafely fay) moft true. For
church-authority, that is, authority refiding in ecclefiaftical perfons, is either of jurifdiction in
church-caufes and matter of fact, or of decifion
in point of church-queftions, and difputable opinion. As for the *firft;* in church-caufes or matter
of fact, ecclefiaftical perfons, in cafes of their cognizance, have the fame authority as any others

have, to whom power of jurifdiction is committed. Their confiftories, their courts, their determinations, ftand upon as warrantable evidence as the decifions of other benches and courts do. I count, in point of decifion of church-queftions, if I fay of the authority of the church, that it was none; I know no adverfary that I have, the church of Rome only excepted: for this cannot be true, except we make the church judge of controverfies; the contrary to which we generally maintain againft that church. Now it plainly appears, that upon this occafion I fpake it; for beginning to fpeak of fchifm arifing by reafon of ambiguous opinion, I brought in nakedly thofe words which gave occafion of offence; which if I had fpoken with due qualification, I had not erred at all. Again, whereas I did too plainly deliver myfelf, *de origine dominii*, and denied it to be founded either in nature or in religion; I am very well content to put off the decifion of this point till Elias comes. In the mean time, whether it be true or falfe, let it pafs for my miftake; for it is but a point of mere fpeculation, which we fall upon when we ftudy Ariftotle's Politics, and in common life and ufe hath no place at all. For authority is not wont to difpute, and it goes but lazily on, when it muft defend itfelf by arguments in the fchools. Whether dominion *in civilibus*, or *in facris*, be κτίσις, &c. or comes in by divine right; it concerns them to look to, who have dominion

committed to them. To others, whose duty it is
to obey (and to myself above all, who am best contented to live and die a poor and private man) it
is a speculation merely useless. Our Saviour questions not Herod's or Augustus's title, and confessed that Pilate had his power from above; which
yet we know came but by delegation from Tibe-
rius Caesar. Let titles of honour and dominion go
as the providence of God will have, yet quiet and
peaceable men will not fail of their obedience: no
more will I of ought, so be that God and good
conscience command not the contrary. A higher
degree of duty I do not see how any man can demand at my hands: for whereas the exception of
good conscience sounds not well with many men,
because oft-times, under that form, pertinacy and
wilfulness is suspected to couch itself; in this case
it concerns every man sincerely to know the truth
of his own heart, and so accordingly to determine
of his own way, whatsoever the judgment of his
superiors be, or whatsoever event befal him. For
since, in case of conscience, many times there is a
necessity to fall either into the hands of men, or
into the hands of God; of these two, whether is
the best, I leave every particular man to judge;
only I will add thus much, It is a fearful thing to
trifle with conscience; for most assuredly, according unto it, a man shall stand or fall at the last.

One thorn more there is, which I would, if I
might, pull out of the foot of him who shall tread

upon that paper : for by reafon of a paffage there, wherein I fharply taxed epifcopal ambition, I have been fufpected by fome, into whofe hands that fchedule fell before ever it came to your Grace's view, that in my heart I did fecretly lodge a malignity againft the epifcopal order; and that, under pretence of taxing the antients, I fecretly lafhed at the prefent times. What obedience I owe unto epifcopal jurifdiction, I have already plainly and fincerely opened unto your Grace; and my truft is, you do believe me: fo that in that regard I intend to fay no more; and the very confideration of the things themfelves, which there I fpeak of, frees me from all fufpicion of fecret gliding at the prefent. For I fpake of fchifms arifing either out of plurality of bifhops in one diocefs, or fuperiority of bifhops in fundry diocefles: both thefe are ftrangers to ours, and proper to the antient times; the *firft* arifing from the unrulinefs of the people, in whofe hands in thofe times the nomination of bifhops was; the *other* from fomewhat (whether good or bad, I know not) in the princes then living, who left the bifhops to themfelves (among whom fome there were no better than other men) and took no keep of the antient canons of the church, by which the limits, orders, and pre-eminences of all diocefles and provinces were fet. But our times have feen a profperous change; for the nomination of bifhops (which was fometimes in the people) is now moft happily devolved into the prince's hand, together with the care of the preſervation of the bounds of biſhops fees, and antient titles of precedency. So that now, ſince that happy change, for well near one hundred years, we have had no experience of any ſuch miſorders, neither are we likely hereafter to fear any, ſo long as ſo good, ſo moderate, ſo gracious a royal hand ſhall hold the ſtern: which God grant may be either in him, or his, till times be no more.

MISCELLANIES.

A

LETTER

CONCERNING THE

LAWFULNESS OF MARRIAGES

BETWIXT

FIRST-COUSINS,

OR

COUSIN-GERMANS.

WORTHY SIR,   September 8, 1630.

IT is too great an honour which you have done
me, to require my judgment (if at leaſt I have
any judgment) in a matter in which yourſelf, both
by reaſon of your ſkill and degree, cannot chuſe
but over-weigh me: yet ſuch as it is, ſince you
are pleaſed to require it, lo, I preſent it to you,
and wiſh it may be for your ſervice.

K

In marriages, two things are moft efpecially to be confidered, conveniency and affection: conveniency, thereby to advance, or otherwife fettle our eftates to our content: affection, becaufe of the fingular content we take in the enjoying of what we love. Now becaufe thefe two are great parties, and fway much in the manage of our temporal actions, by common confent and practice of all men, they freely take their courfe, fave only there where the public laws of God or men have given them fome check and inhibition, for the propagation of mutual love and acquaintance among men. And for avoiding of confufion in blood, God and men have jointly enacted, that it fhall not be lawful for us to make our commodity, our place or affection by way of marriage within certain degrees of propinquity and kindred: but this was with fome reftraint. For as St. Auguftin tells us, *Fuit autem antiquis patribus religiofa cura num ipfa propinquitas fe paulatim propaginum ordinibus dirimens longius abiret, et propinquitas effe defifteret; eam nondum longe pofitam rurfus matrimonii vinculo colligare et quodammodo revocare fugientem.* Now the queftion is, How far in the degrees of propinquity this reftraint doth reach? and where we may begin to couple and lock again?

For the opening of which query, let us a little confider in general of all kinds of propinquity, fo fhall we the better find where we may fafely begin.

All degrees of propinquity amongſt which Moſes * may be ſuppoſed to ſeek a wife, are either of
mothers and daughters; or aunts and nieces; or
ſiſters and couſins. Now as in the aſcending line
of mothers, I may not marry my mother; ſo can
I not marry my grand-mother, nor great-grand-
mother, and ſo infinitely upward: infomuch as if
Eve were now alive, and a widow, no man living
could marry her, becauſe all men are her ſons. In
the deſcending line of daughters, as I may not
marry my daughter, ſo neither my grand-child,
nor great-grand-child, and ſo infinitely down-
wards. Again, in the aſcending line of aunts, I
may not marry my next aunt, ſo nor my great-
aunt, nor her aunt, nor her's, and ſo upwards *in
infinitum*. In the deſcending line of nieces, as I
cannot marry my firſt niece, ſo nor my ſecond,
nor third, nor fourth, unto the thouſandth generation, becauſe I am properly uncle to them all,
how far ſoever diſtant in deſcent. As for marriage with ſiſters, notwithſtanding that the immediate ſons of Adam, becauſe God created only one
woman, were conſtrained to marry their ſiſters;
yet, ever ſince, by general conſent of all nations,
it hath been counted inceſtuous. So then, all marriage with mothers, daughters, nieces, bcing expreſly prohibited; if Moſes will marry within his

* The ſuppoſed perſon of whoſe marriage the author
treats.

kindred, he muſt ſeek his wife amongſt his couſins.

Now here is the queſtion, Where he may firſt adventure to make his choice? If we look to antient laws of God and men, we ſhall find, that in any degree whatſoever marriage was permitted, beginning even from the firſt couſins, or couſingermans. For if we look into Moſes, we ſhall find no reſtraint impoſed upon couſin-germans; and however ſome have pleaded, that there is a degree farther off prohibited, and therefore by conſequence this muſt be taken for prohibited: this (as hereafter I ſhall make plain in the ſequel of my diſcourſe) is but a meer miſtake. And not only myſelf, whoſe inſight into matters may peradventure not be great: but thoſe whoſe ſight is far quicker than mine, could ſee in the law of God no prejudice to the marriage of couſin-germans. For not only Zanchius, * Calvin, † Beza, ‡ Bucer, § Melancthon, in a word, all the divines of the reformed churches, of whoſe judgment and learning we have any opinion, do grant, that firſt-couſins may couple, any thing in God's law notwithſtanding.

I muſt confeſs my ignorance, I know not any of our reformed divines that have written, that have thought otherwiſe. Indeed Calvin having firſt ac-

---

* Levit. 18. † In lib. de repudiis ‡ In Judicum cap. 1. et Matth. c. 4. § De conjugio.

knowledged, that the law of God doth not impeach it; yet gives advice, in regard of the scandal the churches might suffer, to abstain from marriage in that degree; and so accordingly the churches of Geneva, of the Palatinate, of Misnia, Thuringia, and Saxony, have severally by their several constitutions prohibited it. But this toucheth not the case; for I perceive the question is of second-cousins, unto whom those churches (which forbid the first degree) expresly give leave; for I find it recorded, * *In tertio aequalis lineae gradu permitti possunt conjugia:* where that those words, *in tertio gradu,* deceive you not, and make you to think that not second, but third cousins are permitted to marry, you must understand, that second cousins are in the third degree of kindred, and third cousins in the fourth, and so forward, by the account of all lawyers; which that you may see, and because in my ensuing discourse I shall have occasion to refer unto it, I will set down some part of the stem, so much as shall concern our purpose.

* Zepper. de lege Mosaic. l. 4. c. 9.

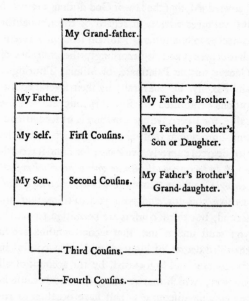

By this rude draught you may fee, that if you count the degrees of kindred betwixt fecond coufins, you fhall find them fix degrees diftant by the civil law, and in the third degree of the canon law. For in the civil law the rule is, *Quot funt perfonae tot funt gradus ftipite dempto;* STIPITEM we call him that ftands at the top, and in whom the cognation firft unites, who here is my grand-father. But, in refpeƈt of the fecond coufins, here is great-grand-father. If then you begin with fecond coufins, and count about till you come to fecond coufins again, leaving out the grand-father, you fhall find them to be fix perfons, and fo diftant fix degrees in kindred. Now two degrees in the civil law, make but one degree in the canon law, where the rule is, that *in linea aequali quoto gradu aiftant à ftipite, toto diftant inter fe* : by which you fee that fecond coufins, being in the third degree from the grand-father, they are three degrees diftant from each other. I have ftood a little upon this, for this caufe, that if any one fhould perchance put you off with the authority of the churches which I have mentioned, you might not be deceived through the equivocation which feems to lurk in thofe words, *in tertio gradu*.

But to return to our queftion of coufin-germans, as there is nothing in the law of God which forbids marriage betwixt them, fo accordingly was the practice of God's own people; for fo we read that the daughters of Zelophehad were married to their uncle's fons; and Caleb gave his daughter Achfah in marriage to his brother's fon; and fundry inftances more in this kind might be given. Now that thofe things fhould be done by difpenfation and permiffion only (which I fee is pleaded by fome men) I know no warrant nor reafon for it: fo that what may be done in this cafe by the law of God, I think is out of queftion.

Let us fee a little what the light of nature taught the Gentiles. Amongft them the wifeft and moft potent were the Romans, whofe laws have

K 4

long been efteemed for the foundeft and beft, by the general approbation of the moft and greateft kingdoms and commonwealths in Europe.

Now amongft thefe, the Romans both by their law and practice did warrant marriages between firft coufins; their law is plain, and thus we read it in their Pandects, about the beginning of the 23. 6. *Si nepotem ex filio, et neptim ex altero filio, in poteftate habeam, nuptias inter eas me folo authore contrahi poffe, Pomponius fcribit, et verum eft.* This one text is fufficient, though I could quote many other teftimonies out of their law concerning this kind of marriage.

What their practice was, thefe inftances which enfue, will be fufficient to fhew: antiently under the firft kings, Dionyfius Halicarnaffeus tells us, that two daughters of Servius Tullius were married to Lucius and Aruns their coufin-germans, nephews to Tarquinius Prifcus. Livy in his 42. 6. brings in one Spurius Liguftinus reporting, that his father had given him for wife his uncle's daughter; and thus he fpeaks to his own praife and commendation, as it will appear, if you pleafe to perufe the place. Tully, in his *Orat. pro Cluentio*, tells us, that Cluentia was married to Melius her coufin-german: *et erant hae nuptiae* (faith he) *plenae dignitatis, plenae concordiae:* which I think he would never have faid, had there lain upon fuch marriages any note of infamy. Auguftus the Emperor gave his daughter Julia in marriage to Marcellus, nephew to Auguſtus by his ſiſter Octavia: and Quintilian tells us, that his ſon (whoſe immature death he doth bewail) was deſigned, when he came to age, to marry his uncle's daughter; and Marcus Brutus was married to his couſingerman, as Plutarch relates.

Out of this heap of inſtances it appeareth, that in the Roman commonwealth, throughout all ages, and amongſt all ſorts of people, marriages between firſt-couſins ran uncontrouled: the firſt that gave reſtraint unto them was Theodoſius the Great, which law of his is yet to be ſeen in that book of his laws, called *Codex Theodoſianus*. But this law continued not long, for his own ſons, Arcadius and Honorius, quickly reverſed it, and in lieu of it made this law, which is extant in the book called Juſtinian's Code, and ſtands for good law amongſt the Civilians at this day, *Celebrandis inter conſobrinos matrimoniis licentia legis hujus ſalubritate indulta eſt, ut revocata priſci juris authoritate, reſtrictiſque calumniarum fomentis, matrimonium inter conſobrinos habeatur legitimum, ſive ex duobus fratribus, ſive ex duabus ſororibus, ſive ex fratre et ſorore nati ſunt: et ex eo matrimonio editi legitimi et ſuis patribus ſucceſſores habeantur.* Thus ſtood the caſe concerning thoſe marriages, until the biſhops of Rome began to grow great, and took upon them to make laws: for then, whether to make way for diſpenſations, whereby to get money, or for what other bye-reſpects, I know not; not only firſt and second coufins, but all coufins until the feventh generation, were exprefly prohibited to marry mutually : till at length the bifhop of Rome freed the three latter degrees, and prohibited marriage only to coufins in four defcents: and fo till this day among thofe that acknowledge the fuperiority of that fee, all marrying within four degrees, except it be by difpenfation, is utterly forbidden.

And if it be lawful for me to fpeak what I think, I verily fuppofe, that not from any reafon, but only by reafon of the long prevailing of the Canon Law, marriages betwixt near coufins were generally forborn. And from hence arofe a fcruple in the minds of many men, concerning the lawfulnefs of fuch marriages : but all caufe of fuch fcruple amongft us is long fince taken away. For at what time we caft off the yoke of the bifhop of Rome, in the thirty-third year of King Henry VIII. a ftatute was enacted in parliament, which was again confirmed in the firft of Queen Elizabeth, that no degrees of kindred fhould be forbidden marriage, but only fuch as were fet down in the Levitical Law, and amongft the degrees fpecified in that act as lawful (if my memory fail me not) coufin-germans are exprefly mentioned.

To fum up all then what hitherto hath been faid, What reafon have we to doubt of the lawfulnefs of that, which the law of God permits, the people of God practifed, the beft and learnedft divines have acknowledged, the wifeft amongft the

Gentiles in their laws and practices have approved, and our own municipal laws, under which we live, exprefly allow.

This had been enough to fatisfy any gain-fayer whatfoever. And indeed I had ended here, but that when your letters came to my hands, there was delivered with them a fchedule, containing reafons perfuading all fuch kind of marriages to be utterly unlawful. Concerning the authority of which difcourfe, to profefs what I think, I take him for a very pious and zealous man; and I earneftly defire of him, if ever he chance to be acquainted with what I write, to conceive of me as one who delights not in oppofition, except it be for the truth, at leaft in opinion. My advice to him is to add knowledge to his zeal, and to call again to account his reafons, and more diligently to examine them. The ftrength of his difcourfe is not fo much his reafon, as his paffion, a thing very prevalent with the common fort, who as they are feldom capable of ftrength of reafon, fo are they eafily carried away with paffionate difcourfe. This thing ought to be a warning to us of the clergy, to take heed how we deal with the people by way of paffion, except it be there where our proofs are found. Paffion is a good dog, but an ill fhepherd. *Tortum digna fequi potius quam ducere funem;* it may perchance follow well, but it can never lead well. I was much amazed to read his refolution of preaching in this cafe fo earneft-

ly, as to break hers or his heart (who defire to
marry) or his own, or all ——— He that ſuffered
himſelf thus far to be tranſported with affection,
ought to have furniſhed himſelf with ſtronger reaſons that any I here can find: but I will let his
paſſion go, for to contend with it were infinite;
for paſſion hath tongue and clamour enough, but
no ears. The reaſons, ſo many as I think require
anſwer, I will take up in order as they lie in the
paper. And *firſt*, I find one phraſe of ſpeech, which
is very predominant, and runs almoſt through the
veins of the diſcourſe; it is this, That Chriſtians
loath, Chriſtians abhor, men, women, and children cry out againſt ſuch kind of marriages. But
who are thoſe Chriſtians of whom he ſpeaks? If
he means the better ſort of learned and judicious
divines, he is certainly deceived, for I have ſhewed already the contrary; and let him for any information, if he can, produce for himſelf ſome
one Proteſtant learned divine. If he mean ſome
of the ordinary ſort: I anſwer, it is the fault of
their guides, who ought better to have informed
them. And whereas toward the latter end of the
diſcourſe, we are told of a dying woman, afflicted
in conſcience, becauſe ſhe had married her couſin:
Firſt, I aſk, of what weight the judgment of a
ſilly woman is? *Secondly*, I anſwer, that this proves
not the thing to be unlawful. Now let our acts
be what they will, good or bad, yet if we do
them, ſuppoſing them to be unlawful, we ſin. It

is a ruled cafe amongſt the Canoniſts, *Confcientia erronea ligat habentem*, he that doth a good action, taking it to be unlawful, to him it is unlawful. If therefore againſt her confcience (though peradventure mifinformed) ſhe married her coufin, ſhe deſerved the torment of mind; and yet marriage between coufin-germans may be lawful enough. Wherefore I pray you advife thofe, concerning whom this queſtion is propoſed, that if they find in themſelves any doubt concerning the lawfulneſs of the action, they forbear to attempt it, until all ſcruple be removed.

But I ſee that the main foundation of this difcourſe is laid in theſe words of Moſes,——' You ' ſhall not approach to any that is near of kin, to '' uncover her nakedneſs.' Levit. xviii. 6. where by near of kin, firſt and ſecond coufins amongſt the reſt are thought to be meant. For anfwer to which, we ſay, That the enumeration of particulars (which Moſes in that place maketh) is a ſufficient comment upon thofe words, and thofe who are reckoned up exprefly together with all others, in whom the ſame reafon is found, are to be eſteemed for near of kin, and befides them no other ; I ſay thofe in whom the ſame reafon is found ; becauſe ſome degrees there are, which are not mentioned by Moſes, and yet are confeffed to be prohibited. It is not forbidden a woman to marry her mother's ſiſter's hufband; yet it is not lawful; for the man is forbidden to marry his father's brother's widow. Now the same reason is there betwixt a man and his father's brother's widow, which is betwixt a woman and her mother's sister's husband, and therefore both are understood as alike forbidden, though both be not alike expressed. But for a full answer to these words, I refer the author of this discourse to Francisc. Hotman, a learned Civilian, and an earnest Protestant, who, in his disputation *de Jure Nuptiarum, cap.* 6. hath these words, *Qui verò propinquorum numero sint, non cujusque hominis nati, sed solius Dei judicium est, qua de causa eadem lege illos ordine nominatim enumerat, ut facilè intelligatur, quos non enumerat, propinquorum numero habendos non esse, quoniam ut dici solet, quod lege prohibitoria vetitum non est, permissum intelligitur.*

Now the better to work us to a conceit, that such marriages are unlawful, the examples of the Gentiles are called to help; and we are informed that Plutarch, a grave writer, tells us of one who was greatly endangered by marrying his cousingerman; certainly it was great want of examples, which moved the gentleman to make choice of this: a worse for his purpose he could not easily have found. For indeed it is true, that Plutarch tells us, that some one (who, or when, he tells not) was publicly questioned for it; but withal he tells us, that he was absolved, and a law made, that for ever after no man should be questioned for so doing. More of these examples were not likely much to prejudice our caufe. For certainly they that abfolved the party, and made a law, that no man ever after fhould be molefted on the like occafion, in likelihood could do it, upon no reafon, but upon conceit, that the accufation was founded upon an error.

But what the authority of Plutarch cannot do, that peradventure the judgment of St. Ambrofe, St. Auguftine, St. Gregory, and no lefs than ten councils, will effect; for all thefe are brought and urged to difcountenance all marriage betwixt near coufins. Firft, for St. Ambrofe and St. Auftin, no marvel if they fpeak fufpicioufly concerning this kind of marriages, fince they lived at the time when the law made by Theodofius in prejudice of them was as yet unrepealed: indeed St. Ambrofe would make us believe, that fuch marriages are againft the law of God; but in that point he was deceived. St. Auftin fpeaks more cauteloufly concerning this kind of marriages, and acknowledging, that by the law of God they were permitted, obferves, that they had been but lately prohibited by human authority. And as for St. Gregory, it is well known that the bifhops of Rome had already began to enlarge their phylacteries, and taken upon them to make laws far more than they needed: and now looking bigger than their fellows, all councils, efpecially in the Weft, were made with fome refpect to what they had decreed. No marvel therefore if fo many councils

are brought to cry down marriages with first and
second cousins, which the Popes had already difcountenanced; we should rather much have mar-
velled if any council had appeared in favour of
them. All therefore that these councils have said
in this point, is in a sort to pass for nothing else
but the will of the bishop of Rome, to which how
much we are to attribute, I leave to the author of
the discourse to judge. And should we attribute
any thing to St. Gregory, his greatest authority
makes nothing against our cause: for he in his answer to Austin our English prelate, forbids the
laws only against first-cousins, against second and
third he hath no quarrel; nay, his words found
quite contrary, *Unde necesse est*, saith he, *ut in ter-
tia*, which is the case, *vel in quarta generatione, fi-
deles sibi licite conjungantur.* So that this authority of St. Gregory may well enough return to the
place where it was taken, for any harm it is likely
to do. The same may be said to St. Ambrose
and St. Austin, that in the case they may be admitted without any danger. For what they say
concerns only first-cousins, which falls a degree
short of the case.

There is yet one reason of some consequence
remains. For we are informed, that it must needs
be that marriage betwixt first-cousins that is forbidden, because a degree farther off is forbidden.
For this purpose we are asked, Is not thy father's
brother's widow farther off, than thy father's bro-

ther's daughter ? I anſwer no ; for my father's
brother's widow is my aunt; but my father's brother's daughter is my couſin-german ; but my
aunt is nearer to me than my couſin. Look but
upon the draught of degrees which I have before
drawn, and if you count from me to my father's
brother, (which is the place of my aunt) you ſhall
find but three degrees : but from me to my couſin german, or firſt-couſin, you ſhall find four degrees. And whereas we are told, that to make a-
mends for this we muſt take notice, that my uncle's widow is tied to me only by outward affinity, but my couſin-german is near to me by blood
and conſanguinity, I anſwer, that the difference
betwixt affinity and conſanguinity in this place
helps not at all : it is confeſſed, that look what
degree of conſanguinity is forbidden, the ſame degree of affinity likewiſe is forbidden, if any be
contracted : for as I may not marry my mother, ſo
I may not marry my father's widow ; my daughter, and my ſon's wife ; my niece, and my nephew's wife ; are all alike forbidden to me. And
by the ſame analogy, as I may not marry my aunt,
ſo I may not marry my uncle's widow. Yet to
help the lameneſs of this reaſon we are told, (but
not for news I trow, for who knew it not ?) that
in conſanguinity, ſome degrees further removed
are excluded marriage ; for inſtance, my brother's
grand-children, to the fourth and fifth generation:
yet all this wind blows no corn ; for it is already

L

granted, that I am excluded the whole line of my nieces, not only to the fourth and fifth, but to all generations possible. And here the line of nieces suffers the same which the line of mothers, of aunts, of daughters doth, which are wholly excluded in the fartheft degree imaginable; so that the total exclusion of nieces proves not the marriage of first and second cousins unlawful; much less doth the exclusion of them to the fourth and fifth generation: so that any law of God, or sound reason notwithstanding, marriage betwixt firstcousins may very well pass for lawful. But whereas some of the antients, and likewise some of the modern churches, out of scrupulofity, have excluded marriage betwixt first-cousins; yet neither any of the antients, nor any churches at this day that I know, (the church of Rome only excepted) have prejudiced the marriage of second-cousins: so that whosoever they be that marry in that degree, if themselves be persuaded of the lawfulness of their action, they have no cause to doubt of the blessing of God upon them and their posterity.

That which remains of the discourse yet untouched, is of no great weight, though of some heat; for indeed it is nothing else but rhetorical and passionate amplification, and to return answer to it were but to lose my labour: if this which I have done give you content, I have my desire. Only this much I request of you for my pains, that you will cause your amanuensis to transcribe a copy of my letters, and at your leifure fend it me. For whereas I was long fince defired to deliver myfelf in this point, in the behalf of a great perfon of this land, who is now with God, I kept no copy of my meditations, by which error I was now as far to feek as ever, which was the caufe which made me flower in returning anfwer to your letters. This courtefy, if you fhall be pleafed to grant me, you fhall for ever oblige unto you,

Your true friend and fervant,

JOHN HALES.

L 2

THE

METHOD

OF READING

PROFANE HISTORY.

IN perufal of hiftory, firft, provide you fome writers in chronology, and cofmography. For if you be ignorant of the times and places, when and where the things you read were done, it cannot chufe but breed confufion in your reading, and make you many times grofly to flip and miftake in your difcourfe. When therefore you fet to your book, have by you Helvicus his Chronology; and a map of the country in which you are converfant; and repair unto them to acquaint you with time and place, when, and where you are. If you be verfing the antient hiftories, then provide you Ptolomy's Maps, or Ortelius his Conatus Geographici: if the latter, then fome of the modern carts.

As for method of reading hiftory, note, that there are in ftory two things efpecially confiderable. *Firft*, the order of the ftory itfelf: and *Se-*

condly, moral, or ſtatical obſervations, for common life and practice.

For the latter of theſe, there needs no method in reading; all the method is in digeſting your reading, by bringing it into heads, or common places, or indices, or the like. For in this kind, read what books, and in what order ye liſt, it matters not; ſo your notes may be in ſome ſuch order as may be uſeful for you. For the former, that is the courſe and order of the ſtory; the order of reading ought to be the ſame with the order of the things themſelves; what was firſt done, that is to be read in the firſt place; what was next, in the next place, and ſo forward; the ſucceſſion and order of time and reading being the ſame. This if you mean to obſerve exactly (which I think it is not ſo neceſſary for you to do) you muſt range your authors according to the times, wherein the things they writ were acted, and in the ſame order read them.

But before you come to read the acts of any people: as thoſe that intend to go to bowls, will firſt ſee and view the ground upon which they are to play; ſo it ſhall not be amiſs for you, firſt, to take a general view of that ground, which you mean more particularly to traverſe, by reading ſome ſhort epitome. So, ere you read the Roman ſtory, (for that way you mean your ſtudies ſhall bend) firſt, read carefully L. Florus, who briefly continues the ſtory from Romulus till Auguſtus fhut the temple of Janus: and if you would yet go lower, add then unto Florus, Eutropius his Breviarium; who from the fame point brings the ftory unto Jovianus the Emperor. This will give you a general tafte of your bufinefs, and add light unto particular authors.

This done, then take Livy in hand. Now becaufe Livy is very much broken and imperfect, and parts of him loft; it may be queftioned, whether were better to read Livy throughout, baulking his imperfections, before you meddle with any other? or when you come to any imperfection, to leave him, and fupply his wants by intercalation of fome other author, and fo refume him into your hands again, *toties quoties?* For anfwer, were it your purpofe exactly to obferve the courfe of the ftory, it were not amifs where Livy fails you, before you go to his next books, to fupply the defect out of fome other authors: but fince this is not that you principally intend, but fome other thing; and again, becaufe variety of authors may trouble you, it will be better for you to read Livy throughout, without interruption. When you have gone him though, then, if you pleafe, you may look back, and take a view of his imperfections, and fupply them out of fome other authors, partly Latin, as Juftin, Salluft, Caefar's Commentaries, Hirtius, Velleius Paterculus: partly Greek, as Polybius, Plutarch, Dionyfius Halicarnaffeus, Appianus Alexandrinus, Dion Caffius: out of which authors you may reasonably supply whatsoever is wanting in Livy.

Having thus brought the story to the change of the empire, you must now begin another course; and first you must take in hand Suetonius Tranquillus, who being carefully perused, your way lies open to the reading of our politicians great apostle Tacitus. Now the same infelicity hath befallen him, which before I noted in Livy: for as *this*, so *that* is very imperfect, and broken, a great part both of his Annals and Histories being lost. And as I counselled you for Livy, so do I for Tacitus, that you read him throughout, without intermingling any other author; and having gone him through, in what you shall see him imperfect, Dion Cassius, or his epitomizer Xiphiline, will help you out: though by reason of your fore-reading of Suetonius, you shall find yourself, for a good part of the story, furnished before-hand.

And thus are you come to the reign of Nerva, where Suetonius and Tacitus ended; hitherto to come is a reasonable task for you yet.

If you shall desire to know the state and story afterward till Constantine's death, and the division of the Empire, or farther, to the fall of the Western Empire, let me understand your mind, and I will satisfy you.

For the editions of those authors hitherto mentioned; your choice is best of those, whom either Lipsius, or Gruterus, or Causabon have set forth:

though if you be careful to buy fair books, you can scarcely chuse amiss; your Greek authors, if you list not to trouble yourself with the language, you shall easily find in Latin sufficient for your use. Only Plutarch, whatever the matter is, hath no luck to the Latin, and therefore I would advise you either to read him in French or in English. But as for Tacitus, the chief cock in the court-basket, it is but meet you take special good advice in reading of him: Lipsius, Savile, Pichena, and others, have taken great pains with him in emaculating the text, in settling the reading, opening the customs, expounding the story, &c. and therefore you must needs have recourse unto them; yet this in only critical, and not courtly learning: Tacitus for your use requires other kind of comments. For since he is a concise, dense, and by repute a very oraculous writer, almost in every line pointing at some state-maxim: it had been a good employment for some good wit, to have expounded, proved, exemplified at large, what he doth for the most part only but intimate. Something our age hath attempted in this kind, though to little purpose. Gruterus hath collected certain places here and there, collected out of him: and Scipio Ammirati hath glossed him in some places according to the shallowness of the new Italian wits. But Annibal Scotus, groom of the chamber to Sixtus Quintus, hath desperately gone through him all, whom I would wish you to look upon, not for any

great good you shall reap by him (for he is the
worst that ever I read) only you shall see by that
which he hath with great infelicity attempted,
what kind of comment it is, which if it were well
performed, would be very acceptable to us.

From the order of reading, we come to the *ex-*
cerpta, and to such things as we observe and gather in our reading. Here are two things to be
marked: *First,* the matters and things which we
collect; *Secondly,* the manner of observing, gathering, registring them in our paper-books for
our speedy use.

To omit all that which belongs to the style and
language wherein your author writes, in which I
suppose you mean not much to trouble yourself;
matters observable in history may be all ranked
under three heads; *First,* there is the story itself,
which usually we gather by epitomizing it. *Second-*
ly, there are *miscellanea,* such as are the names and
genealogies of men ; descriptions of cities, hills,
rivers, woods, &c. customs, offices, magistrates,
prodigies; certain quaint observations, as who was
the first Dictator? when the Romans first began
to use shipping? or to coin gold? what manner of
moneys the antients used ? their manner of war
and military instruments ; and an infinite multitude of the like nature. *Thirdly,* there are *moralia.*

For the *first,* you need not trouble yourself a-
bout it, it is already done to your hand. For there
is almost no story of note, whereof there is not

some epitome, as good as any you can frame of
your own. Indeed, if you did intend any exact
knowledge of history, it were good you did this
yourself, though it were *actum agere :* because
what we do ourselves, sticks best in our memories,
and is most for our use. But since your aim is at
something else, you may spare your own, and
make use of others labours. The *second* head is
pleasant, but is meerly critical and scholastical, and
so the less pertinent to you, and therefore I shall
not need to speak any more of it. The *third,*
which I called morals, is that Penelope which you
must wooe; under this I comprehend all moral sen-
tences and common places, all notable examples
of justice, of religion, &c. apothegms, *Vafre et
simulanter dicta et facta ;* civil stratagems and plots
to bring ends about: censures upon men's persons and actions: considerations upon men's natures and dispositions: all things that may serve
for proof or disproof, illustration or amplification
of any moral place: considerations of the circumstances of actions, the reasons why they prove suc-
cefsful; or their errors, if they prove unfortunate:
as in the second Punic war, why Hannibal still
prevailed by hastening his actions; Fabius, on the
contrary, by delay. And this indeed is one of the
special profits that comes by history. And therefore I have always thought Polybius (might we
have him perfect) one of the best that ever wrote
story. For whereas other historians content them-

felves to touch and point at the true reafons of e-
vents in civil bufinefs ; Polybius, when he hath
hiftorically fet down an action worthy confideration, leaves it not fo, but reviews it, infifts, and,
as it were, comments upon it, confiders all the circumftances that were of any force in the manage
of it; and contents not himfelf, as it were, to caft
its water, but looks into its bowels, and fhews
where it is ftrong, and where difeafed. Wherefore I would have you well acquaint yourfelf with
him, and efpecially with thofe paffages I now fpeak
of, that they may be patterns to you to do the
like, which that you may with greater affurance
and profit do, make fpecial account of thofe who
wrote the things of their own times, or in which
themfelves were agents, efpecially if you find them
to be fuch as durft tell the truth. For as it is
with painters, who many times draw pictures of
fair women, and call them Helen, or Venus; or
of great emperors, and call them Alexander, or
Caefar ; yet we know they carry no refemblance
of the perfons whofe names they bear: fo, when
men write and decypher actions, long before their
time, they may do it with great wit and elegan-
cy, exprefs much politic wifdom, frame very beautiful pieces ; but how far they exprefs the true
countenance and life of the actions themfelves, of
this it were no impiety to doubt: unlefs we were
affured they drew it from thofe who knew and
faw what they did.

One thing more, ere I leave this head, I will admonifh you of. It is a common fcholical error to fill our papers and note-books with obfervations of great and famous events, either of great battles, or civil broils and contentions. The expedition of Hercules his off-fpring for the recovery of Peloponnefe, the building of Rome, the attempt of Regulus againft the great ferpent of Bagradas, the Punic wars, the ruin of Carthage, the death of Caefar, and the like. Mean while things of ordinary courfe and common life gain no room in our paper-books. Petronius wittily and fharply complained againft fchool-mafters in his times, *Adolefcentulos in fcholis ftultiffimos fieri, quia nihil ex iis quae in ufu habemus aut audiunt aut vident, fed piratas cum catenis in littore ftantes et tyrannos edicta fcribentes, quibus imperent filiis, ut patrum fuorum capita praecidant, fed refponfa in peftilentia data ut virgines tres aut plures immolentur;* in which he wifely reproves the error of thofe, who training up youth in the practice of rhetoric, never fuffered them to practife their wits in things of ufe, but in certain ftrange fupralunary arguments, which never fell within the fphere of common action. This complaint is good againft divers of thofe, who travel in hiftory. For one of the greateft reafons that fo many of them thrive fo little, and grow no wifer men, is, becaufe they flight things of ordinary courfe, and obferve only great matters of more note, but lefs ufe. How doth it benefit a

man who lives in peace, to obferve the art how
Caefar managed wars? or by what cunning he a-
fpired to the monarchy? or what advantages they
were that gave Scipio the day againft Hannibal?
Thefe things may be known, not becaufe the
knowledge of thefe things is ufeful, but becaufe it
is an imputation to be ignorant of them; their
greateft ufe for you being only to furnifh out your
difcourfe. Let me therefore advife you in reading, tc have a care of thofe difcourfes which exprefs domeftic and private actions, efpecially if
they be fuch, wherein yourfelf purpofes to venture your fortunes. For if you rectify a little your
conceit, you fhall fee that it is the fame wifdom,
which manages private bufinefs, and ftate affairs,
and that the one is acted with as much folly and
eafe, as the other. If you will not believe me,
then look into our colleges, where you fhall fee,
that I fay not the plotting for an headfhip, for
that is now become a court-bufinefs, but the contriving of a burferfhip of twenty nobles a year, is
many times done with as great a portion of fuing,
fiding, fupplanting, and of other court-like arts,
as the gaining of the fecretary's place; only the
difference of the perfons it is, which makes the
one comical, the other tragical. To think that
there is more wifdom placed in thefe fpecious
matters, than in private carriages, is the fame error, as if you fhould think there were more art required to paint a king, than a country-gentleman:

whereas our Dutch pieces may serve to confute you, wherein you shall see a cup of Rhenish wine, a dish of radishes, a brass pan, an Holland cheese, the fisher-men selling fish at Scheveling, or the kitchen-maid spitting a loin of mutton, done with as great delicacy and choiceness of art, as can be expressed in the delineation of the greatest monarch in the world.

From the order of reading, and the matters in reading to be observed, we come to the method of observation; what order we are for our best use to keep in entering our notes into our paper-books.

The custom which hath most prevailed hitherto, was common-placing; a thing at the first original very plain and simple; but by after-times much increased, some augmenting the number of the heads, others inventing quainter forms of disposing them: till at length common-place-books became like unto the Roman Breviary or Missal, it was a great part of clerkship to know how to use them. The vastness of the volumes, the multitude of heads, the intricacy of disposition, the pains of committing the heads to memory, and last, of the labour of so often turning the books to enter the observations in their due places, are things so expensive of time and industry, that although at length the work comes to perfection, yet it is but like the silver mines in Wales, the profit will hardly quit the pains. I have often doubt-

ed with myself, whether or no there were any neceffity of being fo exactly methodical. *Firft*, Becaufe there hath not yet been found a method of
that latitude, but little reading would furnifh you
with fome things, which would fall without the
compafs of it *Secondly*, Becaufe men of confufed,
dark and cloudy underftandings, no beam or light
of order and method can ever rectify; whereas
men of clear underftanding, though but in a mediocrity, if they read good books carefully, and
note diligently, it is impoffible but they fhould
find incredible profit, though their notes lie never
fo confufedly. The ftrength of our natural memory, efpecially if we help it, by revifing our own
notes; the nature of things themfelves, many times
ordering themfelves, and almoft telling us how to
range them; a mediocrity of care to fee that matters lie not too chaos-like, will, with very fmall
damage, fave us this great labour of being over-
fuperftitioufly methodical. And what though peradventure fomething be loft,

Exilis domus eft, ubi non et plura fuperfunt. Hor.

It is a fign of great poverty of fcholarfhip, where
every thing that is loft, is miffed; whereas rich
and well accomplifhed learning is able to lofe many things with little or no inconvenience. Howfoever it be, you that are now about the noon of
your day, and therefore have no leifure to try and
examine methods; and are to bring up a young
gentleman, who in all likelihood will not be over-

willing to take too much pains; may, as I think,
with moſt eaſe and profit, follow this order.

In your reading excerpt, and note in your
books, ſuch things as you like: going on conti-
nually without any reſpect unto order; and for
the avoiding of confuſion, it ſhall be very profitable to allot ſome time to the reading again of
your own notes; which do as much and as oft as
you can. For by this means your notes ſhalt be
better fixt in your memory, and your memory will
eaſily ſupply you of things of the like nature, if
by chance you have diſperſedly noted them; that
ſo you may bring them together by marginal refe-
rences. But becauſe your notes in time muſt needs
ariſe to ſome bulk, that it may be too great a taſk,
and too great loſs of time, to review them, do
thus, Cauſe a large index to be framed according
to alphabetical order, and regiſter in it your heads,
as they ſhall offer themſelves in the courſe of your
reading, every head under his proper letter. For
thus though your notes lie confuſed in your papers, yet are they digeſted in your index, and to
draw them together when you are to make uſe of
them, will be nothing ſo great pains as it would
be, to have ranged them under their ſeveral heads
at their firſt gathering. A little experience of this
courſe will ſhew you the profit of it, eſpecially if
you did compare it with ſome others that are in
uſe.

A

LETTER

TO AN

HONOURABLE PERSON,

CONCERNING THE

WEAPON-SALVE.

HONOURABLE SIR,

I AM very forry that a gentleman of your quality, fo defirous of information in a point of
obfcure and fubtile learning ; fhould find fo flen-
der means to fatisfy your defire, as to be conftrained to reflect on me, a man of no great capacity,
and by reafon of my privacy, unacquainted abroad,
and of my fmall abilities, not able to make experiments, and try conclufions.

Yet, that I may not feem to neglect your love,
and courtefy, of which, upon all occafions, you
have not failed to make liberal expreffion, I will
rather hazard my judgment with you, than my
good manners, and try what I can deliver unto you

M

concerning the late propofal you made unto me, in the matter of the new devifed cure of wounds, by applying the falve to the weapon that did the mifchief.

Where firft I muft requeft you to confider, that my attempt is weightier in refuting the conceit, than theirs was, who have firft broached it. For firft, I am to prove the negative, a thing in nature and art very difficile. For always the proving part lies upon the affirmer: and he that means to acquaint me with a novelty, muft make account to prove it to me, and not look that I fhould undertake a re-futation of it.

Again, he that undertakes to inform the world with a difcovery of fecrets, and vent paradoxes, fhall never want favourable hearers. For the mind of man much delighting in novelty, accepts eafily and with delight, what fhall be opened in that kind; and every fhew of probability fhall be taken as lawful proof: whereas the refuter muft be fure to look to the ftrength of his reafons, and be they never fo weighty, yet any probable fhew of e-fcape from them, fhall be accounted a fufficient de-feat.

But to leave prefacing, the firft thing I would require you to reform, is your opinion you have conceived concerning the antiquity of weapon-falve; for me-thinks you fpeak of it, as of a thing of fome antiquity and years, whereas indeed it is a child of yefterday's birth.

There have of late appeared in the world a new kind of ſtudents, who, by trying concluſions, and making experiments, eſpecially by the fire, have made diſcovery unto us of many ſtrange and pleaſant effects in nature, which in former ages have not been known. To put on theſe men, and commend them a little more unto us, there hath been, not long ſince, within the compaſs of theſe twenty years, a merry gullery put upon the world, concerning a guild of men, who ſtile themſelves 'The 'Brethren of the Roſy Croſs :' a fraternity, who, what, or where they are, no man yet, no, not they who believe, admire, and devote themſelves unto them, could ever diſcover. Otrebius (a gentleman well acquainted with your great St. Johns-man, the champion for the Weapon-Salve) in a tract of his lately written, *De vita, morte et reſurrectione,* would perſuade us that doubtleſs they are in Paradiſe, which place he ſeateth near unto the region of the moon: well may that be ſome fools paradiſe; for certainly that there is any earthly paradiſe at all, no wiſe man will eaſily believe. Theſe men, whoſoever they are, or their defenders, have taken up that new deviſed learning delivered to us by Chymics and Paracelſians, and now hotly endeavour to poſſeſs the world with it. Wherein I muſt give them this commendation, that they have given us abundance of delightful experiments, and that is the thing that gains them the reputation

M 2

they have. But two things they have attempted with no felicity or good fuccefs.

Firſt, They endeavour to make us believe, that the antient principles of philoſophy, which hitherto great clerks have canonized, are to be rejected, and new from them to be received in their rooms. And ſecondly, That this may be the better effected, they have brought in a new language, which they make by collecting of poetic words and phraſes out of Paracelſus, and adding unto them forms of ſpeech borrowed from the holy ſcriptures, and of theſe have framed us that ſtile of language, which you read not only in the author you write of, but in Paracelſus himſelf, and others who follow him. But all this attempt, upon examination, is proved fruitleſs. For neither have they ſhaken the truth of any principle (I ſay not in the trivials and quadrivials, as old clerks were wont to name them, but neither in phyſical nor metaphyſical learning, which is more ſubject to quarrel) of which the world hath hitherto been perſuaded, nor added any new to increaſe the number of them: only they have ſaid the ſame thing in other words; and, which is ſtrange, all their new experiments, which are the chiefeſt ſtrength of their cauſe, are plainly and evidently demonſtrable out of the antient aphoriſms. The author whom you commend unto me, what a noiſe makes he with his ‘ volatile and eſſential ſalt, balſam of nature, vivifying

' spirit,' and other trim phrases of the same cut ?
Now what is it, think you, that is contained under this abstruse language ? Certainly no more,
but only that mass of moisture and heat in us,
which follow upon the temperature of every mixt
body, and wherein all specification, all vegetation
and animation doth reside, which in our ordinary
schools we call *humidum primogenium*, and *calidum
innatum*. Anatomize other of their new and quaint
phrases, and you evidently deprehend the same sophistry. So that if you desire a definition of this
new learning, you cannot better express it, than by
calling it, ' A translation of vulgar conceits into
' a new language.'

Sir, from these men, amongst many other pleasant phantasies, hath sprung the conceit concerning your wonderful Weapon-salve, which, that I
may shew you upon what firm foundation it stands,
lays claim to three great proofs, but indeed per-
forms none of them: I see reason promised, phrases of scripture used, and experience pretended ;
but I cannot yet discover any thing demonstra-
tively proved, by any of the three.

For the reasons are nothing else but certain ge-
neralities, which prove no more but this, that if
any such thing as curing by Weapon-salve be exi-
stent, such or such concentrics or epicycles of sym-
pathies and antipathies, of eradiations or emanations of spirits, may well be thought to be the causers
of it: whereas true and lively demonstration doth

not only suppose the thing to be, which it endeavours to prove; but shews that necessarily it must be so, and possibly it cannot be otherwise. For this kind of proof arises out of such principles, as which being apprehended by the understanding, leave no room for contradiction, by reason of the light they bring with them.

Scripture is promised, but with worse success, for what proves it in the behalf of Weaponsalve, to plead, that the spirit of God moves in all things? that sanative faculty is of God? that God's power and spirit is not to be confined, but will pass *à termino in terminum,* according as is the will of him that sends it forth? For still it remaineth to be proved that this all-doing spirit of God hath left any such force in things, as is pretended. The discourses which by these kinds of men are made out of scripture, many times are not far dwelling from danger, that I may not say from blasphemy. For what means your Doctor to tell you in one part of his book against Mr. Foster, that the virtue of Elisha his bones, by which he raised the dead to life; the voice of the souls under the altar in the Revelation; is the effect of that volatile balsam of nature, of which he so much treateth? For so he must mean, or else his speech concerning them is impertinent. He must a little temper his language that way, or else as he threatens Mr. Foster with the Star-chamber, so perchance himself may hear from the High-commissi-

on, who fhall do well to take to tafk and cenfure
fpeeches of fuch danger. I underftand you are
well acquainted with the gentleman. I would you
would advife him to beware of fuch uncautelous
fpeeches, in which, whilft he feems to praife the
work of God, in nature, he doth as much difad-
vantage his fupernatural and miraculous acts.

So then, reafon and fcripture being removed,
the only defender of Weapon-falve muft be experience. A proof, I confefs, of great weight, were
there certainty of it. For if our fenfes do deceive
us, which are the firft admitters of all ground of
fcience and fkill, what certainty can we have of
any thing? Befides, that mine Ariftotle hath told
me, I confefs, and I believe him, that it is a true
fign of weaknefs of underftanding, to follow our
reafon againft our fenfes. Here *magnam mihi in-
vidiam fentio effe fubeundam.* For, firft, I fee the
authorities of great and noble perfonages ufed to
gain credit to this conceit: for they are alledged
not only for the belief, but for the practice of it.
Secondly, the frequent experience made of it muft
needs decry all thofe that ftand up againft it. To
the firft (faving all good refpects to all perfons in
their places) I muft crave pardon, if I think that
civil greatnefs ought to have no room in my topics. For in cafe of trial by reafon, I have done
greatnefs all the honour it can demand of me, if I
recede from it with that reverence that I owe. My
reafons muft be tried by peers of the fame rank,

like to true jury-men of the fame country; elfe at the bar of reafon, I fhall except againft civil great-nefs as a ftranger, or demand fome act of parlia-ment by which I may find it to be free denized.

But of this enough. To the experience itfelf, I anfwer, That ftill I doubt, whether there ever were any fuch trial as might certainly plead for it. For it is not only true that Hippocrates tells us, ' Experience is dangerous;' * but, it is as true, that experience is many times very fallacious. For it is hard fo to make trial of any conclufion (at leaft of many) by reafon of divers concurrences, of many particulars, which are feen in moft experi-ments, amongft which concurrents, it is a hard matter to difcover what it is that works the effect: and oftentimes that falls out in nature, which be-fel the poet.

' The verfe was mine, another bore the meid.' †
The effect is wrought by one thing; and another carries the glory of it. A better inftance of this cannot be found, than this very cafe which is now in handling. A man is wounded; the weapon taken, and a wound-working falve laid to it: in the mean while, the wounded perfon is commanded to ufe abftinence as much as may be, and to keep the wound clean; whilft he thus doth, he heals, and the Weapon-falve bears the bell away: where-as it is moft certain, that wounds not mortal (for

* Ἡ δὲ πεῖρα σφαλερὴ.
† Hos ego verficulos feci, tulit alter honores. **Virg.**

I hope their falve cures not mortal wounds) will of themfelves grow whole, if the party wounded abftain as much as poffibly he can, and remove from the wound fuch things as may offend. For nothing hinders wounds from cicatrifing, more than a concourfe of humour to the difeafed part; and keeping things irritatory about the orifice of the wound; the firft of thefe is performed by ab- ftinence, which is naturally a drier: the other by keeping the wound clean : he that can do thefe two things, fhall need no other chirurgery to cure an ordinary wound.

Now whereas it is pleaded, that for further ex- perience fake, it hath been tried, the falve being thus applied, the party grieved hath been at eafe; but immediately upon the removal of the falve, the party hath fallen into torment and pain : who fees not that this only remains to be faid to make the tale good ? For naturally a man would look for this part of the ftory, to hold up the cowples, as King James was wont to fay. And therefore I muft crave pardon for the prefent, if I advife my- felf well ere I pafs any part of my belief unto it.

Hitherto have I only ufed my buckler, and put off the thruft; you perchance would gladly know how I can ufe my weapons. Truly I muft con- fefs, I am not very good at it. I find in myfelf that imperfection, which I fee moft fcholars complain of, that they know better how to refel what is falfe, than to confirm what is true. Yet to give you as good fatisfaction as I may, I will endeavour to draw fuch reafons, as may ferve in fome good meafure to fhew the impoffibility of it.

And firft, I would willingly know, if any fuch thing be, how he that was the firft author of the difcovery of it, came firft, like a fecond Columbus, to take knowledge of it. The ways that lead us to the knowledge of all conclufions, of which we have any knowledge, (for I fpeak not of things taken up hiftorically, and upon truft) are but two: firft, experience; fecondly, ratiocination; and the one of thefe is commonly the way to the other, by comparing one thing with another, and applying actives and paffives, and thence producing fundry conclufions; and making one an occafion of another, as man is in thefe cafes a witty creature. Now I would willingly know from which of thefe two the knowledge of this Weapon-falve was firft derived? From experience it could not be; for fee you not what a multitude of particulars muft concur, ere any fuch experience could be made? Firft, the falve muft be made: a falve of ftrange ingredients: and who would make fuch a falve, except he firft knew it would work this cure? and fuch a knowledge before the making of the falve, cannot poffibly be imagined: for into whofe head could it poffibly fink, that fuch a cure could be thus wrought, except he had formerly collected it by reafon or experience? The firft, it is impoffible he fhould have; the fecond, it is granted he had not: fo that the falve at firft muft be made in likelihood for fome other ufe; and, being made for fome other end, by what chance muft it come, that it is found to cure after this ftrange manner? no man in his right wits could think of applying it to the weapon; fome cafualty muft fall out to difcover this force: as it fared with Bercholdus Swartzius, who firft invented gun-powder, who having made a mixture of nitre and fulphur, by chance it conceived fire, and went off with incredible celerity and noife; and from that chance came he, and others after him, to make that ufe of it that now we fee: even fome fuch chance muft here be. Firft, the falve made for fome other end, muft fall on the weapon, and *that* upon the place where the blood was, and there reft, and then fome man muft obferve it, and find that it wrought the cure. Now who would ever apply himfelf to expect fuch an event? So then, experience could never open this myftery, and therefore reafon much lefs.

It remains therefore, if any fuch thing be, the firft knowledge of it muft come by a kind of revelation, and that muft be either from above or from beneath: and I perfuade myfelf, that this apparent difficulty of the firft difcovery of it, was the caufe of the imputation of fome forcery or witchcraft, which of late hath ftuck upon it. Certainly if any fuch thing be, it will be hard to exclude fome, either fupernatural or unnatural way, by which the firſt diſcovery of it muſt come in ; I would be loath to wrong any man, by fouling him with any vile aſperſion ; and I am yet far enough from it, becauſe I believe not the thing? Yet if any ſuch thing be, I ſhould think the original knowledge of it proceeded from ſome ſuch principle I ſpake of, yet will I not charge any, that either believe or practiſe it, with ſtain of witchcraft. For howſoever, he who firſt knew it, might receive it from ſome ſpirit, (for ſpirits, by reaſon of the ſubtilty of their nature, and long experience, know certainly more myſteries in nature than we do) and therefore might juſtly undergo a hard cenſure: yet thoſe to whom afterwards the knowledge of the myſtery deſcended, might be free from all blame. Upon occaſion of a great plague in Greece, recourſe was had to Apollo's oracle for remedy: where they received this anſwer, That they ſhould double Apollo's altar : now Apollo's altar was a cube: and hence it came to paſs, that ſo many famous mathematicians, both amongſt Ethnics and Chriſtians, both antiently, and even at this day, do labour to find out the demonſtration of doubling the cube, a thing yet never was done. In this action they which firſt conſulted with Apollo were to blame, (for Apollo was the devil) but they which by induſtry would have found it, if they could, were not guilty of the firſt conſulters fault. So might it here well be, that he that firſt diſcovered the Weapon-ſalve might know it by the miniſtry of ſome ſpirit; yet they who afterward practiſed it might be guiltleſs.

But leave we this, and conſider yet ſome other reaſon. I have often much muſed, why this ſalve is called the Weapon-ſalve? For I aſk, Cannot this cure be done, but only by means of the weapon? It may ſeem, by your Doctor's apology, it may: for he tells us, it is done by the blood upon the weapon, and by reaſon of a ſeed of life lurking in it, which by the ſalve is weakned: if this be ſo, then whereſoever the blood falls, there apply your ſalve, and you ſhall work the ſame cure; any linen, or ſtool, or floor, or wall, or whatſoever elſe receives the blood, may receive the ſalve, and work the cure; a thing of which I never yet heard: neither do I think the practice of it ſtretcheth beyond the weapon: elſe we ſhall give the ſalve ſo many names, as chance ſhall allot it places to be applied unto? Whence it follows, that either it is not done by the weapon; or done by a thouſand things as well as it; or that there is ſome ſtrange quality in the weapon to work the cure; which quality yet remains to be diſcovered.

That I kill you not with length of diſcourſe, I will urge but one reaſon more, and that ſhall be drawn from the very cauſe itſelf, unto which your Doctor attributes this curing faculty. He firſt ſuppoſeth ſome eradiation and emanation of ſpirit, or ſecret quality, or whatſoever, to be directed from our bodies to the blood dropped from it.

Secondly, that in the blood thus dropped, there remains a spirit of life, congenious to that in the body; which stirred up by the salve, conveys upon this beam a healing quality from this blood to the body. Thirdly, he grants, that not only in the blood, but in the urine, after it is gone from us, remains the like spirit, which by the like beam from a party sick of the jaundice, conveys a cure to him: for so he tells of a great person, who usually works such magnetical cures of that disease, by a paste made of the ashes of a kind of wood amongst us, (it is the barbery: for that wood, by our new doctrine, *De signaturis rerum*, by reason of the deep yellow by which it is dyed, is thought to have in it something sovereign against the jaundice) mixed with the diseased parties urine. Nay more, our hair, our nails, and skin, pared from us, have the same spirit of life; and from our bodies to them whilst they are subsisting, proceeds the like *radii*: and by such device he thinks a starved member may be recovered, as you may see in his books. Now I suppose if it be thus with the urine, with the hair, and nails, and skin; why then should I not conceive it to be so with our sweat, with our tears, with every excrement that falls from us, as our spittle, and flegm, and the like? For what reason can your Doctor give to confine these things to some part of our excrements, and not enlarge them unto all? As for the amputated members of our bodies, it fares with

them no otherwife, as it appears by the Neapoli-
tan gentleman's nofe, cut out of his fervant's arm,
(one letter altered in that word would have made
the ftory much pleafanter) and of others the like
reported and believed by him.

The vanity of which conceit that you may difcover, let me requeft you to obferve this with me.
Look what way we may be pleafured and conve-
nienced, by the fame way we may be harmed and
wronged. The beams then that pafs from us to
thefe things, which come from our bodies, as they
may be the conveyers of good to us, fo may they
be the minifters of mifchief: for if they encounter
with things good, and fympathizing with them,
they relieve and cherifh us; fo if they meet with
their enemies, with antipathizing materials, may
they not diftrefs and annoy us as much ? Certainly to think otherwife, is meerly voluntary and un-
reafonable. See now, I pray you, into what infinite hazard this doctrine cafts us; there is not a
drop of blood, of fweat, of fpittle, and flegm; not
any part of our flefh, our nails, our hair, our ftool,
but hath in it a fpirit of life, homogenious to that
in our bodies; and beams that emanate perpetually from our bodies to them; but, as they may
comfort us, being well encountred ; fo, if they
meet with ill company, they may diftrefs us: a
thing fo much the more to be feared, by how
much the things that annoy us are in number
more than the things that pleafure us. Now what

mean we then to be thus negligent of our drop-
pings, as to let them fall at random into the earth,
the fire, the water, and God knoweth where, since
there is such danger depends from them? Were
this doctrine true, it were not possible that either
man or beast (for it is the case of beasts too, as
appears by his discourse about an horse) should enjoy one moment of health and safety.

Sir, were I at leasure, and free from other occasions, which at this time of the year especially
attend me by reason of my place, as poor a philo-
sopher as I am, I think I might challenge any reasonable man, at this trial, and not think over-well
of mine own undertakings. This which I now
have commented is very subitany, and I fear con-
fused. Mr. Bagley, who was by me all the time I
wrote it, would not conceive, that the frequent
discourses betwixt his little son and himself, could
be an hindrance to me; and truly, to confess the
truth, I found it not much to further me. And
least I quite weary you out, I will only add this
one thing concerning our admirers of Weapon-
salve.

I have read, that a learned Jew undertook to
persuade Albertus, one of the Dukes of Saxony,
that by certain Hebrew letters and words taken
out of the Psalms, and written in parchment, strange
cures might be done upon any wound: as he one
day walked with the Duke, and laboured him
much to give credit to what he discoursed, in that

argument : the Duke fuddenly drew his fword,
and wounding him much in divers places, tells him,
he would now fee the conclufion tried upon himfelf.   But the poor Jew could find no help in his
Semhamphoras, nor his Hebrew characters, but
was conftrained to betake himfelf to more real chirurgery.   Sir, I wifh no man any harm, and therefore I defire not the like fortune might befal them
who ftand for the ufe of Weapon-falve : only
thus much I will fay, that if they fhould meet
with fome Duke of Saxony, he would go near to
cure them of their errors, howfoever they would
fhift to cure their wounds.   Thus have I freely imparted my judgment to you in this point, which
having done, I leave it to your favourable con-
ftruction, and reft as ever,

Your fervant,

From Eaton College,
  this 23d of No-
  vember, 1630.

JOHN HALES,

N

A

LETTER

T O

Mr. WILLIAM OUGHTRED,

THE MATHEMATICIAN.*

GOOD MR. OUGHTRED,

SINCE your being with us at Eaton, I was but one three days abfent, and then only fell out the opportunity of anfwering your letters, *eruditas, bone Deus! et perhumanas;* which, by being at Oxford, I unfortunately mift. Now verily, Sir, I muft needs confefs, that fuch kindnefs, and fo beneficial, upon fo fmall acquaintance, I never received at the hands of any man, as I have at yours. Either your facility was great, or your pains very much, who could, in fo fhort a fpace, difcharge yourfelf of fo many queries. But howfoever, I efteem your courtefy above all the reft. Amongft all the folutions which you fent me, none there

* This letter was communicated by William Jones, Efq; F. R. S. to the authors of the General Dictionary, and publifhed by them in that work. vol. 5. p. 702.

was which gave me not full and sufficient satisfaction, (and so I persuade myself would have given
to one of deeper skill than myself) one only excepted, and that is concerning the projectures of
an oblique circle. I must confess I cannot well put
by your demonstration; neither indeed, to speak
plainly, do I thoroughly conceive of it, by reason,
I doubt not, of my being unexperienced in these
studies. For if I well conceive the nature of projection, which I take to be nothing else but the repre-
sentation of some shape and figure *in plano*, accordingly as it appears to the eye, I do not see how
your conclusion can be good, except it be granted,
that there is no means to express an oblique circle
according as it appears to the eye *, which is a-
gainst your own experience. For even in the universal Astrolabe there is one only circle fully and
circularly projected into a straight line; all the rest
are either ellipses, or else figures drawing near unto the nature of ellipses composed of two arches of
circles, which I think indeed to be ellipses. For
if so be every meridian in the universal planisphere
be to be projected as a circle, then why are they not

---

* In the General Dictionary the following marginal note
is here added, written, as I presume, by Oughtred. ‘ No, not
‘ as it appears to the eye, but as the visual rays coming from
‘ the eye by the circumference of a circle inscribed upon the
‘ globe, do terminate upon a plane diametrically opposite to
‘ the eye; the eye itself must be understood to be placed in
‘ the very end of the diameter.’

indeed all circles, since that the Astrolabe is nothing else but the projection of all the rest of the
meridians in the plane of one? If I take upon me
to dispute with you, it is but only to learn, and
learn I cannot of you, except I betray my ignorance unto you; and assure yourself I will most
shamefully confess it unto you, that I may receive
information from you. But I would not wish you
to trouble yourself about this business; for I am
now upon going to Oxford, not to return to stay
till about twelve or fourteen days before Christ-
mas, about which time I understand by your father you are purposed to be here. For that private
matter about which you wrote, I must confess I
have thought more upon it than ever I did in my
life; but what the reasons are why I remain irre-
solute, I will thoroughly acquaint you when I can
speak with you. You shall receive by your man
your little compendium of triangles, by which, I
must confess, I have found myself much eased.
And now what is it that I can return you for all
these exceeding courtesies? But I do not love to
compliment; and, if I mistake you not, you do not
expect it. I pray let me be remembered, though
unknown, to Mrs. Oughtred; and so, commend-
ing my love unto you, I commit you to God.

Your true, plain,
and loving friend,

From Eaton College, this
7th of October, 1616.

JO. HALES.

A

LETTER

T O

Mr. JOHN GREAVES.

S I R,

I AM more indebted to your affection than to your judgment, in making me a cenfor of your learned piece. It had not peradventure been much amifs, if you had been fo far at coft as to have afforded us a particular topographical map of the place where thofe *infanae fubftructionum moles* ftand. For by that we might have been able the better to have judged of the difcourfe of a learned gentleman of Bavaria, Johannes Fredericus Herwart, who, in the xxi. chapter of his *Admiranda Ethnicae Theologiae Myfteria*, endeavours to take off from the founders of thofe ftupenduous buildings the fcandal of folly and madnefs, which, in the common judgment of the world, hath ftuck upon them; and would perfuade us that the pyramids are monuments of the fingular wifdom of the raifers of them, and of wondrous ufe and benefit to the country, in maintaining the banks of that part

N 3

of the river upon which the city of Memphis
ſtands, which otherwiſe were in danger to be
ſwept away by the unruly eruptions of the river,
if it were not checkt by thoſe wonderful ſtruc-
tures. If your leiſure will give you leave to write
unto me, give me your judgment upon that diſcourſe of his.

One thing I miſt in your work, which makes
me ſuſpeĉt that it is not of ſuch moment as many
report, becauſe I find not that you do it ſo much
honour as to name it. I mean the Sphynx, which
is wont to be repreſented unto us in the ſhape of
the head and ſhoulders of a woman. When you
liſt to look of much time, let me hear from you
what you have obſerved concerning that piece, if
at leaſt it yielded any thing worth your obſervation. Sir, let not the world be deceived in their ex-
peĉtation to partake of your collections in your
travels. I aſſure myſelf, that as they will greatly
benefit the generality, ſo will they, more particularly,

Your true and faithful friend,

From Eaton College,
  this 18th of Octo-
  ber, 1646.　　　　　JOHN HALES.

This letter was formerly printed in the miſcellaneous works
of Mr. John Greaves. 8vo. 1737. vol. 2　p. 454.

A

LETTER

TO A

PERSON UNKNOWN.*

YOU require of me the ufe of Crellius againft Grotius; I am forry, in mine own behalf, that I cannot pleafure you. My good friend Mr. Chillingworth (a gentleman that borrows books in hafte, but reftores them with advice) hath got it into his hands, and I fear me I fhall hardly fee it again; for he had borrowed it twice: by this fymptom I judge what the iffue will be; for no man ever yet borrowed the fame book twice of me, that ever reftored it again. Belike he found it too much for his own ufe, ever to reftore it again to the owner: but if ever it do return to me, I will not fail to impart it to you; the rather, becaufe I would diftil from you your judgment in fome principal points of the controverfy; for, to my underftanding, both parties are at a lofs. For fince, in common fenfe, fatisfaction and pardon, proper-

* From the original, in the collections of Mr. William Ful-man, rector of Meyfay Hampton in Gloucefterfhire, preferved in the library of Corpus Chrifti College, Oxford.

ly taken, are ἀσύςατα; Socinus, maintaining pardon, denies satisfaction; and we, maintaining satisfaction, take away pardon. For when we teach,
*Deum condonare quidem peccata, sed interveniente
satisfactione*, to my conceit we do, in gentle English, overthrow pardon properly taken. *Sed hunc
ego nodum tuis permitto cuneis.* In your last you
mention Salmasius *de usuris*, a learned treatise lately
set forth, *postrema foetura*, as I think, for I have seen
nothing of his since. It is come to my hands, but
my occasions have yet given me no leave to peruse
it, so as that I cannot pass my judgment upon it.
That he maintains the lawfulness of use, this befals
him by reason he is a Calvinist; for John Calvin
was the first good man, from the beginning of the
world, that maintained use to be lawful; and I
have often wished, that whatsoever his conceit
was, that he had been pleased to conceal it, for
he hath done much hurt: and howsoever he means
and tempers his conclusions with sundry con-
straints, and equitable and pious considerations,
(so that he which practiseth use with Calvin's limits, shall do by it little hurt:) yet, I know not
how, *multos invenit sententiae fautores, pietatis nul-
los.* What conceit of Vedelius I have, and likewise
of Popenburg, shall be the argument of my next
unto you. In the mean time, *si quid fit, in quo te-
nuitas nostra usui tibi esse possit*, ἐξαύδα, μὴ κεῦθε νόῳ,
and you shall not fail of whatsoever is in the power
of your truly affectionate friend.   J. H.

A
LETTER
TO A
LADY.*

GOOD MADAM, my beſt reſpects premiſed,

I AM much diſquieted, that your ladyſhip ſhould demand my judgment in a caſe, wherein it can do you ſo little ſervice: for to ſpeak the truth at firſt, the matter about which you pleaſe to make enquiry, I could never yet incline to favour: it is true, that traffic, and merchandiſe, and all dealings in ſtock of money, will utterly fail, if way be not given to uſury: and therefore, in commonwealths, and ſo in ours, the moderate uſe of it by law is to be rated. But what ſhall we ſay to God himſelf, who every where decries it! What unto all good men, both Ethnic and Chriſtians, who, for many hundred years, have ſtill proteſted againſt it? For let all records be looked into, and it will appear that John Calvin was the firſt good man that ever pleaded the lawfulneſs of it. In-

* Tranſcribed by Mr. William Fulman, and preſerved in the library of Corpus Chriſti College, Oxford.

deed when he had once broken the ice, many good men, at leaft they feem fo, ventured to wade after him ; but with what fuccefs God knows ; for man cannot, till it be too late; fince none can dif-cover what account they have or fhall make at that day. To think it fafe to walk in thefe men's fteps is more than I dare advife you to; fince we live not by example, but by precept. Concerning a-ny church-leafe to be procured, it is a thing in which I have little to fay: they, who hold them, if they be of any value, carry things in fuch a mift, that if any fuch eftate be loofe, we, who are the landlords, are the laft men that know of it.

Madam, my hopes are, that fome other occafi-on may more fortunately offer itfelf, wherein my endeavour may be tried in your behalf with better fuccefs, which as foon as ever I fhall difcover, you fhall not fail to receive fuch fatisfaction, as can be expected from fo poor a perfon, as is

Your humble fervant,

Eaton College, this 11th
 of March, 1640.

JO. HALES.

THE

LAST WILL

OF

Mr. JOHN HALES.

IN *Dei Nomine Amen. Maii decimo nono, anno Domini* 1656. My foul having been long fince bequeathed unto the mercies of God in Jefus Chrift, my only Saviour, and my body naturally bequeathing itfelf to duft and afhes, out of which it was taken; I Hales of Eaton, in the county of Bucks, Clerk, by this my Laft Will and Teftament, do difpofe of the fmall remainder of my poor and broken eftate in manner and form following. Firft, I give to my fifter Cicely Coombs five pounds. More, I give to my fifter Bridgett Gulliford five pounds. More, I give to the poor of the town of Eaton, to be diftributed at the difcretion of my executrix hereafter-named, five pounds. More, I give to fix perfons, to be appointed by my faid executrix, to carry my body to the grave, three pounds, to be diftributed amongft them by even portions. More, I give to Mr. Thomas Mansfield of Windfor, grocer, five pounds. More, I give to Mrs. Mary Collins of Eaton five pounds, to that

end and purpose, that she would be pleased to provide her a ring in what manner she pleaseth, to remain with her in memory of a poor deceased
friend. All which moneys here bequeathed do at
this present rest intrusted in the hands of my singular good friends Mr. William Smith and Mr.
Thomas Mountague. Moreover, All my Greek
and Latin books (except St. Jerom's works, which
I give to Mr. Thomas Mountague) I give to my
most deservedly beloved friend William Salter of
Rich-King, Esq; to whom I further give five
pounds, to this end, that he would provide him a
fair seal-ring of gold, engraven with his arms and
hatchments doubled and mantled, to preserve the
memory of a poor deceased friend. All my English books, together with the remainder of all
monies, goods, and utensils whatsoever, I give and
bequeath unto Mrs. Hannah Dickenson of Eaton,
widow, and relict of John Dickenson lately deceased, in whose house (for her's indeed it is, and
not mine, as being bought with her money, howsoever, for some reasons, I have suffered the public voice to intitle me to it.) In whose house, I
say, I have for a long time (especially since my unjust and causeless extrusion from my college) been
with great care and good respect entertained; and
the said Hannah I do, by these presents, institute
and ordain my sole executrix; and unto this Last
Will I make overseers my very good friends Mr.
Thomas Mountague and Mr. William Smith of

Eaton; and to each of them I give five pounds; humbly requesting them to be assisting to my said executrix with their best advice and help, if so be that she chance to find any trouble. Now, because monies are many times not at command, but may require perchance some time to take them up, I ordain that, in six months after my departure, she see all these my bequeasts and legacies orderly and faithfully discharged. As for my funeral, I ordain, that, at the time of the next even song after my departure (if conveniently it may be) my body be laid in the church-yard of the town of Eaton (if I chance there to die) as near as may be to the body of my little godson Jack Dickinson, the elder; and this to be done in plain and simple manner, without any sermon, or ringing the bell, or calling the people together, without any unseasonable commessation, or compotation, or other solemnities on such occasions usual. And I strictly command my executrix, that, neither of her own head, neither at the importunity or authority of any other, neither upon any other pretence whatsoever, to take upon her to dispense with this point of my Will; for as in my life I have done the church no service, so will I not, that, in my death, the church do me any honour.

Probatum fuit Testamentum praedictum, coram me Richardo Allestree, Sacrae Theologiae Professore, Praeposito Collegii Regalis Beatae Mariae de Eaton, juxta Windsor, in comitatu de Bucks, ordinarii peculiari exempta jurisdictione. Datum vicesimo nono die mensis Martii anno Domini 1666. Ac per me probatum, insinuatum, legitimeque pronunciatum pro eodem. Commissaque est administratio omnium et singularium bonorum dicti defuncti executrici in eodem Testamento nominatae, in juris forma juratae, remedio et interesse cujuscunque in omnibus semper salvis. Datum sub sigillo officii, me Praeposito, die et anno praedicto.

ORATIO FUNEBRIS,

HABITA IN COLLEGIO MERTONENSI A

JOHANNE HALESIO,

MAGISTRO IN ARTIBUS,

ET EJUSDEM COLLEGII SOCIO,

ANNO M.DC.XIII. MARTII 29.

QUO DIE CLARISSIMO EQUITI

D. THOMAE BODLEIO

FUNUS DUCEBATUR.

Ornatissime PROCANCELLARIE, Clarissimi, Doc-
tissimi, Venerabiles Viri ;

FACIETIS mihi, uti spero, inauspicatae oratio-
nis veniam, si quod intus apud me diu sum
commentatus, et tacito tantum praesagio divina-
bam, illud coram apud vos hodierno die praedi-
cem : videri mihi et artium et caeterarum rerum
semper legem esse, idemque, quod reliquis omnibus, Musis etiam literisque senium et interitum
imminere. Non refricabo alicujus antiquioris seculi infortunia : ipsum hoc, quod agimus, incusa-

bo aevum, reliquis impendio infelicius. Nam quam
tandem aetatem majora literatorum dispendia af-
flixerunt? Aut quod unquam seculum tot tamque
continua doctissimorum virorum busta funesta-
runt? Illam auream ubertatem, illam sylvam hominum in omni artium genere praestantissimorum,
quam, non dico majorum aetas, sed pueritia nostra
vidit florentissimam, eam pene omnem juventus
nostra vidit extinctam. Whitakerum, Bezam, Zan-
chium, Rainoldum, Junium, addo etiam alterius
licet Musae, Scaligeros, Lipsiumque cum nondum
per aetatem aestimare potuimus, (proh dolor!) a-
misimus. Scilicet in autumnum quendam incidimus multo infelicissimum, in quo necesse fuit tantam literarum et eruditionis segetem infringi, de-
meti, exarescere. Sed nondum penitus animis frac-
ti concideramus : in mediis bustis, funeribus, et
exequiis spem tamen aluimus impudentem. Nimi-
rum subiit animum, nos humunculos, ubi salillum,
quod habemus, animae expiraverit, totos perire :
literas vero immortale fas habere, nullius aevi se-
nio intermori, nulla invidia carpi, nulla oblivione
sepeliri. Quippe supererant praestantissimi viri, et
in rebus agendis nil nisi immortale cogitare soliti,
qui in eo negotium, in eo otium, in eo vigilias, in
eo etiam somnum reponerent suum, ut mortalita-
tem, quam literatis depellere non possent, ab ipsis
tamen literis pulcherrimis consiliis et operibus
propulsarent. Sed dum nobis faciles adblandi-
remur, et infelicium literarum miseram solitudi-

nem cogitationibus iſtis ſolaremur : neſcio quae
ſolatiis noſtris inſidiata invidia, ut nihil amplius,
non ſpei, non ſpeculae, fieret reliquum, ſubito nobis ſubduxit hunc magnum Muſarum patronum,
et Academiae nihil praeter chariſſimi capitis triſte
deſiderium reliquit. Ergo omnes illi benigniſſimae
naturae flores, illi perennes inexhauſtae munificentiae fontes exaruerunt ? Ergo excellentis animi or-
namenta, et vigorem immortalem, tot diviniſſima-
rum cogitationum foecundum, tot annorum virtutes dies una, hora, momentum abſtulit ? Certe.
Potuit infirmitas et conditio mortalitatis noſtrae,
potuit incerta fortuna, certiſſima natura : auſim
immutare verba mea, et ſic melius errare : potuit
incerta natura, certiſſima fortuna, quae nullo cum
judicio in rebus verſatur, nullo ordine et examine
miſcet fata, confundit merita ; potuit, inquam, a-
liorum ignobile et inutile ſenium improba vivaci-
tate uſque et uſque fatigare: huic vero brevem exi-
gui ſpiritus auraeque communis uſum invidere, qui
ſi annis Neſtorem aequaſſet, nobis tamen fuiſſet in
immaturis. Iis enim qui aeternitatem cogitant, et
ſeſe ampliſſimis operibus poſteritati tranſmittunt,
quae poteſt eſſe non immatura mors ? Nam arcti et
compreſſi pectoris mortales, queis una cura brevem vitam caducis laboribus fatigare, ut vivendi
cauſas quotidie finiunt, ita ſingulis diebus efferun-
tur : at vegeta et experrecta indoles, cui is labor,
ea quies, meditari ampliſſima, et magnifice cogita-
ta ſplendidiſſimis factis honeſtare ; nulla illi mors

O

non repentina eſt, ut quae fundantem arces et ca-
ſtella molientem opprimat, et inceptas turres, et
imperfecta moenia, et ſemper inchoatum aliquid
interrumpat. Erat hoc Bodleii noſtri fatum iniquiſſimum: quem praeclariſſimorum operum, aliorum quidem compotem, aliorum vero candida-
tum, oppreſſit ultima neceſſitas, coëgitque tot la-
bores in ſulco quaſi et ſemine deſtituere. Nos vero quid aliud Divinam Majeſtatem votis votiſque
popoſcimus, quam ut ipſus longa pietate munus
nutriret ſuum; quam ut ſub ipſius, tanquam ſa-
luberrimi ſideris aſpectu laeta beneficii ſeges in a-
riſtam quaſi et fructum matureſceret? Sed ita
averſo numine vota nuncupavimus, ut non modo
nihil annorum apponeretur, ſed nec, quae poſtre-
ma ſolet eſſe defunctorum felicitas, accederet in funere laudator diſertus. Nolebam equidem, Viri
Graviſſimi, et certe iniquiſſimum eſſe ducebam, illam ex omni bonarum artium ingenio collectam
perfectionem, illam munificentiam, quam non modo moribus noſtris non expreſſam, ſed vix libris
deſcriptam habemus, illas reliquas virtutes plane
divinas, quas integras oportuit magnis et decoris
ingeniis reſervari, in unius ingenioli alea pericli-
tari. Sed quoniam qui in hac triſtiſſima rerum fa-
cie moeroris partes habent primas, ſilentii legem,
quam luctui ſuo graviſſimo indixerunt, meo non
non concedunt: ſolabor me obſequii neceſſitate,
et quum vobis rem ipſam non potero, propenſam
tamen emetiar voluntatem.

Mihi vero, Summi Viri laudum immenſum pe-
lagus ingreſſuro, mirari ſubiit eos, qui quum in
praeclariſſimorum virorum laudibus verſentur, atque omnes undique bonae famae auras ambitioſius
colligant, nullis tamen libentius vela implent, quam
quas aut fortunae, aut patriae, aut natalium ſplen-
dor emittit. Equidem ego illum ſterilem verae ſo-
lidaeque laudis ſemper habui, ad cujus gloriae cu-
mulum augendum, aut patriae celebritatem, aut
familiae nobilitatem oportebat accedere. Neque
enim praeſtantiſſimos viros minus honorifica cogi-
tatione proſequi aequum eſt, quia Romae non naſ-
cantur, aut Athenis, aut quia familiae parentes-
que in honore famae et monumentis non legantur:
ut nec ſolem et ſidera minoris ducimus, quia pu-
ros illos coeleſteſque orbes, qui illa nobis exhi-
bent, oculorum acie non conſequamur. Nam ut
corpora ſana et integri ſanguinis ex iiſdem ſpeciem
accipiunt, ex quibus vires: ita verus ille virtutum
profeċtus non adſcititio pigmento, ſed illo ipſo,
quo alitur, ſucco nitet. Si quae tamen ſint apud
eruditos locorum privilegia, is profeċto locus reliquis longe praelucet omnibus, qui votis Academiae
feliciſſimo illuſtrium ingeniorum proventu reſpon-
derit. Atque haec Bodleii noſtri patria fuit.* Is
enim terrarum angulus, cujus feliciſſima ubertas
celeberrimos literarum triumviros, Juellum, Rainoldum, Hookerum, eduxit, Bodleium etiam nobis dedit; providentia quadam ſic diſpenſante, ut

* Devonia.

quae patria tantos daret Marones, hunc etiam daret Maecenatem. Laudabunt ergo, alias terras a-
moena pratorum, laeta fegetem, denfa fylvarum:
hanc vero reliquis omnibus literata fertilitas aeternum reddet beatiorem. In familiae Bodleianae
praeconiis non tam gentilitiam dignitatem nume-
rarim, (quanquam fuit illa perilluftris) quam quod
fuerit pietatis laude florentiffima. Nam quum a-
gerentur illa funeftiffima tempora, quum humanitatem, propriam illam religioforum deam, nufquam magis quam apud religiofos defideraremus;
cum aut fubeundae effent aut adorandae cruces, et
pietati nufquam effet nifi in fuga perfugium: lin-
quenda cenfuit pientiffimus vir, hujus Noftri pater, et domum et terras et placentia pignora, maluitque incertam exterorum humanitatem experiri,
quam fe certiffimae domefticorum crudelitati committere. Fugientium parentum lateri haefit indi-
viduus comes Iulus hic; parvus Iulus, cui jam tum
in literis regnum quoddam fata deftinabant. Jam
cujus eft miraculi, religionis, cujus vix per aetatem fenfum habuit, poenam fubire? Cui demum
animo, non dico molli et tenello, fed robufto plane et exercitato, calamitates illae frangendo non
fuiffent? Ille tamen frui miferiis et exinde animos
virefque recipere, et omni illo triftiffimi exilii taedio ad praeclariffima incepta abuti. Frequentare
nobiliffima gymnafia, ambire illuftrium hominum
familiaritates, audire celeberrimos artium lingua-
rumque profeffores, Beroaldum in Graecis, Cheva-

lerium in Hebraeis, etiam in fanctiore illa et augu-
ftiore theologia Calvinum et Bezam, quorum au-
ditoria jam duodecim annorum auditor implebat.
Neque vero quifquam fingi a me Cyrum aliquem,
potius quam tradi putet, et ad Bodleii virtutes ex-
equendas, votum magis quam hiftoriam commo-
dari. Nam quid poft natam injuriam factum eft
iniquius, quam ad fuam imbecillitatem aliorum vires exigere? Sunt enim magnorum fluminum fontes navigabiles, et generofioris arboris ftatim plan-
ta cum fructu eft. Recolligite potius animis omnia
illa apud antiquos praematurae induftriae miracu-
la: Auguftum jam annorum duodecim aviam pro
roftris laudantem: Tarpam, Pliniumque jam annorum quatuordecim tragoedias fcriptitantes: nam
aut me fallit divini ingenii admiratio, aut nihil habent haec, unicae illi tot linguas percipiendi induftriae comparandum. Nam cujus eft laboris fer-
moni illi, quem jam nafcentes hauriebant, aut rhe-
toricum cultum, aut poëticum nitorem dare? Imo
omnis illa artium exercitatio, quid habet tot linguarum taedio par? Athenis una cum loquela artes ipfas arripiebant: Romae cum Latinis Graeca
conjunxiffe fumma votorum erat. Nos, quibus pa-
trii fermonis paupertas nihil praeftat artium, nifi
Latinis, Graecis, Hebraeis, Gallica, Italica, Hifpa-
nica addamus infuper, nihil egimus. Adeo nobis
major exantlandus labor in aperiendis fontibus,
quam illis in tranandis fluminibus: illis expeditius,

universum artium iter absolvere, quam nobis primas semitas aditusque recludere.

Quamobrem Anglorum licet res saepe fuerint multumque turbatae, Bodleii tamen gloriae et emolumento nunquam magis compositae quietaeque iverunt. Sed quum domi tempestates et procellae detonuissent, et Serenissimae Principis divino beneficio, restinctis animorum incendiis, foro pax, templis sanctitas, juri integritas, omnibus salus esset restituta: protinus collecta est quae toto fuerat orbe sparsa ruina, cujus magna pars Bodleius noster. Reversus itaque Musarum alumnus et ' Centum puer artium †,' nihil habuit antiquius, quam beneficum aliquod sidus experiri, cujus influentiae maturantis illapsu, commissa solo semina in segetem et solidam frugem adolescerent. Sinceram itaque et integram adolescentiam suscepit formandam magnus Theologorum Dux, Humfredus: illum intueri eruditus tyro, illum mirari, sub illo toto pectore artes honestas arripere: ut vel hinc satis esset conjecturae quanta mox cum gloria esset in Musarum castris versaturus, qui sub tantis Imperatoribus prima faceret stipendia, ad tanta exempla tenerum tyrocinium exigeret. Quid infinitum laborem, et quotidianam meditationem, et in omni artium genere exercitationes loquar? Etsi enim quod olim Seneca de Nilo, ' Nilus per septena ostia in ' mare emittitur, quodcunque ex his elegeris, mare ' est:' illud ego de septemplici artium Nilo dixe-

† Horat.

rim, ' septenis canalibus tanquam oftiis in difcipli-
' narum mare emittitur, quodcunque ex his ele-
' geris mare eft,' et folum omnibus tum temporis
tum diligentiae momentis occupandis fufficit: ille
tamen amplius quid divino molimine meditari. Non
eft vifum fatis uno artium rivulo tingi, fed univer-
fo literarum oceano imbui: non unam felegit ar-
tem, quam fibi tanquam fponfam jungeret, fed
commune difciplinarum flumen tentavit, omnium
artium pulcherrimo comitatu pectus implevit, et
ut in aciem omnibus armis inftructus, ita in fcho-
las omnibus artibus armatus exiit. Hae magnificae
cogitationes Bodleio authores fuerunt, unicis Mertoni aedibus reliqua Mufarum templa poftponendi.
Nam quum videret in reliquis ampliffimum illud
per fingula fpaciandi defiderium, angufto unius
profeffionis gyro infringi, hic vero licere tanquam
in latiffimo aequore implere vela, et toto ingenio
vehi: vifum eft hunc Mertoni campum aliorum
femitis et convallibus, amputatae illi difciplinae et
abfciffae, latam hanc et magnificam et excelfam an-
teponere. Fertur enim magni animi torrens, non
ut fontes anguftis fiftulis, fed ut latiffimi amnes totis convallibus; faxa devolvit, pontem indignatur,
ripafque, nifi quas ipfe fibi facit, agnofcit, nullas.
Iftis itaque aedibus inferi et ambivit et obtinuit,
quarum caftigatiffimae difciplinae debentur totius
Europae ingenia celeberrima. Nequeo temperare
mihi quo minus matri meae feliciffimam ubertatem
gratuler. Cui enim debent literae, illa in omni

disciplinarum genere clarissima lumina? in theologia, Wiclefum, Scotum, Occhamum? in opticis
Cantuariensem? in physicis Burlaeum et Suisse-
tum? illum tum in humanis tum divinis aetatis
suae facile principem Bradwardinum? Excipietis
me forsan aliquo aurium convitio, dicam tamen
plane quod sentio. Politissima haec, quae fertur,
aetas non tam veram literaturae faciem praestat,
quam illa quae incultior audit et inornatior. Illam multarum linguarum scientiam, quod nostri
seculi est palmarium, adjunctam licet habeat laudem praeclarissimam, ab ipsis tamen doctrinarum
aris atque adytis arcendam censeo, nec ultra πρό-
ναον admittendam. Quid enim? rerum scientia est,
non vocularum. Illi fortibus, nos fulgentibus armis praeliamur. Apud illos cultissimum fundum,
uberes oleas video, et verum robur: apud nos li-
lia et violas, hortorum amoenitates, quincuncem,
sterilem platanum, tonsasque myrtos. Immo haec
ipsa aetas, quae doctissima audire ambit, si quando
veritatem remotis inanibus notis rerumque pompa
investigandam habet, illos tanquam Democriti pu-
teum consulit, apud illos omnem ubertatem et
quasi sylvam sentiendi sapiendique libens agnoscit.
Ii enim in selectissimis tum theologis tum philoso-
phis arcem tenent, non qui è philologiae spatiis,
sed qui è scholarum officinis instructissimi prodie-
runt. Sed non est idem semper disciplinarum vul-
tus. Nam ut reliqua omnia, ita et literae sua habent momenta, suas periodos, nec eaedem omnium

feculorum palato fapiunt. Agreftem illum et quafi impexum prioris aevi horrorem, politioris aetatis lima reformavit. Secutum eft doctrinarum varie-tatem Athenaeum noftrum, et huic etiam litera-rum elegantiae ornandae eduxit decora ingenia. Nam ut omittam eos, qui fuperfunt adhuc, et ex-ornant feculi noftri gloriam, quorum laudibus li-bera pofteritas plenum teftimonium prolixè cumu-latèque reddet: ut omittam eos, quorum ingeniis fi dignum theatrum, fi fcena acceffiffet, in primis locum habuiffent; ut omittam etiam eos, qui mag-na cum gloria literario pulveri civiles fudores mif-cuerunt: vel unicus hic, quem lugemus defunc-tum, folus aedium noftrarum nomen famae infere-ret, fi in hunc ufque diem laudis et honoris luce caruiffet. Quam enim ille artium regionem non magnis itineribus peragravit? Quo non penetravit illa ignea vis? Aut quis ita affectavit fingula, ut is implevit univerfa? fubtilia Mathefeos, obfcura Phyfices, fublimia Metaphyfices non illi deguftata leviter, fed penitus digefta. O incredibilem indu-ftriam, quae ita fingulis infervire potuit, per uni-verfa diftricta, et univerfa fufcipere in fingulis oc-cupata! Nec vero ille paffus eft divinum ingenium quendam quafi in opaco fitum ducere. Nam vix exceperant aedes noftrae parturientem rofam, et illa ftatim in calathum fundi, et tota rubentium foliorum ambitione pandi. Sic enim oportuit con-fummatiffimum juvenem famam ingredi: non dif-ferre tyrocinium in feneCtutem, fed fructum ftudiorum viridem et adhuc dulcem promere, et prima illa quaſi gemmantis indolis ingeniique germina famae populoque oſtendere. Quamobrem in ipſa quaſi ſtudiorum incude poſitus, et primarum tantum artium laurea conſpicuus, αὐτοχειροͅοͅητὸς effuſiſſimo totius aedis concurſu, Graecarum literarum profeſſorem ſeſe renunciavit. Non enim is eſt inani ſcientiae opinione ſubnixus, ut hodie nonnemo, qui ſi tria verba ſapiat è Lexico, ſtatim ſibi Suidas videtur aut Heſychius : omnem dialeĉtorum varietatem, illam incredibilem verborum et compoſitionum foecunditatem penitus memoria comprehenderat imbiberatque. Statim itaque exploratae utilitatis res adolevit in exemplum, quod ne in poſterum interiret, prudentiſſimi viri praemiis et ſtipendiis caverunt. Sed enim induſtriae Bodleianae admiratio ita me totum occupavit, ut mihi prope morum et probitatis oblivionem induxerit. Videri ſolet multis, ſcio, inter haec tanta induſtriae et ingenii praeconia probitatis laus habere frigus quoddam. Mihi vero, etſi in omni vitae noſtrae ſumma, primum in moribus ponendum calculum exiſtimem, tamen neſcio quo modo honeſtas, in illa ſublimi et plena ſpiritus natura, lumen quoddam habere videtur et nitorem, qui in illis inferioris ſubſellii ingeniis non lucet. Probitas enim ſaepe ſimplicitate quadam naturae conſtat, improbitas ingenio. In illis enim quibus aut conditionis iniquitas occaſiones ſubduxit, aut tenuis et anguſta ingenii vena facultatem non miniſtrat,

exilis laus eft effe moderatos, effe modeftos : ii vero, queis ingenium, facultas, aetas, occafio leno-
cinantur, fi intactos feculi contagio, fi illibatos
mores praeftiterint, quos plaufus merentur ? quae
praeconia ? Atque haec laus Bodleio noftro fere
peculiaris eft. Nam fic profecto eft : poftquam
omnia fummorum virorum exempla evolverimus,
vix millefimus quifque evafit adolefcentiae fenec-
taeque juxta integrae. Illi ipfi, quos non fine ftu-
pore legimus, Themiftocles et Scipiones, aetatis
fuae integritatem non nifi praecerptam vitiis prae-
floratamque, maximis rebus gerendis tranfmife-
runt. Hic vero aetatis fuae lubricum, quum nondum mores in tuto effent, adolefcentiam, quae nulla unquam placuit fine venia, ad maxima obeunda
munia illaefam et facrofanctam confervavit. Quod
fi quid habeant coeleftes cum mortalibus contu-
bernii, fi non prorfus veri vana magnorum effata
authorum ferantur, cafta illa et nullis contacta vitiis pectora deos ipfos maxime habere familiares:
quem praefidentes ftudiis divae propius audirent ?
Cui magis artes fuas aperiret familiare numen Mi-
nerva ? Nunc tandem mirari defino ita pleno numine Mufas ipfi affuiffe. Itaque non modo Athe-
nas, fed et totum illi Orientem indulferunt. Omnia enim illa feu facra Hebraeorum, feu fecreta
Chaldaeorum, feu quicquid habet Syria reconditi,
omnia illi quaefita, meditata, evigilataque erant.
Quanti vero ftudia ifta etiam in aliis aeftimârit,
quamque fuerit eorum, qui hifce literis induftri-

am fuam confecrârint, finus, portus, praemium,
exemplum : ut aliis claris teftimoniis faepe, ita
infigni illo palam fecit, quo eruditum Drufium de
his ftudiis notum, et accivit, et familiariter habuit,
cujus et fovit ftudia, et neceffitatibus fubvenit,
quem etiam difcedentem amiciffimè viatico eft pro-
fecutus. Rem non eminentem quidem difturus
fum, fed tamen folida veraque cognitione maxi-
mam. Erat in Archivis noftris Hebraeis confcrip-
ta literis fyngrapha, negotii olim cum Judaeis ha-
biti teftimonium. Erant literulae vacillantes illae
et perverfae Rabbinorum, et characteris morofitati
accefferat etiam temporis injuria, quae incertos
tantum apices reliquerat, et ἐξίτηλὰ literarum capita. Diu itaque neglefta jacuit, ut Sibyllae foli-
um, cui arbitri et interpretis lumen deeffet. Ubi
vero hic Nofter ingenii quadam face illuxiffet, ftatim patere claufa, lucere tenebrofa, et redire quafi
evanefcens fcriptura, ut quae vix oculis olim, nunc
prope manibus tenerentur. Eft hoc fortaffis minoris, fed tamen numeri. Quaedam enim minima
quidem funt, fed tamen non poffunt nifi à maximis
proficifci. Non enim illa folum pulcherrima, et
omnibus expreffa coloribus tabula, fed et minima
linea Apellem loquitur : neque haec tantum maxima rerum compages, fed nec culices, nec formi-
cae, nec vermiculi ab alio potuerunt, quam ab infinita illa majeftate proficifci. Ego vobis, audito-
res, in illa praeclariffima vitae Bodleianae fumma
non talenta tantum, aut minas, fed, fi liceret, fin-

gulos etiam feftertios numerarem. Equidem nihil
dicam temere, ea tantum loquar, quae viri maxi-
mi aeternis literarum monumentis confignarunt.
'In hominibus praeclariffimis, non folum, quae fpe-
' ciofiffima funt, et omnium oculos convertunt, te-
' nere nos debebant, fed et illa quotidianae necef-
' fitatis munia,' τί ἔφαγον, καὶ πότε ἔφαγον, πότε
ἐκάθισαν, ἢ ποῦ ἐβάδισαν; † Nam ut in omnibus in-
tenta nervis cythara, ita in magnorum hominum
actionibus, fumma infimis incredibili quodam con-
fenfu concentuque refpondent: et altae mentis,
quae in maximis fplendet, radius quidam et velut
ἀπαύγασμα in minimis elucet.

Sed quid ego pluvias, ut inquit Pindarus, a-
quas colligo, fefe undique vivo gurgite offerente?
Illa Bodleii induftria plufquam humana, illa tot
linguarum artiumque infinita comprehenfio, doctos tantum egit in ftuporem: at illa incredibilis
morum fuavitas, ille in congreffibus geftuque toto
lepos et veluti Atticifmus quidam, doctos indoc-
tofque juxta cepit. Sunt quibus lucubrationum
intemperies et pertinacia quicquid eft in moribus
laetum carpit, et omnes amoenos ingenii fuccos
ebibit. Triftes evadunt et difficiles, et dum fe ftudiis humanitatis applicant, ipfi prope fiunt inhu-
mani. Nofter vero continuata ftudia, quorum per-
dius et pernox fatagebat, infinita venuftate quadam et quafi quinta parte nectaris imbuere; et

† Chryfoft. in prooem. in Ep. ad Philemonem.

cum se totum Musis consecrasset, luci tamen et a-
micis et congressibus dare nihilo secius. Unde et
illa supervacua literarum et amoena artium diver-
ticula discere, non habuit insuper: inspicere eos,
quorum ars in manuum vultúsque indiciis dijudi-
candis versatur, scire quicquid oneirocritici somni-
ant de insomniis, istis demum in conventibus, tanquam honesta quadam, et festiva, et erudita alea
lusitare. Hanc autem utramque quam induerat
personam, ita summo egit cum judicio, ut nihil se-
veritati ejus hilaritate, nihil gravitati humanitate
detraheretur: in illis vero quasi supremi coeli disciplinis, quantus fuerit, quam anquisitè sollicitè-
que prudentium consulta, Hippocratis oracula, divina Theologorum scrutatus fuerit, reverentius e-
rit integrum illibatumque secretis vestris cogitationibus reservari, quam carptim breviterque per-
stringi. Illud vero intactum praeterire non possum, quo et altioris eruditionis gloriam, et amoeni
ingenii laudem reportavit. Nam quum in exteris
Academiis ingenii cultum caperet: et incesseret
desiderium, hominum de se voluntates et judicia
explorandi, quantumque ipse posset in Juris scientia experiundi: placuit publice sui specimen exhibere, et in celeberrimo prudentium conventu aliquid controversi Juridicorum more discutere.
Quam rem ita omnibus absolvit numeris; eo judicio authorum expendit opiniones, eo acumine in
intimos recessus penetravit, ea denique autoritate
sententiam tulit, ut qui Scaevolae et Ulpiani audi-

ebant, Bodleium purpura et supremis illius scientiae titulis et insignibus, propensissimis animis et suffragiis cuperent irentque ornatum. Sed non ego illa publici juris faciam, quae ipsi visum est sui tantum pectoris sacrario committere: honores illos attingam potius, in quibus libera tum Academiae tum reipublicae judicia est expertus. Nam judicii in rebus moderandis satis amplum testimonium dedit Universitas, cum eum incredibili omnium ordinum consensu Procuratoriae dignitatis ornamentis honestaret: Literarum vero elegantiae multo amplissimum, cum illum Publici Oratoris munere ornaret, quo ille sic est perfunctus, ut sibi ad illam divinam omnium artium πανοπλίαν non defuisse ostenderet rhetorum vineas et pluteos, et reliquam eruditam vim et oppugnandarum aurium apparatum. Haec autem summa licet apud nos sint munera, quorum illa aetas capax, erant tamen pulcherrimis illis cogitationibus inferiora. Nam quum videret, quanta dignitas, quanta majestas, quantum denique numen esset civilis prudentiae, noluit ulterius in istis officiorum ludicris et umbra velitari, illosque ad veram pugnam natos lacertos, levitate jaculi aut jactu disci vanescere. Protinus ergo Germaniam, Galliam, Italiam peragrare, pulcherrimis exemplis imbui, inde prudentiae haustus bibere, inde civilium rerum usum sumere, quem mox in negotiis et consiliis praestaret. Neque vero illum divinae spes et cogitationes fefellerunt.

Vix enim reverſus eſt, et ſtatim nobiliſſimas obire
legationes, ad Fredericum ſereniſſimum Daniae
Regem, Julium Ducem Brunſvicenſem, Gulielmum
Haſſiae Lantgravium, Henricum Chriſtianiſſimum
Galliarum Regem, funcſtiſſima illa Gallicanae reipublicae tempeſtate, qua Guiſianorum ſcelere et
furiis acta regia civitas clementiſſimum et immeri-
tiſſimum Regem expulit, et pudendo exemplo ultima impulit rerum vitaeque ſuae diſcrimina experiri. Huc accedat celeberrimum illud apud Foe-
deratarum Provinciarum Ordines actum quinquen-
nium, quo turbatis pacem, diſperſis ordinem dedit, quicquid flammarum incenſi animi concepe-
rant, extinxit, et ſi quas tempeſtates concitatae
ſuſpicionibus mentes portendebant, ſerenavit. Hoc
illud tempus eſt, quo honoratiſſimo Viro per Se-
reniſſimam Principem et reliquam Procerum manum, quae ipſi aſſidebat ad gubernacula, ampliſſi-
mum fidei prudentiaeque teſtimonium factum eſt.
Nam quum illa Legatorum pene lex ſit, ex prae-
ſcripto tantum agere, et velut praeformatas infan-
tibus literas perſequi, et ut Graeci dicere ſolent,
' quem mater amictum dedit, ſollicite cuſtodire : '
Ille ſolus nihil fere monitorum accipere, ſuis tantum niti radicibus, et dominus rerum temporum-
que, trahere conſiliis omnia, non ſequi. Haeccine
vobis levia aut ludicra videntur, induere regum
perſonas, indutaſque agere ? Voluntates principum, quas intelligere, immo ſubodorari ſaepe ne-

fas eft, divinare et feliciter antecedere? At non eft
vifum fic Honoratiffimo Seni †, qui tum temporum
principis totiufque reipublicae gratia eft fubnixus.
Ille unicum mirari Bodleium, fummis apud principem laudibus ornare, digniffimum ferre, qui confi-
liis et fecretis interfit, immo illud in animo moliri,
ut Bodleium fibi in officio collegam renunciaret.
Sed quum Illuftriffimus Vir, qui in ea fcena rerum
in principis populique favore partes agebat multo
maximas, Bodleium importunis ubique oneraret
laudibus, quas non ceffabant nimium ingeniofe ma-
levoli magis in aliorum praejudicium, quam in ip-
fius honorem conceptas interpretari: accendit ea
res potentiffimos aemulos, quibus obftinatum in
pofterum Bodleii honores infringere, et, fi quid
ipfi decerneretur honorifici, intercedere. Ego vero te, Bodleie, non illum magis aufpicatum puto
egiffe diem, quo Galliam, Daniam, Germaniam nobiliffimis legationibus peragrares, quam quo libe-
ro de dignitate tua hominum maximorum judicio
fruerere. Tum enim omnes legationum et honorum titulos fupergreffus es. Ambire enim et ge-
rere honores fummos, peffimi et poffunt, et faepe
folent. At frui opinione optimorum, haberi omnibus titulis et honoribus par, is folus poteft, quem
vera virtus internis hominum confcientiis fecit
commendatiffimum. Quamobrem cum eo jam car-
dine prudentiffimus vir res fuas verti comperiffet,
linquendas cenfuit incertas artes, et non femper

† D. Gulielmo Cecilio.

P

finceras magnatum amicitias, removendum fe à fol-
licitudinibus et curis, et neceffitate quotidie aliquid contra animum faciendi: ftatuitque in loca
pura atque innocentia, et in aliquod pulcherrimum
quietis Linternum concedere. Quod divinum Bodleii confilium poftquam innotuiffet, quam aegre?
qua contentione? quo nifu obtinuit? quàm ei pene patria manum injecit? Iterum offerre fefe ce-
leberrimae legationes, iterum Gallia vocare, iterum Germania, nobiliffima Bodleianae virtutis a-
rena, iterum tituli et honores. Sed obduruerat
contemptor ambitionis et infinitae cupiditatis frae-
nator animus, maluitque fecretus et confecratus,
liber ab invidia, procul à contentionibus, famam
in tuto collocare, verumque honorem in hominum
judiciis, quam titulorum fplendore reponere. Quantam vobis haec divinae mentis admirationem exci-
tant? Nam poft damnum temporis et fpes decep-
tas impetu quodam et inftinctu quaerere fecretum,
et hominum famam contemnere, cum te prius fama hominefque contempferint, facile eft. Sed cum
ambit et quafi procatur honor et fecundus magnatum favor, deliberare et caufas expendere, utque
fuaferit ratio, honoris aut fecreti confilium capere
vel ponere, ingentis animi eft. Quamobrem te,
Bodleie, ut actionis flore, ita et feceffionis tuae op-
portunitate, divino confilio ufum arbitror. Eft e-
nim illud fapientis viri et in omni optimi civis officio verfati, finem quoque dignum optimo viro et
opere fanctiffimo facere, et fcire quando definen-

dum. Merito fua riferunt fecula Domitium A-
frum, qui cum olim fori princeps fuiffet, tandem
vero feneƈtute fraƈtus quotidie aliquid autoritatis
perderet, et verfari tamen in orationibus et roftris
vellet, opportuni fcommatis occafionem fecit, 'mal-
' le eum deficere, quam definere.' Noftro ergo cu-
rae fuit, priufquam in has aetatis veniret infidias,
receptui canere, et in portum integra nave perve-
nire, et definere cum defideraretur. Atqui infita
illa coeleftis vis nullo potuit fecreto, nullo feceffu
infringi : fed ut nobiliora animalia, fi caveis in-
cludas, effervefcunt magis ; ita ignea mens eo magis incaluit, quo anguftiore gyro coërceretur. Non
enim otiofa res eft aut quieta magnificus animus,
nec quae importuna quadam modeftia, et veluti
probitate gaudeat. Inquies eft, effraenata, contu-
max, mutat induftriam, non intermittit; pafcitur
operibus, reficitur curis, et quod aliis labor, illi
natura eft. Rem itaque aggreditur Bodleius nec
dicendam nec filendam fine cura. Nam cum memoria recoleret Academiam gentemque togatam,
curas olim fuas et amores; videretque vetuftatem,
non privatam aliquam partem, fed ipfa infignia atque infulas Academiae invafiffe : et locum illum,
quem Mufae tam manifeftae ac praefentes, quam
Parnaffum ac Helicona infident, non modo blattas
et tineas, fed prope vepres et cautes et avia occu-
paffe : cogitavit non modo de hominibus, fed de
teƈtis ipfis bene mereri, fiftere 'ruinas, pellere fo-
litudines, et ingentia opera, eodem quo extruƈta

funt animo, ab interitu vindicare, Mufifque quas priorum temporum immanitas expulerat, quafi fpiritum et fanguinem et patriam refundere. Jam vero quam hoc magni animi, quam augufti, non unum aliquem liberalitate demereri, fed totius literati orbis ambitu munificentiam terminare? Deum ipfum imitari, et beneficia non hominibus, fed humano generi praeftare? fimul omnia perfundere, utque fol et dies, non parte aliqua, fed ftatim totum, nec uni aut alteri, fed omnibus in commune proferri? Quinetiam ut regii tantum muneris erat viam hanc primo difciplinis aperuiffe, librofque publice legendos exhibuiffe: (fic enim literatis Pififtratus, Xerxes, Seleucus, Ptolemaeus omnium primi confuluerunt) ita quofcunque accendit imitationis ardor tanta implere veftigia, regiae plane munificentiae erant et divinae. Patimini, obfecro, Academici doctiffimi, me Mertonenfibus meis iterum celeberrima famae gloriaeque noftrae lumina gratulari. Propemodum enim noftra eft et peculiaris felicitas bibliothecas fumptibus excitare, et ingeniis implere. Nobis enim debetis Kempium illum magnum Archipraefulem, cujus gratiffimam memoriam ad omnes aras et pulvinaria folenni pietate et officiis profequimini. Ille vobis in excelfa illa pyramidum et elegantiffimi operis mole extruenda immenfos fumptus exhaufit; nec in extruenda modo celeberrimam pofuit operam, fed et quingentis infuper inftruxit voluminibus, et intus argumenti fcripturaeque pretio nobiliffimis, et ex-

tra argento auroque operofe fulgidis. Quae omnia
cum in triumphum barbariae et infcitiae ceffiffent,
hinc tanquam è Kempii cinere exortus Bodleius,
ita omnia multo praeftantioribus reponi curavit, ut
ideo cecidiffe videantur, ut hic egregius vindex et
reftitutor accederet. Cogitati operis gloriam cele-
ritatis lenocinium commendavit. Nec enim is erat,
apud quem longis et accuratis precibus erat uten-
dum, aut qui promiffa gravate praeftaret, et im-
putanti fimilis. Illum, demerendis hominibus na-
tum, quifquam ut hortetur? quifquam ut admo-
neat? ut inftiget? eadem opera auras ut vigeant,
ignes ut caleant, maria ut effluant, fuperfluus in-
ftigator admoneret. Ille enim ftatim communicare
Academicis confilia, accerfere peritos, et ne vide-
retur beneficio pondus quaerere, ftatim aggredi.
Memini, femperque meminero illius diei, cum re-
vertentium à confilio publico majorum meorum
fermonibus puer intereffem; Quis tum erat omnium ardor? qui fermo? Veniffe in confeffum ho-
noratiffimum virum; orationem habuiffe, qualem,
Deus bone! quam magnificam? operam Academiae cumulatiffimè promififfe, et immenfos, quos
undique infinitis fumptibus comparaverat, librorum thefauros coram Academiae donaffe. Quae
fuit illius diei laetitia? quis totius civitatis concur-
fus? quae vota pene inferentium coelo manus?
Sic enim affecti fuimus, quafi tum demum veram
Academiae faciem intueremur, et nunquam antea.
Nihil dicam ambitiofius augendae rei caufa, uti-

namque non sim minuendae. Rei literariae ratio-
nibus nemo unquam melius, nemo opportunius ivit
consultum. Nam qui in haec postrema incidimus
tempora atque pessima, ut in rebus civilibus nihil
vidimus usitatius quam inusitata flagitia, ita in
disciplinis infandam sensimus tentari crudelitatem,
et deterrimis nunquam auditam seculis. Parum
scilicet in poenas notae crudelitatis fuit : non est
satis damnatas esse ferro manus et pedes, terga fla-
gris, cervices laqueo et securibus : in ea quae ab
omni patientia rerum natura subduxit, in hominum ingenia, in disciplinarum monumenta saevire,
nostrae aetatis specimen est. Nam qui pietati et
sanctioribus literis abolendis sacramento dixerunt,
postquam nihil fraudis artiumque infamium reli-
querint intentatum, sentiunt tamen sese nihilose-
cius ita durissimis confligere conditionibus atque
ultimis, ut rebus non possint succurrere despera-
tis, nisi in omnia antiquitatis testimonia involent, et
praeclarissimorum virorum monumentis infandam
vim et manus inferant : pristina ingenia alia ex-
tinxerunt penitus, alia mutilarunt, alia faece et
scoria infecerunt, omnia immundo contactu pol-
luerunt. ' Dii talem terris avertite pestem.' Sed-
enim labes illa et funesta disciplinarum pestis, quae
ubique praela occupaverat, irrepserat in Bibliothecas, nec jam secretis molitionibus, sed palam mul-
titudine et authoritate munita volitabat, nullis potuit, ne Vulcaniis quidem armis penitius confodi,
quam est per Bodleium, confecta atque trucidata,

quum tutiffimum illud fcriptoribus afylum confe-
craret. Quamobrem graffentur qua volunt Poffe-
vinus et Gretferus, qui in corrumpendis libris do-
minantur: cudant, recudant, inhibeant, corrigant,
corrumpant, corrodant, Bodleii tamen immortalis
munificentiae divinum munus inviolata antiquo-
rum monumenta omni pofteritati dabit. Sed dum
vobis impenfius faveo, quae ego et quanta praeter-
mitto? Perpetuos illos et opimos reditus, quibus
operis fui aeternitati profpexit: leges illas et falu-
berrima inftituta, quibus, quantum erat humanae
opis, hominum et temporum injuriis ivit obviam:
reliqua illa, quae fingula etiam difpenfata jufti vo-
luminis inftar exigunt? Facile enim fentio oratio-
nis meae taedium, et longae attentionis veftrae
martyrium. Sed quid faciam? aut quem ego fta-
tuam orationi meae finem, quum hic beneficiis fta-
tuat nullum? Inftat et onerat priora fequentibus,
nec fatis actum putat, nifi fuis immenfis fumptibus futurorum liberalitatem invitet. Nam quum
campliffimum prioris feculi opus pofterorum muni-
ficentia feliciter anguftum feciffet, regiis plane im-
penfis campliffimo auxit frontifpicio; cui cum ul-
timam manum impofuiffet, Divina Majeftas eum
coelo vindicavit, ne poft illud immortale factum,
mortale aliquid faceret. Enimvero, Bodleie, fuerit
haec maximo operi tuo debita veneratio, ut novif-
fimum effet: fuerit etiam fortaffis felicitatis tuae
pulcherrimo operi immori: at quid reipublicae re-
fpondebimus, quam tractafti? quid Academiae,

quam inftaurafti, quae in mediis tuis Maufolaeis et
monumentis et bibliothecis te cogitat, te defiderat:
quae te ut infigne quoddam naturae monumentum
fufpexit, te omni artium fupellectile inftructiffi-
mum, ut vivam et fpirantem bibliothecam femper
habuit. Cui jam noftrum fudabit ingenium? Cui
literulae noftrae placere geftient? quicquid dixe-
rimus, quicquid meditabimur, quia ille non audit,
mutum videtur. Monumenta illa quidem atque beneficia manent, aeternumque manebunt, nec ulla
unquam labaffent innumerabili annorum ferie et
fuga temporum. Sed admirabiles illos et fpirantes
amores, quibus Academiam prolixiffime eft ample-
xus, fidelibus icti defideriis quaerimus. Nam qui
diffimulare poffumus, quas ille curas in caufis ne-
gotiifque academicis fufceperit? Quam illa ultima
deficientis fpiritus momenta circa folam Academiam habuerit? Nam cum certus obeundi media jam
morte teneretur, et de illa, quam fcholis publicis
imponere ftatuerat, coronide fermo incidiffet: 'E-
'go,' inquit, 'fi vixero, ipfe praeftabo, fin mihi
'aliquid accidat humanitus, teftamento cavebo.'
Atque hic cum aliquis ex intimis novas vires et
longam falutem voto magis quam fpe ominaretur:
'Immo vero, ego,' inquit, 'morior. Nam quam-
'diu mihi cor vegetum manfit et erectum, vitae
'fpem fovi: ac nunc mihi ipfum cor labafcit, et
'mors certiffima imminet.' Tibi cor ut labafcat,
Bodleie, aut unquam illud pulcherrimorum confi-
liorum domicilium frigus et torpor ut occupet?

Tuumne, ô praefidium noftrum et dulce decus, frigidum et exangue corpus tenemus, videmus, et chariffimam nobis fanctiffimamque memoriam poftremis officiis hodierno die profequimur? Tenè, quem deum queùdam et parentem ftatuimus fortunae, nominifque noftri, intuemur hodie fine nomine cadaver, truncum, cineres, nihil? Atque ille quidem, obiit, plenus annorum μετρητῶν ἀμετρήτωντι, plenus honorum, etiam illorum quos recufavit: Candidatus aeternitatis et exempli, quod imitabitur nemo, etfi omnes fateantur imitandum*. Vos vero, fanctae reliquiae et quicquid reftat Bodleii, eruditi cineres, quos hodie poftremum videmus, heu poftremum videmus, falutamus, falvete aeternum, aeternumque valete.

* Naz. in funere Fratris.

Q

O F

ECCLESIASTICAL

JURISDICTION.*

A LETTER TO A FRIEND.

I TAKE it for a maxim that all jurisdiction is civil. By jurisdiction I understand all power to make law, to command, to conveen, to null, to restrain, to hear and determine doubts, and other things of like quality. Now, whereas we hear often mention made of ecclesiastical authority, and speak of it as a thing distinct from civil, we must know that it is but an error of common speech; for indeed ecclesiastical authority is nothing but some part of civil government committed to the managing of ecclesiastical persons : and if we

* The following tract was communicated to the editor by the reverend Mr. Thomas Percy, a gentleman well known in the literary world. It was found among the papers of Anthony Farringdon, B. D. in the possession of John Orlebar, Esq; of Hinwick in Bedfordshire. This tract, transcribed by Farringdon, is, in all probability, the work of Hales. Farringdon was his friend and admirer. [See letter prefixed to the first edition of *the Golden Remains.*] Upon the margin of this tract Far-

should conceive (a thing which may and doth come oft to pass) some part of authority delegated either to a merchant, or physician, or grammarian, or geometrician, we might, by as good analogy, de- nominate it by an epithet derived from the profes- sion or quality of the person that bears it. For to think that either by divine or natural, or other o- riginal right, any point of authority beyond ἔλεγ- ξον, ἐπιτίμησον, παρακάλεσον, be annexed to the ministry of preaching the gospel, is but an error, though, perhaps, it be both common and antient. The Author and first preachers of our faith nei- ther claimed nor practised any such thing. But, by consent of Christians, whether upon suppositi- on of their integrity, or for the honour of the mi- nistry, or for what other cause I know not, coer- cive authority, and power to meddle in seculars, hath been committed to the preachers of the go- spel ; First, by ordaining sundry clergy degrees, and subordinating the one unto another. Second- ly, by subjecting the laity, in some cases, to their courts, and impropriating certain pleas to their cognisance. Thirdly, by giving way to clerks to

ringdon has marked a short but expressive eulogium, ' A letter ' from a friend ὁ πάνυ.' This tract has all that freedom of thought by which the writings of Hales are distinguished, it is composed in his spirited and masculine style: the reader, upon comparing it with the sermon *Peace, the Legacy of Christ,* vol. iii. p. 17. and p. 26. will perceive the strongest internal evidence that both are the composition of one author.

end cause by appeal, compromise, umpirage, or the like, as appears in that title of the first book of the Code, *De Episcopali Audientia:* Further than all this, princes have thought good to employ in business of higher nature, as embassages, and the like, as our books shew us that Ambrose was sent embassador by Gratian the Emperor to Eugenius. And, if we look to latter times, we shall see the highest places of the kingdom, as the chancellorship, treasurership, &c. managed by cardinals, bishops, and canons of churches; yea poor Capuchin friars, Father Ney and Father Joseph, have been thought the fittest instruments for treaties and secret councils of highest nature.

Now I perceive your curiosity inclines you to enquire upon what good policy this was done, and how princes and ecclesiastical persons may interchangeably serve themselves one of another mutually to advance each others ends; the prince of his clergy, by using them to bow the hearts of his people to his will, or by giving honour to them, so to bias his secular nobility. The clergy again of the prince, by gaining, through his countenance, estimation among the people, by raising themselves in wealth, honours, and promotions. This is a speculation which I never studied, because I never delighted in it. Foreign countenance and favour is but an staff unto the lame, and those who fail of inward strength; resolution, virtue, sanctity are the true means to gain authority and respect unto the clergy; so they be well supported by these, it is not material though they never see the inside of the court, or with poor Mycillus in·Lucian, they know not whether a penny be square or round. After that the world and outward state began to side with the church, that fell out which St. Jerom complained of, *Potentia et divitiis major facta est, virtutibus minor.* And indeed to teach the clergy a way to comply with princes is the directest means to produce the same effect. If in this point I satisfy not your expectation, you must remember the oracle, *Male respondent coacta ingenia.*

Now whereas to strengthen yourself as you hoped, and to draw me on to a liking of intercourse betwixt princes and priests, you have drawn some testimonies out of Isidorus Pelusiota and Pope Leo, I would willingly speak a little unto them, but for Isidore, I am bound to keep silence, for I know not where to find the text you quote, and the words seem to me too secular than to proceed from so abstracted a person. As for Leo's smooth assertion, you must consider who speaks what. He was a vain ambitious person, every where cracking of the pre-eminence of his chair, casting about to bring all bishops causes to his cognizance, oiling himself with fond pretences of Peter's power, and Peter's pre-eminence, so to abuse the name of that great apostle to further his vain ambition. Hence came that fond speculation, that the world's safety

and good could not confift if prince and prieft confpire not in defence of Chrift. For what means he
by the world's good? The flourifhing and gilded
eftate of men in peace and profperity? Like e-
nough he did; for by his pulfe I perceive he was
inclinable enough to dote on fuch painted trumpe-
ry: or did he mean the difperfion and propagating
of Chriftian religion, which is indeed the greateft
good that ever befell the world: if he did fo, as
indeed he fhould have done, then hath he abufed
you with a grofs falfhood. For caft back your eye
upon the times forgoing Chriftianity, when the
crown and the mitre (as you fpeak) were at defiance, and you fhall fee with your eyes that Chriftianity increafed and fpread itfelf through Europe,
Afric, and Afia, in far greater proportion in 300
years before that prince, than it hath done in
1300 years fince. If you wonder at this conclufion, you will much more wonder at the reafon.
You conceive that peace is a great friend to the
propagation of the gofpel: deceive not yourfelf;
this commendation belongs to perfecution. Peace
bribes men, and makes them delight in houfe and
home; perfecution occafions difperfion, and difperfion fpreads the gofpel. You may fee in the
Acts of the Apoftles, that whilft the apoftles and
brethren had peace, the gofpel went not out of the
gates of Jerufalem; but when, by reafon of perfecution raifed upon the death of Stephen, men difperfed and fhifted for themfelves, then preached

they the gospel to the neighbouring cities to which they fled for safety. Those troublesome and tempestuous times before Constantine constrained good men to fly from city to city, from country to country; who endeavouring to persuade all with whom they could acquaint themselves, in so short a space spread the gospel in so large a compass, as that so many ages since have added little in proportion to it. *Nihil interest evangelii quam bene quam male inter se conveniat principibus et presbyteris, interest principum ut evangelio faveant.* Assure yourself, deep discourse of mutual intercourse and interchange of good offices betwixt kings and priests are but politic essays helping forward, not the gospel of Christ, but the avarice and ambition of clergymen.

And now, since for your sake I have examined an ambitious piece of Leo, let me request you, for my sake, but more for your own, to take into consideration a more mortified piece of Hilary (another man than Leo) out of his book against Auxentius the Arian bishop of Milan. I will transcribe it. *Ac primum misereri* &c. [See vol. iii. p. 26, 27.]

ERRATA.

Vol. i. P. 146. num, r. cum.

P. 184. l. 18. meid, r. meed.

P. 203. l. 6. I Hales, r. I, John Hales.

Vol. ii. P. 41. folvit, r. folvet.

P. 48. perpauculo, r. pauperculo.

P. 86. fubmittendum, r. fubmittendo.

P. 136. poft modum, r. poftmodum.

Vol. iii. P. 26. miferari, r. mifereri.

P. 26. ad dignationem, r. a dignatione.

P. 93. ἴδοκα, r. ἴδωκα.

P. 152. relinquendos, r. relinquendi.

THE

CONTENTS

OF THE

FIRST VOLUME.

CONTENTS.

THE

WORKS

OF THE

EVER MEMORABLE

MR. JOHN HALES

OF

EATON.

NOW FIRST COLLECTED TOGETHER.

IN THREE VOLUMES.

The wifdom that is from above, is firft pure, then peaceable,
gentle, and eafy to be intreated, full of mercy and good
fruits, without partiality, and without hypocrify, and the
fruit of righteoufnefs is fown in peace of them that make
peace. JAMES iii. 17, 18.

VOL. II.

GLASGOW:

PRINTED BY ROBERT AND ANDREW FOULIS.

SOLD BY J. TONSON, A. MILLAR, AND D. WILSON,
LONDON; J. BALFOUR, EDINBURGH; AND
R. AND A. FOULIS, GLASGOW.
M.DCC.LXV.

CONTENTS.

CONTENTS.

A B U S E S

OF

H A R D   P L A C E S

OF

S C R I P T U R E.

2 Pet. iii. 16.

*Which the unlearned and unstable wrest, as they do the
other scriptures, unto their own destruction.*

THE love and favour which it pleased God to
bear our fathers before the law, so far prevailed with him, as that without any books and
writings, by familiar and friendly conversing with
them, and communicating himself unto them, he
made them receive and understand his laws: their
inward conceits and intellectuals being after a
wonderful manner, as it were, ' figured and cha-
ractered*,' (as St. Basil expresses it) by his Spirit,
so that they could not but see, and consent unto,
and confess the truth of them. Which way of
manifesting his will, unto many other gracious pri-

---

* Φαντασιυμένη τῇ ἡγεμονικῇ τῶν ἀνθρώπων ὡς ἂν ἀκμὴν βύλη-
ται τῆς ἰδίας φωνῆς ὁ Θεος. Basil. Homil. in Psalm. 28. §. 3.

vileges which it had, above that which in after-
ages came in place of it, had this added, that it
brought with it unto the man, to whom it was
made, a preſervation againſt all doubt and heſitan-
cy, a full aſſurance, both who the author was, and
how far his intent and meaning reacht. We that
are their off-ſpring, ought, as St. Chryſoſtom tells
us, ſo to have demeaned ourſelves, that it might
have been with us as it was with them, that we
might have had no need of writing, no other
teacher but the Spirit, * no other books but our
hearts, no other means to have been taught the
things of God, ' except thoſe internal and ſweet
' leſſons of divine inſpiration, where truth ſpeaks
' without words or writing, and where the more
' ſecret the information, the more delightful † ; '
as ſaith Fulgentius. ' For it is a great argument
' of our ſhame and imperfection, (ſaith Iſidorus
' Peluſiota) that the holy things are written in
' books ‡.' For as God, in anger, tells the Jews,
that he himſelf would not go before them as hitherto he had done, to conduct them into the pro-
miſed land, but would leave his angel with them

---

* —— ὕτως ὀφείλοντας ζῆν κάθαρως, ὡς μηδὲ δῶσθαι γραμμ-
μάτων, ἀλλ' ἀντὶ βιβλίων παρέχων τὰς καρδίας τῷ πνεύματι.
In Matth. Praefat. Hom. 1.

† Niſi inſpirationis divinae internam ſuavioremque doctri-
nam, ubi ſine ſonis ſermonum et ſine elementis literarum, eo
dulcius quo ſecretius veritas loquitur.   L. 3. Epiſt. 106.

‡ Ἔγκλημα γὰρ τῶν γραμμάτων δῶσθαι.

as his deputy, Exod. xxxiii. so hath he dealt with us, the unhappy posterity, degenerated from the antient purity of our fore-fathers. When himself refused to speak unto our hearts, because of the hardness of them, he then began to put his laws in writing. Which thing, for a long time, amongst his own people, seems not to have brought with it any sensible inconvenience. For amongst all those acts of the Jews, which God in his book hath registered for our instruction, there is not one concerning any pretended ambiguity or obscurity of the text and letter of their law, which might draw them into faction and schism; the devil, belike, having other sufficient advantages on which he wrought. But ever since the gospel was committed to writing, what age, what monument of the church's acts, is not full of debate and strife, concerning the force and meaning of those writings, which the Holy Ghost hath left us to be the law and rule of faith? St. Paul, one of the first pen-men of the Holy Ghost, who, in paradise, heard words which ' it was not lawful for man to utter,' 2 Cor. xii. 4. hath left us words in writing, which it is not safe for any man to be too busy to interpret. No sooner had he laid down his pen, almost ere the ink was dry, were there found, such as St. Ambrose spake of †, ' who thought there could be no greater dis- ' paragement unto them, than to seem to be igno-

† Syllabarum aucupes, qui nescire aliquid erubescunt, et per occasionem obscuritatis tendunt laqueos deceptionis.

'rant of any thing, and under pretence of inter‑
' preting obfcure places, laid gins to entrap the un‑
' cautelous:' who, taking advantage of the obfcu‑
rity of St. Paul's text, made the letter of the go‑
fpel of life and peace, the moft forcible inftrument
of mortal quarrel and contention. The growth
of which, the Holy Ghoft, by the miniftry of St.
Peter, hath endeavoured to cut up in the bud, and
to ftrangle in the womb, in this fhort admonition,
which but now hath founded in your ears,' Which
' the unlearned and unftable wreft, as they do the
' other fcriptures, unto their own deftruction.' In
which words, for our more orderly proceeding,
we will confider, *Firft*, the fin itfelf that is here re‑
prehended, *wrefting of fcripture* : where we will
briefly confider what it is, and what caufes and
motioners it finds in our corrupt underftandings.
Secondly, the perfons guilty of this offence, decy‑
phered unto us in two epithets, *unlearned, unftable*.
Laft of all, the danger, in the laft words, *unto their
own damnation*.

And *firft*, of the fin itfelf, together with fome
of the fpecial caufes of it. *They wreft*, ςρεβλȣσι.
They deal with fcripture as chimics deal with na‑
tural bodies, torturing them to extract that out of
them which God and nature never put in them.
Scripture is a rule which will not fit itfelf to the
obliquity of our conceits, but our perverfe and
crooked difcourfe, muft fit itfelf to the ftraight‑
nefs of that rule. A learned writer in the age of

our fathers †, commenting upon fcripture, fpake moſt truly, when he faid, ' That his comments ' gave no light unto the text, the text gave light ' unto his comments.' Other expofitions may give rules and directions for underſtanding their authors, but fcripture gives rules to expofition itſelf, and interprets the interpreter. Wherefore ' when ' we contend not for the authority of fcripture, ' but for the authority of our own interpretati- ' ons ‡,' as St. Auſtin fpeaks: when we ſtrive to give into it, and not receive from it the fenſe : when we factiouſly contend to faſten our conceits upon God ; and, like the harlot in the book of Kings, 1 Kings iii. 20. take our dead and putrified fancies, and lay them in the boſom of fcripture, as of a mother; then are we guilty of this great fin of wreſting of fcripture. The nature of which will the better appear, if we confider a little, fome of thoſe motioners which drive us upon it.

One very potent and ſtrong mean, is the exceeding affection and love unto our own opinions and conceits. For grown we are unto extremities on both hands: we cannot with patience, either admit of other men's opinions, or endure that our own ſhould be withſtood. As it was in the Lacedemonian army, almoſt all were captains § ; fo, in theſe difputes, all will be leaders : and we take our-

† Faber. ‡ Non pro fententia divinarum fcripturarum, fed pro noſtra ita dimicantes ut ea velimus fcripturarum effe quae noſtra eſt. De Genefi ad literam. lib. i. 37. § Schol. in Thucyd.

felves to be much difcountenanced, if others think
not as we do. So that the complaint which one
makes concerning the diffenfion of phyficians a-
bout the difeafes of our bodies, is true likewife in
thefe difputes which concern the cure of our fouls.
' From hence have fprung thofe miferable conten-
' tions about the diftemper of our *fouls*, fingula-
' rity alone, and that we will not feem to ftand as
' cyphers to make up the fum of other men's opi-
' nions, being caufe enough to make us difa-
' gree.*' A fault antiently amongft the Chriftians
fo apparent, that it needed not an apoftolical fpirit
to difcover it, the very heathen themfelves, to our
fhame and confufion, have juftly, judicioufly, and
fharply taxt us for it. Ammianus Marcellinus paffing his cenfure upon Conftantius the Emperor :
' The Chriftian religion,' faith he, and they are
' words well worth your marking, ' the Chriftian
' religion, a religion of great fimplicity and per-
' fection, he troubled with dotage and fuperftiti-
' on. For going about rather perplexedly to fearch
' the controverfies, than gravely to compofe them,
' he raifed great ftirs, and by difputing, fpread
' them far and wide, whilft he went about to make
' himfelf fole lord and commander of the whole
' profeffion †.' Now (that it may appear where-

* Hinc illae circa aegros miferae fententiarum concertatio-
nes, nullo idem cenfente, nè videatur acceffio alterius. Plin.
Nat. Hift. lib. xxix c. 5.

† Chriftianam religionem abfolutam et fimplicem anili fu-

fore I have noted this) it is no hard thing for a
man that hath wit, and is ſtrongly poſſeſt of an
opinion, and reſolute to maintain it, to find ſome
places of ſcripture, which by good handling will
be wooed to caſt a favourable countenance upon
it. Pythagoras's ſcholars having been bred up in
the doctrine of numbers, when afterward they diverted upon the ſtudies of nature, fancied unto
themſelves ſomewhat in natural bodies like unto
numbers, and thereupon fell into a conceit, that
numbers were the principles of them. So fares it
with him, that to the reading of ſcripture comes
fore-poſſeſt with ſome opinion. As Antipheron
Orietes in Ariſtotle* thought, that every where he
ſaw his own ſhape and picture going afore him :
ſo in divers parts of ſcripture where theſe men
walk, they will eaſily perſuade themſelves, that
they ſee the image of their own conceits.

It was, and is to this day, a faſhion in the hot-
ter countreys, at noon, when the ſun is in his
ſtrength, to retire themſelves to their cloſets or
beds, if they were at home, to cool and ſhady places, if they were abroad, to avoid the inconvenience of the heat of it. To this the Spouſe in the

perſtitione confundens. In qua ſcrutanda perplexiùs quam
componenda gratiùs, excitavit diſſidia plurima, quae progreſſa
fuſiùs aluit concertatione verborum,——dum ritum omnem ad
ſuum trahere conatur arbitrium. Lib. xxi. c. 16.

* Meteor. lib. iii. c. 4. ibique Alexander Aphrodiſæus et
Olympiodorus.

Canticles alluding, calls after her beloved as after a
shepherd, ' Shew me, O thou, whom my soul loveth,
' where thou feedest thy flock, where thou doest rest
' at noon.' Cant. i. 7. The Donatists conceiting unto themselves, that the church was shut up in them
alone, being urged by the fathers to shew how the
church, being universal, came on a sudden thus to
be confined to Afric: they had presently their scripture for it, for so they found it written in the Canticles, ' Shew me, O thou whom my soul loveth,
' where thou feedest thy flock, where thou dost rest
' at noon.' In which text, *meridies*, ' noon,' doubtless, as they thought, was their southern country of
Afric, where the shepherd of Israel was, and no
where else, to feed his flocks. I may not trouble
you with instances in this kind: little observation
is able to furnish the man of slenderest reading
with abundance. The texts of Scripture which
are specially subject to this abuse, are those that
are of ambiguous and doubtful meaning. For as
Thucydides observes of ' the fat and fertile places
' of Greece, that they were evermore the occasions
' of stirs and seditions * :' the neighbouring nations every one striving to make itself lord of them;
so is it with these places that are so fertile, as it
were, of interpretation, and yield a multiplicity of
sense : they are the school of exercises for good

---

* Μάλιςα δὲ τῆς γῆς ἡ ἀρίςη ἀεὶ τὰς μεταϐολὰς τῶν οἰκητόρων
ἤχεν. Lib. i. c. 2.

wits to prove masteries in, where every one desires
to be lord and absolute.

A *second* thing occasioning us to transgress a-
gainst scripture, and the discreet and sober handling
of it, is our too quick and speedy entrance upon
the practice of interpreting it, in our young and
green years, before that time and experience have
ripened us, and settled our conceits. For that
which in all other business, and here likewise doth
most especially commend us, is our cautelous and
wary handling it. But this is a flower seldom seen
in youth's garden; Aristotle differencing age and
youth, makes it a property of youth, ' to sup-
' pose they know all things, and to be bold in af-
' firming * : ' and the Heathen rhetorician could
tell us, that by this so speedy entring upon action,
and so timely venting our crude and unconcocted
studies, ' a thing which in all cases is most pernici-
' ous; presumption is greater than strength † ; '
after the manner of those, who are lately recovered
out of some great sickness, in whom appetite is
stronger than digestion. These are they who take
the greatest mysteries of Christian religion, to be
the fittest arguments to spend themselves upon. So
Eckius in his Chrysopaffus, a work of his so term-
ed, wherein he discusses the question of predestination, in the very entrance of his work tells us,

* Πάντα εἰδέναι οἴεσθαι ⁊ διϊσχυρίζεσθαι Rhet. lib. ii. c. 14.
† Quod est ubique perniciosissimum, praevenit vires fidu-
cia. Quintil. Inst. Orat. lib. xii. c. 6.

That he therefore enterprized to handle this argument, becaufe, forfooth, he thought it to be the fitteft queftion in which he might ' exercife his ' youthful and ardent fancy*.' The antient mafters of fence amongft the Romans, were wont to fet up a poft, and caufe their young fcholars to practife upon it, and to foin and fight with it, as with an adverfary. Inftead of a poft, this young fencer hath fet himfelf up one of the deepeft myfteries of our profeffion, to practife his frefhmanfhip upon. Which quality, when once it finds fcripture for its object, how great inconvenience it brings with it, needs no large difcourfe to prove. St. Jerom, a man not too eafily brought on to acknowledge the errors of his writings, among thofe few things which he doth retract, cenfures nothing fo fharply as the miftake of his youth in this kind: He thought it one of the greateft fins of his youth, ' That being carried away through an inconfide-
' rate heat in his ftudies of fcripture, he adventu-
' red to interpret Obadiah the prophet allegorical-
' ly, when as yet he knew not the hiftorical mean-
' ing †.' Old men, faith our beft natural mafter, by reafon of the experience of their often miftakes, are hardly brought conftantly to affirm any thing, ' they will always cauteloufly interline their fpeech-

* Juveniles calores exercere.

† In adolefcentia provocatus ardore et ftudio fcripturarum, allegoricè interpretatus fum Abdiam prophetam cujus hiftoriam nefciebam.   Praefat. in Abdiam.

' es with *it may bees*, and *peradventures* *,' and o-
ther such particles of wariness and circumspection.
This old men's modesty, of all other things best
fits us in perusing those hard and obscure texts of
holy scripture. Out of which conceit it is, that we
see St. Austin, in his books *de Genesi ad literam*, to
have written only by way of questions and inter-
rogations, after the manner of Aristotle in his Problems, ' That he might not ' (for so he gives his
reason) ' by being over positive prejudice others,
' and peradventure truer interpretations: that e-
' very one might chuse according to his liking;
' and where his understanding cannot attain unto
' the sense of it, let him give that honour and re-
' verence which is due unto the scripture, and car-
' ry himself with that awe and respect which be-
' fits him †.' Wherefore not without especial providence it is, that the Holy Ghost, by St. Paul, giving precepts to Timothy, concerning the quality of
those who were to be admitted to the distributing
of God's holy word, expresly prescribes against a
young scholar, ' lest, saith he, he be puft up.' 1 Tim.
iii. 6. For as it hath been noted of men, who are

---

* Προστιθέασιν ἀεὶ τὸ ΊΣΩΣ ᾗ τὸ ΤΑ'ΧΑ.   Arist. Rhet.
lib. ii. c. 15.

† Non aliquid unum temere affirmans cum praejudicio alterius expositionis fortasse melioris, ut pro suo modulo eligat
quisque quod capere possit: ubi autem intelligere non potest,
scripturae Dei det honorem, sibi timorem.   De Genesi ad literam. lib. i. 40.

lately grown rich, that they differ from other rich
men only in this, ' That commonly they have all
' the faults that rich men have, and many more*:'
fo is it as true in thofe who have lately attained to
fome degree and mediocrity of knowledge. Look
what infirmities learned men have, the fame have
they in greater degree, and many more befides.
Wherefore if Hippocrates in his Phyfician required thefe two things, ' great induftry, and long
' experience,' the one as tillage to fow the feed,
the other as time and feafon of the year to bring
it to maturity † : then certainly by fo much the
more are thefe two required in the fpiritual phyfician, by how much he is the phyfician to a more
excellent part.

I will add yet one *third* motioner to this abufe
of fcriptures, and that is, The too great prefumption upon the ftrength and fubtilty of our own
wits. That which the Roman prieft fometimes
told an over-pleafant and witty Veftal Virgin,
' The Gods ought to be worfhipped, not curiouf-

---

* Τῷ ἅπαντα μᾶλλον ἢ φαυλότερα κακὰ ἔχειν τὺς νεοκλύτυς.
Arift. Rhet. lib. ii. c. 18.

† Ἔτι δὲ ΦΙΛΟΠΟΝΙΉΝ προςενέγκασθαι ἰς ΧΡΟΝΟΝ
ΠΟΛΎΝ, ὅκως ἡ μάθησις ἐμφυσιωθῆσα, δέξιως τε καὶ εὐαλδίως
τὺς καρπὺς ἐξενέγκηται. Ὁκοίη γὰρ τῶν ἐν τῇ γῇ φυομίνων θεωρίη,
τοίηδε καὶ τῆς ἰατρικῆς ἡ μάθησις, ἡ μὲν γὰρ φύσις ἡμίων, ὁκοῖον ἡ
χώρη, τὰ δὲ δόγματα τῶν διδασκόντων, ὁκοῖον τὰ σπέρματα, ἡ δὲ
παιδομαθίη, τὸ, καθ' ὥρμην αὐτὰ πεσεῖν ὡς τὴν ἀρύραν. Hippocrat. Lex.

' ly, but in the simplicity of a pious mind*,' hath
in this great work of exposition of scripture an
especial place. The holy things of God must be
handled with fear and reverence, not with wit and
dalliance. The dangerous effects of this have appeared, not in the green tree only, in young heads,
but in men of constant age, and great place in the
church. For this was that which undid Origen, a
man of as great learning and industry, as ever the
church had any ; whilst in the sublimity of his
wit, in his comments on scripture, conceiving meteors and airy speculations, he brought forth those
dangerous errors, which drew upon his person
the church's heaviest censure, and upon posterity
the loss of his works. Subtile-witted men in nothing so much miscarry as in the too much pleasing themselves in the goodness of their own conceits ; where the like sometimes befals them which
befel Zeuxis the painter, who having to the life
pictured an old woman, so pleased himself with
the conceit of his work, that he died with laugh-
ing at it. Heliodorus bishop of Tricca in Thessaly,
the author of the Ethiopic story, a polite and elegant, I confess, but a loose and wanton work, being summoned by a provincial synod, was told, that
which was true, That his work did rather endanger the manners, than profit the wits of his reader, as nourishing loose and wanton conceits in

---

* Coli Deos sancte magis quam scite.

the heads of youth : and having his choice given
him, either to abolish his work, or to leave his
bishopric ; not willing to lose the reputation of
wit, chose rather to resign his place in the church,
and as I verily think, his part in heaven †. And
not in private persons alone, but even in whole
nations, shall we find remarkable examples of miscarriage in this kind. The Grecians, till barbarism began to steal in upon them, were men of
wondrous subtility of wit, and naturally over-in-
dulgent unto themselves in this quality. Those
deep and subtile heresies concerning the Trinity,
the divinity of Christ, and of the Holy Ghost, the
union and division of the Divine Substance and
persons, were all of them begotten in the heat of
their wits; yea, by the strength of them were they
conceived, and born, and brought to that growth,
that if it had been possible for the gates of hell to
prevail against the church, they would have prevailed this way. Wherefore as God dealt with his
own land, which being sometimes the mirror of
the world for fertility and abundance of all things,
now lies subject to many curses, and especially to
that of barrenness : so at this day is it with Greece,
where sometimes was the flow and luxury of wit,
now is there nothing but extreme barbarism and

---

† Would that the author had not drawn a conclusion so
harsh from a tale of such dubious credit as this related by Ni-
cephorus alone.   Vid. Valesium ad Socrat. Hist. Ecclef. lib. v.
c. 22.

ftupidity. It is in this refpect fo degenerated, that it fcarcely for fome hundreds of years hath brought forth a child that carries any fhew of his father's countenance: God as it were purpofely plaguing their miferable pofterity with extreme want of that, the abundance of which their fathers did fo wantonly abufe.

The reafon of all, that hitherto I have in this point delivered, is this, fharpnefs of wit hath commonly with it two ill companions, pride, and levity. By the firft it comes to pafs, that men know not how to yield to another man's reafonable pofitions; by the fecond, they know not how to keep themfelves conftant to their own. It was an excellent obfervation of the wife Grecian, ' Sad ' and dull fpirited men ufually manage matters of ' ftate better than quick and nimble wits *.' For fuch for the moft part have not learned that leffon, the meaning of that voice that came to the Pythagorean, that was defirous to remove the afhes of his dead friend out of his grave, ' Things lawful-' ly fettled and compofed muft not be moved †.' ' Men over bufy,' faith Julian, ' are by nature un-' fit to govern ‡:' for they move all things, and leave nothing without queftion and innovation:

* Οἵ τε φαυλότεροι τῶν ἀνθρώπων, πρὸς τὺς ξυνετωτέρυς, ὡς ἐπιτοπλεῖσον ἄμεινον οἰκῦσι τὰς πόλεις. Thucyd. lib. iii. §. 37.

† Ἀχῦσαι φωνῆς ἐδόξα, τὰ ἀκίνητα μὴ κινεῖν. Plutarch. de Daemon. Socrat.

‡ Ἀνεπιτήδεος φύσει προγατεύειν δῆμυ πολυπράγμων ἀνήρ.

' Making the right ſomewhat righter,' as Nazianzen ſpeaks, out of deſire to amend what is already well *. And therefore we ſee that for the
moſt part ſuch, if they be in place of authority; by
unſeaſonable and unneceſſary tampering, put all
things into tumult and combuſtion. Not the commonwealth alone, but the church likewiſe hath received the like blow from theſe kind of men. Nazianzen, diſcourſing concerning the diſorders committed in the handling of controverſies, ſpeaks it
plainly, ' Great wits, hot and fiery diſpoſitions have
' raiſed theſe tumults. From theſe it is' (ſaith he)
' that Chriſtians are ſo divided. We are no longer
' a tribe and a tribe, Iſrael and Judah, two parts
' of a ſmall nation : but we are divided kindred a-
' gainſt kindred, family againſt family, yea, a man
' againſt himſelf †.'

But I muſt haſten to my ſecond general part,
The perſons here accounted guilty of abuſe of
ſcripture.

The perſons are noted unto us in two epithets,
' unlearned, unſtable.' *Firſt*, ' unlearned.' It was
St. Jerom's complaint, that practitioners of other

* Τῦ δεξιῦ ποιώμενοί τι δεξιώτερον.

† Φύσεις θερμαὶ ᚼ μεγάλαι τῆς ταραχῆς ταύτης αἴτιον——
ᚼ τῦτό ἐςιν ὡς ἐπιτοπλεῖςον, ὃ διέσπασε μέλη —— ᚼ γεγόναμεν ᚼ
φυλὴ ᚼ φυλὴ καθ᾽ ἑαυτήν, ὃ πάλαι ὁ Ισραὴλ ὠνειδίζετο, οὐδὲ Ισραὴλ
ᚼ Ιύδας, τὰ δύο ᚼ ἑνὸς ἔθνυς ᚼ μικρῦ τύτυ τμήματα, κατ᾽ οἴκυς καὶ
συζυγίας τὰς ἀναγκαίας, καὶ οἷον πρὸς ἑαυτὸν ἕκαςος ἐμερίσθημεν.
Orat. xxvi.

arts could contain themſelves within the bounds of
their own profeſſion, ' The art of interpreting the
' ſcriptures is the only art, whereof every one,
' without diſtinction, aſſumes the knowledge. This
' the talkative old woman, the aged dotard, the
' wordy ſophiſt, this all men confidently take upon
' themſelves, mangling the ſcriptures, and pre-
' tending to teach, untaught *.' Every one pre-
ſumes much upon his ſkill, and therefore to be a
teacher of ſcripture : as if this great myſtery of
' Chriſtianity' (ſo Nazianzen ſpeaks) ' were but
' ſome one of the common, baſe, inferior, and con-
' temptible trades †.' I ſpeak not this as if I en-
vied, that all, even the meaneſt of the Lord's
people ſhould prophecy : but only that all kind of
men may know their bounds, that no unlearned
beaſt touch the hill, leſt he be thruſt through with
a dart. It is true which we have heard, ' The un-
' learned ariſe and take the kingdom of heaven by
' violence :' they ariſe indeed, but it is as St. Paul
ſpeaks of the reſurrection, ' every man in his own
order.' 1 Cor. xv. 23. Scripture is given to all,
to learn : but to teach, and to interpret, only to a
few. This bold intruſion therefore of the unlearned into the chair of the teacher, is that which

---

* Sola ſcripturarum ars eſt, quam ſibi omnes paſſim vindi-
cant. Hanc garrula anus, hanc delirus ſenex, hanc ſophiſta
verboſus, hanc univerſi praeſumunt, lacerant, docent antequam
diſcant.

† Ὡς κινδυνεύων τεχνύδριον ἀναι τὸ μέγα ἡμῶν μυςήριον.

here, with our blessed apostle, I am to reprehend.
Learning in general is nothing else, but the competent skill of any man in whatsoever he professes.
Usually we call by this name only our polite and
academical studies ; but indeed it is common to
every one, that is well skilled, well practised in his
own mystery. 'The unlearned,' therefore, whom
here our apostle rebukes, is not he that hath not
read a multiplicity of authors, or that is not as
Moses was, skilful in all the learning of the Egyp-
tians: but he that taking upon him to divide the
word of God, is yet but raw and unexperienced;
or if he have had experience, wants judgment to
make use it. Scripture is never so unhappy, as
when it falls into these men's fingers. That
which old Cato said of the Grecian physicians, 'If
'those men once bring in their learning among us,
'they will corrupt all things *,' is most true of
these men; whensoever they shall begin to tam-
per with Scripture, and vent in writing their raw
conceits, they will corrupt and defile all they
touch. 'For what trouble and anguish these rash
'presumers' (as St. Austin complaineth) 'bring
'unto the discreeter sort of the brethren, cannot
'sufficiently be exprest; when being convinced of
'their rotten and ungrounded opinions, for the
'maintaining of that which with great levity and

---

* Quandocunque ista gens literas suas dabit, omnia cor-
rumpet. Plin. Hist. Nat. lib. xix. c. 1.

' open falfhood they have averred, they pretend
' the authority of thefe facred books, and repeat
' much of them even by heart, as bearing witnefs
' to what they hold: whereas indeed they do but
' pronounce the words; but underftand not ei-
' ther what they fpeak, or of what things they do
' affirm †.' Belike as he that bought Orpheus's
harp, thought it would of itfelf make admirable me-
lody, how unfkilfully foever he touched it: fo
thefe men fuppofe, that fcripture will found wonderful mufically, if they do but ftrike it, with how
great infelicity and incongruity foever it be. The
reafon of thefe men's offence againft fcripture, is
the fame with the caufe of their mifcarriage in civil actions: 'Rude men,' (faith Thucydides) 'men
' of little experience, are commonly moft peremp-
' tory: but men experienced, and fuch as have
' waded in bufinefs, are flow of determination ‡.'
Quintilian making a queftion, why unlearned men
feem many times to be more copious than the

---

† Quid enim moleftiae triftitiaeque ingerant prudentibus
fratribus temerarii praefumptores, fatis dici non poteft; cum
fi quando de prava et falfa opinione fua reprehendi et convinci
coeperint ab eis, qui noftrorum librorum auctoritate non te-
nentur, ad defendendum id quod leviffima temeritate et aper-
tiffima falfitate dixerunt, eofdem libros fanctos, unde id pro-
bent, proferre conantur, vel etiam memoriter, quae ad teftimonium valere arbitrantur, multa inde verba pronunciant, non
intelligentes neque quae loquuntur, neque de quibus affirmant.
De Genefi ad literam, lib. i. 39.

‡ Ἀμαθία μὲν θράσος, λογισμὸς δὲ ὄκνον φέρει. Lib. ii. §. 40.

learned, (for commonly such men never want matter of discourse) answers, That it is, because whatsoever conceit comes into their heads, without care
or choice they broach it; 'whereas learned men
' are choice in their invention, and lay by much
' of that which offers itself *.' 'Wise hearted
' men, in whom the Lord hath put wisdom and
' understanding, to know how to work all man-
' ner of work for the service of the sanctuary,'
Exod. xxxvi. 1. like Bezaleel and Aholiab, refuse
much of the stuff which is presented them. But this
kind of men, whom here our Apostle notes, are
naturally men of bold and daring spirits, as St. Je-
rome speaks, 'Whatsoever conceit is begotten in
' their heads, the Spirit of God is presently the fa-
' ther of it‡.' But to leave these men, and to speak a
little more home unto mine own auditory: let us a
little consider, not the weakness of these men, but
the greatness of the business, the manage of which
they undertake. So great a thing as the skill of
exposition of the word and gospel is, so fraught
with multiplicity of authors, so full of variety of
opinion, must needs be confest to be a matter of
great learning, and that cannot, especially in our
days, in short time, with a mediocrity of indu-

---

* Cum doctis est electio et modus. Inst. Orat. lib. ii. c. 12.
‡ Quicquid dixerint hoc legem Dei putant; nec scire dig-
nantur quid prophetae, quid apostoli senserint, sed ad suum sen-
sum incongrua aptant testimonia. Epist. lib. ii. Paulino.

ſtry, be attained. For if in the Apoſtles times,
when as yet much of ſcripture was ſcarcely written, when God wrought with men miraculouſly,
to inform their underſtanding, and ſupplied by
revelation what man's induſtry could not yield ;
if, I ſay, in theſe times St. Paul required ' dili-
' gent reading,' 1 Tim. iv. 13. and expreſly for-
bad greenneſs of ſcholarſhip : much more then
are theſe conditions required in our times, wherein God doth not ſupply by miracle our natural
defects, and yet the burden of our profeſſion
is infinitely encreaſt. All that was neceſſary in
the Apoſtles times, is now neceſſary, and much
more. For if we add unto the growth of Chriſtian learning, as it was in the Apoſtles times, but
this one circumſtance (to ſay nothing of all the
reſt) which naturally befals our times, and could
not be required at the hands of thoſe who guided
the firſt ages of the church: that is, the knowledge of the ſtate and ſucceſſion of doctrine in the
church from time to time; a thing very neceſſary
for the determining the controverſies of theſe our
days: how great a portion of our labour and induſtry would this alone require ? Wherefore if
Quintilian thought it neceſſary to admoniſh young
men, that they ſhould not preſume themſelves ' ſuf-
' ficiently provided with knowledge, and as hav-
' ing the ſanction of the learned in their favour,
' merely by being maſters of ſome ſhort and com-

' mon manual of rhetoric †.' If he thought fit
thus to do in an art of so inferior and narrow a
sphere, much more is it behoveful, that young stu-
dents, in so high, so spacious, so large a profession, be advised not to think themselves sufficiently
provided, upon their acquaintance with some *notitia*, or system of some technical divine. Look
upon those sons of Anak, those giant-like voluminous writers of Rome, in regard of whom, our
little tractates, and pocket-volumes in this kind,
what are they but as grashoppers? I speak not this
like some seditious or factious spy, to bring weakness of hands, or melting of heart, upon any of
God's people: but to stir up and kindle in you
the spirit of industry, to inlarge your conceits, and
not to suffer your labours to be copst and mued up
within the poverty of some pretended method. I
will speak as Joshua did to his people, ' Let us not
' fear the people of that land, they are as meat
' unto us, their shadow is departed from them :
' the Lord is with us, fear them not.' Numb. xiv. 9.
Only let us not think, that the conquest will be
gotten by sitting still and wishing all were well ‡ :
or that the walls of these strong cities will fall
down, if we only walk about them, and blow rams

---

† —— Satis instructos, si quem ex iis, qui breves circumfe-
runtur, artis libellum edidicerint, et velut decretis technicorum
tutos putent. Inst. Orat. lib. ii. c. 13.

‡ Stultitia est sedendo aut votis debellari credere posse.
Liv. hist. lib. xxii. c. 14.

horns. But as the voice of God's people sometime was, ' by the fword of God and of Gideon,' Judg. vii. 18. fo that which here gives the victory muft be the grace of God and our induftry. For by this circumcifed, narrow, and penurious form of ftudy, we fhall be no more able to keep pace with them, than a child can with Hercules. But I forbear, and pafs away unto the *fecond* epithet, by which thefe rackers of fcriptures are, by St. Peter, ftiled ' unftable.'

In the learning which the world teaches, it were almoft a miracle to find a man conftant to his own tenets. For not to doubt in things in which we are converfant, is either by reafon of excellency and ferenity of underftanding, thoroughly apprehending the main principles on which all things are grounded, together with the defcrying of the feveral paffages from them unto particular conclufions, and the diverticles and blind by-paths which fophiftry and deceit are wont to tread; and fuch a man can nature never yield: or elfe it is through a fenfelefs ftupidity, like unto that in the common fort of men, who converfing among the creatures, and beholding the courfe of heaven, and the heavenly hoft, yet never attend them, neither ever finks it into their heads to marvel, or queftion thefe things fo full of doubt and difficulty. Even fuch a one is he, that learns theology in the fchool of nature, if he feem to participate of any fettlednefs or compofednefs of confcience; either it never comes into his head to doubt of any of those things, with which the world hath inured him: or if it doth, it is to no great purpose, he may smother and strangle, he can never resolve his doubt. The reason of which is this, it lies not in the world's power to give, in this case, a text of sufficient authority to compose and fix the thoughts of a soul, that is disposed to doubt. But this great inconvenience, which held the world in uncertainty, by the providence of God is prevented in the church. For unto it is left a certain, undoubted, and sufficient authority, able to exalt every valley, and lay low every hill, to smooth all rubs, and make our way so open and passable, that little enquiry serves. So that as it were a wonder in the school of nature, to find one settled and resolved; so might it seem a marvel that in the church any man is unstable, unresolved. Yet notwithstanding, even here is the unstable man found too, and to his charge the apostle lays this sin of wresting of scripture. For since that it is confest at all hands, that the sense and meaning of scripture is the rule and ground of our Christian tenets, whensoever we alter them, we must needs give a new sense unto the word of God. So that the man that is unstable in his religion, can never be free from violating of scripture. The especial cause of this levity and flitting disposition in the common and ordinary sort of men, is their disability to discern of the strength of such reasons, as may be framed against

them. For which caufe they ufually ftart, and many times fall away, upon every objection that is
made. In which too fudden entertainment of objections, they refemble the ftate of thofe, who are
lately recovered out of fome long ficknefs, who
never more wrong themfelves, than by fufpecting
every alteration of their temper, and being affrighted at every little paffion of heat, as if it were
an ague-fit *. To bring thefe men therefore unto
a right temper, and to purchafe them a fettlednefs
of mind ; that temper that St. Auftin doth require in him that reads his book, ' I would wifh,'
fays he, ' to have for judges of my writings, men
' who do not require an anfwer to every objection
' that is made againft them.' The fame temper
muft be found in every reader of fcripture ; he
muft not be at a ftand, and require an anfwer to
every objection that is made againft them. For as
the philofopher tells us, that mad and fantaftical
men ate very apprehenfive of all outward acci-
dents, becaufe their foul is inwardly empty and un-
furnifhed of any thing of worth which might hold
the inward attention of their minds : fo when we
are fo eafily pozed and amazed with every fophifm,

* Qui cum reliquias effugerint, fufpicionibus tamen inquietantur, et omnem calorem corporis fui calumniantur. Senec.
de tranq. anim. ii.

† Tales meorum fcriptorum velim judices, qui refponfio-
nem non femper defiderent, quum his quae leguntur audierint
aliquid contradici.

it is a certain argument of great defect of inward
furniture and worth, which fhould, as it were, ba-
lance the mind, and keep it upright againft all outward occurrents whatfoever. And be it that many times, the means to open fuch doubts be not
at hand, yet, as St. Auftin fometime fpake unto
his fcholar Licentius, concerning fuch advice and
counfel as he had given him: fo much more muft
we thus refolve of thofe leffons which God teacheth us; ' the reafons and grounds of them, though
' they might be given, yet it fits not that credit
' and truft which we owe him, once to fearch in-
' to, or call in queftion *.' And fo I come to the
third general part, the danger of wrefting of fcripture, in the laft words, ' unto their own damna-
' tion.'

The reward of every fin is death. As the worm
eats out the heart of the plant that bred it, fo whatfoever is done amifs, naturally works no other end
but deftruction of him that doth it. As this is
true in general, fo it is as true, that when the fcripture doth precifely note out unto us fome fin, and
threatens death unto it, it is commonly an argument, that there is more than ordinary, that there
is fome efpecial fin, which fhall draw with it fome
efpecial punifhment. This fin of wrefting of fcripture in the eye of fome of the antients, feemed fo

* Nolo te caufas rationefque rimari, quae etiamfi reddi
poffint, fidei tamen, qua mihi credis non eas debeo.   Epift.
xxvi.

ugly, that they have ranged it in the same rank with the sin against the Holy Ghost. And therefore they have pronounced it a sin ' greater than can be ' pardoned *.' For the most part of other sins are sins of infirmity or simplicity, but this is a sin of wit and strength: the man that doth it, doth it with a high hand; he knows, and sees, and re-solves upon it.

Again, Scripture is the voice of God: and it is confest by all, that the sense is scripture, rather than the words. It cannot therefore be avoided, but he that wilfully strives to fasten some sense of his own upon it, other than the very nature of the place will bear, must needs take upon him the person of God, and become a new inditer of scrip-ture: and all that applaud and give consent unto any such, in effect cry the same that the people did to Herod, ' The voice of God, and not of man.' Acts xii. 22. If he then that abases the prince's coin deserves to die, what is *his* desert, that instead of the tried silver of God's word, stamps the name and character of God upon Nehushtan, upon base brasen stuff of his own?

Thirdly, ' No scripture is of private interpre-' tation,' saith the Apostle, 2 Pet. i. 20. There can therefore be but two certain and infallible in-terpreters of scripture; either itself, or the Holy

---

* Οἱ τὰς θείας χρησμὺς παραποιοῦντες, ἢ πρὸς τὸ οἰκεῖον βούλη-μα ἐκβιαζόμενοι, ΣΥΓΓΝΩ'ΜΗΣ 'ΑΜΑΡΤΑ'ΝΟΤΣΙ ΜΕΙ'ΖΟΝΑ. Isidor. Pelusiota. lib. ii. epist. 454.

Ghoſt the author of it. Itſelf doth then expound itſelf, when the words and circumſtances do ſound unto us the prime, and natural, and principal ſenſe. But when the place is obſcure, involved, and intricate ; or when there is contained ſome ſecret and hidden myſtery, beyond the prime ſenſe; infallibly to ſhew us this, there can be no interpreter but the Holy Ghoſt that gave it. Beſides theſe two, all other interpretation is private. Wherefore, as the lords of the Philiſtines ſometime ſaid of the kine that drew the ark unto Bethſh'emeſh, 'If they ' go of themſelves, then is this from God; but if ' they go another way, then it is not from God, ' it is ſome chance that hath happened unto us.' 1 Sam. vi. 9. ſo may it be ſaid of all pretended ſenſe of ſcripture. If ſcripture come unto it of itſelf, then is it of God: but if it go another way, or if it be violently urged and goaded on, then is it but a matter of chance, of man's wit and invention. As for thoſe marvellous diſcourſes of ſome, framed upon preſumption of the Spirit's help in private, in judging or interpreting of difficult places of ſcripture, I muſt needs confeſs, I have often wondered at the boldneſs of them. The Spirit is a thing of dark and ſecret operation, the manner of it none can deſcry. As underminers are never ſeen till they have wrought their purpoſe, ſo the Spirit is never perceived but by its effects. The effects of the Spirit (as far as they concern knowledge and inſtruction) are not particular information for refolution in any doubtful cafe (for this were plainly revelation) but, as the angel which was fent unto Cornelius informs him not, but fends him to Peter to fchool: fo the Spirit teaches not, but ftirs up in us a defire to learn; defire to learn makes us thirft after the means: and pious fedulity and carefulnefs makes us watchful in the choice, and diligent in the ufe of our means. The promife to the Apoftles of the Spirit which fhould ' lead them into all truth,' John xvi. 1 3. was made good unto them by private and fecret informing their underftandings, with the knowledge of high and heavenly myfteries, which as yet had never entered into the conceit of any man. The fame promife is made to us, but fulfilled after another manner. For what was written by revelation in their hearts, for our inftruction have they written in their books. To us for information, otherwife than out of thefe books, the Spirit fpeaks not. When the Spirit regenerates a man, it infufes no knowledge of any point of faith, but fends him to the church, and to the fcriptures. When it ftirs him up to newnefs of life, it exhibits not unto him an inventory of his fins, as hitherto unknown; but either fuppofes them known in the law of nature, of which no man can be ignorant; or fends him to learn them from the mouth of his teachers. More than this in the ordinary proceeding of the Holy Spirit, in matter of inftruction, I yet

could never defcry. So that to fpeak of the help
of the Spirit in private, either in dijudicating, or
in interpreting of fcripture, is to fpeak they know
not what. Which I do the rather note, firft, becaufe by experience we have learnt, how apt men
are to call their private conceits the Spirit: and
again, becaufe it is the efpecial error with which
St. Auftin, long ago, charged this kind of men:
' By fo much the more prone are they to kindle
' fchifm and contention in the church, by how
' much they feem to themfelves to be endued with
' a more eminent meafure of Spirit than their bre-
' thren *;' whilft (as St. Bafil fpeaks) ' under pre-
' tence of interpretation they violently broach their
' own conceits †.' Great then is the danger in
which they wade, which take upon them this bufinefs of interpretation. ' The rafhnefs' (faith
St. Auftin) ' of thofe that aver uncertain and doubt-
' ful interpretations, for catholic and abfolute, can
' hardly efcape the fin of facrilege ‡.'

But whereas our apoftle faith, ' their own de-
' ftruction ,' is the deftruction only their own ?
this were well if it ftretched no farther. The antients much complain of this offence, as an hin-

* Tanto funt ad feditionem faciliores, quanto fibi videntur
fpiritu excellere.

† Ἐν προςποιήσει ἐξηγήσεως τὰ ἑαυτῶ παρεισάγωσιν.

‡ Temeritas afferendae incertae dubiaeque opinionis, difficile facrilegii crimen evitat.

derer of the falvation of others. There were in
the days of Ifidorus Pelufiota fome that gave out,
that all in the Old Teftament was fpoken of Chrift,
belike out of extreme oppofition to the Manichees,
who on the other fide taught, that no text in the
Old Teftament did foretel of Chrift. That father,
therefore, dealing with fome of that opinion, tells
them how great the danger of their tenet is: ' For
' if,' faith he, ' we ftrive with violence to draw
' and apply thofe texts to Chrift, which apparent-
' ly pertain not to him, we fhall gain nothing but
' this, to make all the places that are fpoken of
' him fufpected; and fo difcredit the ftrength of
' other teftimonies, which the church ufually ur-
' ges for the refutation of the Jews*.' For in thefe
cafes, a wrefted proof is like unto a fuborned witnefs; it never doth help fo much whilft it is prefumed to be ftrong, as it doth hurt when it is difcovered to be weak. St. Auftin fharply reproves
fome Chriftians, who out of fome places of fcripture mifunderftood, framed unto themfelves a kind
of knowledge in aftronomy and phyfiology, quite
contrary unto fome part of heathen learning in
this kind, which were true and evident unto fenfe.
A man would think that this were but a fmall error, and yet he doubts not to call it ' Exceeding-
' ly fhameful, pernicious, and above all things to

* Τὰ γὰρ μὴ εἰς αὐτὸν εἰρημένα ἐκβιαζόμενοι, καὶ τὰ ἀβιάσως
εἰρημένα ὑποπλέεσθαι παρασκευάζωσιν. Lib. ii. Epift. 195.

' be avoided †.' His reafon warrants the round-
nefs of his reproof; for he charges fuch to have
been a fcandal unto the word, and hinderers of the
converfion of fome heathen men that were fcholars: ' For how,' faith he, ' fhall they believe our
' books of fcripture, perfuading the refurrection
' of the dead, the kingdom of heaven, and the reft
' of the myfteries of our profeffion, if they find
' them faulty in thefe things, of which themfelves
' have undeniable demonftration?' Yea, though
the caufe we maintain be never fo good, yet the
iffue of difeafed and crazy proofs brought to maintain it, muft needs be the fame. For unto all caufes, be they never fo good, weaknefs of proof,
when it is difcovered, brings great prejudice, but
unto the caufe of religion moft of all. St Auftin
obferved, that there were fome, ' who, whenever
' *any* Chriftian is falfely reported or actually pro-
' ved to be guilty of a crime, endeavour with un-
' remitting diligence, to make it believed that *all*
' Chriftians are alike guilty ‡.' It fares no otherwife with religion itfelf, than it doth with the profeffors of it. Divers malignants there are, who lie
in wait to efpy where our reafons on which we

† Turpe nimis, et perniciofum et maxime cavendum. De
Genef. ad Literam. lib. i. 39.

‡ Qui cum de aliquibus, qui fanctum nomen profitentur, aliquid criminis vel falfi fonuerit, vel veri patuerit, inftant, fata-
gunt, ambiunt ut de omnibus hoc credatur. Epift. lxxviii.
§. 6.

build are weak, and having deprehended it in some, will earneſtly ſolicit the world to believe that all are ſo, if means were made to bring it to light: as Nazianzen ſpeaks, ' uſing for advantage againſt ' us no ſtrength of their own, but the vice and im- ' becillity of our defence †.' The book of the Re- velation is a book full of wonder and myſtery: the antients ſeem to have made a religion to meddle with it, and thought it much better to admire with ſilence, than to adventure to expound it: and therefore amongſt their labours in expoſition of ſcripture, ſcarcely is there any one found that hath touched it. But our age hath taken better heart; and ſcarcely any one is there, who hath entertain- ed a good conceit of his own abilities, but he hath taken that book as a fit argument to ſpend his pains on. That the church of Rome hath great cauſe to ſuſpeƈt herſelf, to fear leſt ſhe have a great part in the prophecies in that book, I think the moſt partial will not deny. Yet unto the expoſi- tors of it, I will give this advice, that they look that that befal not them, which Thucydides ob- ſerves to befal the common ſort of men: who though they have good means to acquit themſelves like men, yet when they think their beſt hopes fail them, and begin to deſpair of their ſtrength, com- fort themſelves with interpretations of certain dark and obſcure prophecies. Many plain texts of ſcrip-

† Οὐκ ἐν τοῖς ἑαυτῶν δόγμασι τὴν ἰσχὺν ἔχοντες, ἀλλ' ἐν τοῖς ἡμετέρων σαθροῖς ταύτην θηρεύοντες.

ture are very pregnant, and of fufficient ftrength
to overthrow the points maintained by that church
againft us. If we leave thefe, and ground ourfelves upon our private expofitions of this book,
we fhall juftly feem in the poverty of better proofs,
to reft ourfelves upon thofe prophecies ; which,
though in themfelves they are moft certain, -yet
our expofitions of them muft (except God give yet
further light unto his church) neceffarily be mixt
with much uncertainty, as being at the beft but
improbable * conjectures of our own. Scarcely can
there be found a thing more harmful to religion,
than to vent thus our own conceits, and obtrude
them upon the world for neceffary and abfolute.
The phyfician's fkill, as I conceive of it, ftands as
much in opinion, as any that I know whatfoever ;
yet their greateft mafter Hippocrates tells them directly, ‘ Than the phyfician's prefumption upon
‘ opinion, there is not one thing that brings either
‘ more blame to himfelf, or danger to his pati-
‘ ent †.’ If it be thus in an art, which, opinion
taken away, muft needs fall ; how little room then
muft opinion have in that knowledge, where nothing can have place but what is of eternal truth,
where if once we admit of opinion, all is overthrown ? But I conclude this point, adding only

---

* Ought not we to read *probable ?*

† Οἴησις γάρ μάλιςα ἐν ἰντρικῇ, αἰτίην μὲν τοῖσι κιχρημίνοι-
σιν, ὄλεθρον δὲ τοῖσι χρεομίνοισιν ἐπιφέρει. Hippocrat. de decenti
habitu. c. 2.

this general admonition, That we be not too peremptory in our politions, where expreſs text of ſcripture fails us; that we lay not our own collections and concluſions with too much precipitancy. For experience hath ſhewed us, that the error and weakneſs of them being afterwards diſcovered, brings great diſadvantage to Chriſtianity, and trouble to the church. The Eaſtern Church, before St. Baſil's time, had entertained generally a conceit, that thoſe Greek particles, ἐν, σὺν, διά, and the reſt, were ſo divided among the Trinity, that each of the perſons had his particle, which was no way appliable to the reſt. St. Baſil having diſcovered this to be but a niceneſs and needleſs curioſity, beginning to teach ſo, raiſed in the church ſuch a tumult, that he brought upon himſelf a great labour of writing many tracts in apology for himſelf, with much ado, ere matters could again be ſettled. The fault of this was not in Baſil, who religiouſly fearing what by way of conſequence might enſue upon an error, taught a truth; but in the church, who formerly had with too much facility admitted a concluſion ſo juſtly ſubject to exception. And let this ſuffice for our *third* part.

Now becauſe it is apparent, that the end of this our apoſtle's admonition is to give the church a caveat how ſhe behave herſelf in handling of ſcripture, give me leave a little, inſtead of the uſe of ſuch doctrines as I have formerly laid down, to ſhew you, as far as my conceit can ſtretch, what

courſe any man may take to ſave himſelf from offering violence unto ſcripture, and reaſonably
ſettle himſelf, any pretended obſcurity of the text
whatſoever notwithſtanding. For which purpoſe,
the diligent obſerving of two rules ſhall be throughly available: Firſt, The literal, plain, and uncon-
troverſable meaning of ſcripture, without any addition or ſupply by way of interpretation, is that
alone which for ground of faith we are neceſſarily
bound to accept, except it be there where the Holy
Ghoſt himſelf treads us out another way. I take not
this to be any peculiar conceit of mine, but that
unto which our church ſtands neceſſarily bound.
When we receded from the church of Rome, one
motive was, becauſe ſhe added unto ſcripture her
gloſſes as canonical, to ſupply what the plain text
of ſcripture could not yield. If in place of her's,
we ſet up our own gloſſes, thus to do, were nothing elſe but to pull down Baal, and ſet up an
ephod ; to run round, and meet the church of
Rome again in the ſame point in which at firſt we
left her. But the plain, evident, and demonſtra-
tive ground of this rule, is this : *That* authority
which doth warrant our faith unto us, muſt every
way be free from all poſſibility of error. For let
us but once admit of this, that there is any poſſibility that any one point of faith ſhould not be
true; if it be once granted that I may be deceived
in what I have believed, how can I be aſſured that
in the end I ſhall not be deceived? If the author

of faith may alter, or if the evidence and affurance
that he hath left us be not pregnant, and impoffible to be defeated, there is neceffarily opened an
inlet to doubtfulnefs and wavering, which the nature of faith excludes.

That faith therefore may ftand unfhaken, two
things are of neceffity to concur. Firft, That the
author of it be fuch a one as can by no means
be deceived, and this can be none but God. Secondly, That the words and text of this author
upon whom we ground, muft admit of no ambiguity, no uncertainty of interpretation. ' If the
' trumpet give an uncertain found, who fhall pro-
' vide himfelf to battle.' 1 Cor. xiv. 8. If the
words admit a double fenfe, and I follow one, who
can affure me that that which I follow is the truth?
For infallibility either in judgment, or interpretation, or whatfoever, is annext neither to the fee of
any bifhop, nor to the fathers, nor to the councils, nor to the church, nor to any created power
whatfoever. This doctrine of the literal fenfe was
never grievous or prejudicial to any, but only to
thofe who were inwardly confcious that their pofitions were not fufficiently grounded. When Cardinal Cajetan, in the days of our grandfathers, had
forfaken that vein of poftilling and allegorifing on
fcripture, which for a long time had prevailed in
the church, and betaken himfelf unto the literal
fenfe ; it was a thing fo diftafteful unto the church
of Rome, that he was forced to find out many

shifts, and make many apologies for himself. The truth is, (as it will appear to him that reads his writings) this sticking close to the literal sense was that alone, which made him to shake many of those tenets, upon which the church of Rome and the reformed churches differ. But when the importunity of the reformers, and the great credit of Calvin's writings in that kind, had forced the divines of Rome to level their interpretations by the same line: when they saw that no pains, no subtilety of wit was strong enough to defeat the literal evidence of scripture, it drave them on those desperate shelves, on which at this day they stick, to call in question, as far as they durst, the credit of the Hebrew text, and countenance against it a corrupt translation ; to add traditions unto scripture, and to make the church's interpretation, so pretended, to be above exception. As for that restriction which is usually added to this rule, that the literal sense is to be taken, if no absurdity follow, though I acknowledge it to be found and good, yet my advice is that we entertain it warily. St. Basil thought the precept of Christ to the rich man in the gospel, ' Go ' sell all that thou hast, and give unto the poor,' Matth. xix. 21. to be spoken as a command universally and eternally binding all Christians without exception. And making this objection, how possibly such a life could be amongst Christians, since where all were sellers, none could

be buyers: 'Afk not me,' faith he, 'the fenfe of
'my Lord's commands. He that gave the law,
'can provide to give it poffibility of being kept,
'without any abfurdity at all *.' Which fpeech
howfoever we may fuppofe the occafion of it to be
miftaken, yet it is of excellent ufe to reprefs our
boldnefs, whereby many times, under pretence of
fome inconvenience, we hinder fcripture from that
latitude of fenfe, of which it is naturally capable.
You know the ftory of the Roman captain in Gellius, and what he told the fhip-wright, that chofe
rather to interpret, than to execute his lord's command; 'The office of the commander is then fet
'at nought, when the commanded, inftead of due
'obedience, gives unafked advice †.' It will certainly, in the end, prove fafer for us to entertain
God's commandments with the refpect which is
due, than to interpret them with a nicety which is
not required. Thofe other ways of interpretation,
whether it be by allegorifing, or allufion, or whatfoever, the beft that can be faid of them, is that
which St. Bafil hath pronounced, 'We account of
'them as of trim, elegant, and witty fpeeches, but
'we refufe to accept of them, as of undoubted

---

* Μὴ ἐρώτα με διάνοιαν δεσποτικῶν προςταγμάτων. οἶδεν ὁ νο-
μοθετήσας, χ̀ τὸ ἀδύνατον συναρμόσαι τῷ νόμῳ. Homil. in Divites. § 3.

† Corrumpi atque diffolvi omne imperantis officium, fi quis
ad id quod facere juffus eft non obfequio debito, fed confilio
non defiderato refpondeat.

C 4

' truths*.' And though of fome part of thefe, that
may be faid which one faid of his own work, ' In
' refpect of any profit comes by them, they are
' but fport, but in refpect of the pains taken in
' making of them, they are labour and travel†:' yet
much of them is of excellent ufe in private, either
to raife our affections, or to fpend our meditations,
or (fo it be with modefty) to practife our gifts of
wit to the honour of him that gave them. For if
we abfolutely condemn thefe interpretations, then
muft we condemn a great part of antiquity, who
are very much converfant in this kind of interpreting. For the moft partial for antiquity cannot
chufe but fee and confefs thus much, that for the
literal fenfe the interpreters of our own times, becaufe of their skill in the original languages, their
care of preffing the circumftances and coherence
of the text, of comparing like places of fcripture
with like, have generally furpaft the beft of the
antients. Which I fpeak not to difcountenance antiquity, but that all ages, all perfons may have
their due. And let this fuffice for our firft rule.

The Jewifh Rabbins, in their comments on
fcripture, fo oft as they met with hard and intricate texts, out of which they could not wreft
themfelves, were wont to fhut up their difcourfe

---

* Ὡς κεκομψευμίνον μὲν τὸν λόγον ἀποδεχόμιθα, ἀληθῆ δὲ ἔναι
ȣ πάνυ δώσομεν.

† Quod ad ufum pertinet, lufi, quod ad moleftiam laboravi.
Aufon. Technopaeg. xii.

with this, ' Elias fhall anfwer this doubt when he
' comes *.' Not the Jews only, but the learned
Chriftians of all ages have found many things in
fcripture, which yet expect Elias. For befides
thofe texts of fcriptures, which by reafon of the
hidden treafures of wifdom, and depth of fenfe
and myftery laid up in them, are not yet conceived,
there are in fcripture of things that are feemingly
confufed, carrying femblance of contrariety, ana-
chronifms, metachronifms, and the like, which
brings infinite obfcurity to the text: there are, I fay,
in fcripture more of them, than in any writing that
I know, fecular or divine. If we mean not to fettle
ourfelves till all thefe things are anfwered, let us
take heed left the like be faid to us, which St. Auftin faid to fome of the Gentiles, who refufed to
believe till all objections were fatisfied, ' innumer-
' able are the things not to be afcertained before
' we believe, left our life end before we believe†.'
The Areopagites in Athens, when they were troubled in a doubtful cafe, in which they durft not
proceed to fentence, were wont to put it off till a
day of hearing for fome hundred years after ; a-
voiding, by this means, the further being importuned with the fuit. To quiet ourfelves in thefe
doubts, it will be our beft way, to put them to
fome day of hearing afar off, even till that great

* Elias cum venerit, folvit dubia.

† Sunt enim innumerabiles quae non funt finiendae ante
fidem, ne vitae finiatur fine fide.

day, till Chrift, our true Elias, fhall come, who
at his coming fhall anfwer all our doubts, and
fettle all our waverings. Mean while, till our Elias
come, let us make ufe of this fecond rule, In places of ambiguous and doubtful, or dark and intricate meaning, it is fufficient if we religioufly admire, and acknowledge, and confefs : ufing that
moderation of St. Auftin, ' not feeking to fupport
' or to overturn either opinion, but only reftrain-
' ing ourfelves from prefumptuous confidence in
' our own judgment*.' ' To underftand,' (faith
one) ' belongs to Chrift, the author of our faith; to
' us is fufficient the glory of believing†.' Wherefore we are to advife, not fo much how to attain
unto the underftanding of the myfteries of fcripture, as how it beft fits us to carry ourfelves, when
either the difficulty of the text, or variety of opinions fhall diftract us. In the fixth general council, Honorius bifhop of Rome is condemned for a
Monothelite. Two epiftles there are of his, which
are produced to give evidence againft him. For
the firft, I have nothing to fay. For the fecond,
(I fpeak with fubmiffion to better judgments) notwithftanding the fharp proceeding of the council
againft him, I verily fuppofe that he gives unto
the church the beft counfel, that ever yet was given for the fettling of doubts, and final decifion

---

* Neutram partem affirmantes five deftruentes, fed tan-
tummodo ab audaci affirmandi praefumptione revocantes.

† Qui credit, fatis eft illi quod Chriftus intelligat.

of controverſy. For that which he teaches in that
epiſtle, at leaſt in thoſe parts of it which *there* are
brought , ſounds to no other purpoſe but this,
' That whereas there was lately raiſed in the church
' a controverſy concerning the duality or unity of
' wills in Chriſt ; ſince that hitherto nothing in
' the church concerning either part hath been ex-
' preſly taught, his counſel was, That men would
' rather ceaſe to doubt, than to be curious to
' ſearch for any ſolution of their doubtings; and ſo
' abſtain from teaching doctrinally either part, and
' content themſelves with that expreſs meaſure of
' faith, with which the church hath hitherto reſt-
' ed ſatisfied *.' This, to my conceit, is the drift
of his epiſtle. How this advice of the biſhop's was
appliable, or how it fitted the queſtion then in
controverſy, or what reaſon moved the council to
think that it was abſolutely neceſſary for them to
give an expreſs deciſion, and determine for the one
part, belongs not to me to diſcuſs. But I verily
perſuade myſelf, that if it had pleaſed thoſe, who
in all ages have been ſet to govern the church of
God, betimes to have made uſe of this advice, to
have taught men rather not to have doubted, than
to have expected ſtill ſolution of their doubtings :
to have ſtopped and dammed up the originals and
ſprings of controverſies, rather than by determining for the one part, to give them, as it were, a

* Vid. Harduin. concil. tom. iii. p. 1319. et ſeq.

pipe and conduit to convey them to pofterity, I
perfuade myfelf, the church had not fuffered that
inundation of opinions, with which, at this day, it is
over·run. Is it not St. Paul's own practice, when
having brought in a queftion concerning God's
juftice in predeftination, he gives no other anfwer
but this, 'O man, who art thou that difputeft with
' God?' Rom. ix. 20. Is it not his plain purpofe
to advife the difputer, rather not to make the queftion, than to require a determination of it at his
hands? How many of the queftions even of our
own times, even of thofe that are at home amongft
us, might by this way long fince have been determined? I have, I confefs, the fame difeafe that
my firft parents in paradife had, a defire to know
more than I need. But I always thought it a very
judicious commendation, which is given to Julius
Agricola, ' That he knew how to bridle his de-
' fire in purfuit of knowledge*.' ' I would wifh,'
as St. Auftin faith, ' to underftand thofe things
' concerning which you have enquired of me, but
' fince to this I have not hitherto attained, I ra-
' ther chufe cautioufly to confefs my ignorance,
' than to arrogate to myfelf a knowledge which I
' have not †.' It fhall well befit our Chriftian mo-

---

* Retinuitque, quod eft difficillimum, ex fcientia modum.
Tacit. vit. Agricolae. c. 4.

† Mallem quidem eorum quae à me quaefivifti habere fcientiam, quam ignorantiam ; fed quia id nondum potui, magis
eligo cautam ignorantiam confiteri, quam falfam fcientiam pro-
fiteri.

defty to participate fomewhat of the Sceptic, and to ufe their withholding of judgment, till the remainder of our knowledge be fupplied by Chrift: ' againft whom, if we are indeed believers in him, ' we ought not to murmur, although he fhould ' not always open unto us even when we knock*.' To conclude, St. Auftin in his cxcix. epiftle, difcourfing of the fpeedy or flow coming of our Saviour to judgment, to fhew that it is the fafeft way to teach neither, but to fufpend our belief, and confefs our ignorance, ranging himfelf with men of this temper ' fuch as I am,' faith he to Hefychius, to whom he writes that epiftle, ' fuch as ' I am, I befeech you, defpife me not †.' So give me leave to commence the fame fuit to you. Let me requeft you bear with me, if I be fuch a one as I have St. Auftin for example. For it is not depth of knowledge, nor knowledge of antiquity, or fharpnefs of wit, nor authority of councils, nor the name of the church, can fettle the reftlefs conceits that poffefs the minds of many doubtful Chriftians: only to ground for faith on the plain uncontroverfable text of fcripture, and for the reft, to expect and pray for the coming of our Elias, this fhall compofe our waverings, and give final reft unto our fouls.

Thus inftead of a difcourfe which was due un-

* In quem fi credimus, ut fi aliqua nobis non aperiat etiam pulfantibus, nullo modo adverfus eum murmurare debeamus.

† Obfecro te ut me talem non fpernas.

to this time, concerning the glorious refurrection of our bleſſed Saviour, and the benefits that come unto us by it, I have diverted myſelf upon another theme, more neceſſary, as I thought, for this auditory, though leſs agreeable with this ſolemnity. Thoſe who have gone afore me in that argument have made ſo copious a harveſt, that the iſſue of my gatherings muſt needs have been but ſmall, except I had with Ruth gleaned out of their ſheaves, or ſtrained my induſtry which is but ſmall, and my wits which are none, to have held your attentiveneſs with new and quaint conceits. In the mean time, whether it be I or they, or whatſoever hath been delivered out of this place, God grant that it may be for his honour, and for the church's good, to whom both it and we are dedicate. ' To ' God the Father, &c.'

OF

DEALING

WITH

ERRING CHRISTIANS.

Preached at St. Paul's Crofs.

Rom. xiv. 1.

Him that is weak in the faith receive, but not to doubtful difputations.

MIGHT it fo have pleafed God, that I had in my power the choice of my ways, and the free management of my own actions, I had not this day been *feen*, (for fo I think I may better fpeak : *feen* may I be of many, but to be *heard* with any latitude and compafs, my natural imperfection doth quite cut off :) I had not, I fay, in this place this day been feen ; ambition of great and famous auditories I leave to thofe whofe better gifts and inward endowments are admonitioners unto them of the great good they can do, or otherwife thirft after popular applaufe. Unto my-

felf have I evermore applied that of St. Jerom *,
a fmall, a private, a retired auditory, better ac-
cords both with my will and my abilities. Thofe
unto whofe difcretion the furniture of this place
is committed, ought efpecially to be careful, fince
you come hither to hear, to provide you thofe who
can be heard; for the neglect of this one circumftance, how poor foever it may feem to be, is no
lefs than to offend againft that ' faith which com-
' eth by hearing;' and to fruftrate, as much as in
them is, that end for which alone thefe meetings
were ordained. We that come to this place, as
God came to Elias in the mount, in a foft and ftill
voice, to thofe which are near us, are that which
the grace of God doth make us, unto the reft we
are but ftatues: fuch therefore as my imperfection in this kind fhall offend, fuch as this day are
my fpectators only, know, I truft, whom they are
to blame. At my hands is only required truth in
fincerely difcharging a common care, at others,
care of profitably delivering a common truth. As
for me, the end of whofe coming is to exhort you
to a gracious interpreting of each others imperfections, having firft premifed this apology for myfelf, it is now time to defcend to the expofition of
that fcripture, which I have propofed, ' Him that
' is weak in the faith receive, but not to doubtful
' difputations.'

* Mihi fufficit cum auditore et lectore perpauculo in angulo
monafterii fufurrare.

Goodnefs, of all the attributes by which a man may be ftiled, hath chief place and fovereignty; goodnefs, I fay, not that metaphyfical conceit which we difpute of in our fchools, and is nothing elfe but that perfection which is inwardly due unto the being of every creature, and without which, either it is not at all, or but in part, that whofe name it bears: but that which the common fort of men do ufually underftand, when they call a man good; by which is meant nothing elfe, but ‘ a foft, and fweet, and flexible difpofition *.’ For all other excellencies and eminent qualities which raife in the minds of men fome opinion and conceit of us, may occafion, peradventure, fome ftrong refpect in another kind; but impreffion of love and true refpect, nothing can give but this: greatnefs of place and authority may make us feared, depth of learning admired, abundance of wealth may make men outwardly obfequious unto us; but that which makes one man a god unto another, that which doth tie the fouls of men unto us, that which like the eye of the bridegroom, in the book of Canticles, iv. 9. ‘ ravifhes the heart of him ‘ that looks upon it,’ is goodnefs: without this, mankind were but (as one fpeaks) ‘ Stones heapt ‘ together without mortar, or pieces of boards ‘ without any cement to combine and tie them to- ‘ gether †:’ For this it hath fingular in it, above

* Ἥγρὸν ᾗ μειλίχον ἦθος.

† Lenius comptiufque fcribendi genus adeo contemnens, ut

all other properties of which our nature is capable, that it is the moſt available to human ſociety, incorporating, and, as it were, kneading us together by ſoftneſs of diſpoſition, by being compaſſionate, by gladly communicating to the neceſſity of others, by transfuſing ourſelves into others, and receiving from others into ourſelves. All other qualities, how excellent ſoever they are, ſeem to be ſomewhat of a melancholic and ſolitary diſpoſition; they ſhine then brighteſt, when they are in ſome one alone, or attained unto by few; once make them common, and they loſe their luſtre: but goodneſs is more ſociable; and rejoiceth in equalling others unto itſelf, and loſes its nature, when it ceaſes to be communicable. The Heathen, ſpeaking of God, uſually ſtile him by two attributes, *Optimus* and *Maximus*, the one importing his goodneſs, the other his power. In the firſt place they called him *Optimus*, a name ſignifying his goodneſs, giving the precedency unto it; and in the ſecond place *Maximus*, a name betokening his power: yea, goodneſs is that wherein God himſelf doth moſt delight himſelf; and therefore all the acts of our Saviour, while he converſed on earth among men, were purely the iſſues of his tenderneſs, without any aſperſion of ſeverity, two only excepted: I mean his chaſing the prophaners out of the temple, and the curſe laid upon the in-

Senecam tum maxime placentem *commiſſiones meras* componere et *arenam* eſſe *ſine calce* diceret.   Sueton. Calig. c. 53.

nocent fig-tree: and yet, in both thèſe, mercy re-
joiced againſt judgment, and his goodneſs had the
preheminence. For the firſt brought ſome ſmart
with it indeed, but no harm at all, as fathers uſe
to chaſtiſe their children by means that fear them,
more than hurt them. The ſecond of itſelf was
nothing, as being practiſed on a creature dull and
ſenſeleſs of all ſmart and puniſhment; but was
meerly exemplary for us. Chriſt whips our fruit-
leſſneſs in the innocent fig-tree*; like as the manner was among the Perſians, when their great men
had offended, to take their garments and beat
them. Now that gracious way of goodneſs, which
it pleaſed our Saviour thus to tread himſelf before
us, the ſame hath he left behind him to be gone by
us, and hath ordained us a courſe of religious and
Chriſtian ſervice unto him, known by nothing
more than goodneſs and compaſſion. The very
Heathen themſelves, though utter enemies unto it,
have candidly afforded us this teſtimony. Ammianus Marcellinus taxing Georgius, a factious and
proud biſhop of Alexandria, for abuſing the weakneſs of Conſtantius the Emperor, by baſe tale-
bearing, and privy informations, notes preciſely that
he did it, 'quite beſides the meaning of his profeſ-
' ſion, whoſe eſpecial notes were gentleneſs and
' equity †.' And Tertullian tells us, that antient-

---

* Sterilitas noſtra in ficu vapulat.

† Oblitus profeſſionis ſuae, quae nil niſi juſtum ſuadet et
lene. Lib. xxii. c. 11.

ly among the Heathen, the profeffors of Chriftianity were called, not *Chriftiani*, but *Chreftiani*, from
a word fignifying benignity and fweetnefs of difpofition *. The learned of our times, who for our
inftruction have written *de Notis Ecclefiae*, by what
notes and figns we may know the church of Chrift,
may feem to have but ill forgotten this, which the
Heathen man had fo clearly difcovered. For what
reafon is there, why that fhould not be one of the
chiefeft notes of the church of Chrift, which did
fo efpecially characterize a Chriftian man, except
it were the decay of it at this day in the church ?
of this thing therefore, fo excellent in itfelf, fo
ufeful, fo principally commended by the precept
and example of our bleffed Saviour, one efpecial
part is, if not the whole, which here by our A-
poftle is commended unto us, when he fpeaks unto us of kindly intreating, and making much of
fuch, who are, as he calls them, ' weak in the faith.'
' Him that is weak in the faith receive, but not to
' doubtful difputations.'

To know the natural ground and occafion of
which words, it fhall be very pertinent to note unto you, that with the church of Chrift, as it fignifies a company of men on earth, it fares no otherwife than it doth with other focieties, and civil
corporations. One thing there is unavoidable, and

* Cum perperam *Chreftianus* pronunciatur a vobis (nam
nec nominis certa eft notitia penes vos) de fuavitate vel benig-
nitate compofitum eft.   Apologet. adv. Gentes.

natural to all focieties, which is the greateft occa-
fioner, yea, the very ground of difunion and dif-
fent; I mean, inequality of perfons and degrees.
All are not of the fame worth, and therefore all
cannot carry the fame efteem and countenance: yet
all, even the meaneft, are alike impatient of difcountenance and contempt, be the perfons never
fo great from whence it proceeds. Wherefore we
find that in ftates governed by the people, nothing
did more exafperate the common fort, than the
conceit of being contemned by men of greater
place. For the taking away therefore of tumult
and combuftion, which through this inequality
might arife, it was antiently counted an excellent
policy in the Roman ftate, that men of greater account and place did, as it were, fhare the inferior
fort amongft themfelves, and every one, according
to his ability, entertained fome part of them as
clients, to whom they yielded all lawful favour and
protection. Even thus it fares with the church
of God, it cannot be that all in it fhould be of e-
qual worth, it is likewife diftinguifhed into *people*
and *nobles*. Some there are, and thofe that either
through abundance of fpiritual graces, or elfe of
natural gifts, do far outftrip a great part of other
Chriftians; thefe are the nobles of the church,
whom our Apoftle fomewhere calls ' ftrong men
' in Chrift *.' Others there are, and thofe moft in

* *It is probable that the author here alludes to 1 Cor. iv. 10.
where mention is made of ' wife in Chrift.'*

number, who either becaufe God hath not fo liberally bleft them with gifts of underftanding and
capacity, or by reafon of fome other imperfections, are either not fo deeply fkilled in the myfteries of Chrift, and of godlinefs, or otherwife weak
in manners and behaviour; and thefe are the many of the church, whom our Apoftle fometimes
calls 'brethren of low degree †,' fometimes 'babes
'in Chrift,' 1 Cor. iii. 1. and here in my text 'the
'weak and fick in faith.' Men by nature queru-
lous, and apt to take exception; 'A fick man,'
faith Electra in the tragedy, 'is a pettifh and way-
'ward creature, hard to be pleafed ‡;' as therefore with the fick, fo are we now to deal with a
neighbour, weak and fick of his fpiritual conftitution, and much we are to bear with his froward-
nefs, where we cannot remedy it. For, as Varro
fometimes fpake of the laws of wedlock, 'Either a
'man muft amend, or endure the faults of his
'wife; he that amends them makes his wife the
'better, but he that patiently endures them makes
'himfelf the better §:' fo is it much more true in
dealing with our weak brethren, if we can by our
behaviour remedy their imbecillities, we make
them the better; if not, by enduring them we fhall

† *This paffage is in St. James* i. 9.

‡ Δυσχρεςον οἱ νοσῦντες ἀπορίας ὑπο. Eurip. Oreft. v. 232.

§ Vitium uxoris aut tollendum aut ferendum eft; qui tol-
lit vitium, uxorem commodiorem praeftat; qui fert, fefe meli-
orem facit. A. Gell. lib. i. c. 17.

make ourselves the better; for so shall we increase
the virtue of our patience, and purchase to ourselves, at God's hand, a more abundant reward. A
great part of the lustre of a Christian man's virtue
were utterly obscure, should it want this mean of
shewing itself. For were all men strong, were all
of sufficient discretion, to see and judge of conveniency, where were the glory of our forbearance?
As well therefore to increase the reward of the
strong man in Christ, as to stop the whining and
murmuring of the weaker sort, and to give content at all hands, our Apostle, like a good Tri-
bune, in this text gives a rule of Christian popula-
rity, advising the man of worthier parts, to avoid
all slighting behaviour, to open the arms of tenderness and compassion, and to demerit by all courtesy the men of meaner rank, so to prevent all inconvenience that might arise out of disdainful and
respectless carriage. For God is not like unto mortal princes, jealous of the man whom the people
love; in the world, nothing is more dangerous for
great men than the extraordinary favour and ap-
plause of the people; many excellent men have
miscarried by it. For princes stand much in fear
when any of their subjects hath the heart of the
people. It is one of the commonest grounds upon which treason is raised; Absalom had the art
of it, who by being plausible, by commiserating
the peoples wrongs, and wishing their redress;
' O that I were a judge to do this people good!'

2 Sam. xv. 4. by putting out his hand, and em-
bracing, and kiffing every one that came nigh him;
fo ftole away the hearts of the people, that he
had well-nigh put his father befides his kingdom.
But what alters and undoes the kingdoms of this
world, *that* ftrengthens and increafes the kingdom
of God; Abfalom, the popular Chriftian, that hath
the art of winning men's fouls and making himfelf
beloved of the people, is the beft fubject in the
kingdom of grace, for this is that which our A-
poftle expreffes in the phrafe of ' receiving the
' weak.'

Now it falls out oftentimes, that men offend
through intempeftive compaffion and tendernefs, as
much as by over much rigidnefs and feverity; as
much by familiarity, as by fupercilioufnefs and
contempt: wherefore even our love and courtefy muft be managed by difcretion. St. Paul faw
this well, and therefore he prefcribes limits to our
affections; and having in the former part of my
text counfelled us, as Chrift did St. Peter, to let
loofe our nets to make a draught; to do as Jofeph
did in Egypt, open our garners and ftore-houfes,
that all may come to buy, to admit of all, to exclude none from our indulgence and courtefy: in
this fecond part, ' But not to doubtful difputati-
' ons;' he fet the bounds how far our love muft
reach.   As Mofes, in the xix. of Exodus, fets
bounds about Mount Sinai, forbidding the people,
that they go not up to the hill, or come within

the borders of it; so hath the Apostle appointed
certain limits to our love and favour, within which
it shall not be lawful for the people to come. Enlarge we the phylacteries of our goodness as broad
as we list, give we all countenance unto the meaner fort, admit we them into all inwardness and
familiarity ; yet unto disputations and controversies, concerning profounder points of faith and
religious mysteries, the meaner sort may be by
no means admitted. For give me leave now to
take this for the meaning of the words; I know
they are very capable of another sense : as if the
Apostle's counsel had been unto us, to entertain
with all courtesy our weaker brethren, and not
over-busily to enquire into, or censure their secret
thoughts and doubtings, but here to leave them
to themselves, and to God who is the judge of
thoughts : for many there are, otherwise right
good men, yet weak in judgment, who have fallen
upon sundry private conceits, such as are unnecessary differencing of meats and drinks, distinction
of days, or (to exemplify myself in some conceit of
our times) some singular opinions concerning the
state of souls departed, private interpretations of
obscure texts of scripture, and others of the same
nature : of these or the like thoughts, which have
taken root in the hearts of men of shallow capacity, those who are more surely grounded may not
presume themselves to be judges; many of these
things of themselves are harmless and indifferent,

only to him that hath some prejudicate opinion of them, they are not so; and of these things, they who are thus or thus conceited, shall be accountable to God, and not to man, to him alone shall they stand or fall; wherefore, bear (saith the Apostle) with these infirmities, and take not on you to be lords of their thoughts, but gently tolerate these their unnecessary conceits and scrupulosities. This though I take to be the more natural meaning of the words, (for indeed it is the main drift of our Apostle's discourse in this chapter) yet chuse I rather to follow the former interpretation. First, because of the authority of sundry learned interpreters; and, secondly, because it is very requisite that our age should have something said unto it concerning this over-bold intrusion of all sorts of men into the discussing of doubtful disputations. For disputation, though it be an excellent help to bring the truth to light, yet many times, by too much troubling the waters, it suffers it to slip away unseen, especially with the meaner sort, who cannot so easily espy when it is mixed with sophistry and deceit. ' Him that is weak in the faith re-' ceive, but not to doubtful disputations.'

This my text therefore is a spiritual regimen and diet for these who are of a weak and sickly constitution of mind, and it contains a recipe for a man of crazy and diseased faith. In which, by that which I have delivered, you may plainly see there are two general parts. *First,* An admonition of

courteous entertainment to be given to the weaker
sort, in the firſt words, ' Him that is weak in the
' faith receive.' *Secondly*, The reſtraint and bound
of this admonition, how far it is to extend, even
unto all Chriſtian offices, excepting only the hearing of ' doubtful diſputations.'

In the *firſt* part we will conſider; *Firſt*, who
theſe weak ones are of whom the Apoſtle ſpeaks,
and how many kinds of them there be, and how
each of them may be the ſubjeċt of a Chriſtian man's goodneſs and courteſy. *Secondly*, Who
theſe perſons are, to whom this precept of entertaining is given, and they are two; either the private man, or the public magiſtrate. In the ſecond general part we will ſee what reaſons we may
frame to ourſelves, why theſe weak ones ſhould
not be admitted to queſtions and doubtful diſputations. Which points ſeverally, and by themſelves, we will not handle, but we will ſo order
them, that ſtill as we ſhall have in order diſcovered
ſome kind of weak man, whom our Apoſtle would
have received, we will immediately ſeek how far
forth he hath a right to be an hearer of ſacred diſputation, and this as far only as it concerns a private man: and for an upſhot in the end, we will
briefly conſider by itſelf, whether, and how far
this precept of bearing with the weak pertains to
the man of public place, whether in the church, or
in the commonwealth.

And *firſt*, Concerning the weak, as he may be

a fubject of Chriftian courtefy in private. And
here, becaufe that in comparifon of him that is
ftrong in Chrift, every man, of what eftate foever,
may be faid to be weak, that ftrong man only excepted, we will in the number of the weak contain
all perfons whatfoever. For I confefs, becaufe I
wifh well to all, I am willing that all fhould reap
fome benefit by my text. As therefore the woman
in the gofpel, who in touching only the hem of
Chrift's garment, did receive virtue to cure her
difeafe ; fo all weak perfons whatfoever, though
they feem to come behind, and only touch the hem
of my text, may peradventure receive fome virtue
from it to redrefs their weaknefs; nay, as the king
in the gofpel, that made a feaft, and willed his fervants to go out to the highways fide, to the blind,
and the lame, and force them in, that his houfe
might be full: fo what lame or weak perfon foever he be, if I find him not in my text, I will go
out and force him in, that the doctrine of my text
may be full, and that the goodnefs of a Chriftian
man may be like the widow's oil, in the book of
Kings, that never ceafed running fo long as there
was a veffel to receive it. Wherefore to fpeak in
general, there is no kind of man, of what life, of
what profeffion, of what eftate and calling foever,
though he be an Heathen, and idolater, unto whom
the fkirts of Chriftian compaffion do not reach.
St. Paul is my author , ' Now whilft you have
' time' (faith he) ' do good unto all men, but e-

' fpecially to the houfhold of faith.' Galat. ii. 4. The houfhold of faith indeed hath the prehemi- nence; it muft be chiefly, but not alone refpected. The diftinction that is to be made, is not by ex- cluding any, but not participating alike unto all. God did fometime indeed tye his love to the Jew- ifh nation only, and gave his laws to them alone: but afterward he enlarged himfelf, and inftituted an order of ferving him promifcuoufly, capable of all the world. As therefore our religion is, fo muft our compaffion be, catholic. To tye it either to perfons, or to place, is but a kind of moral Ju- daifm. Did not St Paul teach us thus much, com- mon reafon would. There muft of neceffity be fome free intercourfe with all men, otherwife the paffages of public commerce were quite cut off, and the common law of nations muft needs fall. In fome things we agree, as we are men, and thus far the very Heathen themfelves are to be recei- ved. For the goodnefs of a man, which, in Solo- mon's judgment, extendeth even to a beaft, much more muft ftretch itfelf to a man of the fame na- ture with him, be his condition what it will. St. Paul loved the Jews, becaufe they were ' his bre- ' thren according to the flefh;' Rom. ix. 3. We that are of the Heathen, by the fame analogy, ought to be as tenderly affected to the reft of our brethren, who though they be not as we are now, yet now are that which we fometimes were. ' It ' is an eafy thing,' faith St. Auftin, ' to hate evil

' men, becaufe they are evil; but to love them as
' they are men, this is a rare and a pious thing *.'
The offices of common hofpitality, of helping diftreffed perfons, feeding the hungry, and the like,
are due not only betwixt Chriftian and Chriftian,
but between a Chriftian and all the world. Lot,
when the angels came to Sodom, and fate in the
ftreets; Abraham, when he faw three men coming
toward him, ftood not to enquire who they were,
but out of the fenfe of common humanity, ran
forth and met them, and gladly entertained them,
not knowing whom they fhould receive. St. Chryfoftom confidering the circumftances of Abraham's
fact, that he fate at his tent door, and *that* in the
heat of the day, that he came to meet them, thinks,
he therefore fate in public, and endured the inconvenience of the heat, even for this purpofe, that
he might not let flip any occafion of being hofpital.
The writings of the fathers run much in commendation of the antient monks, and were they fuch
as they report, well did they deferve to be commended; for their manner was to fit in the fields,
and by the highway fides, for this end, that they
might direct wandering paffengers into the way,
that they might relieve all that were diftreffed by
want, or bruifing or breaking of any member, and
carry them home into their cells, and perform un-

* Facile eft atque proclive, malos odiffe quia mali funt;
rarum autem et pium eofdem ipfos diligere, quia homines funt.
Epift. cliii. §. 3.

to them all duties of humanity. This serves well to tax us, who affect a kind of intempestive prudence, and unseasonable discretion, in performing that little good we do, from whom so hardly, after long enquiry and entreaty, drops some small benevolence, like the sun in winter, long ere it rise, and quickly gone. How many occasions of Christian charity do we let slip, when we refuse to give our alms, unless we first cast doubts, and examine the persons, their lives, their necessities, though it be only to reach out some small thing, which is due unto him, whatsoever he be. It was antiently a complaint against the church, that the liberality of the Christians made many idle persons. Be it that it was so, yet no other thing befel them than what befals their Lord, who knows and sees that his sun-shine and his rain is every day abused, and yet the sun becomes not like sackcloth, nor the heavens as brass; unto him must we, by his own command, be like: and whom then can we exclude, that have a pattern of such courtesy proposed to us to follow? We read in our books of a nice Athenian being entertained in a place by one given to hospitality, finding anon that another was received with the like courtesy, and then a third, growing very angry; I looked, said he, for a friend's house, but I am fallen into an inn to entertain all comers, rather than a lodging for some private and especial friends. Let it not offend any that I have made Christianity rather an inn to re-

ceive all, than a private houfe to receive fome few.
For fo both the precepts and examples I have
brought, teach us to extend our good, not to this
or that man, but to mankind; like the fun that
arifeth not on this or that nation, but on the whole
world. Julian obferves of the fig-tree, ' That a-
' bove all trees it is moft capable of grafts and fcy-
' ons of other kinds, fo far, as that all variety will
' be brought to take nourifhment from one ftock*.'
Beloved, a Chriftian muft be like unto Julian's
fig-tree, fo univerfally compaffionate, that fo all
forts of grafts, by a kind of Chriftian inoculation,
may be brought to draw life and nourifhment from
his root.

But I am all this while in a generality only, and
I muft not forget, that I have many particular fick
patients, in my text, of whom every one muft have
his recipe, and I muft vifit them all ere I go. But
withal, I muft remember my method, which was,
ftill as I fpake of receiving the weak, to fpeak likewife of excluding them from difputation. So muft
I needs, ere I pafs away, tax this our age, for giving fo general permiffion unto all, to bufy themfelves in doubtful cafes of religion. For nothing
is there that hath more prejudiced the caufe of re-

---

* Θεόφραςος ——— πάντων, οἶμαι, τῶν φυτῶν μᾶλλον ἐπαινῶ
τῆς συκῆς τὸ δένδρον, ὡς ἄν τι ποικίλης ᾗ διαφόρου γενέσεως δεκλικὸν,
ᾗ μόνον τῶν ἄλλων εὔκολον παντοίοις γένεσιν ἐνεγκεῖν βλάςην, εἴ τις αὐτῦ τῶν κλάδων ἐκτεμὼν ἕκαςον, ἦτα ἐκρήξας, ἄλλην ἐς ἄλλο τῶν
πρίμνων ἐμφυῆ γονὴν ἐναρμόσειεν. Julian. epiſt. 24.

ligion, than this promifcuous and carelefs admiffion of all forts to the hearing and handling of controverfies, whether we confider the private cafe of
every man, or the public ftate of the church. I
will touch but one inconvenience which much an-
noys the church, by opening this gate fo wide to
all comers ; for by the great prefs of people that
come, the work of the Lord is much hindered.
Not to fpeak of thofe, who out of weaknefs of underftanding fall into many errors, and by reafon
of liberty of bequeathing their errors to the world
by writing, eafily find heirs for them. There is a
fort that do harm by being unneceffary, and though
they fow not tares in the field, yet fill the Lord's
floor with chaff: for what need this great breed
of writers, with which in this age the world doth
fwarm? how many of us might fpare the pains in
committing our meditations to writing, contenting
ourfelves to teach the people *viva voce*, and fuffering our conceits quietly to die in their birth ?
The teaching the people by voice is perpetually
neceffary, fhould all of us every where fpeak but
the fame things. For all cannot ufe books, and all
that can, have not the leifure. To remedy therefore the want of fkill in the one, and of time in
the other, are we fet in this miniftry of preaching.
Our voices are confined to a certain compafs, and
tied to the individuating properties of *here* and
now: our writings are unlimited. Neceffity therefore requires a multitude of fpeakers, a multitude

of writers not so. G. Agricola, writing *de ani-*
mantibus subterraneis, reports of a certain kind of
spirits that converse in minerals, and much infest
those that work in them; and the manner of them
when they come, is, to seem to busy themselves
according to all the customs of workmen; they
will dig, and cleanse, and melt, and sever metals;
yet when they are gone, the workmen do not find
that there is any thing done †: so fares it with a
great part of the multitude, who thrust themselves
into the controversies of the times; they write
books, move questions, frame distinctions, give
solutions, and seem sedulously to do whatsoever the
nature of the business requires; yet if any skilful
workman in the Lord's mines shall come and examine their work, he shall find them to be but spirits
in minerals, and that with all this labour and stir
there is nothing done. I acknowledge it to be very true, which St. Austin spake; ' It is a thing
' very profitable, that divers tracts be written by
' divers men, after divers fashions, but according
' to the same analogy of faith, even of the same
' questions, that some might come into the hands
' of all, to some on this manner, to another after

---

† In subterraneorum animantium, seu, quod placet, theologis, substantiarum numero haberi possunt daemones, qui in
quibusdam versantur fodinis——quum nihil agant, in omni la-
borum genere videntur se exercere: quasi modo fodiant venas,
modo in vasa infundant id quod effossum est: modo versent
machinam tractoriam. Agricola de animant. subterr. ad. fin.

' that†.' For this may we think to have been the counsel of the Holy Ghost himself, who may seem even for this purpose, to have registered the self-same things of Christ, by three of the Evangelists, with little difference. Yet notwithstanding, if this speech of St. Austin admit of being qualified, then was there no time which more than this age required should be moderated, which I note, because of a noxious conceit spread in our universities, to the great hindering of true proficiency in study, springing out from this root. For many of the learned themselves are fallen upon this preposterous conceit, That learning consisteth rather in variety of turning and quoting of sundry authors, than in soundly discovering and laying down the truth of things. Out of which arises a greater charge unto the poor student, who now goes by number rather than weight, and the books of the learned themselves, by ambitiously heaping up the conceits and authorities of other men, increase much in the bulk, but do as much imbase in true value. Wherefore as Gideon's army of two and thirty thousand, by prescript from God, was brought unto three hundred; so this huge army of disputes might, without any hazard of the Lord's battles, be well contracted into a smaller

† Utile est plures libros à pluribus fieri diverso stilo, sed non diversa fide, etiam de quaestionibus iisdem, ut ad plurimos res ipsa perveniat ad alios sic, ad alios vero sic. De Trinitate lib. i.

number. Juftinian the Emperor, when he found that the ftudy of the civil law was furcharged, and much confufed, by reafon of the great heaps of unneceffary writings, he calls an affembly of learned men, caufed them to fearch the books, to cut off what was fuperfluous, to gather into order and method the fum and fubftance of the whole law : Were it poffible that fome religious Juftinian might, after the fame manner, employ the wits of fome of the beft learned in examining the controverfies, and felecting out of the beft writers what is neceffary, defaulting unneceffary and partial difcoufes, and fo digeft into order and method, and leave for the direction of pofterity, as it were, Theological Pandects, infinite ftore of our books might well lie by, and peaceably be buried, and after-ages reap greater profit with fmaller coft and pains But that which was poffible in the world, united under Juftinian, in this great divifion of kingdoms, is peradventure impoffible. Wherefore having contented myfelf to fhew what a great and irremediable inconvenience this free, and uncontroulable venturing upon theological difputes hath brought upon us, I will leave this project as a fpeculation, and pafs from this general doctrine unto fome particulars. For this generality, and heap of fick perfons, 1 muft divide into their kinds, and give every one his proper recipe.

The firft in this order of weak perfons, fo to be received and cherifhed by us, is one of whom queſtion may be made, whether he may be called weak or no; he may ſeem to be rather dead: for no pulſe of infuſed grace beats in him. I mean, ſuch a one who hath but ſmall, or peradventure no knowledge at all in the myſtery of Chriſt, yet is, otherwiſe, a man of upright life and converſation, ſuch a one as we uſually name a moral man. Account you of ſuch a one as dead, or how you pleaſe, yet methinks I find a recipe for him in my text. For this man is even to be woed by us; as ſometimes one Heathen man wiſhed of another, ' Being what thou art, would that thou wert ' ours *.' This man may ſpeak unto a Chriſtian, as Ruth does unto Boaz, ' Spread the skirt of thy ' garment over me, for thou art a near kinſman.' Ruth iii. 9. Two parts there are that do compleatly make up a Chriſtian man, a true faith, and an honeſt converſation. The firſt, though it ſeem the worthier, and therefore gives unto us the name of Chriſtians, yet the ſecond, in the end, will prove the ſurer. For true profeſſion, without honeſt converſation, not only ſaves not, but increaſes our weight of puniſhment: but a good life, without true profeſſion, though it brings us not to heaven, yet it leſſens the meaſure of our judgment: ſo that a moral man, ſo called, is a Chriſtian by the ſurer ſide. As our Saviour ſaith of one in the goſpel, that had wiſely and diſcreetly

* Talis cum ſis, utinam noſter eſſes.

E 3

anſwered him, ' Thou art not far from the king-
' dom of heaven;' Matth. xii. 3 4. ſo may we ſay of
theſe men, Suppoſe that as yet they be not of, yet
certainly far from the kingdom of heaven they cannot be. Yea, this ſincerity of life, though ſevered
from true profeſſion, did ſeem ſuch a jewel in the
eyes of ſome of the antient fathers, that their opinion was, and ſo have they in their writings (er-
roneouſly doubtleſs) teſtified it, That God hath
in ſtore for ſuch men not only this mitigating mercy, of which but now I ſpake, but even ſaving
grace, ſo far forth as to make them poſſeſſors of
his kingdom. Let it not trouble you, that I intitle them to ſome part of our Chriſtian faith, and
therefore without ſcruple to be received as weak,
and not to be caſt forth as dead. Salvianus diſ-
puting what faith is, ' What might this faith be?'
(ſaith he) ' I ſuppoſe it is nothing elſe, but faith-
' fully to believe Chriſt, and this is to be faithful
' unto God, which is nothing elſe but faithfully to
' keep the commandments of God †.' Not therefore only a bare belief, but the fidelity and truſti-
neſs of God's ſervants, faithfully accompliſhing the
will of our Maſter, is required as a part of our
Chriſtian faith. Now all thoſe good things which
moral men by the light of nature do, are a part
of God's will written in their hearts; wherefore

† Quid eſt igitur credulitas vel fides? opinor fideliter ho-
minem Chriſto credere, id eſt, fidelem Deo eſſe, hoc eſt fideliter Dei mandata ſervare.

so far as they were conscientious in performing them (if Salvianus his reason be good) so far have they title and interest in our faith. And therefore Regulus, that famous Roman, when he endured infinite torments, rather than he would break his oath, may thús far be counted a martyr, and witness for the truth. For the crown of martyrdom sits not only on the heads of those who have lost their lives, rather than they would cease to profess the name of Christ, but on the head of every one that suffers for the testimony of a good conscience, and for righteousness sake. And here I cannot pass by one very general gross mistaking of our age. For in our discourses concerning the notes of a Christian man, by what signs we may know a man to be one of the visible company of Christ, we have so tied ourselves to this outward profession, that if we know no other virtue in a man, but that he hath conned his creed by heart, let his life be never so profane, we think it argument enough for us to account him within the pale and circuit of the church : on the contrary side, let his life be never so upright, if either he be little seen in, or peradventure quite ignorant of the mystery of Christ, we esteem of him but as dead ; and those who conceive well of those moral good things, as of some tokens giving hope of life, we account but as a kind of Manichees, who thought the very earth had life in it. I must confess that I have not yet made that proficiency in the schools

of our age, as that I could fee, why the fecond
table, and the acts of it, are not as properly the
parts of religion and Chriftianity, as the acts and
obfervations of the firft. If I miftake, then it is
St. James that hath abufed me; for he defcribing
religion by its proper acts, tells us, that ' True re-
' ligion, and undefiled before God and the Father,
' is, to vifit the fatherlefs and the widow in their
' affliction, and to keep himfelf unfpotted of the
' world.' Jam. i. 27. So that the thing which in
an efpecial refined dialect of the new Chriftian
language fignifies nothing but morality and civili-
ty, *that* in the language of the Holy Ghoft imports true religion. Wherefore any difference that
the Holy Ghoft makes notwithftanding, the man
of virtuous difpofitions, though ignorant of the
myftery of Chrift, be it Fabricius, or Regulus, or
any antient Heathen man, famous for fincerity and
uprightnefs of carriage, hath as fure a claim and
intereft in the church of Chrift, as the man deepeft fkilled in, moft certainly believing, and openly
profeffing all that is written in the holy books of
God, if he endeavour not to ' fhew his faith by
' his works.' Jam. ii. 18. The antients therefore,
where they found this kind of men, gladly received them, and converft familiarly with them, as
appears by the friendly intercourfe of epiftles of
St. Bafil with Libanius, of Nazianzen and Auftin,
with fundry others; and antiquity hath either left
us true, or forged us falfe epiftles betwixt St. Paul

himself and Seneca. Now as for the admitting of
any of these men to the discussing of the doubts in
our religious mysteries, who either know not, or
peradventure contemn them, there needs not much
be said: by a canon of one of the councils of Carthage it appears, it had sometimes been the erroneous practice of some Christians to baptize the
dead, and to put the sacrament of Christ's body into their mouths *. Since we have confest these
men to be in a sort dead, as having no supernatu-
ral quickening grace from above, to put into their
hands the handling of the word of life at all,
much more of discussing of the doubtful things in
it, were nothing else, but to baptize a carcase, and
put the communion bread into the mouth of the
dead. Wherefore leaving this kind of weak person to your courteous acceptance, let us consider
of another, one quite contrary to the former; a
true professor, but a man of profane and wicked
life, one more dangerously ill than the former :
have we any recipe for this man? May seem for
him there is no balm in Gilead, he seems like unto
the leper in the law, unto whom no man might
draw near. And by so much the more dangerous
is his case, because the condition of conversing
with Heathen men, be they never so wicked, is
permitted unto Christians by our Apostle himself,
whereas with this man, all commerce seems, by
the same Apostle, to be quite cut off. For in the

* Concil. Carthag. iii, can. 6. apud Harduin. vol. i. p. 961.

1 Cor. v. St. Paul having forbidden them former⸗
ly all manner of converfing with fornicators, infamous perfons, and men fubject to grievous crimes;
and confidering at length how impoffible this was,
becaufe of the Gentiles with whom they lived, and
amongft whom neceffarily they were to converfe
and trade, he diftinguifhes between the fornicators of this world, and the fornicators which were
brethren. I meant not (faith the bleffed Apoftle,
expounding himfelf) ' that ye fhould not admit of,
' the fornicators of this world ; ' 1 Cor. v. 10.
that is, fuch as were Gentiles, for then muft ye
have fought a new world. So great and general a
liberty at that time had the world affumed for
the practice of that fin of fornication, that ftrict-
ly to have forbidden them the company of fornicators, had almoft been to have excluded them the
fociety of mankind. But, faith he, ' If a brother
' be a fornicator, or a thief, or a railer; with fuch
' a one partake not, no not fo much as to eat.'
1 Cor. v. 11. Wherefore the cafe of this perfon
feems to be defperate; for he is not only mortally
fick, but is bereft of all help of the phyfician. Yet
notwithftanding all this, we may not give him o-
ver for gone; for when we have well fearched
our boxes, we fhall find a recipe even for him too.
Think we that our Apoftle's meaning was, that
we fhould acquaint ourfelves only with the good,
and not the bad; as phyficians in the time of pe-
ftilence look only to the found, and fhun the dif-

eafed? Our Saviour Chrift familiarly converft, eat,
and drank with publicans and finners, and gives
the reafon of it, becaufe he ' came not to call the
' righteous, but finners to repentance.' Matth.
ix. 13. Is Chrift contrary to Paul? This reafon of our Saviour concerns every one on whom
the duty of faving of fouls doth reft. It is the
main drift of his meffage, and unavoidably he
is to converfe, yea, eat and drink with all forts
of finners, even becaufe he is to call, not the
righteous, but finners to repentance. Neceffary it
is that fome means be left to reclaim notorious offenders, let their difeafe be never fo dangerous.
' I know not whether ought that can be tried, in
' the extremity of danger, will prove falutary;
' certainly to try nothing, muft be deftructive *.'
Who can tell whether in this extremity, were it at
the laft caft, it may fome way profit to receive
him; but this we all know, that altogether to caft
him out of the fociety of good men, is to cut him
off from all outward means of health. The leper
in the law, though he were excluded the multitude, yet had he accefs unto the prieft. Beloved,
the prieft in the new law hath much greater privilege than the antient had; he was only a judge,
and could not cure; but this is both a judge and a
phyfician, and can both difcern and cure the lepro-
fy of our fouls; wherefore he is not to be exclud-

* Nefcio an in extremis aliquid tentare medicina fit, certe
nihil tentare perditio eft.

ed from the moſt deſperately ſick perſon. Neither
doth this duty concern the prieſt alone; for, as
Tertullian ſometimes ſpake in another caſe, ' A-
' gainſt traitors and public enemies every man is a
' ſoldier *;' ſo is it true in this. Every one who
is of ſtrength to pull a ſoul out of the fire, is for
this buſineſs, by counſel, by advice, by rebuking,
a prieſt, neither muſt he let him lie there to expeсt
better help. Again, no man ſo ill, but hath ſome
good thing in him, though it breaks not out, as
being clouded and darkened with much corruption. We muſt take heed, that we do not miſtake in
thinking there is nothing elſe but evil, where we
often ſee it. We muſt therefore entertain even near
friendſhip with ſuch a one to diſcover him. ' No
' man is perfectly diſcovered,' ſaith St. Auſtin, ' but
' by his inward acquaintance†.' As therefore they
who ſeek for treaſure, give not over by reaſon of
clay and mire, ſo long as there is any hope to ſpeed;
ſo may we not caſt off our induſtry, though it labour in the moſt polluted ſoul; that ſo at length,
through charitable patience and long-ſuffering, we
may diſcover in him ſome good things which may
content us for the preſent, and give hope of better things to come ‡.' For as they that work in

* In majeſtatis reos et publicos hoſtes omnis homo miles
eſt. Apolog. c. 2.

† Nemo enim niſi per amicitiam cognoſcitur.

‡ Ut ad quaedam ſana in quorum delectatione acquieſcamus
per charitatis tolerantiam perducamur.

gold and coftly matter, diligently fave every little
piece that falls away; fo goodnefs, wherefoever it
be, is a thing fo precious, that every little fpark
of it deferves our care in cherifhing. Many mif-
carry through the want of this patience in thofe
who undertake them, whilft they defpair of them
too foon: Whilft they rebuke us, as if they hated, and upbraid rather than reprehend *.   As
unfkilful phyficians, who fuffer their patients to
die under their hands, to hide their error, blame
their patients intemperance †: fo let us take heed,
left it be not fo much the ftrength of the difeafe,
as the want of fkill in us, which we ftrive to cover
and vail over with the names of contumacy, intemperance, or the like. David received an exprefs meffage from the prophet, that the child
conceived in adultery fhould furely die ; yet he
ceafed not his prayers, and tears, and fafting, as
long as there was life in it. We receive no fuch
certain meffage concerning any man's mifcarriage,
and why then fhould we intermit any office which
Chriftian patience can afford ? Wherefore, what
Maecenas fometime fpake loofely in another fenfe,
that we may apply more properly to our purpofe,
Let our weak perfon here be lame, hand and foot,
hip and thigh, fick in head and heart; yet fo long

---

* Dum ita objurgant quafi oderint.

† Tranfit convitium et intemperantia culpatur, uterque qui
periere arguuntur.

as there is life in him, there is no caufe we fhould
defpair ‡. How knoweft thou how potent the
word of God may be through thy miniftry, ' out
' of thefe ftones to raife up children unto Abra-
' ham ?' Luke iii. 8. I cannot therefore perfuade
myfelf, that this prohibition of St. Paul, of which
we but now fpake, fo far extended, as that it quite
interdicted good men the company of the finners,
be they never fo grofs. For when he delivered
men unto Satan, (the greateft thing that ever he
did in this kind) it was, ' to the mortifying of the
' flefh, that fo the fpirit might be fafe in the day
' of the Lord.' 1 Cor. v. 5. But this is worfe, for
by this peremptory excluding the grofs finner from
the good, a greater gap is opened to the liberty of
the flefh, and a more immediate way could not be
found to bring final deftruction on him at that
day. The extent therefore of St. Paul's precept,
though given in fhew to all, I take to reach no
farther than the weak, and fuch as are in danger

‡ Inde illud Mecaenatis turpiffimum votum, quo et debili-
tatem non recufat, et deformitatem, et noviffimè acutam cru-
cem, dummodo inter haec mala fpiritus prorogetur.

Debilem facito manu,
    Debilem pede, coxa:
Tuber adftrue gibberum,
    Lubricos quate dentes.
Vita dum fupereft, bene eft.
    Hanc mihi vel acutâ
Si fedeam cruce, fuftine.

Senecae epiftol. 101.

of infection; for the weaker fort of men are always evermore the moft, and a charge given unto the moft, is commonly given under the ftile of all. Our Apoftle therefore jealous of the tenderer fort, whom every unwholfome blaft doth eafily taint, feems, what he intended for the moft, to make general to all. The reafon which the Apoftle gives does warrant this reftraint; ' See ye not,' faith he, ' that a little leaven fours the whole lump ? ' 1 Cor. v. 6. If therefore there be any part of the lump out of fhot and danger of fouring and contagion, on it this precept can have no extent: and furely fome wrong it were to the church of Chrift, to fuppofe that all were neceffarily fubject to fouring and infection, upon fuppofal of fome admiffion of leaven. Evil indeed is infectious, but neither neceffarily, nor yet fo, that it need fright us from thofe who are difeafed with it. Contagious difeafes which feize on our bodies, infect by natural force and means, which we cannot prevent: but no man drinks down this poifon, whofe will is not the hand that takes the cup: fo that to converfe with men of difeafed minds, infects us not, except we will. Again, Ariftotle, in his problems, makes a queftion, ' Why health doth not infect as well ' as ficknefs.' For we grow fick many times by incauteloufly converfing with the difeafed, but no man grows well by accompanying the healthy. Thus indeed it is with the healthinefs of the body; it hath no tranfient force on others. But the

ftrength and healthinefs of the mind carries with it
a gracious kind of infection: and common experience tells us, that nothing profits evil men more
than the company of the good. So that ftrength
of mind, accompanied with the prefervative of the
grace of God, may not only, without fear of contagion, fafely converfe with ungracious finners,
but by fo doing, as it were infect them, and make
them fuch as himfelf is. No caufe therefore hitherto, why the true profeffors, though notorious
finners, fhould not be partakers of our Chriftian
courtefies. And therefore as of the former, fo of
this my conclufion is, we muft receive him. Only
let me add St. Paul's words in another place, ' Ye
' that are ftrong receive fuch a one *.'

Having thus far fpoken of his admiffion, let us
now a little confider of his reftraint, and fee whether he may have any part in hearing and handling
religious controverfies; where plainly to fpeak my
mind, as his admiffion before was, fo his exclufion
here is much more neceffary: the way to thefe
fchools fhould be open to none, but to men of
upright life and converfation: and *that* as well in
regard of the profane and wicked men themfelves,
as of the caufe which they prefume to handle: for
as for themfelves, this is but the field wherein
they fow and reap their own infamy and difgrace.
Our own experience tells us, how hard a thing it

* *This feems an allufion, from memory, to Rom.* xv. 1.

is for men of behaviour known to be spotless, to avoid the lash of those men's tongues, who make it their chief fence to disgrace the persons, when they cannot touch the cause. For what else are the writings of many men but mutual pasquils and satires against each others lives, wherein digladiating like Eschines and Demosthenes, they reciprocally lay open each others filthiness to the view and scorn of the world. The fear therefore of being stained, and publicly disgraced, might be reason enough to keep them back from entering these contentions. And as for the cause itself, into which this kind of men do put themselves, needs must it go but ill with it: for is it possible that those respects, which sway and govern their ordinary actions, should have no influence upon their pens? It cannot be, that they who speak, and plot, and act wickedness, should ever write uprightly. Doubtless, as in their lives, so in the causes they undertake, they nourish hopes full of improbity*. Besides all this, the opinion of the common sort is not to be contemned, whom no kind of reason so much abuses, and carries away, as when the discredit of the person is retorted on the cause; which thing our adversaries here at home amongst us know very well, a master-piece of whose policy it is, to put into the hands of the people such pamphlets which hurt not our cause at all, but only

* Sicut in vita, ita in causis quoque spes improbas habent. Quintil. inst. orat. lib. xii. c. 1.

difcredit our perfons. St. Chryfoftom obferves
out of the antient cuftoms of the Olympic Games,
that whenfoever any man offered himfelf to contend in them, he was not to be admitted till public proclamation had been made throughout the
multitude to this purpofe. Whether any man
knew him to be either a fervant, or a thief, or o-
therwife of infamous life. And if any imputation
in this kind were proved againft him, it was fufficient to keep him back *. Had the Heathen this
care that their vanities fhould not be difcredited ?
how great then muft our care be, that they which
enter into thefe exercifes be of pure and upright
condition ? Let men's fkill and judgment therefore be never fo good, yet if their lives be notori-
oufly fubjeἐt to exception, let them know, that
there is no place for them in thefe Olympics. Men
indeed, in civil bufinefs, have found out a diftinction, between an honeft man, and a good com-
monwealths-man: and therefore Fabricius, in the
Roman ftory, is much commended, for nominating
to the confulfhip Ruffinus, a wicked man, and his
utter enemy, becaufe he knew him to be ferviceable to the commonwealth, for thofe wars which
were then depending. But in the bufinefs of the
Lord, and commonwealth of God, we can admit

* Οἱ γὰρ μέλλοντες ἐς τὸ ϑεάτρον ἕλκεσθαι ἐκεῖνο, ὁ πρότερον
καθιάσιν εἰς τὺς ἀγῶνας, ἕως ἀν αὐτὺς ὁ κῆρυξ λαϐὼν ὑπὸ τοῖς ἀ-
πάντων ὀρθαλμῖς περιαγάγη βόων ᾗ λέγων, ΜΗ' ΤΙ'Σ τύτυ κατή-
γορει. Ad Illuminandos Catechefis. ii.

of no such diftinction. For God himfelf, in the
book of Pfalms, ftaves them off with a ' What haft
' thou to do to take my words into thy mouth,
' fince thou hateft to be reformed?' Pf. l. 17.
The world, for the managing of her matters, may
employ fuch as herfelf hath fitted: ' But let every
' one who names the name of God, depart from
' iniquity.' 2 Tim. ii. 19. For thefe reafons
therefore it is very expedient, that none but right
good men fhould undertake the Lord's quarrels,
the rather, becaufe there is fome truth in that
which Quintilian fpake, ' As impoffible it is that
' good and bad thoughts fhould harbour in the
' fame heart, as it is for the fame man to be joint-
' ly good and bad *.' And fo, from the confideration of this fick perfon, let us proceed to vifit the
next.

The weak perfons, I have hitherto treated of,
are the feweft, as confifting in a kind of extreme.
For the greateft fort of men are in a mediocrity;
of men, eminently good, or extremely ill, the number is fmalleft; but this rank of fick perfons, that
now we are to view, is an whole army, and may be,
every one of us, if we do well examine ourfelves,
fhall find ourfelves in it: for the weak, whom we
now are to fpeak of, is he that hath not that degree and perfection of faith, and ftrength of fpi-

* Cogitare optima fimul ac deterrima, non magis eft unius animi, quam ejufdem hominis bonum effe ac malum. Inft.
Orat. lib. xii. c. 1.

ritual conftitution, that he ought to have. Where‑
fore our recipe here muft be like the tree of life
in the book of the Revelation, it muft be medicine
to heal whole nations. For who is he amongft
men that can free himfelf from this weaknefs?
Yea, we ourfelves, that are fet over others for their
cure, may fpeak of ourfelves and our charge, as
Iolaus, in Euripides, doth of himfelf and Hercules's children, ' We take care of thefe, ourfelves
' ftanding in need of others care for us *.' Hippocrates counfels his phyfician, to look efpecially
that himfelf be healthy, ' fair of colour, and full
' of flefh †.' For otherwife, faith he, how can
he give comfort and hope of fuccefs to a fick patient, who, by his ill colour and meagrenefs, bewrays fome imperfection of his own. But what
phyfician of foul and manners is capable of this
counfel? or who is it, that, taking the cure of
others, doth not in moft of his actions bewray his
own difeafe? Even thus hath it pleafed God to
tye us together with a mutual fenfe of each others
weaknefs; and as ourfelves receive and bear with
others; fo for ourfelves interchangeably muft we
requeft the fame courtefy at others hands. Notwithftanding, as it is with the health of our bo-

* Σάζω τά δ'αὐτὸς δεόμενος σωτηρίας. Eurip. Heracl. v. 11.

† 'Ιἡτρν μὲν ἔναι προσασίην, ὁρῆν "ΕΥΧΡΩΣ ΤΕ ΚΑΙ' "ΕΤ-
ΣΑΡΚΟΣ "ΕΣΤΑΙ πρὸς τὴν ὑπέρχασαν αὐτῷ φύσιν, ἀξιῦνται γὰρ
ὑπὸ τῶν πολλῶν οἱ μὴ εὖ διακείμενον τὸ σῶμα ὕτως, ὡς ὑδ' ἀν ἑτέ-
ρων ἐπιμεληθῆναι καλῶς. Hippocr. de Medico. c. 1.

dies, no man at any time is perfectly well, only he goes for an healthy man, who is least sick : so fares it with our souls. God hath included all under the name of weak, some peradventure are less weak than others, but no man is strong. It is but a miferable comfort to judge our own perfections only by others defects, yet this is all the comfort we have *.

Let us leave therefore those, who, by reason of being less crazy, pass for healthy, and consider of those whom some sensible and eminent imperfection above others hath ranked in the number of the weak. And of those there are sundry kinds, especially two. One is weak, because he is not yet fully informed, not so sufficiently catechized in the mysteries of faith, whom farther institution may bring to better maturity : The other peradventure is sufficiently grounded for principles of faith, yet is weak, by reason either of some passion, or of some irritatory and troublesome humour in his behaviour. There is no man so perfect, but hath somewhat in his behaviour that requireth pardon †.

As for the imperfection of the former of these, it is the weakness of infancy and childhood in faith, rather than a disease : and with this weak man we are especially to bear above all others. For as for him that is weak through gross and wilful igno-

* Infeliciffimum confolationis genus eft de miferiis hominum peccatorum capere folatia.

† Nullum unquam ingenium placuit fine venia.

rance, or contumacy, or the like, it is pardonable,
if fometimes we yield him not that meafure of
courtefy which were meet; but to be cruel againft
infancy and childhood were inhumani:y. The
manner of our recipe for thefe men, our Apoftle
fomewhere expreffes, where he tells us of fome
that muft ' be fed with milk, and not ftrong meat:'
1 Cor. iii. 2. unto thefe we muft rather be as nur-
fes than phyficians ; by gently fubmitting ourfelves to the capacity of the learner, by lending
our hand, by leffening our fteps to keep them in
equi-pace with us, till they come up to their full
growth *. As Chrift, being God, emptied himfelf, and became man like to us, fo muft we lay
down our gifts of wit, in which we flatter ourfelves, and take ourfelves to be as gods, and in
fhew and fafhion become like one of them. Grave
men have thought it no difparagement to have
been feen with their little fons, toying and prac-
tifing with them their childifh fports † : and if
any take offence at it, thcy are fuch as know not
what it is to be fathers. Thofe therefore who
bear the office of fathers amongft other men, to
bring up the infancy of babes in Chrift, muft not
blufh to practife this part of a father, and out of
St. Paul's leffon of ' becoming all to all,' 1 Cor.
iv. 22. learn to become a child to children; do it

* Submittendum nos ad menfuram difcentis, et manum
dando et gradum noftrum minuendo.

† Ludere par impar, equitare in arundine longa. Horat.

he may very well, without any impeachment to himſelf. He that helps one up that is fallen, throws not himſelf down to lie by him, but gently ſtoops to lift him up again * ; but of this weak perſon I have little need, I truſt, to ſpeak. For no man in theſe days can be long weak, but by his own de-fault, ſo long and careful teaching as hath been, and every day is, muſt needs take from men all pretence of weakneſs in this kind: for what is the end of all this labour and pains in teaching, but that ye might at length not need a teacher †. Wherefore from this I come unto that other weak perſon, ſtrong in faith, but weak in carriage and behaviour.

Having before proved, that Chriſtian courteſy ſpreads itſelf to all ſorts of men, to the infidel, to the groſs notorious ſinner, then will it, without any ſtraining at all, come home to all the infirmi-ties of our weaker brethren : for that which can endure ſo great a tempeſt, how can it be offended with ſome ſmall drops. Is Chriſtian patience like unto St. Peter's reſolution, that durſt manfully en-counter the high prieſt's ſervant, yet was daunted at the voice of a ſilly maiden ; whatſoever it is that is irkſome unto us in the common behaviour of our brethren, it were ſtrange we ſhould not be

* Non ſe projicit, ut ambo jaceant; ſed incurvat tantum, ut jacentem erigat.

† Nam quid aliud agimus docendo vos, quam ne ſemper docendi ſitis.

able to brook. Epictetus confidering with himfelf
the weaknefs which is ufual in men, ftill to make
the worft of what befals us, wittily tells us, that
every thing in the world hath two handles, one
turned toward us, which we may eafily take, the
other turned from us, harder to be laid hold of ;
the firft makes all things eafy, the fecond not fo ;
the inftance that he brings is my very purpofe ;
' Be it,' faith he, ' thy brother hath offended
' thee, here are two hand-fafts, one of the of-
' fence, the other of thy brother.   If thou take
' hold of that of the offence, it will be too hot
' for thee, thou wilt not eafily endure the touch
' of it : but if thou lay hold of that of thy bro-
' ther, this will make all behaviour tolerable. There
' is no part of our brother's carriage towards us,
' but if we fearch it, we fhall find, fome hand-
' faft, fome circumftance, that will make it eafy
' to be born *.'   If we can find no other, the circumftance of our Saviour Chrift's example will
never fail : an example which will not only make
us to endure the importunity of his ordinary behaviour, but all his outragious dealing whatfoever.
For, faith St. Chryfoftom, ' Didft thou know that
' thy brother intended particular mifchief againft
' thee, that he would embrue his hand in thy
' blood, yet kifs that hand ; for thy Lord did not
' refufe to kifs that mouth that made the bargain

---

* A paraphrafe of Epictet. Enchir. c. 39.

' for his blood *.' It is ſtoried of Protagoras,
that being a poor youth, and carrying a burthen of
ſticks, he ſo piled them, and laid them together
with ſuch art and order, that he made them much
more light and eaſy to be born. Beloved, there
is an art among Chriſtians, like unto that of Protagoras, of ſo making up and ordering our burthens, that they may lie with much leſs weight
upon our ſhoulders; this art, if we could learn it,
would make us take all in good part at our brother's hand, were he as bad as Nabal was, of whom
his own ſervant complained, that he was ' ſuch a
' man of Belial, that no man could ſpeak unto him.'
1 Sam. xxv. 17.

Wherefore, leaving you to the ſtudy and learning of this moſt Chriſtian art, I will a little conſider for what reaſons we may not admit of theſe
two ſorts of weak men to controverſy. For firſt,
as for the unlearned, in private, nothing more u-
ſual with them than to take offence at our diſſen-
tions, and to become more uncertain and unjointed
upon the hearing of any queſtion diſcuſt: it is their
uſual voice and queſtion to us, Is it poſſible that
we ſhould be at one in theſe points in which yourſelves do diſagree? thus caſt they off on our backs
the burthen of their back-ſliding and neutrality;
wherefore to acquaint them with diſputation in
religion, were, as it were, to blaſt them in their

* Αὐτὴν φίλησον τὴν δεξίαν.

infancy, and bring upon them some improsperous diseale to hinder their growth in Chrift.

Secondly, What one faid of other contentions, ' In civil wars no man is too weak to do a mif- ' chief *,' we have found too true in thefe our holy wars; no man is too weak (I fay not) to do mifchief, but to be a principal agent and captain in them. Simple and unlearned fouls, trained up by men of contentious fpirits, have had ftrength enough to be authors of dangerous herefies; Prifcilla and Maximilla, filly women laden with iniquity, were the chief ring-leaders in the errors of the Montanifts; and as it is commonly faid,'Weak- ' lings are able to begin a quarrel, but the profe- ' cution and finifhing is a work for ftronger men†;' fo hath it fared here. For that quarrel which thefe poor fouls had raifed, Tertullian, a man of great wit and learning, is drawn to undertake: fo that for a Barnabas to be drawn away to error, there needs not always the example and authority of a Peter.

A third reafon is the marvellous violence of the weaker fort in maintaining their conceits, if once they begin to be opinionative. For one thing there is that wonderfully prevails againft the reclaiming of them, and that is, The natural jealoufy they have of all that is faid unto them by men of better wits, ftand it with reafon never fo good, if it

* In bellis civilibus audacia etiam valet fingulorum.

† Bellum inchoant inertes, fortes finiunt.

found not as they would have it. A jealousy founded in the sense of their weakness, arising out of
this, that they suspect all to be done for no other
end, but to circumvent and abuse them. And
therefore when they see themselves to be too weak
in reasoning, they easily turn them to violence.
The monks of Egypt, otherwise devout and religious men, antiently were for the most part unlearned, and generally given over to the error of
the Anthropomorphitae, who held, that God had
hands and feet, and all the parts that a man hath,
and was in outward shape and proportion like to
one of us. Theophilus, a learned bishop of A-
lexandria, having fallen into their hands, was so
roughly used by them, that ere he could get out
of their fingers, he was fain to use his wits, and
to crave aid of his equivocating sophistry, and
soothly to tell them, ' I have seen your face as the
' face of God.' Now when Christian and religious
doubts must thus be managed with wilfulness and
violence, what mischief may come of it is already
so plain, that it needs not my finger to point it out.
Wherefore let every such weak person say unto
himself, as St. Austin doth, ' Let others reason, I
' will marvel; let others dispute, I will believe *.'

As for the man strong in passion, or rather
weak, for the strength of passion is the weakness
of the passionate; great reason hath the church to

---

* Tu ratiocinare, ego mirer; disputa tu, ego credam.

except againſt him. For firſt of all, from him it
comes, that our books are ſo ſtuft with contumelious malediction, no Heathen writers having left
the like example of choler and groſs impatience.
An hard thing I know it is, to write without affection and paſſion in thoſe things which we love,
and therefore it is free ſo to do, to thoſe who are
lords over themſelves. It ſeems our Saviour gave
ſome way to it himſelf. For ſomewhat certainly
his kinſmen ſaw in his behaviour, when, as St.
Mark reports, they went forth to lay hold upon
him, ' thinking he was beſide himſelf.' Mark iii. 2 1.
But for thoſe who have not the command of
themſelves, better it were they laid it by; St.
Chryſoſtom excellently obſerveth, that the prophets of God, and Satan, were by this notoriouſly
differenced, that they which gave oracles by motion from the devil, did it with much impatience
and confuſion, with a kind of fury and madneſs;
but they which gave oracles from God by divine
inſpiration, gave them with all mildneſs and temper; if it be the cauſe of God which we handle in
our writings, then let us handle it like the prophets of God, with quietneſs and moderation, and
not in the violence of paſſion, as if we were poſſeſſed, rather than inſpired. Again, what equity
or indifferency can we look for in the carriage of
that cauſe, that falls into the handling of theſe
men : What man, overtaken with paſſion, remembers impartially to compare cauſe with cauſe,

and right with right; on what caufe he happens,
that is he refolute to maintain*; as a fencer to the
ftage, fo comes he to write, not upon confcience
of quarrel, but becaufe he propofes to contend;
yea, fo potently hath this humour prevailed with
men that have undertaken to maintain a faction, that it hath broken out to the tempting of
God, and the difhonour of martyrdom. Two fri-
ers in Florence, in the action of Savonarola, voluntarily, in the open view of the city, offered to
enter the fire: fo to put an end to the controverfy, that he might be judged to have the right, who,
like one of the three children in Babylon, fhould
pafs untouched through the fire †. But I haften
to vifit one weak perfon more, and fo an end.

He whom we now are to vifit, is a man weak
through heretical and erring faith; now whether
or no we have any receit for him, it may be
doubtful: for St. Paul advifes us to avoid the
man that is a maker of fects, knowing him to be
damned ‡. Yet, if as we fpake of not admitting to
us the notorious finner, no not to eat, fo we teach
of this, that it is delivered refpectively to the
weaker fort, as juftly for the fame reafons we may

* Quis conferre duces meminit, qui pendere caufas?
   Qua ftetit inde favet.

† See Burchardi Diar. in the appendix to Gordon's life of
Pope Alexander VI. where the tenor of this extraordinary
challenge is recorded.

‡ *Alluding to Tit.* iii. 10, 11.

do: we shall have a recipe here for the man that errs in faith, and rejoiceth in making of sects: which we shall the better do, if we can but gently draw him on to a moderation to think of his conceits only as of opinions; for it is not the variety of opinions, but our own perverse wills, who think it meet, that all should be conceited as ourselves are, which hath so inconvenienced the church. Were we not so ready to anathematize each other, where we concur not in opinion, we might in hearts be united, though in our tongues we were divided, and that with singular profit to all sides. It is ' the unity of the Spirit in the bond of peace,' Ephes. iv. 3. and not identity of conceit, which the Holy Ghost requires at the hands of Christians. I will give you one instance, in which, at this day, our churches are at variance; the will of God, and his manner of proceeding in predestination, is undiscernible, and shall so remain until that day, wherein all knowledge shall be made perfect; yet some there are, who, with probability of scripture, teach, that the true cause of the final miscarriage of them that perish, is that original corruption that befel them at the beginning, increased though the neglect or refusal of grace offered. Others, with no less favourable countenance of scripture, make the cause of reprobation only the will of God, determining freely of his own work, as himself pleases, without respect to any second cause whatsoever. Were we not ambitiously mind-

ed, every one to be lord of a sect, each of these
tenets might be profitably taught and heard, and
matter of singular exhortation drawn from either;
for on the one part, doubtless it is a pious and religious intent, to endeavour to free God from all
imputation of unnecessary rigour, and his justice
from seeming injustice and incongruity : and on
the other side, it is a noble resolution, so to humble
ourselves under the hand of Almighty God, as that
we can with patience hear, yea, think it an honour, that so base creatures as ourselves should become the instruments of the glory of so great a
Majesty, whether it be by eternal life, or by eternal death, though for no other reason but for
God's good will and pleasure's sake. The authors
of these conceits might both freely (if peaceably)
speak their minds, and both singularly profit the
church : for since it is impossible, where scripture
is ambiguous, that all conceits should run alike,
it remains, that we seek out a way, not so much to
establish an unity of opinion in the minds of all,
which I take to be a thing likewise impossible, as
to provide, that multiplicity of conceit trouble not
the church's peace. A better way my conceit cannot reach unto, than that we would be willing to
think, that these things, which with some shew of
probability we deduce from scripture, are at the
best but our opinions : for this peremptory manner
of setting down our own conclusions, under this
high commanding form of necessary truths, is ge-

nerally one of the greateft caufes, which keeps the churches this day fo far afunder; when as a gracious receiving of each other, by mutual forbearance in this kind, might peradventure, in time, bring them nearer together.

This peradventure, may fome man fay, may content us in cafe of opinion indifferent, out of which no great inconvenience, by neceffary and evident proof, is concluded: but what recipe have we for him that is fallen into fome known and defperate herefy ? Even the fame with the former. And therefore antiently, heretical and orthodox Chriftians, many times, even in public holy exercife, converft together without offence. It is noted in the ecclefiaftick ftories, that the Arrians and right believers fo communicated together in holy prayers, that you could not diftinguifh them till they came to the Doxology, which the Arrians ufed with fome difference from other Chriftians. But thofe were times of which we read in our books, but we have loft the practice of their patience *. Some prejudice was done unto the church by thofe, who firft began to intermingle with public ecclefiaftical duties, things refpective unto private conceits. For thofe Chriftian offices in the church ought, as much as poffibly they may, be common unto all, and not to defcend to the differences of particular opinions. Severity a-

---

* Quorum lectionem habemus, virtutem non habemus.

gainſt, and ſeparation from heretical companies,
took its beginning from the heretics themſelves:
and if we ſearch the ſtories, we ſhall find, that the
church did not, at their firſt ariſing, thruſt them
from her, themſelves went out: and as for ſeverity, that which the Donatiſts ſometimes ſpake in
their own defence; ' She was the true church, not
' which raiſed, but which ſuffered perſecution *,'
was *de facto* true for a great ſpace. For when hereſies and ſchiſms firſt aroſe in the church, all
kinds of violence were uſed by the erring factions;
but the church ſeemed not for a long time to have
known any uſe of a ſword, but only of a buckler,
and when ſhe began to uſe the ſword, ſome of
her beſt and chiefeſt captains much miſliked it.
The firſt law in this kind that ever was made, was
enacted by Theodoſius againſt the Donatiſts, but
with this reſtraint, that it ſhould extend againſt
none, but only ſuch as were tumultuous, and till
that time they were not ſo much as touched with
any mulct, though but pecuniary, till that ſhame-
ful outrage committed againſt Biſhop Maximian,
whom they beat down with bats and clubs, even
as he ſtood at the altar: ſo that not ſo much the
error of the Donatiſts, as their riots and mutinies
were by imperial laws reſtrained. That the church
had afterward good reaſon to think, that ſhe
ought to be rather ſalutary than pleaſing; that

* Illam eſſe veram eccleſiam quae perſecutionem patitur,
non quae facit.

sometimes there was more mercy in punishing than
forbearing, there can no doubt be made. St. Austin (a man of as mild and gentle spirit as ever bare
rule in the church) having, according to his natural sweetness of disposition, earnestly written a-
gainst violent and sharp dealing with heretics, being taught by experience, did afterward retract,
and confess an excellent use of wholesome severity
in the church. Yet could I wish that it might be
said of the church, which was sometimes observed
of Augustus, ' He had been angry with, and se-
' verely punished many of his kin, but he could
' never endure to cut any of them off by death *.'
But this I must request you to take only as my private wish, and not as a censure, if any thing have
been done to the contrary. When Absalom was
up in arms against his father, it was necessary for
David to take order to curb him, and pull him on
his knees; yet we see how careful he was he
should not die, and how lamentably he bewailed
him in his death : what cause was it that drove
David into this extreme passion ? Was it doubt of
heir to the kingdom ? that could not be; for Solomon was now born, to whom the promise of the
kingdom was made : Was it the strength of natural affection ? I somewhat doubt of it; three years
together was Absalom in banishment, and David
did not very eagerly desire to see him : the scrip-

* In nullius unquam suorum necem duravit. Tacit. Annal: i. 6.

ture indeed notes, that the king longed for him; yet in this longing was there not any such fierceness of passion, for Absalom saw not the king's face for two years more after his return from banishment to Jerusalem: What then might be the cause of his strength of passion, and commiseration in the king? I persuade myself it was the fear of his son's final miscarriage, and reprobation, which made the king (secure of the mercies of God unto himself) to wish he had died in his stead, that so he might have gained for his ungracious child some time of repentance. The church, who is the common mother of us all, when her Absaloms, her unnatural sons, do lift up their hands and pens against her, must so use means to repress them, that she forget not that they are the sons of her womb, and be compassionate over them, as David was over Absalom, loth to unsheath either sword, but most of all the temporal; for this were to send them quick dispatch to hell.

And here I may not pass by that singular moderation of this church of ours, which she hath most Christianly exprest towards her adversaries of Rome, here at home in her bosom, above all the reformed churches I have read of. For out of desire to make the breach seem no greater than indeed it is, and to hold communion and Christian fellowship with her, so far as we possibly can, we have done nothing to cut off the favourers of that church. The reasons of their love and respect to the church of

Rome we wifh, but we do not command, them to lay down : their lay-brethren have all means of inftruction offered them. Our edicts and ftatutes, made for their reftraint, are fuch as ferve only to awaken them, and caufe them to confider the innocency of that caufe, for the refufal of communion in which they endure (as they fuppofe) fo great loffes Thofe who are fent over by them, either for the retaining of the already perverted, or perverting others, are either returned by us back again to them, who difpatched them to us; or, without any wrong unto their perfons, or danger to their lives, fuffer an eafy reftraint; which only hinders them from difperfing the poifon they brought. And had they not been ftickling in our ftate bufinefs, and medling with our prince's crown, there had not a drop of their blood fallen to the ground; unto our fermons, in which the fwervings of that church are neceffarily to be taxt by us, we do not bind their prefence ; only our defire is, they would join with us in thofe prayers and holy ceremonies, which are common to them and us. And fo accordingly, by fingular difcretion was our Service-book compiled by our fore-fathers, as containing nothing that might offend them, as being almoft merely a compendium of their own Breviary and Miffal; fo that they fhall fee nothing in our meetings, but that they fhall fee done in their own ; though many things which are in theirs, here, I grant, they fhall not find. And here in-

deed is the great and main difference betwixt us.
As it is in the controverfy concerning the canonical books of fcripture : whatfoever we hold for
fcripture, that even by that church is maintained,
only fhe takes upon her to add much, which we
cannot think fafe to admit : fo fares it in other
points of faith and ceremony ; whatfoever it is we
hold for faith, fhe holds it as far forth as we : our
ceremonies are taken from her ; only fhe, over and
above, urges fome things for faith, which we take
to be error, or at the beft but opinion ; and for
ceremony, which we think to be fuperftition : fo
that to participate with us, is, though not throughout, yet in fome good meafure, to participate with
that church ; and certainly were that fpirit of charity ftirring in them, which ought to be, they
would love and honour us, even for the refemblance of that church, the beauty of which themfelves fo much admire. The glory of thefe our
proceedings, even our adverfaries themfelves do
much envy ; fo that from hence it is, that in their
writings they traduce our judiciary proceedings a-
gainft them, for fanguinary and violent ; ftriving
to perfuade other nations, that fuch as have fuffered by courfe of public juftice for religion only,
and not for treafon have died, and pretend we what
we lift, our actions are as bloody and cruel as their
own : wherefore if a perfect pattern of dealing
with erring Chriftians were to be fought, there
were not any like unto this of ours ; which, as it

takes not to itself liberty of cruelty, so it leaves not unto any the liberty of deftroying their own fouls in the error of their lives *. And now that we may at once conclude this point concerning heretics, for prohibiting these men accefs to religious difputations, it is now too late to difpute of that; for from this, that they have already unadvifedly entered into these battles, are they become that which they are: let us leave them therefore as a fufficient example and inftance of the danger of intempeftive and immodeft medling in facred difputes.

I fee it may be well expected, that I fhould, according to my promife, add inftruction for the public magiftrate, and fhow how far this precept in receiving the weak concerns him.

I muft confefs I intended, and promifed fo to do, but I cannot conceive of it, as a thing befitting me to ftep out of my ftudy, and give rules for government to commonwealths, a thing befitting men of greater experience to do. Wherefore I hope you will pardon me if I keep not that promife, which I fhall with lefs offence break than obferve: and this I rather do, becaufe I fuppofe this precept to concern us efpecially, if not only, as private men, and that in cafe of public proceeding, there is fcarce room for it. Private men may pafs over offences at their pleafure, and may be, in not

---

* In qua nec faeviendi, nec errandi pereundique licentia permittitur.

doing it, they do worfe; but thus to do, lies not in the power of the magiftrate, who goes by laws, prefcribing him what he is to do. Princes and men in authority do many times much abufe themfelves, by affecting a reputation of clemency, in pardoning wrongs done to other men, and giving protection to fundry offenders, againft thofe who have juft caufe to proceed againft them. It is mercy to pardon wrong done againft ourfelves, but to deny the courfe of juftice to him that calls for it, and to protect offenders, may peradventure be fome inconfiderate pity, but mercy it cannot be. All therefore that I will prefume to advife the magiftrate is, a general inclinablenefs to merciful proceedings.

And fo I conclude, wifhing unto them who plentifully fow mercy, plentifully to reap it at the hand of God, with an hundred-fold encreafe, and that the blefting from God, the father of mercies, may be upon them all, as on the fons of mercy, as many as are the fands on the fea-fhore in multitude. The fame God grant, that the words which we have heard this day, &c.

O F

D U E L S,

PREACHED AT THE HAGUE.

Numb. xxxv 33.

*And the land cannot be cleanfed of blood that is
fhed in it ; but by the blood of him that fhed it.*

THESE words are like unto a fcorpion : for
as in that, fo in thefe, the felf-fame thing
is both poifon and remedy : blood is the poifon,
blood is the remedy; he that is ftricken with the
fcorpion, muft take the oil of the fcorpion to cure
him; he that hath poifoned a land with the fin of
blood, muft yield his own blood for antidote to
cure it. It might feem ftrange, that I fhould amongft
Chriftians thus come and deliver a fpeech of blood.
For when I read the notes and characters of a
Chriftian in holy fcriptures, methinks it fhould be
almoft a fin for fuch a one to name it. ' Poffefs
' your fouls in patience.' Luke xxi. 19. ' By this
' fhall men know that ye are my difciples, if ye
' love one another.' John xiii. 35. ' Peace I leave
' with you.' John xiv. 27. ' The fruit of the Spi-

'rit is love, joy, peace in the Holy Ghoft.' Rom. xiv.
17. ' Let your moderation be known to all men.'
Philip. iv. 5. ' The wifdom that is from above is
' firft pure, then peaceable, gentle, eafy to be en-
' treated, full of mercy.' Jam. iii. 17. It is reported of Avenzoar, a great phyfician, that he was fo
tender-hearted, that he could not endure to fee a
man let-blood: he that fhould read thefe paffages
of fcripture, might think that Chriftians were like
Avenzoar, that the fight of blood fhould be enough
to affright them. But is the common Chriftian fo
foft, fo tender-hearted? is he fo peaceable, fo tame
and tractable a creature? You fhall not find two
things of more different countenance and complexion, than that Chriftianity which is commended unto us in the writings of the apoftles and e-
vangelifts, and that which is current in ufe and
practice of the times. He that fhall behold the true
face of a Chriftian, as it is decyphered and painted
out unto us in the books of the New Teftament,
and impartially compare it with that copy or coun-
terfeit of it, which is expreft in the life and demeanour of common Chriftians, would think them
no more like, than thofe fhields of gold which Solomon made, were unto thofe of brafs which Re-
hoboam made in their ftead: and might fuppofe
that the writers of thofe books had brought wifhes rather than precepts, had rather fancied to
themfelves fome admirable pattern of a Chriftian,
fuch as they could wifh, than delivered rules and

laws, which ferioufly and indeed ought or could be practifed in common life and converfation. St. James obferves, that ' he which beholds his natu-
' ral face in a glafs, goes his way, and immediately
' forgets what manner of man he was.' i. 23. Be-
loved, how careful we are to look upon the glafs, the books of holy fcriptures, I cannot eafily pro-
nounce; but this I am fure of, we go our ways, and quickly forget what manner of fhape we faw there. As Jacob and Efau had both one father, Ifaac; both one mother, Rebecca; yet the one was fmooth and plain, the other rough and hairy, of harfh and hard countenance and condition: fo thefe two kinds of Chriftians, of which but now I fpake, though both lay claim to one father and mother, both call themfelves the fons of God, and the fons of the church, yet are they almoft as unlike as Jacob and Efau; the one fmooth, gentle, and peaceable, the other rough and harfh. The notes and characters of Chriftians, as they are de-
fcribed in holy fcriptures, are patience, eafily put-
ting up and digefting of wrongs; humility, pre-
ferring all before ourfelves: and St. James tells us, that ' the wifdom that is from above, is firft
' pure, then peaceable, gentle, eafy to be entreat-
' ed.' iii. 17. St James indeed hath given the firft place unto purity, and it were almoft a fin to compare Chriftian virtues together, and make them ftrive for precedency and place. For what Solomon faith upon another occafion, is here much

more true, 'Say not, Why is this thing better than
' that? for every thing in its time is seasonable.'
Ecclef. vii. 10. Yet he that shall mark how every
where the scriptures commend unto us gentleness
and meeknefs, and that peace is it, ' which,' as
Tertullian speaks, ' the apostles endeavour with all
' the strength and force of the Holy Ghost to plant
' amongst us *,' might a little invert the words of
St. James, and read them thus, ' The wisdom that
' is from above, is first peaceable, then pure.' The
Son of God, who is the Wisdom of the Father,
and who for us men came down from heaven, first,
and before all other virtues, commended this unto the world: for when he was born, the song of
the angels was, ' Peace upon earth, and good will
' towards men.' Luke ii. 14. All his doctrine was
peace, his whole life was peaceable, and ' no man
' heard his voice in the streets;' Matth. xii. 19.
his last legacy and bequest left unto his disciples
was the same; ' Peace,' faith he, ' I leave unto you,
' my peace I give unto you:' John xiv. 27. As
Christ, so Christians. In the building of Solomon's
Temple, there was no noise of any hammer, of any
instrument of iron; so in the spiritual building and
frame of a Christian, there is no sound of iron, no
noise of any weapons, nothing but peace and gentlenefs. ' Unadvised anger,' faith St. Austin, ' by
' the law of faith is as great a sin, as murther was

* Quam nobis apostoli totis viribus Spiritûs Sancti com-
mendant. De Patientia c. 12.

' by the law of Mofes *.' As fome phyficians have
thought, that in man's body, the fpleen hath
very little ufe, and might well be fpared; and
therefore in dealing with fundry difeafed perfons,
they endeavour by phyfic to abate, and take away
that part in them, as much as may be; fo if we
look into a Chriftian man, as he is propofed to us
in the gofpel, we may juftly marvel to what purpofe God hath planted in him this faculty and
paffion of anger, fince he hath fo little ufe of it;
and the gofpel, in a manner, doth fpiritually diet
and phyfic him for it, and endeavours much to a-
bate, if not quit to purge out, that quality.

Beloved, we have hitherto feen who Jacob is,
and what manner of man the Chriftian is, that is
defcribed unto us in holy fcripture. Let us a little
confider his brother Efau, the Chriftian in paffage, and who commonly, in the account of the
world, goes for one. Is he fo gentle and tractable
a creature? Is his countenance fo fmooth, his body fo free from gall and fpleen? To try this, as
the devil fometimes fpake unto Job, ' Touch him
' in his goods, touch him in his body, and fee if
' he will not curfe thee to thy face:' Job i. 10.
ii 9. fo touch this man a little in his goods, touch
him in his reputation and honour, touch him in
any thing that he loves, (for this is the only way
to try how far thefe commands of peace, and for-

* Ex praecepto fidei non minus rea ira eft fine ratione fuf-
cepta, quam in operibus legis homicidium.

bearance, and long suffering prevail with us) and
see if he will not forget and lose all his patience.
Which of us is there that understands the words
and precepts of our Saviour in their literal sense,
and as they lie? The precepts of suffering wrong,
rather than to go to law; of yielding the coat to
him that would take the cloak, of readiness to receive more wrongs, than to revenge one : these
and all the evangelical commands of the like nature we pervert by our comments: we have found
out favourable interpretations and glosses, restric-
tions and evasions, to wind ourselves out of them,
to shift them all off, and put them by, and yet
pass for sound and current Christians : we think
we may be justly angry, continue long suits in law,
call to the magistrate for revenge, yea, sometimes
take it into our own hands: all this and much more
we think we may lawfully, and with good reason
do, any precept of Christ to the contrary notwithstanding. And as it usually comes to pass, the
permitting and tolerating lesser sins opens way
to greater, so by giving passage and inlet to those
lesser impatiences and discontents, we lay open a
gap to those fouler crimes, even of murther and
bloodshed. For as men commonly suppose, that
all the former breaches of our patience, which but
now I mentioned, may well enough stand with
the duties of Christians : so there are who stay not
here, but think that in some cases it may be lawful, yea, peradventure necessary, at least very par-

donable, for Chriſtians privately to ſeek each o-
ther's blood, and put their lives upon their ſwords,
without any wrong to their vocation; out of this
have ſprung many great inconveniences, both private and public.

Firſt, Laws made too favourable in caſe of bloodſhed. *Secondly*, A too much facility and eaſineſs in
princes and magiſtrates ſometimes to give pardon
and releaſe for that crime. *Thirdly* and chiefly (for
it is the ſpecial cauſe indeed that moved me to ſpeak
in this argument) An over-promptneſs in many
young men, who deſire to be counted men of valour and reſolution, upon every ſlight occaſion to
raiſe a quarrel, and admit of no other means of
compoſing and ending it, but by ſword and ſingle
combat. Partly therefore to ſhew the grievouſneſs
and greatneſs of this ſin of bloodſhed, and partly
to give the beſt counſel I can for the reſtraint of
thoſe conceits and errors which give way unto it,
I have made choice of theſe few words out of the
Old Teſtament which but now I read. In the New
Teſtament there is no precept given concerning
bloodſhed. The apoſtles ſeem not to have thought
that Chriſtians ever ſhould have had need of ſuch
a prohibition; for what needed to forbid thoſe to
ſeek each other's blood, who are not permitted to
ſpeak over haſtily one to another. When therefore I had reſolved with myſelf to ſpeak ſomething
concerning the ſin of bloodſhed, I was in a manner conſtrained to reflect upon the Old Teſtament,

and make choice of thefe words; ' And the land
' cannot be purged of blood that is fhed in it, but
' by the blood of him that fhed it.'

In which words, for my more orderly proceeding, I will obferve thefe two general parts: *Firft*,
The greatnefs of the fin. *Secondly*, The means to
cleanfe and fatisfy for the guilt of it. The firft,
that is, the greatnefs of the fin, is expreffed by
two circumftances. *Firft*, By the generality, extent, and largenefs of the guilt of it: and *fecondly*,
By the difficulty of cleanfing it. The largenefs
and compafs of the guilt of this fin is noted unto
us in the word *land*, ' and the land cannot be purged.' It is true, in fome fenfe, of all fins, ' no man
' fins in private, and to himfelf alone*; ' for as
the fcripture notes of that action of Jeptha, when
he vowed his daughter unto God, ' That it be-
' came a cuftom in Ifrael,' Judg. xi. 39. fo is it
in all fins: the error is only in one perfon, but the
example fpreads far and wide; and thus every man
that fins, fins againft the whole land, yea, againft
the whole world. For who can tell how far the
example and infection of an evil action doth
fpread ? In other fins the infection is no larger
than the difeafe, but this fin like a plague; one
brings the infection, but thoufands die for it †;
yet this fin of blood diffufes and fpreads itfelf a-
bove all other fins; for in other fins the guilt of

* Nemo fibi uni errat.   Seneca de Vita Beata. c. i.

† 'Ολίκοντο δὲ λαοὶ.   Hom. Iliad. A. v. 9.

them is confined to the perſon that committed
them*; God himſelf hath pronounced of them,
' The ſon ſhall not bear the ſins of the father, the
' ſoul that ſinneth ſhall die the death : ' Ezech.
xviii. 20. But the ſin of blood ſeems to claim an
exception from this law ; if by time it be not purged, like the frogs of Egypt, the whole land ſtank
of them ; it leaves a guilt upon the whole land in
which it is committed. Other ſins come in like rivers, and break their banks to the prejudice and
wrong of private perſons; but this comes in like
a ſea, raging and threatening to overwhelm whole
countries. If blood in any land do lie unrevenged,
every particular ſoul hath cauſe to fear, leſt part
of the penalty fall on him. We read in 2 Sam xxi.
that long after Saul's death, God plagued the land
of Jewry with three years famine, becauſe Saul in
his life-time had, without any juſt cauſe, ſhed the
blood of ſome of the Gibeonites ; neither the famine ceaſed, till ſeven of Saul's nephews had died
for it. In this ſtory there are many things rare,
and worth our obſervation. Firſt, The generality
and extent of the guilt of bloodſhed, (which is
the cauſe for which I urged it,) it drew a general
famine on the whole land. Secondly, The continuance and length of the puniſhment; it laſted
full three years and better. Thirdly, The time
of the plague ; it fell long after the perſon of-

---

* Noxa ſequitur caput.

fending was dead. Fourthly, Whereas it is said in
my text, ' That blood is cleansed by the blood of
' him that shed it : ' here the blood of him that
did this sin sufficed not to purge the land from it ;
that desperate and woful end that befel both Saul
and his sons in that last and fatal battle upon Mount
Gilboa, a man may think had freed the land from
danger of blood : yet we see that the blood of the
Gibeonites had left so deep a stain, that it could
not be sponged out without the blood of seven
more of Saul's off-spring. So that in some cases it
seems we must alter the words of my text, ' The
' land cannot be purged of blood, but by the
' blood of him and his posterity that shed it.' St.
Paul tells us, that ' some men's sins go before them
' into judgment, and some men's sins follow after.'
1 Tim. v. 24. Beloved, here is a sin that exceeds
the members of this division, for howsoever it
goes before or after us unto judgment, yet it hath
a kind of ubiquity, and so runs afore, so follows
us at the heels, that it stays behind us too, and
calls for vengeance long after that we are gone.
Blood unrevenged passes from father to son like an
heirlome or legacy : and he that dies with blood
hanging on his fingers, leaves his off-spring and
his family as pledges to answer it in his stead. As
an engineer that works in a mine, lays a train, or
kindles a match, and leaves it behind him, which
shall take hold of the powder long after he is gone;
so he that sheds blood, if it be not betimes pur-

ged, as it were kindles a match, able to blow up not only a parliament, but even a whole land, where blood lies unrevenged.

Secondly, Another circumstance serving to express unto us the greatness of this sin, I told you, was the difficulty of cleansing it, intimated in those words, ' cannot be cleansed but by the blood of ' him that shed it.' Most of other sins have sundry ways to wash the guilt away; as in the Levitical Law, the woman that was unclean by reason of child-bearing, might offer a pair of turtle-doves, or two young pigeons: so he that travels with other sins, hath either a turtle or a pigeon, he hath more ways than one to purify him: prayer unto God, or true repentance, or satisfaction to the party wronged, or bodily affliction, or temporary mulct. But he that travels with the sin of blood, for him there remains no sacrifice for sin, but a fearful expectation of vengeance; he hath but one way of cleansing, only his blood, ' the blood of ' him that shed it.'

The *second* general part which we considered in these words, was, that one mean which is left to cleanse blood, exprest in the last words, ' the ' blood of him that shed it.' The Apostle to the Hebrews, speaking of the sacrifices of the Old Testament, notes, that without blood there was no cleansing, no forgiveness. He spake it only of the blood of beasts, of bulls and goats, who therefore have their blood, that they may shed it in man's service, and for man's use. But among all the Levitical sacrifices, there was not one to cleanse the manslayer; for the blood of the cattle upon a thousand hills was not sufficient for this, yet was that sin to be purged with blood too, and *that* by a more constant and perpetual law than that of sacrifices. For the cleansing of other sins by blood is done away; the date of it is out; but to cleanse blood by blood remains as a law to our times, and so shall unto the world's end: out of blood no way to get but by blood*. 'Hast thou shed blood?' saith St Basil, ' wouldst thou be free from the ' guilt of it? thy best way is to be a martyr, and ' shed thy blood for Christ's sake †.'

Now that what I have to say may the better be conceived and lodged up in your memories, I will comprehend and order all that I will speak under three heads. *First*, I will, in general, yet a little further, briefly shew how great a sin the sin of blood is. *Secondly*, I will speak of the redress of some misorders very frequent in our age, which give way to this sin, especially private revenge and single combat. *Thirdly*, I will touch at the means of taking the guilt of blood away, which here the Hold Ghost commends to those which are set in authority to that purpose.

And *first*, of the greatness of the crime and sin of blood. Of sins in holy scripture there be two

* ——Sanguine quaerendi reditus. Aeneid. ii. 118.

† 'Εφονευσας; μαρτυρησον.

forts recorded. One fort is a filent, dumb, and quiet fin ; God doth, as it were, feek after it to find it, as the people did after Saul, when he was hidden amongft the ftuff: of this nature are the ordinary fins of our life, which do more eafily find pardon at the hands of God ; but there is a fecond fort of fin, which is a vocal and a crying fin, a fin, like that importunate widow in the gofpel, that will not fuffer the judge to be quiet, till he hath done juftice ; and thofe are the more heavy and grievoufer fins of our lives: of this fecond fort, there are two fins, to which the fcripture doth attribute this crying faculty. Firft, the fin of Sodom ; for fo God tells Abraham, ' The cry of So- ' dom and Gomorrha is come up before me.' Gen. xviii. 20. The fecond is the fin of which I am now to fpeak, the fin of bloodfhed ; for fo God tells Cain, ' The voice of thy brother's blood cries ' unto me from the earth.' Gen. iv. 10. The fin of Adam in paradife doubtlefs was a great and heinous fin, which hath thus made us all the children of death ; yet it feems to be but of the rank of mute fins, and to have had no voice to betray it ; God comes unto Adam, convents him, examines him, as if he had not known it, and feems not to believe any fuch thing was done, till himfelf had confeffed it. But blood is an unmannerly, importunate, and clamorous fin, God fhall not need to come and enquire after it, it will come up unto him, and cry as the fouls do under the altar

in the Revelation, 'How long, Lord, how long?'
it suffers not God to forget judgment, or entertain
a thought of mercy *. To satisfy therefore the cry
of this importunate sin, and to shew men the grie-
vousness of it, the laws of God and men have wonderfully conspired in the avenging of blood, by
what means, or by what creature soever it were
shed. Beasts, unreasonable creatures, though whatsoever they do, they cannot be said to sin : for
whatsoever they do, they do by force of that natural instinct, by which they are guided and led as
by their proper law; yet man's blood, if they shed
it, is revenged upon them : God himself is the author of this law, (Gen. ix. 5.) where he tells Noah,
' The blood of your lives I will require, at the hands
' of every beast will I require it :' and accordingly
in Exodus, he precisely enacts a law of the ox that
goreth, ' If an ox gore a man that he die, the ox shall
' be slain, and the flesh cast away as an abominati-
' on.' xxi. 2 8. The laws of natural men, who had
no knowledge of God, come little behind this; yea,
they may seem to have gone before it in severe revenging of blood : for amongst the laws by which
Athens, that famous city of Greece, was governed,
there was one, that if a wall by chance had fallen
down, and slain a man, as the tower of Siloam
did, of which we read in the gospel; that then the
judges should sit, and formally arraign that wall,

---

* Neque per nostrum patimur scelus
Iracunda Jovem ponere fulmina.   Horat. od. i.

condemn it, and throw the ſtones of it out of the country*. This ſo formal proceeding againſt un-reaſonable, againſt dull and ſenſeleſs creatures, hath been thus jointly both by God and man prac-tiſed, only for our example, to teach us how pre-cious the life of man ought to be in our eyes: and it reſembles that action of Chriſt in the goſpel, where, for our inſtruction, he curſes the barren fig-tree †.

Now as exemplary juſtice is ſeverely done on theſe creatures for man's inſtruction; ſo much more if man himſelf keep not his hands clean from blood, did the laws of God proceed with much ſtrictneſs and ſeverity: for to ſay nothing of groſs, malicious, and wilful murther; if a man only in his haſte ſtrook another with a weapon, or with a ſtone, ſo that he died, though the ſtriker intended but to hurt, yet he was to die for it. That he did it in anger, that he did it in his drink, that he did it provoked, that he did it in defence of his honour and reputation, none of all theſe pretences might excuſe him. Nay, which is yet more, God him-ſelf propounds the caſe; ' If,' ſaith he, ' a man ' cleaving wood, his ax head flie off, and hit his ' neighbour, ſo that he kills him,' Deut. xix. 5. except he could recover one of the cities of re-fuge, he was to die; and having recovered a city of refuge, if before the death of the high prieſt he

* Vid. Petit. in Leg. Attic. lib. vii. tit. 1. p. 523.
† Sterilitas noſtra in ficu vapulat.

were taken without the walls of the city, he was
to die. So ſtrict was God in the caſe of chance-
medley, (as they call it) in a caſe which he takes
unto himſelf, and makes himſelf the author of.
For in the xxi. of Exodus 13. ſpeaking of the man
that thus ſheds blood by chance and unwittingly,
his words are theſe, ' If a man lie not in wait, but
' God put him into his hands, I will appoint him a
' city of refuge to flie unto.' In which words God
acknowledges, that he who thus dies by chance,
dies by his providence, and not by the ſin of him
that ſlew him. ' If God (ſaith he) ſhall put him
' into his hands;' yet you ſee what a penalty he
lays upon the innocent inſtrument of ſuch bloodſhed. The blood that is ſhed in battle, and in
times of lawful war, you all ſuppoſe as lawfully
ſhed; yet notwithſtanding, Moſes, in the xvi. of
Numbers, gives charge, that the ſoldiers returning from battle, ſhould ſtay a while without the
camp, even ſeven days, until they were cleanſed:
again, when David adviſed with himſelf about the
building of an houſe unto God, he ſends him
word to lay by all thought of that, he was no fit
perſon to do it; and he gives the reaſon of it,
' For thou art a man haſt ſhed much blood, and
' fought many battles.' 1 Chr. xxviii. 3. Beloved, the battles which David fought were called
the Lord's battles, and therefore whatſoever he
did in that kind, he had doubtleſs very good warrant to do; and yet you ſee, that it is an impu-

tation to him, that he fhed blood, though lawfully; fo that it feems blood cannot be juftly fhed,
but that it brings with it fome ftain and fpot of
injuftice †.

All this I have faid to raife up in you, as much
as poffibly I can, a right conceit of the height and
heinoufnefs of this fin, and further, yet to effect
this in you, as in the beginning and entrance into
my difcourfe, I briefly toucht at two reafons, fhewing the greatnefs of this fin, occafioned thereunto
by the words of my text: fo will I as briefly touch
at the two more tending to the fame purpofe; one
drawn from the refpect of the wrong, which by
this fin is done unto God; another from the wrong
done to ourfelves.

And *firft*, what wrong is done unto God: God
himfelf fhews us in the ix. of Genefis ; where
giving this for an everlafting law, ' He that fhed-
' deth man's blood, by man let his blood be fhed;'
he prefently adds the reafon of it, ' for in the image
' of God made he man.' v. 6. We fhall the better underftand the force of this reafon, if we look
a little into civil actions. It is the ufual manner of
fubjects, when they rebel againft the prince, to
think they cannot more effectually exprefs their
hate, than by difgracing, breaking, throwing down
the ftatues and images erected to his honour: The
citizens of Antioch, in a fedition againft Theodo-

† Ut fundi fanguis ne jufte quidem, fine aliqua injuftitia
poffit.

fius the Emperor, in one night difgracefully threw down all his ftatues; which fact of theirs caufed St. Chryfoftom, at that time preacher to that city, to make thofe famous fermons, which from that action to this day are called ' his ftatues*.' This by fo much the more is counted a great offence, becaufe, next unto wronging and difgracing the very perfon of the prince, a greater infolence cannot be offered : for it expreffeth with what welcome they would entertain him, if they had him in their power. Beloved, man is the image of his Maker, erected by him as a ftatue of his honour : he then that fhall defpitefully handle, batter, and deface it, how can he be counted otherwife than guilty of the higheft treafon againft his Maker. ' Rebel-' lion,' faith Samuel to Saul, ' is like the fin of ' fuperftition and idolatry.' 1 Sam. xv. 23. The fin of blood therefore equals the fin of idolatry, fince there cannot be a greater fin of rebellion a-gainft God, than to deface his image. Idolatry, through ignorance, fets up a falfe image of God, but this fin, through malice, defaces, pulls down the true. Amongft the Heathen, fometimes the ftatues of the Emperors were had in fuch refpect, that they were accounted fanctuaries, and fuch as for offence fled unto them, it was not lawful to touch. Beloved, fuch honour ought we to give unto a man, that if he have offended us, yet the image of God which fhines in him ought to be as

* Ἀνδριάντες.

a sanctuary unto him, to save him from our violence, an admonitioner unto us, that we ought not to touch him.

A *second* reason, yet further shewing the heinousness of this sin, is drawn from the wrong which is done to ourselves. All other wrongs, whatsoever they be, admit of some recompence; honours, wealth, preferments, if they be taken from us, they may return, as they did unto Job, in far greater measure, and the party wronged may receive full and ample satisfaction; but, what recompence may be made to a man for his life? When that is gone, all the kingdoms which our Saviour saw in the mount, and the glory of them, are nothing worth, neither is all the world, all the power of men and angels, able to give the least breath to him that hath lost it. Nothing under God is able to make satisfaction for such a wrong: the revenge that is taken afterward upon the party that hath done the wrong, cannot be counted a recompence; that is done to the terror of the living, not for the aid of the dead †; it serves to deter the living from committing the like outrage, but it can no way help him that is dead: David at the same time committed two sins, great sins, murther and adultery; the reward of either of which, by God's law, is nothing else but death; yet for his adultery he seems to make some satisfaction to the party wronged; for the text notes, that

† In terrorem viventium, non in subsidium mortuorum.

David took her to his wife, made her his queen,
and that he went in unto her, and comforted her:
all which may well be counted at leaft a part of recompence. But for dead Urias, what means could
David make to recompence, to comfort him? For
this caufe I verily fuppofe it is, that in his peniten-
tial pfalm, wherein he bewails his fin, he makes
no particular confeffion, no mention of his adultery; but of the other, of blood, he is very fenfible, and exprefly prays againft it: ' Deliver me
' from blood-guiltinefs, O God, thou God of my
' falvation;' Pf. li. 14. as if adultery in comparifon of murder were no crime at all.

I am forry I fhould have any juft occafion a-
mongft Chriftian men, fo long to infift upon a
thing fo plain; and fhew that the fin of blood is a
great and heinous fin: but, he that fhall look into
the neceffities of thefe times, fhall quickly fee that
there is a great caufe why this doctrine fhould be
very effectually preft: for many things are even
publicly done, which in part argue that men e-
fteem of this fin much more flightly than they
ought. Ariftotle obferved it of Phaleas, one that
took upon him to prefcribe laws by which a commonwealth might, as he thought, be well governed, ' That he had taken order for the preventing
' of fmaller faults, but he left way enough open
' to greater crimes *.' Beloved, the error of our

* "Ωϛι πρὸς τὰς μικρὰς ἀδικίας βοηθητικὸς μόνον ὁ τρόπος
τῆς Φαλίν πολιτείας. Polit. lib. ii. c. 7.

laws is not fo great as that of Phaleas was;
yet we offend too, though on the contrary, and
the lefs dangerous fide; for great and grievous
fins are by them providently curbed, but many inferior crimes find many times too free paffage.
Murther, though all be abominable, yet there are
degrees in it, fome is more heinous than other.
Grofs, malicious, premeditated, and wilful murther, are by our laws, fo far as human wifdom can
provide, fufficiently prevented: 'but murders done
in hafte, or befides the intent of him that did it,
or in point of honour and reputation, thefe find a
little too much favour; our laws in this refpect
are fomewhat defective, both in preventing that it
be not done, and punifhing it when it is done;
men have thought themfelves wifer than God, pre-
fuming to moderate the unneceffary feverity (as
they feem to think) of his laws. And hence it comes
to pafs, that in military companies, and in all great
cities and places of mart and concourfe, few months,
yea, few weeks, pafs without fome inftance and
example of bloodfhed, either by fudden quarrel, or by challenge to duel and fingle combat. How
many examples, in a fhort fpace, have we feen of
young men, men of hot and fiery difpofition, mutually provoking and difgracing each other, and
then taking themfelves bound in high terms of valour, and honour, to end their quarrels by their
fwords? That therefore we may the better difcover the unlawfulnefs of challenge and private

combat, let us a little enquire and examine in what cafes blood may lawfully, and without offence, be fhed; that fo we may fee where, amongft thefe, fingle combat may find its place.

The Manichees were of opinion, that it was not lawful to violate any thing in which there was life; and therefore they would not pull a branch from a tree, becaufe, forfooth, there was life in it. To think that man's life may in no cafe be taken from him, is but a branch of Manicheifm : and the words of my text do directly crofs it, where it is laid down, that for the cleanfing of blood, blood may and muft be fhed. For the a-voiding therefore of the extreme, we are to note, that the lawful caufes of bloodfhed are either pu-blic or private: public cafes are two; firft, in cafe of juftice, when a malefactor dies for his fin by the hand of the magiftrate. Secondly, in cafe of public war and defence of our country; for the doctrine of Chrift is not, as fome have fuppofed, an enemy to foldierfhip and military difcipline. When John the Baptift began to preach repen-tance and amendment of life, amongft thofe that came forth to underftand and learn their duty, the text faith, that ' the foldiers came and afked him, ' Mafter, what fhall we do?' Luke iii. 14. And John wills them not to lay down their weapons, or to take another courfe of life (which he ought and would have done, if that courfe had been unlaw-ful) but he inftructs them rather in their calling;

for, he gives them thefe two leffons, ' Do no man
' wrong ; and, Be content with your pay, your
' wages;' than which there could not have been
better, or more pertinent counfel given to foldiers,
thefe being the two principal vices of foldiers, to
wrong places where they live, by forage and pil-
lage, and to mutiny in diflike of their pay. When
St. Peter came to preach to the Centurion in the
Acts, we find not a fyllable in all that fermon prejudicial to a foldier's profeffion. And therefore,
accordingly, in the times of the primitive church,
Chriftians ferved even under Heathen Emperors,
and *that* with the approbation of God himfelf.

For in the ecclefiafic ftory we read of the *Le-
gio fulminatrix*, of a band of foldiers called the
Thundering Band, becaufe that at what time Marcus the Emperor lying with his army in Germany,
was afflicted with a great drought, and in great
danger of the enemy, when they were now about
to join battle, the Chriftian foldiers (that band) fell
flat on their faces, and by their inftant prayers ob-
tained of God a great tempeft, which to the Emperor and his army brought ftore of cold refrefh-
ing water; but upon the enemy nothing elfe but
fire and whirl-wind. The Emperor's epiftle, in
which this ftory is related, is this day extant, recovered by Juftin Martyr, who lived about the
time the thing was done † : wherefore we may not

† This ftory of the Thundering Legion is generally exploded among the learned. That the Roman army was relie-

doubt of the lawfulnefs of that profeffion, which
it hath pleafed God thus to grace, and honour with
fuch a miracle. Befides thefe two, there are no other
public caufes of bloodfhed. As for the caufes in
private, I know but one, and that is, when a man
is fet upon, and forced to it, in his own defence.
If a thief be robbing in the night, and be flain,
the law of God acquits him that did it : and by
the Roman laws it was lawful to kill a thief by
night at any hand, and by day if he ufed his weapon *. Of private bloodfhed there is no caufe but
this, and this we muft needs allow of. For in
all other private neceffities into which we may be

ved by a plentiful rain feems undeniable; but that this rain
was procured by the prayers of Chriftian foldiers is not probable. Eufebius, after having related this incident in the words
of Tertullian, adds, But of this let every one judge as he
thinks fit. ἀλλὰ ταῦτα μὲν ὅπη τις ἐθέλη τίθεσθω. Hift. Ecclef.
lib. v. c. 5. With refpect to the Emperor's epiftle, here mentioned, it is univerfally confeffed to be a forgery, and that of
a much later date than the age of Juftin Martyr. Even Hue-
tius, credulous and incorrect as he is, gives it up. His words
are, ' Habetur harum literarum exemplar apud Juftinum, ad
' calcem Apologiae fecundae ; fed ejus νοθείαν et κιβδηλίαν,
' tam etiam novitatem, quod Juftiniano recentius fit, tot ar-
' gumentis approbarunt viri eruditi, et criticae artis principes,
' Jofephus Scaliger et Salmafius, ut nihil contra opponi poffit.'
Demonft. Evangel. propof. iii. §. 19.

* Lex duodecim tabularum *furem noctu deprehenfum occi-*
dere permittit; ut tamen id ipfum cum clamore teftificetur.
Interdiu autem *deprehenfum ita permittit occidere, fi is fe telo*
defendat, ut tamen aequè cum clamore teftificetur. L. iv.
§. 1. Dig. ad Leg. Aquil.

driven, the law and magiftrate have place, to whom we muft repair for remedy: but in cafe of defence of life againft fudden onfet, no law can be made, except we would make a law to yield our throats to him that would cut them, or our laws were like the prophet that came to Jeroboam at Bethel, and could dry up men's arms that offered violence. Wherefore all caufe of death, one only excepted, is public, and that for great reafon. For to die is not a private action to be undertaken at our own, or at any other private man's pleafure and difcretion: for, as we are not born unto ourfelves alone, but for the fervice of God, and the commonwealth in which we live; fo no man dies to himfelf alone, but with the damage and lofs of that church or commonwealth of which he is a member: wherefore it is not left to any private man's power to difpofe of any man's life, no not to our own, only God and the magiftrate may difpofe of this. As foldiers in the camp muft keep their ftanding, neither may they move or alter, but by direction from the captain; fo is it with us all: our life is a warfare, and every man in the world hath his ftation and place, from whence he may not move at his own, or at another man's pleafure, but only at the direction and appointment of God, his general, or of the magiftrates, which are as captains and lieutenants under him. Then our lawful times of death are either when our day is come, or to fall in battle, or for mifdemeanour to be cut off by the public hand of juſtice, ' that ' the public might profit by the death of thoſe, ' who, while living, would not be uſeful *.' He which otherwiſe dies, comes by ſurreption and ſtealth, and not warrantably, unto his end.

And though we have ſpoken ſomething in apology and defence of war, yet you may not think, that in time of war your hands are looſe, and that you may at your pleaſure ſhed the blood of your enemy: ' Even in war and battle (ſaith St. Auſtin) ' there is room for thoughts of peace and ' mercy †;' and therefore many of the antient heroes, renowned ſoldiers and captains, were very conſcientious of ſhedding the blood of their enemies, except it were in battle, and when there was no remedy to avoid it. In that mortal battle, 2 Sam. ii. 22, 23. between the ſervants of David and the ſervants of Iſboſheth, the ſcripture reports that Abner fled, and Azahel, Joab's brother, following him hard at heels to kill him, Abner adviſes him twice, ' Turn aſide,' ſaith he, ' why ſhould ' I ſmite thee to the ground;' but when Azahel would not hearken, but followed him ſtill for his blood, then he ſtruck him with his ſpear that he died: in the time of war, when he might lawfully have done it, in the fury of the battle, Abner

* Ut qui vivi prodeſſe noluerunt, eorum morte reſpublica utatur.

† Miſericorditer enim, ſi fieri poſſet etiam bella gererentur a bonis. Epiſt. cxxxviii.

would not shed blood, but by constraint. Xenophon would make us believe, that the soldiers in
Cyrus his army were so well disciplined, that one
of them in time of the battle, having lift up his
arm to strike his enemy, hearing the trumpet to
begin to sound the retreat, let fall his arm, and
willingly lost his blow, because he thought the
time of striking was now past * : so far were these
men from thinking it lawful to shed the blood of
a subject in time of peace, that they would not
shed the blood of an enemy in time of war, except it were in the field. Julius Caesar was one of
the greatest and stoutest captains that ever was in
the world, he stood the shock of fifty set battles,
besides all sieges and out-roads ; he took a thousand cities and walled towns ; he over-run three
hundred several countreys, and in his wars were
slain well near twelve hundred thousand men, besides all those that died in the civil wars, which
were great numbers ; yet this man protested of
himself, and that most truly, ' that he never drew
' blood but in the field, never slew any man, but
' in a set battle † :' I have been a little the bolder,
in bringing these instances of Heathen men ; First,
because the doctrine of Christ, through error, is

* This is related of a Spartan by Plutarch. Apotheg. La-
con. in fin.

† Quod dicere solebat, praestitit, neminem occidit nisi ar-
matum. *Seneca de Benef. lib.* v. c. 16. Neminem nisi acie
consumptum civem patria desideravit. *Vell. Paterc. lib.* ii.

counted an enemy to policy of war and martial discipline: Secondly, because we have found out many distinctions and evasions to elude the precepts of our blessed Saviour and his apostles: for as it hath been observed of the god-makers, I mean the painters and statuaries among the Heathen, they were wont many times to paint their goddesses like their mistresses, and then think them most fair, when they were most like what they best loved: so is it with many professors of Christian religion, they can temper the precepts of it to their liking, and lay upon them glosses and interpretations as it were colours, and make it look like what they love: Thirdly, because it is likely that the examples of these men will most prevail with those to whom I speak, as being such to whom above all they affect to be most like; except therefore it be their purpose to hear no other judgment, but only their own unruly and misorderly affections, it cannot but move them to see the examples of men, guided only by the light of reason, of men, I say, the most famous in all the world for valour and resolution, to run so mainly against them.

To come then unto the question of duels; both by the light of reason, and by the practice of men it doth appear, that there is no case wherein subjects may privately seek each other's lives: there are extant the laws of the Jews, framed by God himself; the laws of the Roman em-

pire, made partly by the Ethnic, partly by Christian princes; a great part of the laws of Sparta and
Athens (two warlike commonwealths, especially
the former) lie dispersed in our books; yet a-
mongst them all is there not a law or custom that
permits this liberty to subjects: the reason of it,
I conceive, is very plain; the principal thing, next
under God, by which a commonwealth doth stand,
is the authority of the magistrate, whose proper
end is to compose and end quarrels between man
and man, upon what occasion soever they grow;
for were men peaceable, were men not injurious
one to another, there were no use of government:
wherefore to permit men in private to try their
own rights, or to avenge their own wrongs, and
so to decline the sentence of the magistrate, is
quite to cut off all use of authority. Indeed it hath
been sometimes seen, that the event of a battle, by
consent of both armies, hath been put upon single
combat, to avoid further effusion of blood; but
combats betwixt subjects for private causes, till
these latter ages of the world, was never allowed:
yet, I must confess, the practice of it is very antient; for Cain, the second man in the world, was
the first duelist, the first that ever challenged the
field; the text saith, that Cain spake unto his brother, and when they were in the field, he arose
and slew him. Gen. iv. 8. The Septuagint, to
make the sense more plain, do add another clause,

and tell us what it was he faid unto his brother;
' Let us go out into the field*;' and when they were
in the field, he arofe and flew him: ' Let us go
' out into the field,' it is the very form and proper language of a challenge. Many times indeed
our gallants can formalize in other words, but e-
vermore the fubftance, and ufually the very words
are no other but thefe of Cain, ' Let us go out
' into the field.' Abel, I perfuade myfelf, underftood them not as a challenge; for had he fo done,
he would have made fo much ufe of his difcretion,
as to have refufed it; yet can we not chufe but
acknowledge a fecret judgment of God in this,
that the words of Cain fhould ftill be fo religioufly kept till this day, as a proeme and introduction
to that action, which doubtlefs is no other than
what Cain's was. When therefore our gallants are
fo ready to challenge the field, and to go into the
field, let them but remember whofe words they
ufe, and fo accordingly think of their action.

Again, notwithftanding duels are of fo antient
and worfhipful a parentage, yet could they never
gain fo good acceptance as to be permitted, much
lefs to be counted lawful, in the civil part of the
world, till barbarifm had over-ran it. About five
or fix hundred years after Chrift, at the fall of the
Roman empire, abundance of rude and barbarous
people brake in and poffeft the civiler part of the

* Διήλθωμεν εἰς τὸ πεδίον.

I 3

world; who abolifhing the antient laws of the empire, fet up many ftrange cuftoms in their rooms.
Amongft the reft, for the determining of quarrels
that might arife in cafe of doubtful title, or of
falfe accufation, or the like, they put themfelves
upon many unufual forms of trial; as, to handle
red hot iron, to walk bare-foot on burning coals,
to put their hands and feet in fcalding water, and
many other of the like nature, which are reckoned up by Hottoman a French lawyer : for they
prefumed fo far on God's providence, that if the
party accufed were innocent, he might do any of
thefe without any fmart or harm. In the fame cafes, when by reafon of unfufficient and doubtful
evidence, the judges could not proceed to fentence, as fometimes it falls out, and the parties
contending would admit of no reafonable compo-
fition, their manner was to permit them to try it
out by their fwords; that fo the conqueror might
be thought to be in the right. They permitted,
I fay, thus to do; for at the beft it was but a permiffion to prevent farther mifchief; for to this
end fometimes fome known abufes are tolerated :
fo God permitted the Jews upon flight occafions
to put their wives away, becaufe he faw, that o-
therwife their exorbitant lufts would not be
bounded within thefe limits, which he in paradife
in the beginning had fet. And it is obferved of
the wife men which had the managing and bringing up of Nero the Emperor, that they fuffered

him to practise his lusts upon Acte, one of his mother's chamber-maids, ' Left if he were forbidden
' that, he should turn his lust upon some of the
' noblewomen †.' Permission and toleration warrants not the goodness of any action. But, as
Caiaphas said, ' Better one man die, than all the
' people perish;' John xi. 50. so they that first
permitted duels seem to have thought, better one
or two mutinous persons, and disorderly, die in
their folly, than the whole commonwealth be put
into tumult and combustion: yet even by these
men it was never so promiscuously tolerated, that
every hasty couple, upon the venting of a little
choler, should presently draw their swords; but
it was a public or solemn action, done by order,
with inspection, either of the prince himself, or of
some other magistrate appointed to order it. Now
certainly there can be no very great reason for that
action, which was thus begun by Cain, and continued only by Goths and Vandals, and mere barbarism.

Yet that we may a little better acquaint ourselves with the quality of it, let us a little examine
the causes and pretences which are brought by
them who call for trial by single combat. The
causes are usually two; First, disdain to seem to
do or suffer any thing for fear of death: Se-

† Ne in stupra foeminarum illustrium perrumperet, si illa
libidine prohiberetur. Tacit. Annal. xiii. c. 12.

condly, point of honour, and not to suffer any contumely and indignity, especially if it bring with it disreputation, and note of cowardise. For the first, disdain to fear death; I must confess I have often wondered with myself, how men durst die so ventrously, except they were sure they died well: in other things which are learned by practising, if we mistake, we may amend it; for the error of a former action may be corrected in the next: we learn then by erring, and men come at length not to err, by having often erred: but no man learns to die by practising it; we die but once, and a fault committed then, can never afterward be amended, because the punishment immediately follows upon the error †. To die is an action of that moment, that we ought to be very well advised when we come to it; on that moment hangs eternity: you may not look back upon the opinion of honour and reputation which remains behind you: but rather look forward upon that infinite space of eternity, either of bliss or bale, which befals us immediately after our last breath. To be loth to die upon every slight occasion, is not a necessary sign of fear and cowardise: he that knew what life is, and the true use of it, had he many lives to spare, yet would he be

† In aliis rebus siquid erratum est, potest post modum corrigi, quia poena statim sequitur errorem. *Alluding to a saying of Cato recorded by Vegetius.* lib. i. c. 13.

loth to part with one of them upon better terms,
than thofe our books tell us, that Ariftippus a
philofopher being at fea in a dangerous tempeft,
and bewraying fome fear, when the weather was
cleared up, a defperate ruffian came and upbraided
him with it, and tells him, That it was a fhame
that he, profeffing wifdom, fhould be afraid of his
life ; whereas himfelf, having had no fuch education, expreft no agony or dread at all. To whom
the philofopher replied, there was fome difference
between them two : ‘ I know,’ faith he, ‘ my life
‘ may be profitable many ways, and therefore am
‘ I loth to lofe it ; but becaufe of your life you
‘ know little profit, little good can be made, you
‘ care not how eafily you part with it †.’ Beloved, it may be juftly fufpected, that they who e-
fteem thus lightly of their lives, are but worth-
lefs and unprofitable men : our own experience
tells us, that men who are prodigal of their money in taverns and ordinaries, are clofe-handed
enough, when either pious ufes, or neceffary and
public expence requires their liberality ; I have
not heard that prodigals ever built churches. So
thefe men that are fo prodigal of their lives in
bafe quarrels, peradventure would be coward-
ly enough, if either public fervice, or religion
did call for their help ; I fcarcely believe any of
them would die martyrs, if the times fo requi-

† Diog. Laert. vita Ariftip. A. Gellius. lib. xix. c. 1.

red it. Beloved, I do do not go about to perfuade any man to fear death, but not to contemn life; life is the greateft bleffing God gives in this world, and did men know the worth of it, they would never fo rafhly venture the lofs of it: but now lightly prizing both their own and others blood, they are eafily moved to fhed it; as fools are eafily won to part with jewels, becaufe they know not how to value them. We muft deal with our lives, as we do with our money, we muft not be covetous of it, defire life for no other ufe but to live, as covetous perfons defire money, only to have it: neither muft we be prodigal of life, and trifle it away upon every occafion; but we muft be liberal of our lives, know upon what occafion to fpare, upon what occafion to fpend them. To know where, and when, and in what cafes to offer ourfelves to die, is a thing of greater fkill than a great part of them fuppofe, who pretend themfelves moft forward to do it; for brutifhly to run upon and haften unto death, is a thing that many men can do; and we fee that brute beafts many times will run upon the fpears of fuch as purfue them: but wifely to look into, and weigh every occafion, and, as judgment and true difcretion fhall direct, fo to entertain a refolution either of life or death; this were true fortitude and magnanimity *. And indeed,

* Nam impetu quodam et inftinctu currere ad mortem commune cum multis; deliberare vero et caufas ejus expen-

this prodigality and contempt of life is the greateſt ground of this quarrellous and fighting humour. There is a kind of men, who, becauſe they con-temn their own lives, make themſeves lords and commanders of other men's, eaſily provoking o-thers to venture their blood, becauſe they care not how they loſe their own *. Few places of great reſort are without theſe men, and they are the greateſt occaſioners of bloodſhed, you may quick-ly know them; there are few quarrels wherein they are not either principals, or ſeconds, or ſome way or another will have a part in them. Might there be public order taken for the reſtraint of ſuch men, that make a practice of quarrelling, and becauſe they contemn their own lives, carry them-ſelves ſo inſolently and imperiouſly towards others: it will prevent much miſchief, and free the land of much danger of blood-guiltineſs.

The ſecond cauſe which is much alledged in defence of duels, I told you was point of honour, a conceit that it is diſhonourable for men of place and faſhion quietly to digeſt and put up contume-ly and diſgrace; and this they take to be a reaſon of that authority and ſtrength, as that it muſt ad-mit of no diſpenſation.

For anſwer, Firſt, the true fountain and origi-

dere utque ſuaſerit ratio vitae mortiſque conſilium ſuſcipere, vel ponere ingentis eſt animi. Plin. Epiſt. lib. i. c. 22.

* Quiſquis ſuam vitam contempſit, tuae dominus eſt. Se-nec. Epiſt 4.

nal of quarrel are of another kind, and honour is abufed as a pretence : the firft occafioners of a great part of them are indeed very difhonourable; let there an inventory be taken of all the challenges that have been made for fome time paft, and you fhall find that the greateft part by far were raifed either in taverns, or dicing-houfes, or in the ftews : pardon me, if in a cafe of this nature I deal a little plainly ; drinking, gaming, and whores, thefe are thofe rotten bones that lie hid under this painted fepulchre and title of honour.

Laftly, to conclude, It is a part of our profeffion, as we are Chriftians, to fuffer wrong and difgrace. Therefore to fet up another doctrine, and teach that honour may plead prefcription againft Chrift's precepts, and exempt you from patient enduring of contumely and difgrace, you withftand Chrift, and deny your vocation ; and therefore are unavoidably apoftates. But we lofe our labour, who give young men and unfettled perfons good advice and counfel; the civil magiftrate muft lay to his hand and pity them, who want difcretion to pity themfelves: for as bees, though they fight very fiercely, yet if you caft a little duft amongft them, are prefently parted ; fo the enacting and executing fome few good laws, would quickly allay this greatnefs of ftomach and fighting humour. How many have been cenfured for fchifmatics and heretics, only becaufe by probable confequence, and afar off, they feemed to overthrow fome Chriftian principle? But here are men, who walk in our ftreets, and come to our churches, who openly oppofe that great point of Chriftianity, which concerns our patience, and yet for their reftraint, no fynod is called, no magiftrate ftirs, no church-cenfure is pronounced. The church of Rome hath, long ago, to the difgrace of the reformed churches, fhut them out of the number of Chriftians, and pronounced them all excommunicated perfons, who, upon what pretence foever, durft enter the field for duel and fingle combat.

Theodofius the Emperor enacted it for a law, and it is extant at this day in the Code, a book of laws, that if any man fpake difgracefully of the Emperor ' from levity, it fhould be defpifed, if ' from madnefs, held worthy of pity, but if with ' an injurious intention, forgiven *.'

So great a virtue is patience, that for the attaining of it, it is God's will we fhould fuffer ourfelves to be contemned as cowards †.

Chrift is an example to us of fuffering difgrace; let us as the Ifraelites look up to this ferpent, and all the ftinging of fiery ferpents fhall do us no harm.

---

† Si ex levitate procefferit, contemnendum eft, fi ex infania, miferatione digniffimum, fi ex injuria, remittendum. Cod. Theodof. l. ix. T. 4. l. 1.

* Summa virtus habenda patientia eft, quam ut caperet homo juftus voluit illum Deus pro inerte contemni. Lactant. de vero cultu. lib. vi. c. 18.

We muſt forſake all and follow Chriſt: there-fore honour and reputation too; if we be aſhamed of this pattern of patience, Chriſt will be aſhamed of us.

Now that God may give a bleſſing to what hath been delivered, let us &c.

THE
DANGER
OF RECEIVING
OUR GOOD THINGS
IN
THIS LIFE.

Preached at Shrove-tide at Eaton-College.[*]

Luke xvi. 25.

*San, remember that thou in thy life-time receivedſt
thy good things.*

FIRST SERMON ON THE TEXT

THAT man of miſery, whoſe woful end occaſioned this diſcourſe in St. Luke, whence
I have choſen out theſe few words as my ſubject
to treat of at this time, much deſires that one

---

[*] *The Author entitles this ſermon, ‘ The Rich Man’s Recepiſti ;’ and conſtantly uſes the word in the Vulgate recepiſti, ‘ thou
‘ haſt received,’ as a noun. Such modes of ſpeech were common
in the age of the author, but now they appear uncouth and pe-
dantic. The editor therefore has preſumed to vary the phraſe,*

from the dead might be fent unto his brethren, to
give them warning that they come not into that
place of torment in which himfelf was.   May I
not at this time juftly feem to be that meffenger?
For methinks I come into the pulpit, as young Po-
lydore, in the tragedy, enters the ftage, and may
fpeak unto you as he did unto his auditors in another
language, ' I come from the pit of the dead, from
' the gates of utter darknefs, where the devil hath
' his manfion far removed from God *.' Firft, the
fadnefs of the meffage with which I come might
eafily tempt you to think fo, as being very unwelcome to the ears of flefh and blood; for, where
death is not reft, where fhall we find reft? in what
fhall we joy, if the good things of our life deceive
us? Certainly fo difconfolate a piece of news could
never come, but from fome place of extreme fadnefs.   Secondly, the unfitnefs of the time might
help on well to this conceit: there is, faith Abraham in this fcripture, ' there is a great gulph be-
' twixt you and us.'   Beloved, the difference betwixt thofe two places here mentioned is not
much greater, than is the diftance betwixt my
text and this time; for the time invites you to
that, from which my text affrights you: eating,

and, inftead of a recepifti, _has ufed the expreffions,_ ' _an expro-_
' _bation for having received, — the doom thou haft received,_' _or_
others of like import.

* Ἥκω νεκρῶν κευθμῶνα καὶ σκότυ πύλας——Διπὼν, ἵν' Ἅδης
χωρὶς ὤκισαι Θιῶν.   Eurip. Hecub. v. 1.

drinking, merry-making, all the reſt of this rich man's daily ſervice*, theſe are the ſubjeſt of the time; but my text pulls you by the ear, and bids you beware, leſt even theſe good things (for ſo men commonly call them) may be amongſt thoſe things, which when time comes, may draw after them this ' remember ;' you may be told, Remember you had your Shrove-tide; for what elſe, I beſeech you, was the whole life of this miſerable man here, but in a manner a perpetual ſhroving?

But neither the ſourneſs of the meſſage, nor any pretended unſeaſonableneſs of the times, muſt hinder us from communicating unto you what the Spirit of God ſhall put into our hearts. Let it be unwelcome, what then? Sick perſons muſt not look for ſmoothing, and much-making, but for that which fits their malady †. And if you plead intempeſtivity and unſeaſonableneſs, for this the Apoſtle's rule muſt be my warrant, ' in ſeaſon, out ' of ſeaſon. 2 Tim. iv. 2. Indeed Solomon tells us, that there is a ſeaſon, a fitting time for all things; Eccleſ. iii. 1. and our moral books tell us of a vice which they call intempeſtivity ‡, an indiſcretion by which unwiſe and unexperienced men ſee not what befits times, perſons, occaſions. But, beloved, the miniſters of God's word, who break to you the bread of life, are ſecure in this

---

* Totum choragium Epicureum.

† 'Ο νοσίων ὁ ζητᾶτχι τὸν καλλοπισμὸν, ἀλλὰ τὸ σναφέρον.

‡ 'Ακαιρία.

K

regard; they can never be in danger of any intempeſtivity, indiſcretion, ſo the leſſon they teach be
true. We need not to ſtand removing and fitting
our ſails, all winds blow for us; for every good
ſeaſon is at all times, with all perſons, upon all
occaſions, upon no occaſion, profitable. Are you
ignorant of your duty? it ſerves to inform you;
Do you already know your duty? it ſerves to com-
memorate, and to make you record it; Are you
peccant? it ſerves to reprove you; Are you innocent? it ſerves to admoniſh you, and teaches you
prevention. ' Jupiter's dice,' we ſay, ' always run
' fortunately *.' The word of God, whereſoever,
whenſoever, by whomſoever ſown, never returns
back fruitleſs unto him that ſent it. St. Bernard,
commenting upon the Canticles, takes occaſion
much to bewail his brother's death; and by reaſon of that digreſſion, delivers many profitable leſſons concerning our common mortality. But one
Berengarius, a bitter enemy unto him, ſcoffing at
him for ſo doing, aſks him in ſcorn, ' What hath
' a funeral to do with a marriage-ſong †?' By his
leave that made it, this was but a fooliſh queſtion;
for indeed our Chriſtian ſongs are ſet to a muſic, in
which there is no fear of diſcords. As it is ſaid
of truth, ' All truths agree ‡;' ſo in our Chriſtian
muſic, every note, bound it as you liſt, is ſtill in

---

* Ἀεὶ γάρ εὖ πίπτυσιν οἱ Διὸς κύϛοι.

† Quid funeri cum nuptiis?

‡ Omne verum vero conſonat.

tune. Let therefore no cavilling Berengarius ask me, What hath a funeral to do with a marriage-song? What hath a sad sermon to do with Shrove-tide. For, when the Spirit will, who, as we hope, guides us in our choice, the pleasant Canticles shall yield fit matter for a funeral sermon, and times of pleasure and merriment shall well enough combine with sad and melancholic discourses.

Yet one word more, to fit my text to my au-ditors; a thing here somewhat the more difficult, because of the manner of the phrase, ' Remember ' thou hast received:' for memory is of things past, and ' thou hast received' is not of things in expectation, but of things already received by us. But we are yet in expectation; what shall befal us we know not; as yet therefore I cannot say as our Saviour doth, ' This day is this scripture fulfilled ' in your ears,' Luke iv. 21. let that time never be! for, should we stay to hear from Abraham a *remember*, it would be too late then to preach un-to you: yet we must find a way to apply this scripture to us, even for the present; and indeed it is not hard to do it. I have read in my books of a painter, who being desired to picture an horse wallowing in the dust, painted him galloping; and being required why he did so, he answered, Turn the picture. and it will be as you would have it. Beloved, I come this day to give you a *beware*, not a *remember;* to advise you that you beware how you receive your good things in your life, not to remember that you have done fo. And this will I do without any wrong to my text, for do but turn the picture, that which feems to gallop will wallow; do but alter the time, and *remember* will immediately become *beware*. Ariftotle tells us, that expectation and memory are but the fame thing; for what memory is in regard of things paft, that expectation is in regard of things to come. Expectation is but memory antedated, and memory is expectation whofe date is out. As it is betwixt expectation and memory, fo ftands the cafe betwixt *remember* and *beware.*: *beware* is but *remember* antedated; what *remember* is in regard of things paft, that is *beware* in regard of things to come. Let us then turn memory into warinefs and prevention, and exprobration into counfel and admonition; and forthwith you fhall fee, that ' Remember that thou haft received,' will become ' Beware that thou receive not;' and fo the text will exactly fit us. So come I to the words, ' Son, remember that thou in thy life-time ' receivedft thy good things.' I will branch them into two parts: *Firft*, a preface, in the firft word *fon*. *Secondly*, the body of the words themfelves, ' Remember thou haft received,' &c. The words we will further divide, if need fhall be, when we come to confider of them. In the mean time we will confider of the preface, *Son*.

I have heard that Abraham was a great fcholar; what portion of clerkfhip he hath otherwife and

upon other occasion exprest, I know not; sure I am
that here he hath shewed us a wondrous piece of
his rhetoric: for, two things most contrary, sweetness and bitterness, compassion and exprobration,
in two or three words so strangely couched and
mixed together, I have not lightly found ; ' Son,
' remember;' two words near in site and place, but
in sense and power infinitely distant : *Son*, a word
of bowels, mercy, sweetness; a word in which nature and custom hath summed up and concluded
all which lies disperfed in all the names of goodness. Contrarily, *remember*, a word (as here it
lies) of bitterness, of sarcasm, of exprobration: for,
unto this miserable man here in torments, what
could have been more irksome, than to be twitted
with, and constrained to remember, his sometime
happiness? Could he have learned the art of obli-
vion, and quite forgotten that ever he was happy,
his misery had been yet somewhat less. Never to
have tasted happiness abates a great part of misery; but, were there no other misery, yet this were
misery enough, to have been happy. It was observed of Domitian the Emperor, that when he
made a preface of mercy, it was a certain note he
would use the greatest severity: shall we conceive
so of Abraham, that to his *son* he added a *remember*, to his preface of mercy he under-joins a sentence of harshness and severity, so to add misery
to the enough already miserable, and increase his
wo? Reverence to so great a man must teach us

K 3

well to weigh what we speak or what we think †.
Certainly thus to suppose, were much to wrong
so excellent a person. If we shall a little enquire of
the learned, whence it comes that Abraham useth
this gracious compellation of *son* unto a damned
ghost; some will tell us, that he doth it by way
of retaliation: the man with whom he speaks had
called him father, out of complement therefore and
formality he calls him *son*. But this carries a countenance of courtship and levity. Others will say,
that he calls him by the name of *son*, because indeed
he was so, though by the flesh only; which proves
the weaker side. But this had been unprofitable,
neither from it could we have raised, for our use,
any instruction. Others have thought that Abraham did this out of his natural goodness, and that
he therefore used this gentle compellation of *son*,
to one utterly cast off, and to be now for ever left
under the eternal wrath of God, to teach us this
lesson, That in all cases, how desperate soever, unto all persons, though never so forlorn, unto the
greatest delinquent, how sinful soever, yet still we
must open some window, at least some small cre-
vice, to let our goodness shine through. St. Chrysostom was the man that told me thus, and I must
confess I believed him. Saith the great Roman o-
rator, ' Nature hath made me good, but my coun-
* try and the public good made me to be severe;

† Ἀφίσαμαι. ἀχίρδεια λίλογχεν
Θαμινὰ κακηγόρως.   Olymp. i. 84.

' but neither nature nor my country permit me to
' be cruel *.' Abraham here hath well expreſt
this, for *ſon*, *remember*, they are no other than
' nature and my country:' *Son* comes from his
bowels and natural goodneſs; *remember* is but occaſioned out of his duty to God and public good;
to teach us ſtill to temper our neceſſary ſeverity
with ſome goodneſs; for mere ſeverity is nothing
elſe but cruelty, which neither God nor nature requires at our hands. The maſter of the feaſt in
the goſpel, when he came in to his gueſts, and ſaw
one there without a wedding-garment, though he
ſaw he was conſtrained to pronounce a ſharp and
ſevere doom, yet he uſeth Abraham's method,
' Friend (ſaith he) how comeſt thou hither.' Matth.
xxii. 12. *Son, Friend:* Here is the true art of
chiding, this is the proper ſtyle wherein we ought
to reprove. A fair pattern for us, Beloved, who
in no caſe more miſtake ourſelves than in this duty of check and reproof; who are wont ſo to chide
as if we hated, who think foul words to be but
ornaments of ſpeech, and enchaſe our diſcourſe
with bitter language as with pearls, and never think
we reprove except we be contumelious.

Amongſt the antient Roman inſcriptions which
are preſerved unto poſterity, I find one written upon a Roman gentleman, where, amongſt other his
commendations, it is recorded, ' He knew not how

* Me natura miſericordem, patria ſeverum, crudelem nec
patria nec natura eſſe volunt.

' to speak contumeliously to any man †: ' and I have heard it reported of Philip the second, that famous King of Spain in our own memory, that he so wonderfully could contain himself, that in his whole life he never gave any man a harsh word. And indeed I have often wondered with myself, whether there were (not any necessary use, for that I know there is not) but any use at all of opprobrious and reviling language : if there be, it must be either in reproof, or in the administration of justice; if there be a third thing, my experience is too narrow to prompt me with it. But neither reproof, nor chastisement of justice require it, but are best performed without it. It cannot therefore stand either with our judgment, or with our goodness, to make any use of so useless, of so unwelcome a superfluity. It hath been observed of the antient Cornish language, that it afforded no forms of oaths, no phrases to swear in. I should never think our language the poorer, if it were utterly destitute of all forms and phrases of reviling and opprobrious speech. And what then can we conceive why any man should delight in the use of vile language ? for it is so useless and so unprofitable a vice, that except a man did love a vice for its own sake, he can give no reason why he doth affect it. On the contrary, the opposite quality is, first, a most welcome virtue ; for nothing more ingratiates us with men than that bles-

* Nescivit quid esset maledicere.

ſing of Nepthali, gracious language, which offends
not even thoſe whom it condemns †. Secondly, it
is ſo cheap a virtue; good words are afforded at
the ſame price that evil are. Laſtly, it is a prevailing and a winning virtue, even in civil actions. I
know you have heard the parable of the north
wind and the ſun; the wind, with all his raging
and bluſtering, could not make the wayfaring man
lay down his cloak; but when the ſun had diſ-
played his beams, ſent forth his heat, and wrought
a while upon him, he makes him retire to the
ſhade, and unbrace himſelf.

Beloved, as we much deſire to be the ſons of
Abraham the faithful, ſo let us no leſs deſire to be
the ſons of Abraham the good: and if we will be
the ſons of Abraham, then let us follow our Saviour's counſel, and do the works of Abraham; let
us ſtrive on all occaſions ſome way or other to expreſs our goodneſs, and uſe no more ſeuerity than
we muſt needs. Abraham could not releaſe this
poor man of his pain, he could not ſo much as procure a mitigation of it, he found no means to provide him a drop of cold water; yet he found a
way to expreſs his goodneſs, and affords him the
appellation of *ſon*. Love, you ſay, will creep where
it cannot go; it will expreſs itſelf in ſmall matters, where greater will not permit. This courteſy of Abraham was the leaſt of all; yet what of
that? The leaſt is enough where the leaſt is all

† Quae ne illos quidem quos damnat offendit.

that can be had. Though it do no service to the party for whom it is intended, yet it doth him service that affords it; For, in all our actions we must consider, not only what is good for others, but what becomes us to do, though no benefit accrue to others.

The Psalmist tells us, that 'the mercy of God 'is over all his works;' Psf. cxlv. 9. and I infer, therefore over his works of judgment too. And who knows then, whether or no the very damned spirits have not some taste of his goodness? Let us imitate God and Abraham; and love we our goodness so well, that even the most undeserving creature may have some experience of it. If we cannot relieve him, yet it shall be some part of goodness to give him the appellation of *son*, to give him good words; that, as God's, so our mercy too may be over all our works. The very faults of men, though they deserve correction, yet withal they deserve pity; and therefore though they demand justice, yet they exclude not goodness, but even naturally call for it. Horace the poet tells us of a painter, who having a good faculty in painting a cypress-tree, delighted on all occasions to shew his skill there; insomuch that being requested to express a shipwrack, he asked if he should paint withal a cypress-tree *. Beloved, let our oc-

_____

* ———————— fortasse cupressum
   Scis simulare: quid hoc, si fractis enatat exspes
   Navibus, aere dato qui pingitur?

                              Horat. de Arte Poëtica. v. 19.

cafions be as different as the fea and a cyprefs-
tree, yet, if we love our art of goodnefs, as well
as he did his art of painting the cyprefs, there will
be room enough to exprefs it, if we fhall be willing to lay hold of the occafion. So, from the preface, I come to the words, ' Remember thou haft
' received thy good things.'

You may remember I begged leave of you ere
while, for the better ufe and application I am to
make of them, to change the words; and as the
crafty fteward in the gofpel, who advifed the creditor to take his book, and inftead of an hundred
to write down fifty; fo I advifed you inftead of
remember to write *beware*. For, as the apothecary, when he finds himfelf at a lofs, and cannot
procure the drug he would have, takes a *quid pro
quo*, as they call it, another drug or fimple that
fhall be of the fame, or the like force, to cure the
difeafe; fo fares it with me, who now am to cure
a fpiritual difeafe in you; *remember*, as it lies in
the text, can never cure you: if it could, then
might our rich man here have hope to recover
heaven; for Abraham applies to him long ago.
For your ufe therefore, I am conftrained to lay by
remember, and take in *beware*, for a *quid pro quo*,
becaufe it ferves beft for the cure I have in hand :
that therefore you may not hereafter, when it is
too late, hear from Abraham, ' Remember thou
' haft received,' let me intreat you this day, whilft
it is yet time to hear from me, ' Take heed thou

'receive not thy good things in thy life:' For practise but this *beware*, and you shall never hear of *remember;* but if *beware* come not in time, you must unavoidably expect a *remember.* Read we therefore our text thus, ' Beware thou receive not thy good things.' Now, Beloved, this word *beware*, though in place and situation it reflect only upon the word *receive*, yet indeed it hath immediate influence upon every word I read. First, here is the word *receive*, here is a *beware* put upon that to your hand : in some sense therefore or other you may not receive the good things of this life, otherwise why is it cast in this man's dish that he received them ? The next word is, ' thy good ' things:' *thy*, put a *beware* there too ; for indeed they are not thine. When we call the things of the world *ours*, ours is but a word of usurpation ; we peradventure may be some emphyteuticaries, or farmers, or usufructuaries; but the propriety is in another person. The next word is, ' good things; *good*, put a *beware* there too : advise well how you call them *good*. Were our rich man asked what now he thought ? I persuade myself he would pass another censure of them ; for how good soever they were in themselves, yet to him they were not good. I have heard of a statue of Venus so cunningly framed, that as men came toward it, it seemed to smile, but as they turned from it, it seemed to frown. The things of this life are somewhat akin to the statue of Venus, as they come toward you they fmile upon you, they are good ; but as you turn from them, or they from you, many times they frown, they look with another countenance. The next word is ' things, ' good things ; ' put a *beware* there too. Take heed how thou calleft them *things ;* for indeed they are not things, but nothings. The laft word is ' thy life ;' *life*, put a *beware* there too. Take heed how thou call this prefent ftate of things ' thy ' life.' Nature taught Euripides the poet to afk this queftion, ' Who knows whether to live be to die, '. and to die to live * ?' But grace taught St. Paul to anfwer it, ' Now we live not, for our life is hid ' with Chrift in God.' Colof. iii. 3. So I return to refume the words again, and to confider a little more largely of them ; ' Take heed you receive ' not.'

What is this I hear ? Muft I not receive the good things of this life ? If either right of patrimony and inheritance devolve them to me, or fome cafual providence of God caft them upon me, or my labour and induftry woo and win them, muft I bid defiance, and fhut the doors againft them ? Is this precept here like to the command of old Euclio in the comedy, who wills his fervant to keep his doors fhut, and open to none, no though good

---

* Τίς δ' οἶδεν εἰ ζῆν τῦθ', ὃ κέκληται θανεῖν,
Τὸ ζῆν δὲ θνήσκειν ἐςί;

Euripid. apud Stobaeum.

fortune herſelf ſhould come and knock* ? Beloved, here I am in an uncertainty.

For anſwer to this queſtion; it is reported of Ariſtippus the famous philoſopher, that travelling over ſome parts of Afric, with his ſervants overladen with gold, when they complained of their burthen, and told him that they were ſo loaded, they ſhould never reach their journey's end; he bad them lay down their burthens, and take up ſo much as they thought themſelves conveniently enabled to bear, and leave the reſt to the next that came that way †. From this example I draw my anſwer; Wouldſt thou know whether thou ſhouldſt receive the good things of the world ? Try thy ſtrength; art thou able to confront occaſions, to converſe amongſt men, to wreſtle with temptations, and take no foil ? In a word, art thou able, with the three in Daniel, to go through the fire, and come out untouched ? Do as Ariſtippus's ſervants did, take up thy gold, receive the bleſſings that offer themſelves, entertain them, welcome them. On the contrary, art thou weak, or ſuſpecteſt thou thy ſtrength ? will fears, or hopes, or pleaſures over-maſter thee ? canſt thou not touch pitch but thou muſt be defiled with it ? Then do as Ariſtippus's ſervants did, leave thy gold behind thee; theſe goodly glittering things, refuſe them,

---

* Ne ſi bona quidem fortuna venerit.

† —— ſervos projicere aurum
In mediâ juſſit Lybiâ.   Horat.

though they drop into thy lap. Briefly, two ways is this question answered : hast thou strength of mind ? receive them ; hast thou not ? refuse them. The first is the wisest way, the second is the safest ; He that receives them doth well, but he that receives them not doth better.

I will begin with the first ; ' Receive them.' I know that this seems a riddle unto you, for my text seems to command you not to receive them ; and I have told you, that one way to put this precept in use, is to receive them. This is true, receive them we may, but yet so as if we received them not. Many of the saints of God, yea Abraham himself, received large portions of the good of this world : and how then shall they, with Abraham himself, avoid this bitter exprobration, ' thou hast received,' but that some way or other even they that have received them, may justly be said not to have received them ? Julius Caesar, when he had considered of his estate, and summed it up, and found for how great a sum he was in debt, beyond what he was worth, he merrily said, ' So much must I have, to have nothing †;' so much must I have that I may give every man his own, and myself have nothing. As Caesar found a way to have much, and yet to have nothing ; so thou must find out a way to receive much at the hands of God, and yet have received nothing : for whatsoever it be that thou hast received from God,

† Tantum me oportet habere ut nihil habeam.

thou art but in debt for it, thou art but intrufted
with it; look what it is thou haft, and fay unto
thyfelf as Caefar did, So much I have that I may
have nothing. In debt, I fay, thou art for all thou
haft; and wilt thou know who are thy creditors?
even every man that needs thee. The hungry man
begs at thy gate, he is thy creditor, thou art in
debt to him for his dinner: the naked man in the
ftreets, he is thy creditor, thou art in debt to him
for his garment: the poor oppreffed prifoner, he
is thy creditor, thou art in debt to him for his relief: the wronged captive, he is thy creditor, thou
art in debt to him for his redemption. Be then
like the widow's oil in the book of Kings, run as
long as there is a veffel to receive thee; pay all
thefe thy debts, and leave thyfelf nothing, and lo,
thou haft found the wonderful art of receiving
much at the hands of God, and yet receiving nothing. Had our rich man here done thus, he had
never heard of this, ' thou haft received;' for, to
receive here is not to take that which God offers,
but to impropriate, to enjoy alone the gifts of
God, either by difpending them on thyfelf, or thy
vanities, or locking them up, and neither enjoying them thyfelf, nor fuffering any other fo to do;
by making them ' thy good things,' and placing
thy felicity in them; this is to receive. Thou fitteft at thy full table, and crammeft thyfelf with
meats and drinks, whilft Lazarus ftarves at thy
gate, ' thou haft received;' thou cladeft thyfelf

with fuperfluous and gaudy apparel, whilft thy
naked brother freezes in the ftreet, ' thou haft received; thou refrefheft thyfelf with dainty reftor-
ing phyfic, whilft the fick indeed perifh for want
of care, ' thou haft received.' Take heed, every
vanity, every fuperfluity, every penny that thou
haft mifpent to the prejudice of him that wants,
when the time comes, fhall cry out unto thee,
' Thou haft received.' On the contrary, to have
received, but not unto thyfelf, to have fpent thyfelf for others good; he that doth thus, to him there
can be no more objected a having received, than
there can unto the fun that he received his beams,
which he hath communicated to the world; or to
the fountain, that it received it fprings, wherewith it hath watered the earth for which it was
given.

Erewhile, when I confidered the words in particular, I advifed you to put a *beware* upon the
word *thy*, ' thy good things:' for indeed, here is
the ground of all abufe and error, that we take
upon us to think and call any thing *ours*. For now
we think, by and by we may infer, May we not do
with our own what we lift? We think we are not
anfwerable to any one, no action of account lies
againft us, we fear no charge of having received.
Beloved, there is more danger in the ufe of that
word than you are aware of; *ours*, *mine*, is a grofs,
a crafs, a fecular term, eafily taken up by world-
lings, by better men not fo eafily. When Laban

had overtaken Jacob, and began to chide with
him, ' Thefe daughters,' faith he, ' are my daugh-
' ters, thefe children are my children, thefe cattle
' are my cattle, and all that thou feeft is mine.'
Gen. xxi. 43. Jacob had done enough to ftile
them his, he had bargained, he had ferved, he had
watched, he had fweat, he had freezed for them;
and yet he would not take up that word, nor
count any thing his. Nabal, a man of the fame
letters, and of the fame garb and quality with Laban, when David fent unto him to require relief
of him, fpeaks in the fame fibboleth; ' Shall I
' take,' faith he, ' my bread, and my water, and
' my flefh, which I have killed for my fhearers,
' and give it unto men whom I know not?' 1 Sam.
xxv. 11. Neither is it any wonder that they thus
fpeak; for this is the language which they learned
of their father, of their prince, of their god, even
the prince which ruleth in the air, the god of this
world, the devil; for he fetting upon our Saviour
in the gofpel, courts him in the fame manner; for,
fhewing him all the kingdoms of the earth, and
the glory of them, he tells him, ' All this is mine,
' and to whom I will, I give it*.' He lies, I doubt
not, when he thus fpake, (but that is no marvel)
yea, and all thofe who take up the dialect, are no
whit truer of their word. If the tongues of the
children of light have fometimes tript that way,
and fallen upon fome of the fame language, it is

* Alluding to Matth. iv. 9.

but out of contagion, an error of conversation, such as befel Joseph, who conversing with the E-gyptian courtiers, learned of them to swear by the life of Pharaoh : for, as walking in the sun disco-lours us, so walking in spiritual darkness will bring upon us swarth and blackness. But the sons of God, in their better thoughts, speak in another dialect : when David had, with great providence, with great hazard of person, treasured up much for the use of the house of the Lord, and was now come to dedicate it, and offer it up unto God, he dares not say, *mine*, but *thine;* ' out of thine own ' we present unto thee.' 1 Chron. xxix. 14. Now whereas the Holy Ghost is pleased here to use the phrase to the rich man, and call them ' thy good ' things,' this is but an irony and scorn; for, as they were originally, so still continue they to be God's, if abuse do not alter the property, for it is abuse only that makes them to be called *ours :* as the poet told his friend, ' The book, my friend, ' you read is mine; but if once you read it amiss, ' it is now *yours*, and no longer *mine*.*' We read in the book of Joshua, that the gold and silver which was in Jericho was all God's, and was to be brought into his treasury; but when Achan had once purloined a part of it, and endeavoured to turn it to unlawful ends, God owns it no longer, but it is brought forth and burnt, and buried with

* Quem recitas meus est, ô Fidentine, libellus,
    Sed male dum recitas incipit esse tuus.   Mart.

him, and no more thought worthy to be employ-
ed in holy ufe. Parallel to this is there a notable
example in St. Jerom ; for he, writing of the
monks of Egypt, reports of one of them, that labouring with his hands, and living without fcandal, at length he dies; and when the brethren
came to do their laft duty to him; they found about
him, as my author tells me, an hundred pieces of
gold, which was of our money about fifty pounds;
and mufing much to find there fuch a fum, and long
confulting what to do, at length they all agreed
in this, they took the party and laid him in his
grave, and laid his money by him, with this fare-
well, ' Thy money perifh with thee †.' It feems
therefore that things abufed either to fuperfluity
and wantonnefs, or to covetous and unprofitable
ends, are no longer fit for God, or good men's fervice ; therefore they perifh with the abufers. Ufe
them as God requires, and they remain ftill God's;
thou haft not received them, they are not thine :
abufe them once to folly or avarice, God owns
them not ; thou haft received them, and made
them thy good things, by abufing them.

Yet that we may defcend a little more particularly into this queftion of propriety, would thou
know indeed what it is of which thou mayeft juftly
fay unto thyfelf, It is mine‡? Examine thyfelf, find

---

† Argentum tuum tecum in perditionem.   Epift. 18. ad
Euftoch.

‡ Quod poffis dicere jure, meum eft.

out thine own meafure, fo much as thou needeft
is *thine*, the reft thou art but entrufted withal for
others good. That part of the beam of light which
fhines in thine eye is thine, all the reft is another's;
that which thou eateft to fuffice thine hunger is
thine, all the reft is thy neighbour's; that water
which thou drinkeft of thy well is thine, all the
reft is the property of the next comer. If thy
barns and ftorehoufes, thy wardrobes, thy treafu-
ries, imprifon and detain any thing, thou art but
a common enemy, and offendeft againft a common
profit. It is the bread of the hungry that thou de-
taineft, it is the garment of the naked that thou
lockeft up in thy wardrobe, it is the fhoe of the
bare foot that rots by thee, it is the poor's money,
and the talent of thy Lord, which thou hideft under the ground ; look how many thou haft not
furnifhed, fo many haft thou wronged*. It is well
that the providence of God hath left in common
the light, the heat, the influence of heaven, and
the water, and the air, patent unto all †; for, if
fome men had their will, even thefe fhould fuffer
inclofure and reftraint, neither fhould we freely enjoy the benefit of light and air. For, I know not

---

* Τῦ πεινῶντός ἐϛιν ὁ ἄρτος ὅν σὺ κατέχεις, τῦ γυμνητεύοντος
τὸ ἱμάτιον ὅ σὺ φυλάσσεις ἐν ἀποθήκαις, τῦ ἀνυποδήτυ τὸ ὑπόδημα
ὁ παρά σοι κατασήπεται, τῦ χρῆζονῖος τὸ ἀργύριον ὅ σὺ κατορύξας
ἔχεις, ὥϛε τοσ\u{0301}ϊτοις ἀδικεῖς ὅσοις παρίχεν ἰδύνασο. Bafil. Hom.
in Luc. xii. v. 18.

† —— cunctis undamque auramque patentem.

how it falls out, that whereas there are two pages, two parts of every account, the receipt, and the expence, there is a reigning madnefs amongft men to increafe their receipts, whilft, in the mean time, they are fecure of their expence; whereas it is the expence that moft concerns us; for what we fhall receive is in the care and will of our mafter, but all our care and providence is feen in our expence. Now I know not how it comes to pafs, that many feem to leffen the reputation of thrift and good hufbandry with God, and therefore they treafure and lock up their receipts, as if they thought to clear their accounts, and fave themfelves from a charge of having received, by returning God his own again. But the account with God is in one circumftance very different from that with men; the fteward that hath received his Lord's money, when he comes to his audit, if he repay what he hath not expended, he hath his acquittance, and all is well: but in our great audit with God there is no refunding, all muft be difpended. Could we pay back again our Lord's money which we have not laid out, yet ftill the account depends, ftill we are in danger of a charge of having received; for nothing clears our accounts with God, but pariation of expences with receipts; God's account muft have no remain. Secular thrift is feen in faving, but divine thrift is beft feen in fpending: whether therefore thou fpendeft amifs, or whether thou faveft amifs, thou art ftill liable to a charge of having received.

THE
DANGER

OF RECEIVING

OUR GOOD THINGS

IN

THIS LIFE.

Preached on Eafter-day at Eaton-College.

Luke xvi. 25.

Son, remember that thou in thy life-time receivedft thy good things.

SECOND SERMON ON THE TEXT.

I HAVE heard a proverb to this found, ' He ' that hath a debt to pay at Eafter, thinks the ' Lent but fhort :' how fhort this Lent hath feemed to me, who ftand indebted to you for the remainder of my meditations upon thefe words, is no matter of confequence; to you peradventure it may have feemed fo long, that what you lately heard at Shrove-tide, now at Eafter you may, with pardon, have forgotten. I will therefore recall in-

to your memories fo much of my former medita-
tations, as may ferve to open unto me a convenient way to purfue the reft of thofe leffons, which
then, when I laft fpake unto you, the time and
your patience would not permit me to finifh. But
ere I do this, I will take leave a little to fit my
text unto this time of folemnity.

This time, you know, calls for a difcourfe concerning the refurrection of our Lord and Saviour
Jefus Chrift; of this you hear no found in the
words which I have read, and therefore you conclude it a text unbefitting the day. Indeed, if you
take the refurrection for that glorious act of his
omnipotency, by which, through the power of
his eternal Spirit, he redeems himfelf from the
hand of the grave, and triumphs over death and
hell, you fhall in thefe words find nothing pertinent; but if you take this refurrection for that
act, by which, through the power of faving grace,
Chrift the fun of righteoufnefs rifes in our hearts,
and raifes us from the death of fin, unto the life
of righteoufnefs, here in thefe words you may,
perchance, find a notable branch of it. For to
raife our thoughts from this earth, and clay, and
from things beneath, (and fuch are thofe which
here Abraham calls, ' the good things of our life')
and to fet them above, where ' Chrift fits at the
' right-hand of God,' Colof. iii. 1. this is that
practic refurrection, which above all concerns us;
that other of Chrift in perfon, in regard of us, is

but a refurrection in fpeculation; for to him that
is dead in fin and trefpaffes, and who places his
good in the things of this life, Chrift is, as it were,
not rifen at all ; to fuch a one he is ftill in the
grave, and under the bands of death : but to him
that is rifen with Chrift, and feeks the good things
that are above, to him alone is Chrift rifen : to
know and believe perfectly the whole ftory of
Chrift's refurrection, what were it, if we did not
practife this refurrection of our own ? God will
not reckon with thee, how much thou knoweft,
but how well thou haft lived *. Epictetus, that
great philofopher, makes this pretty parable, Should
a fhepherd, faith he, call his fheep to account how
they had profited, would he like of that fheep,
which brought before him his hay, his grafs, and
fodder ; or rather that fheep, which having well
digefted all thefe, expreft himfelf in fat, in flefh,
and wool † ? Beloved, you are the flock of Chrift,
and the fheep of his hands ; fhould the great Shepherd of the flock call you before him, to fee how
you have profited, would he content himfelf with
this, that you had well conned your Catechifm,
that you had diligently read the Gofpel, and exactly knew the whole ftory of the refurrection ?
would it not give him better fatisfaction to find
Chrift's refurrection expreft in your's, and as it

* Cogita non exacturum à te Deum, quantum cognoveris,
fed quantum vixeris.

† Epictet. Encheir. c. 42.

were digested into flesh and wool? To have read Chrysippus his book, this is not virtue *: To have read the Gospel, to have gathered all the circumstances of the resurrection of Christ, this is not Christianity: to have risen, as Christ hath done, so to have digested the resurrection of Christ, as that we have made it our own, this is rightly to understand the doctrine of the resurrection of Christ. For this cause have I refused to treat this day of that resurrection, in the doctrine of which I know you are perfect, and have reflected on that, in the knowledge of which I fear you are imperfect: which that I might the better do, I have made choice to prosecute my former meditations, begun when I last spake unto you in this place; for so doing, I shall open unto you one of the hardest points of your spiritual resurrection, even to raise your thoughts from the things of this life, and seat them with Christ above.

To make my way more fair to this, I will take leave to put you in mind, in short, how I proceeded in the opening of these words, when I last spake unto you out of this place: you may be pleased to remember, that after some instruction drawn from the first word, *son*, I proceeded to consider the ensuing words, wherein having by an alchimy, which then I used, changed the word *remember* into *beware*; and so read my text thus,

* Οὐ γάρ ἀρετὴ τῦτο ἐςὶ, Χρύσιππον ἀναγνωκίναι.

' Beware thou receive not thy good things in this
' life,' I fhewed you, that we had never greater
caufe to confult our beſt wits, what we are to do,
and how we are to carry ourfelves, than when the
world, and outward bleſſings come upon us; upon
this I moved this queſtion, Whether or no, if the
things of this world fhould, by fome providence
of God, knock and offer themfelves to us, are we
bound to exclude them and refufe them? or, might
we open and admit of them? I divided my anfwer
according to the divers abilities and ſtrengths of
men: Firſt, he that hath ſtreugth and fpiritual
wifdom to manage them, let him receive them :
but in the fecond place, he that is weak, let him
let ſtrong diet alone, and feed on herbs, let him
not intangle himfelf with more than he can manage; let him try what his ſtrength can endure,
what not *. To the firſt, the fum of what I fpake
was this, Receive them we may, and that without
danger of an exprobration for having received;
firſt, if we fo received them, as if we received them
not; fecondly, if we efteemed them not good;
thirdly, if we did not efteem them ours: and here
the time cut me off, and fuffered me not to defcend unto the *fecond* part, upon which now I am
about to fall, ' Take heed thou receive not thy
' good things.'

In this matter of receiving and entertaining
thefe outward and foreign good things, there have

* —— quid valeant humeri, quid ferre recufent. Horat.

been two ways commended to you, the one the more glorious, to receive them; of this we have spoken. The other the more safe, not to receive them; of this we are now to speak. These ways are trodden by two kinds of persons; the one is the strong man, and more virtuous; the other is weaker, but more cautelous; the one encounters temptation, the other avoids it: we may compare them to the two great captains, Hannibal and Fabius, the one ever calling for the battle, the other evermore declining it. In one of these two ranks must every good man be found; if we compare them together, we shall find, that the one is far more excellent, the other far more in number: for to be able to meet and check our enemy, to encounter occasions, to act our parts in common life upon the common stage, and yet to keep our uprightness; this indeed is truly to live, truly to serve God and men, and therefore God the more, because men. On the contrary to avoid occasions, to follow that other kind of victory which is attained by declining the combat *, to overcome the world by contemning and avoiding it, this argues a wise indeed, but a weak and fainting spirit: I have often wondered at antiquity, which doting extremely upon a sequestered, a solitary, retired, and monkish life, sticks not to give out, that all perfection is in it, whereas indeed there is no greater argument of imperfection in good men,

* Vincendi genus, non pugnare.

than not to be able to endure the fun and the croud *; not to be able, without offence, to walk the public ways, to entertain the common occafions, but to live only to God and to themfelves: men of no great public ufe, but excellent for themfelves †; faints indeed in private, but being called forth into common life, are like bats in the fun, utterly ignorant of public practice; like Scheubelius a great mathematician, but by book only, and not by practice, who being required fometime in an army to make ufe of his quadrant, knew not the difference between *umbra recta* and *umbra verfa :* yet, beloved, becaufe this kind of good men is by far the greateft in number; and fecondly, becaufe it is both an ufual and a dangerous error of many men, to pretend to ftrength, when they are but weak, and fo forgetting their place, range themfelves among the firft, whereas they ought to have kept ftation among the fecond fort, I will take leave both to advife myfelf, and all that hear me, to like better of the fafer, though the weaker fide, and to avoid the exprobration of having received here in my text, fimply by not receiving, not admitting at all of the outward, lower, and temporal good things, rather than by an improvident fool-hardinefs to thruft ourfelves upon occafions which we are unable to manage without offence. This I am the more wil-

* Quam non poffe pati folem, non multitudinem.

† Utilis ipfe fibi fortaffis, inutilis orbi.

ling to do, becaufe there is not among men a
greater error committed, and more frequent, than
in this kind; for in moft things in the world, men
that have no fkill in them, will be content to acknowledge their ignorance, and to give place to
better experience: fhould we put the difcuffion of
fome point of fcholarfhip to the plough-hind, or
a cafe in law to the phyfician, or a point in phyfic
to the lawyer, none of thefe will offer to interpofe, but will advife to confult with every one in
his proper myftery; but let offer be made of moneys, lands, places of honour and preferment, and
who will excufe himfelf, who will acknowledge
his ignorance, or weaknefs to manage them?
Whereas in all the arts and fciences there are not
fo many errors committed, as in the unfkilful ufe
of thefe things, and yet our errors are no where
fo dangerous: it is therefore a thing moft neceffary, that in this behalf we advife men, either to
know their weaknefs, or to fufpect their ftrength;
better to be cautelous and wary, than ftrong and
hardy; the ftrong man hath been often captiva-
ted, but the wary man very feldom *. We read
in many places of Mofes and Samuel, of a race of
men greater in bulk and ftature than the ordinary
men, unto whom men of common inches feemed
but as grafhoppers; fuch were the Anakims, the
Emims, the Horims, the Zamzummims, the Re-

---

* Malo cautior effe quam fortior; fortis faepe captus eft,
cautus rariffime.

phaims, and the like: but if you read the fcriptures, you fhall find it obferved unto your hand,
that the men of leffer bodies always drove them
out; if you demand the reafon, experience will anfwer you, that the one went upon the opinion of
ftrength and hardinefs, the other of wary wit and
policy: it fares no otherwife with thefe two orders of men, of which I have fpoken, there is the
Anakim, the man that goes forth in the conceit of
his ftrength and valour; there is the man of mean
ftature, whofe ftrength is his warinefs; were there
a furvey taken of both thefe, it would be found,
that more by far have perifhed by unadvifed ad-
venturing upon the things of this world, than by
difcreet and fober retiring.

Wherefore, doft thou find that thou comeft on,
and thriveft in the world? that the good things
of this world wooe thee, and caft themfelves into
thy lap? that wealth, that honours, that abundance waits upon thee? take heed how thou prefume of thy ftrength to manage them, look well
upon them, and fee if there be not written on the
fore-head of every one of them, ' thou haft recei-
' ved.' But, Beloved, I perceive I deceive myfelf,
for thefe gay things of the world carry not their
exprobration of having received in their fore-heads;
as they come towards us, they are fmooth and
fair: you can prognofticate nothing by their countenance but ferene and Summer weather: our
great mafter Ariftotle hath told us, That if our

pleasures did look upon us when they come to us, as they do when they turn their back and leave us, we would never entertain them; these goodly things have their exprobration of having received written in 'their back; it is never discovered till it be too late to mend it, when death summons us, when the world, the flesh, the glory and pomp of life turns its back and leaves us, then shall you read ' thou haft received. *Beware* therefore, presume not, but be wary; and that thou mayest avoid a charge for having received, be sure that thou receive not: how many of those, think you, who out of their opinion of skill and strength, have given free entertainment to the world, have made large use of the world, lived abundantly, fared costly, dwelt sumptuously, clothed themselves richly, when their time and hour came, would rather have gone out of some poor cottage, than out of a princely palace, and lived with no noise in the world, that so they might have died in some peace? See you not, what some great persons in the church of Rome have often done? Charles V, the Prince of Parma, sundry others, though they lived in all pomp and state, yet at their death they desired to be buried in a poor Capuchin's hood; miserable men! If to die in a state of perfect sequestration from the world were so precious, so available a thing; how much more precious, more available had it been to live in it! For thus to die, not having thus lived, is nothing else but to give

fentence againſt their own life; for we ſhall not
appear before God as we died, but as we lived.
To profeſs hate and deſertion of the world at our
death, as moſt do; to put on humiliation at our
death, that live at eaſe and in ſtate all our life;
this is but to be buried in a Capuchin's hood:
What is it, Beloved, that thus reforms our judg-
mènt, and clears our ſight at that hour? Nothing
but this, all our pleaſures, all our honours, all the
May-games of our life, they now ſhall ſhew themſelves unto us, and every one cry out unto us,
' Thou haſt received thy good things.'

Now, Beloved, that I may a little the better
ſtrengthen, with good reaſon, this my advice of
retiring from, and rejecting, the goodly things of
the world, give me leave a little to conſult with
my topics, and to try out of what place I may
draw ſome arguments to bring you on the eaſier.

And *firſt* of all, were there no other reaſon to perſuade you, yet the very reading of this ſtory, where
I have taken my text, would afford arguments e-
nough; for what meant Abraham, I beſeech you,
when he told the rich man, he had received his
good things? Did he uſe ſome obſcure and unknown phraſe, which no circumſtance of the ſtory could open? It ſtands not with the goodneſs
of the Holy Ghoſt, to tell us of our danger in unknown language; ſomething therefore certainly
we ſhall find to open the meaning: caſt back your
eye upon the deſcription of the perſon, whom

Abraham charges with this error, and fee if you find not a paraphrase there ; the man to whom this phrase is applied, is described by the properties, of which I understand not that any one is a virtue; first, it is said, he was rich; secondly, he wore scarlet and soft linen; thirdly, he was jovial, and feasted liberally every day: doth not this accurate description of the person shew his error? For to what other purpose else could this description serve? Either here is his error, or this character is in vain; it seems therefore we must conclude, that to be rich, to cloath ourselves costly, to fare deliciously, thus to do, is ' to receive the good ' things in our life,' except some favourable interpretation do help us out; but we must take heed how we do dally with, and elude, scripture by interpretations; as it is written so do thou understand *. When St. John describes the world, which he forbids us to follow, he makes three parts of it, ' the lust of the flesh, the lust of the ' eye, and the pride of life.' 1 John ii. 16. Do not all these three appear here in the character of our man? Where is ' the lust of the eye,' if it be not in gaudy apparel? Where is ' the lust ' of the flesh,' at least one great branch of it, if it be not in the use of dainty diet? Where is ' the pride of life,' if not in riches? And what reason have you now to doubt, what should be

---

* Νοώσθω ὡς γίγραπται. Basil. Hom. ix. de Terrestribus. §. 1.

the meaning of ' thou haſt received thy good
' things?' He then that fears to hear an exprobration for having received, if he be rich, let him not
forget to diſtribute, and empty thoſe bags which
lie up by him; if he be coſtly clad, let him turn
his ſcarlet into ſackcloth; if he feed deliciouſly,
let him turn his coſtly diſhes into temperance and
faſting : otherwiſe, what can we plead for ourſelves, that we ſhould not, as well as this man in
my text, when our time comes, hear our doom,
' thou haſt received ?'

But I ſee what it is, peradventure, that troubles you; you will aſk me, Whether I will avouch
it to be a ſin to be rich? I muſt walk warily, leſt I
lay myſelf open to exception : Pelagius grounding
himſelf upon that of our Saviour, ' It is impoſſible
' for a rich man to enter into the kingdom of hea-
' ven,' taught that leſſon indeed, as the words do
lie, and would by no means grant that a rich man
could be ſaved; but for this the church noted him
for an heretic; for among his hereſies this is ſco-
red up for one, together with that, that it is not
lawful to ſwear; but if Pelagius had never otherwiſe erred, the church might very well have pardoned him that hereſy. Many times it falls out, by
the reaſon of the hardneſs of our hearts, that there is
more danger in preſſing ſome truths, than in maintaining ſome errors : that it is lawful ſometime to
ſport ourſelves, that it is lawful to feaſt at Chriſt-
mas, that it is lawful to ſwear, and many other

M 2

things of the like nature, are all truths; yet there is no neceſſity we ſhould preſs them in our ſermons to the people, for there is no fear the people will ever forget theſe; better to labour that they do not too much remember them*; he that will labour in repreſſing the abuſes, which people ground upon theſe truths, muſt remember the old rule, ' Seek what is not thy due, that thou mayeſt re- ' ceive what is †;' he muſt go very near to teach for truth the contrary falſhood. To return then from this digreſſion to our rich man; Pelagius, I grant, was deceived, when he ſhut all rich men out of the kingdom of heaven : but ſuppoſe we that he had prevailed in this doctrine, that he had wrought all the world to this bent, that the church had received it for catholic doctrine, ſhew me, he that can, what inconvenience would have attend- ed this error? If every rich man ſhould ſuddenly become liberal, and diſburſe his moneys where his charity directed him; if every painted gallant did turn his peacocks feathers into ſackcloth; if every glutton left his full diſhes, and betook himſelf to temperance and faſting, yea, and thought himſelf in conſcience bound ſo to do, out of fear, leſt he might hear of ' thou haſt received;' I perſuade myſelf the ſtate of Greece would never ſuffer the more for this; but the ſtate of Chriſtianity would have thrived the more. Well had it been for our

---

* Cavendum eſt ne nimium meminerint.

† Iniquum petendum eſt, ut aequum feras.

rich man here, if he had been a Pelagian; for this
point of Pelagianifm is the fureſt remedy, that I
know, againſt an exprobration of having received;
whereas, on the contrary ſide, by reaſon of the
truth, many rich and covetous perſons flatter
themſelves in their ſin, whereof they die well conceited, from which they had been freed, had it
been their good fortune to have been thus far deceived, and been Pelagians. Let men therefore
either quite refuſe riches, if they offer themſelves,
which is the advice I give, or if they will give
them acceptance, let them believe, that if they be
rich, they may be ſaved; but let them ſo live, as
if they could not; for the one ſhall keep them
from error in their faith, the other from ſin in
their actions.

A *ſecond* reaſon, perſuading us to the neglect of
theſe ſo much admired things of the world, is the
conſideration of certain abuſes, which they put upon us, certain fallacies, and falſe gloſſes, by which
they delude us; for I know not how, the world hath
cried them up, and hath given them goodly titles*;
men call them bleſſings, and favours, and rewards,
and think thoſe men moſt bleſt of God, who enjoy moſt of them; theſe goodly titles ſerve for
nothing, but to ſet men on longing after them, and
ſo fill thoſe that have them with falſe perſuaſions,
and thoſe that have them not with deſpair and

---

* Ut vel lactis gallinacei ſperare poſſis hauſtum, *as Pliny*
ſpeaks, Hiſt. Nat. lib. i. c. 2.

difcontents. Were they indeed bleffings, were they
rewards, then were our cafe·very ill, and we our
felves in greater danger of the fentence, 'thou haft
' received,' than before: for as Abraham here tells
the man of, ' thou haft received thy good things,'
fo our Saviour tells, more than once, of fome who
have their reward; if then we fhall beg, and receive thefe things at the hands of God, as a reward of our fervice, we fhall be no more able,
when we come to appear before our God, to fhelter ourfelves from an ' thou haft had thy reward,'
you have your reward, then the rich man here
could defend himfelf from a ' thou haft received
' thy good things.' They may indeed pafs for rewards, and bleffings, and that truly too, but to a
fad and difconfolate end; for there is no man,
though never fo wicked, but that fome way or
other doth fome good, fome cup of cold water
hath been given, fome fmall fervice enterprized e-
ven by the worft of men: now God, who leaves no
fervice unrewarded, no good office unrefpected,
therefore preferves thefe fublunary bleffings of
purpofe to clear accounts wi:h men here, who o-
therwife might feem to claim fomething at his
hand at that great day. It is the queftion Ahafuerus makes, ' What honour and dignity hath been
' done to Mordecai for this?' Eft. vi. 3. God is
more careful of his honour than Ahafuerus was;
none more careful than he to reward every fervice
with fome honour: Nebuchadnezzar was no faint,

I trow, yet becaufe of his long fervice in the fub-
duing of Tyre, God gives him Egypt for his reward, they are the prophet Ezekiel's words, xxix.
20. when therefore thou feeft God willing to bring
the world upon thee, to enrich thee, to raife thee
to honours, as Tertullian faith, ' Be jealous of
' this courtefy of God * ;' or rather cry out with
St. Bernard, ' O Lord, I will none of this kind of
' mercy† :' for how knoweft thou whether he reward not thee, as he did Nebuchadnezzar, only to
even accounts with thee, and fhew thee that he is
not in thy debt, that thou mayeft hear at the laft
either a ' thou haft received,' or ' thou haft thy re-
' ward ?' ' O how great a reward,' faith St. Jerom, ' might many men receive at the hand of
' God, if they did not anticipate their reward, and
' defire it in this life ‡ ?' Why do we capitulate
with him for our fervices? Why not rather, out
of pious ambition, defire to have God in our debt?
He that doth God the greateft fervice, and receives
here from him the leaft reward, is the happieft
man in the world. There goes a ftory of Aquinas,
that praying once before the crucifix, the crucifix miraculoufly fpeaks thus unto him, ' Thou haft
' written well of me, Thomas, what reward doft
' thou defire ?' To whom Aquinas is made to an-

* Sufpectam habe hanc Domini indulgentiam.

† Mifericordiam hanc nolo, Domine.

‡ O quanta apud Deum merces, fi in praefenti praemium
non fperarent. Epift. 34. ad Nepotianum.

M 4

fwer, ' No reward, Lord, but thyfelf *.' It is
great pity this tale is not true, it doth fo excellently teach what to afk of God for our reward in his
fervice. Let God but affure thee of this reward,
thou mayeft very well pardon him all the reft.
Let us therefore amend our language, and leave off
thefe folecifms, and mifapplied denominations of
bleffings, and favours, and rewards, names too
high for any thing under the moon, and at our
leifure find out other names to exprefs them; as
for this great efteem which we make of the things
below, it comes but from this, that we know not
the value of things above ; did we believe ourfelves to be the heirs and the fons of God, and
knew the price of our inheritance in heaven, it
could no be that we fhould harbour fo high and
honourable conceits of earthly things. It is a famous fpeech of Martin Luther, ' Did a man in-
' deed believe that he is a fon and heir unto God,
' it could not be that fuch a man fhould long
' live, but forthwith he would be fwallowed up,
' and die of immoderate joy †. And certainly either our not believing, or not rightly valuing the
things of God, or howfoever, not knowing them,
is the caufe of this our languifhing, and impatient

---

* Bene de me fcripfifti, Thoma, quam ergo mercedem ac-
cipies?—Nullam, Domine, praeter teipfum.

† Homo perfecte credens fe effe haeredem et filium Dei,
non diu fuperftes maneret, fed ftatim immodico gaudio abfor-
beretur.

longing after earthly things. It is but a plain com-
parison which I shall use, yet because it fits the
person to whom I will apply it, and because it is
Theophylact's in his comments on St. Luke's Gospel, I will not be ashamed to make use of it ;
' Swine, saith he, have their eyes so framed, that
' they cannot look up to heaven ; their keepers,
' therefore, when they find themselves troubled
' with their crying, are wont to cast them upon
' their backs, and so make them cease their cry-
' ing ; for that beast being amazed to see the frame
' and beauty of heaven, which before he had ne-
' ver seen, being stricken with admiration, forgets
' his crying* :' the eyes of many men seem to be
framed like those of swine, they are not able to
cast them up to heaven ; for would they but cast
themselves upon their backs, turn their face from
earth, and view the beauty of things above, it could
not be, but all this claim, or rather clamour after
earthly things should utterly cease.

Again, (yet the more to quicken one to the neglect of these things below) among many other
fallacies, by which they delude us, I have made

---

* Τῦ χοίρυ γὰρ οἱ ὀφθαλμοὶ ὑδέποτε τὰ ἄνω βλέπων δύνανται,
ἀλλοκότῃ διαπλάσεως τυχόντες· ὅθεν ᾧ οἱ χοιροβοσκοὶ ἐπειδὰν χοῖ-
ρον κατέχοντες, ὑ δύνωνται παύειν αὐτὸν βοῶντα, ἀναςρέψαντες
ὕπτιον, μετριώτερον αὐτὸν πέθυσι βοᾶν. οἱονεὶ γὰρ ὡς θέαν ἐλθὼν
ὧν ὑκ ἔδέ ποτε, ᾧ τὰ ἄνω βλέπων ἐκπλήττεται, ᾧ σιγᾷ. τοιῦτοι
οἱ ὀφαλμοὶ τῶν τοῖς φαύλοις ἐντριφομένων, ὑδέποτε τὰ ἄνω ὁρῶσι.
Theophylact. in Lucam. c. xv.

choice of one more: they prefent themfelves unto
us, fometimes as neceffaries, fometimes as ornaments unto us in our courfe of virtue and happinefs; whereas they are but mere impertinences,
neither is it any way material whether we have
them, yea or no: ' Virtue and happinefs require
' nothing elfe but a man * :' thus fays the Ethnics,
and Chriftianity much more: for it were a ftrange
thing that we fhould think, that Chrift came to
make virtue more chargeable: in regard of virtue
and piety, all eftates, all conditions, high and low,
are alike. It is noted by Petronius for the vanity
of rich men; ' Thofe men, whofe minds are fet
' upon wealth and riches, would have all men be-
' lieve that it is beft fo to do †.' But riches and
poverty make no difference, for we believe him
that hath told us, ' there is no difference, Jew and
' Gentile, high and low, rich and poor, all are one
' in Chrift Jefus.' Galat. iii. 28. Colof. iii. 11.
St. Ambrofe faith, ' Poverty, as men call it, is but
' a fancy ‡;' there is no fuch thing indeed, it is but
a figment, an idol; men firft framed and fet it up,
and afterwards feared it; as fome naturalifts tell us,
that the rainbow is a thing framed only by the eye:

* Virtus non eligit domum nec cenfum, nudo homine con-
tenta eft.   Senec. de Benef. lib. iii. c. 18.

† Qui folas divitias extruere curant, nihil volunt inter homines melius credi, quam quod ipfi tenent. Satyr. c. 84.

‡ Non naturae paupertas, fed opiuionis eft.   Epift. Claff.
i. 63. §. 90.

fo this difference betwixt rich and poor is but the creature of the eye. Smyndyrides the Sybarite was grown fo extremely dainty, that he would grow weary with the fight of another man's labour, and therefore when fometime he faw a poor man digging, and painfully labouring, he began to faint and pant, and required to be removed *. Beloved, when we are thus offended to fee another man meanly clad, meanly houfed, meanly traded, all this is but out of a Sybaritifh ridiculous daintinefs, for all this is but to grow weary at the fight of another man's labour; would we follow our Saviour's precept, and put out this eye of ours, the greateft part of all this vanity were quite extinguifhed; for what were all outward ftate and pomp imaginable, were no eye to fee or regard it?

Now, Beloved, yet to fee this more plainly, what is the main end of our life? what is it, at which, with fo much pain and labour, we ftrive to arrive? It is, or fhould be nothing elfe but virtue and happinefs: now thefe are alike purchafable in all eftates; poverty, difeafe, diftrefs, contumely, contempt; thefe are as well the object of virtue as wealth, liberty, honour, reputation, and the reft of that forefpoken rank: happinefs therefore may as well dwell with the poor, miferable, and diftreffed perfons, as with perfons

---

* Athen. lib. xii. 3. Seneo. de Ira. lib. ii. c. 25.

of better fortune, since it is confest by all, that happiness is nothing else but a leading of our life according to virtue.   As great art may be exprest in the cutting of a flint, as in the cutting of a diamond, and so the workman do well express his skill, no man will blame him for the baseness of the matter, or think the worse of his work : Beloved, some man hath a diamond, a fair and glittering fortune; some man hath a flint, a hard, harsh, and despicable fortune; let him bestow the same skill and care in polishing and cutting of the latter, as he would or could have done on the former, and be confident it will be as highly valued (if not more highly rewarded) by God, who is no accepter of persons, but ' accepteth every man according to that he hath, and not according to that ' he hath not.' 2 Cor. viii. 1 2. To him let us commit ourselves: To him be all honour and praise, now and for ever.   Amen.

O F

S⊤. PET·ER'S FALL.

Matth. xxvi. 7 5.

And he went forth, and wept bitterly.

THUS to commit to writing, as here our E-
vangelift hath done, and fo to lay ópen to
all pofterity the many flips and errors which have
much blemifhed and difgraced the lives and aftions
of the beft and moft excellent men, may feem, in
the judgment of a reafonable man, to participate of
much envy and uncharitablenefs: fo that their good
life had remained upon record for our example, we
might very well have fuffered their errors to have
flept and been buried with their bodies in their
graves. St. Peter makes it the property of charity
to ' hide the multitude of fins;' 1 Pet. iv. 8. whofe
property then is it thus to blazon them at mid-day,
and to fill the ears of the world with the report
of them? Conftantine, the firft-born among Chriftian Emperors, fo far mifliked this courfe, that he
profeffed openly, if he found any of his bifhops
and clergy, whom it efpecially concerned to have
a reputation pure and fpotlefs, committing any
grievous fin, to hide it from the eye of the world,

he would cover it with his own garment; he knew well that which experience had long ago observed, ' Things well said, well done, do nothing ' so much profit and further us, as the examples ' of ill speeches, ill actions, do mischief and incon- ' venience us * :' and men are universally more apt from the errors and scapes of good men to draw apologies for their own, than to propose their good deeds for examples and patterns for themselves to follow. Neither is this my own speculation, St. Austin observed it long since, who discoursing upon the fall of David, complains, that from his example, many framed unto themselves this apology, ' If David did thus, then why not I? ' Thou dost (saith he) prepare thy heart to sin; ' thou providest thyself of purpose; thou dost look ' into the book of God, even therefore that thou ' mightest sin; the scriptures of God thou dost ' therefore hear, that by the example of those that ' fell, thou mayest learn to do that which is dis- ' pleasing unto God †.' Yea, the greater is the person offending, the more dangerous is the example; for greatness is able of itself, as it were, to legitimate foul acts, to add authority and credit unto ill doings. Whosoever he be,' saith Seneca

---

* Non tam juvare quae bene dicta sunt, quam nocere quae pessime.

† Si David, cur non et ego? Praeparas te ad peccandum, disponis peccare; librum Dei ut pecces inspicis; scripturas Dei ad hoc audis, ut facias quod displicet Deo.

of Cato, ' that objects drunkenness to Cato, shall
' more easily prove drunkenness to be a virtue,
' than that Cato, who used it, was to blame *.'
When St. Peter, Galat. ii. 13. had halted in his
behaviour betwixt the Gentiles and those of the
circumcision, St. Paul notes, that many of the
Jews, yea ' Barnabas himself, was carried away
' with their dissimulation : ' and to speak truth,
whom would not the authority and credit of St.
Peter have drawn into an error? So easily the
faults of great men grow up and become exemplary, and so full of hazard is it, to leave unto the
world a memorial of the errors and scapes of worthy persons. Yet notwithstanding all this, the Holy Spirit of God, who bringeth light out of darkness, and worketh above and against all means,
hath made the fall of his saints an especial means
to raise his church: and therefore hath it pleased
him, by the penmen of the lives of his saints in
holy scripture, to lay open in the view of the
world many gross faults and imperfections, even
of the most excellent instruments of his glory.
That which he tells the woman in the gospel,
who anointed him before his passion, that ' where-
' soever the gospel shall be preached, this fact of
' hers should be recorded in memorial of her : '
Matth. xxvi. 13. the same, as it seems, was his

*. Catoni ebrietas objecta est: at facilius efficiet, quisquis
objecerit, hoc crimen honestum, quàm turpem Catonem. Seneca de Tranquil. Anim. 15.

intent concerning his faints; that wherefoever the
word of life fhould be taught, there likewife
fhould be related the grievous fins of his fervants.
And therefore accordingly, fcarcely is there any
one faint in the whole book of God, who is not
recorded in one thing or other to have notably o-
verfhot himfelf. Sometimes he hath made the
faints themfelves the proclaimers of their own
fhame: fo he makes Mofes to regifter his own infidelity; fo David in his one and fiftieth pfalm,
by the inftinct of God's Spirit, leaves unto the
church, under his own hand, an evidence againft
himfelf for his adultery and murther: fometimes
he makes their deareft friends the moft exact chro-
niclers of their faults; for fo St. Chryfoftom obferves of St. Mark, the companion and fcholar of
St. Peter, who hath more particularly regiftered
the fall of his mafter, than any of the other Evangelifts, ' Who would not marvel,' faith he, ' that
' St. Mark not only concealed not the grofs efcape
' of his mafter; but hath more accurately than
' any of the reft recorded the particulars of it, e-
' ven becaufe he was his difciple * ;' as if he could
have done his mafter no better fervice, than to deliver a moft exact relation of his fault. There are
yet two things further to be noted in this difpenfation of Almighty God; the firft, in regard of us;

---

* Ὅθεν μάλιϲα ἄν τιϲ αὐτὸν ἐκπλαγείη, ὅτι ἠ μόνον ὐκ ἔνρυψε
τὸ ἐλάτΙωμα, ἀλλὰ κ, τῶν ἄλλων σαφίϲερον ἀπήγγειλεν, αὐτῷ
τύτῳ τῷ μαθητῇ.   Hom. 86.

the fecond, in regard of the faints, whofe errors
are recorded: for the firft, who can but marvel,
that fince all things that are written, are written
for our inftruction; that if they be good, they may
ferve for our imitation; if otherwife, for warning to us: yet, many finifter actions of the faints
of God are fo expreft in fcripture, without cenfure, without note, that it were almoft fome danger to pronounce of them? Abraham's equivocating with Abimelch, Jacob's deluding his blind
father, Rachel abufing Laban with a lie, Jephthah
his facrificing his daughter, Sampfon killing himfelf with the Philiftines; thefe, and many other
befides, are fo fet down, that they may feem to have
been done rather by divine inftinct, than out of
human infirmity. Wherein the Holy Ghoft feems
to me to fet upon us out of ambufh, to ufe a kind
of guile, to fee whether we have fpiritual difcretion, to try whether we will attribute more to men's
examples, than to his precepts. Secondly, in regard of the faints themfelves: it is worth our
noting, that God feems to have had more care to
difcredit them, than to honour them, in that their
faults are many times particularly regiftered, but
their repentance is wrapt up in filence; fo the ftory
of Noah is concluded with his drunkennefs; after
the report of Lot's inceft, there is not a word of
him throughout the fcriptures; as foon as the
ftory of Solomon's idolatry is related, it immediately follows in the text, ' and Solomon flept with

'his fathers.' 1 Kings xi. 43. We ſhould very much wrong theſe men, if we ſhould think that they paſt out of this life without repentance, becauſe their repentance is concealed. Doubtleſs if we were worthy to ſearch the myſteries of the Spirit, we ſhould find that the Holy Ghoſt hath left ſomething for our inſtruction even in this particular; for nothing in ſcripture is done by chance: but, as St. Chryſoſtom is wont ſometime to tell his auditory, that he will not reſolve all doubts, but leave ſome to meditate on by themſelves; ſo will I now deal with you, I will leave this to your private conſiderations, to practiſe your wits in the depths of Chriſtianity, and ſo to frame reaſons unto yourſelves of this proceeding of the Holy Spirit.

In the New Teſtament, the Holy Ghoſt conſtantly holds the ſame courſe of relating the fall of the ſaints: and ſo accordingly by all the four Evangeliſts ſets down at large, the fearful ſin of St. Peter in denying and forſwearing his maſter. But as it pleaſed him in mercy to give him repentance, ſo in theſe words which I have read unto you, hath it pleaſed him to leave unto the church a memorial of it. Our firſt note therefore, before we come to the words, ſhall be a note of that exceeding uſe and profit, which hath redounded to the church by the regiſtering of St. Peter's repentance; for this is done by the Holy Ghoſt, to ſignify unto us the neceſſity and force of repentance, and ſorrow for ſin. The concealing of Solomon's

reclaim hath occafioned fome, upon acknowledgment of the neceffity of repentance, to fuppofe
that Solomon paft away without it, and fo received the final reward of the impenitent. But he
that fhould have read this ftory of St. Peter, and
obferved what authority he had afterwards, what
efpecial favour our Saviour did him after his refurrection, notwithftanding his fall, if the manner
of his recovery had not been recorded, might eafily have entertained a conceit very prejudicial to
repentance. Who might not hope to regain the
favour of God without fhedding a tear, if St. Peter, notwithftanding fo grievous a crime, without
repentance, fhould again be reconciled? We might
therefore, with excufe, have prefumed upon a non-
neceffity of repentance, as if it had been enough
in cafe of fin to practife that which common morality teaches, barely to relinquifh it, without any
more ado. *That* therefore which we learn by this
regiftering of St. Peter's repentance, is this, That
for the clearing of a Chriftian man's account unto
God, it is not fufficient barely to ceafe from doing
ill, to fatisfy the law which we broke, either with
our life, or with our goods; to make recompence
to our neighbour for wrong done him; all this
and much more wafhes not away the guilt of fin
before God. Thefe are things which the very
light of nature teaches us to do. It was not to be
thought that David to his former adulteries and
murther, would have added new: he that hath

been forced to reſtore fourfold that which he had
taken away by ſtealth, will, peradventure, take
warning to ſteal no more: but this doth not ſuffice him: there is a further duty, a duty of repentance required of every Chriſtian man, a duty
proper to him alone.   For this doctrine of repentance Nature never taught in her ſchool, neither
was it ever found in the books of the learned; it
is particular to the Book of God, and to the doctrine that came down from heaven.   In the ſins
againſt the firſt table we offend immediately and
only againſt God; but in the ſins againſt the
ſecond table, there is a double guilt contracted,
one againſt God, another againſt our neighbour;
in theſe ſins, as there is a double fault, ſo there
is a double ſatisfaction to be made, one unto
God, another to our neighbour: for this ſecond
ſatisfaction between man and man, many Heathen commonwealths have been very ſufficient-
ly furniſhed with ſtore of excellent laws; but
of an atonement, over and above, to be made to
God, they ſcarce ſeem to have had any thought:
and indeed to ſpeak truth, to what purpoſe had it
been to trouble their heads about it? it is impoſſible that it ſhould ever fall within the conceit of
any reaſonable creature, to pronounce what ſatisfaction was to be made for offence committed a-
gainſt God: he is of infinite majeſty, holding no
proportion, no correſpondence, with any created being; what recompence then can he receive

from the hands of duſt and aſhes? Ten thouſand
worlds, were we able to give them all, could not
make ſatisfaction for any part of the ſmalleſt offence we have committed againſt him: when
therefore the inventions of men were thus at a
ſtand, when all diſcourſe, all reaſon were poſed, it
pleaſed God in mercy to open his pleaſure in his
word, and to accept of true and unfeigned repentance, as the only means to waſh away the guilt
of ſin againſt his majeſty: a thing in the eye of
fleſh and blood altogether ridiculous. And therefore Julian, that accurſed apoſtate, ſcorning Con-
ſtantine the Emperor for betaking himſelf to the
Chriſtian religion, in contempt and deriſion of baptiſm and repentance, thus ſpeaks: ' Hô, whoſo-
' ever is a corrupter and a defiler of women, who-
' ſoever is a manſlayer, whoſoever is an impure
' and unclean perſon, let him from henceforth be
' ſecure, and care for nothing; I will ſhew him a
' little water, in which, if he do but dip himſelf,
' he ſhall be forthwith clean: yea, though he de-
' ſperately run again into the ſame crimes, I will
' give him this gift, if he but knock his breaſt and
' ſtrike his forehead (which are the geſtures of the
' penitent) he ſhall, without any more adoe, be-
' come as pure as glaſs *.' It is true indeed, in

---

* Ὅστις φθορεὺς, ὅστις μιαιφόνος, ὅστις ἐναγὴς ᾗ βδελυρὸς, ἴτω
θαῤῥῶν, ἀποφανῶ γὰρ αὐτὸν τυτῳ τῷ ὕδατι λύσαξ, αὐτίκα καθα-
ρόν. κᾂν πάλιν ἔνοχος τοῖς αὐτοῖς γένηται, δώσω τὸ ςῆθος πλήξανλι,
ᾗ τὴν κεφαλὴν πατάξανλι, καθαρῷ γενέσθαι. **Caeſares. in fin.**

ſpight of unbelieving miſcreants, it hath pleaſed
God, through the fooliſhneſs of baptiſm and repentance, to ſave thoſe that are his. The water of
baptiſm and the tears of true repentance, creatures
of themſelves weak and contemptible, yet, through
the wonderful operation of the grace of God annext unto them, are able, were our ſins as red as
twice-died ſcarlet, to make them as white as ſnow.
The ſentence of God denounced unto Adam,
' What day thou eateſt of the tree, thou ſhalt die,'
Gen. ii. 17. certainly was abſolute and irrevocable,
neither could any repentance of Adam's totally
have reverſed it : yet Abulenſis cries out, ' O how
' happy ſhould mankind have been, if Adam after
' his fall had uſed the benefit of repentance, and
' in time acknowledged his ſin unto God : ' yea,
he goes further, and ſeems to intimate, that it had
been of force almoſt to reſtore us unto our primitive purity; for this way his words ſeem to look,
when he ſaith, ' If he had accuſed himſelf, doubt-
' leſs he had freed us all from accuſation and a
' curſe * : ' whatſoever his meaning was, thus
much without danger we may think, that if our
firſt parents had not ſo ſtrangely ſhuffled their
fault from the one to the other, the man to the

---

* Quod ſi ſeipſum accuſaſſet, nos omnes ab accuſatione et
judicio liberaſſet.

By *Abulenſis* is meant *Alphonſus Toſtatus biſhop of Avila in
Spain. The editor has had no opportunity of conſulting the writings of this voluminous author.*

woman, the woman to the ſerpent; but had freely acknowledged it, and humbly begged pardon
for it, God, whoſe mercies were then as many
and as ready as now they are, would, if not altogether have revoked, yet doubtleſs much have
qualified and mitigated the ſentence of the curſe;
if Adam had uſed more ingenuity in confeſſing,
God would have uſed leſs rigour in puniſhing. Out
of all this I draw this one leſſon for your inſtruction; Whoſoever he be that thinks himſelf quit of
ſome ſins into which, either through weakneſs or
careleſſneſs, he hath fallen, let him not preſently
flatter himſelf, as if for this his book of debt unto
God were cancelled, as if he were in a ſtate of
grace and new birth; but let him examine his
own conſcience, and impartially ſift all the manner
of his reclaim: he may, peradventure, find that,
upon ſome moral reſpect, he hath broken off the
practice of his ſin; he may find that he hath ſatisfied his neighbour, contented the law, done many acts by which he hath purchaſed reconciliation
with the world: but, if he find not this paſſage
of repentance and hearty ſorrow betwixt God and
his own ſoul, let him know, that God is yet unſa-
tisfied, that he is yet in his ſin; his ſin is yet unrepented of, and therefore ſtill remains.

Thus from the neceſſity of regiſtering St. Peter's repentance, I come to the words wherein it is
regiſtered, ' And he went forth, and wept bitter-
'ly.' In theſe words we will conſider four things;

First, the person, *he*, ' He went forth;' or, ' and
' going forth he wept.' *Secondly*, the preparative
to the repentance, ' he went forth.' *Thirdly*, the
repentance itself, comprised in the word *wept*.
Fourthly, the extent, measure, and compass of this
repentance, in the last word, *bitterly*.

First, He. The way of man's life is a slippery
way; no man whilst he is in it hath the privilege
of not sliding; just and unjust, thus far, are of like
condition; both fall: but here they differ, the just
man riseth again. Not the eminency of St. Peter's
person, nor his great understanding in the mystery of Christ, nor his resolution in our Saviour's
quarrel, nor the love and respect his master bare
him, kept him from falling: but St. Peter being
fallen, provides himself to rise, and therefore in
the *second* place, ' he went forth,' saith my text:
St. Peter was now in the High-priest's court, a
place very unfit for one in St. Peter's case. Princes courts are no place for repentance: to wear
soft raiment, to fare deliciously every day, this is
courtiers guise; but the shirt of hair, the tears of
repentance *; this is the habit of the penitent.
But, *thirdly*, Wherefore went St. Peter out? Did
he, as our Saviour observes of the Scribes and Pharisees, go out into the wilderness to see, to gaze
and look about him? No, his eyes now must do
him other service; he went out as Joseph did from

* Τὸ τριχινὸν ῥάκος, ὃ τὸ τῆς μετανοίας δάκρυον.

the face of his brethren, to feek a place to weep.
Maldonat the Jefuit thinks it would have been a
more goodly thing, and far more befeeming St.
Peter's refolution, if in the place he had offended,
in the fame he had repented: if before thofe he
had made a conftant confeffion of Chrift, before
whom he had denied him. But be the reafons
what they will which moved St. Peter to go forth,
we will not prefcribe unto the faints a form of repentance; we will ceafe therefore to difpute what
St. Peter fhould have done, and rather gather leffons for ourfelves out of what he did. *Fourthly,*
and laft of all, as St. Peter's fault was great, fo he
contends that his repentance may be as ferious.
The tears therefore he fheds are not flight and
perfunctory, fhed only only for fafhion's fake, fuch
as Quintilian fpake of, ' Nothing fooner grows dry
' than tears * :' but, as the text faith, ' He wept
' bitterly :' to fummon up a fort of Chriftians,
who never had tear drop from their eye to witnefs
their repentance † : to teach us to enlarge the
meafure of our forrow for our fins, and in cafe of
grievous relapfe, not mince out our repentance,
but to let loofe the reins unto grief. And thus I
come to handle the parts in order more particularly : and *firft* of the perfon, *he.*

* Nihil facilius quam lacrymas inarefcere.   Inft. Orat.
lib. vi. c. 1.

† Siccoculum genus Chriftianorum.   *Alluding to Plautus,*
Pfeud. i. *v.* 75. Genus noftrum femper ficcoculum fuit.

Amongſt all the ſaints of God, whoſe errors
are ſet down in holy ſcriptures, there is none
whoſe perſon was more eminent, or fall more dangerous, than St. Peter's. That which wiſe men
have obſerved in great and eminent wits, that they
evermore exceed; either they are exceeding good,
or elſe they are exceeding bad, in St. Peter was
true both ways. His gifts of faith, of underſtanding in the myſtery of godlineſs, of reſolution to
die in our Saviour's cauſe, were wonderful: but
yet his errors were as many and as ſtrange; yea,
ſo much the more ſtrange, becauſe in that thing
he moſt offended, in which he was moſt eminent.
It was a great argument of his faith, when in the
tempeſt meeting our Saviour on the waters, he
calls out unto him, 'If it be thou, command me
' to come unto thee on the waters;' Matth. xiv.
28. but no ſooner was he come out of the ſhip,
but through infidelity he began to ſink. Again,
of his great underſtanding in the myſtery of Chriſt
he gave a notable inſtance, when being queſtioned
by our Saviour ' whom men took him to be?'
he gave the firſt evident, plain, and open teſtimony that ever was given him by man, ' Thou art
' Chriſt, the Son of the living God.' Matth. xvi.
16. St. John indeed gave teſtimony, and ſo
did St. Simeon, and ſo did many more; but it
was more involved, done in more covert terms,
more dark: whence we may, and that not without ſome probability, argue, that the underſtand-

ing of thefe men was not fo evidently, fo fully, fo
perfpicuoufly enlightened as was St. Peter's. It is
a great argument that a man doth paffing well underftand himfelf, when he is able perfpicuoufly and
plainly to fpeak to the underftanding of another*:
this confeffion therefore of St. Peter, that carries
with it greater light and perfpicuity than any yet
that ever was given, doth not obfcurely intimate,
that he had a greater meafure of illumination than
any of his predeceffors. Yet to fee the wonderful
difpenfation of the Holy Ghoft, fcarce was this
confeffion out of his mouth, but in the very next
bout, where our Saviour begins further to inform
him in the particulars of his paffion, and death,
and defpiteful handling by the Jews, the edge of
his conceit was quite turned, quite blunted and
dull: poor man, as if he had been quite ignorant
of the end of Chrift's coming, out of a humane
conceit and pity, he takes upon him to counfel
and advife our Saviour; ' Sir, favour yourfelf,
' thefe things fhall not come unto you:' Matth.
xvi. 23. and for this pains he is rewarded with no
lefs reproachful a name than that of Satan, of a
feducer, of a devil: he that fhall perufe the ftory
of the gofpel, and here ftay himfelf, might think
that that which we read, St. John vi. 70. fpoken
of Judas, ' Have I not chofen you twelve, and one
' of you is a devil,' were here fulfilled in St. Pe-

* Signum eft intelligentis poffe docere.

ter. Laſt of all, his love to Chriſt, and reſolution
in his quarrel, he gave an evident teſtimony, when
he proteſted himſelf ready to lay down his life for
him ; ' Greater love than this;' in the Apoſtle's
judgment, ' no man hath, than to lay down his
' life for his friend * :' this St. Peter had, if we
may believe himſelf : yea, he began to expreſs
ſome acts of it, when, in defence of his maſter,
he manfully drew his ſword, and wounded the ſervant of the high prieſt. But ſee how ſoon the ſcene
is changed ; this good champion of our Saviour,
as a lion that is reported to be daunted with the
crowing of a cock, is ſtricken out of countenance,
and quite amazed with the voice of a ſilly damſel ;
yea, ſo far is he poſſeſſed with a ſpirit of fear,
that he not only denies, but abjures his maſter,
and perjures himſelf, committing a ſin not far behind the ſin of Judas ; yea, treading it hard upon the heels. But the mercy of God, that leaves
not the honour of his ſervant in the duſt of death,
but is evermore careful to raiſe us up from the
death of ſin, unto the life of righteouſneſs, ſuffers
not this rock, this great pillar of his church to be
overthrown. He firſt admoniſhes him by the crowing of a cock ; when that would not ſerve, himſelf (full of careful love and goodneſs) though in
the midſt of his enemies, forgets his own danger,
and remembers the danger of his ſervant ; himſelf

* The author ought to have ſaid ' in the judgment of our
' Lord himſelf;' for he alludes here to John xv. 13.

was now ' as a sheep before the shearer, dumb,
' and not opening his mouth ;' Isaiah liii. 7. yet
forgets he not, that he is that great shepherd of
the flock, but, David like, rescues one of his fold
from the mouth of the lion, and from the paw of
the bear; ' He turns about, and looks upon him,'
faith the text; he cries louder unto him with his
look, than the cock could with his voice: of all
the members in the body, the eye is the most moving part; *that* oft-times is spoken in a look, which
by no force of speech could have been uttered ;
this look of Christ did so warm St. Peter, almost
frozen dead with fear, that it made him well-near
melt into tears: as if he had cried out with the
Spouse, ' O turn away thine eyes, for they have
' overcome me;' Cantic. vi. 5. he grows impatient of his looks, and seeks for a place to weep ;
what a look was this think you? St. Jerom dif-
coursing with himself what might be the cause
that many of the disciples, when they were called
by our Saviour, presently without further consul-
tation arose and followed him, thinks it not improbable, that there did appear some glory and
majesty in his countenance, which made them believe he was more than a man that thus bespake
them: whatsoever then appeared in his looks,
doubtless in this look of his was seen some sovereign power of his Deity, that could so speedily
recover a man thus almost desperately gone: a
man that had one foot in hell, whom one step

more had irrecoverably caſt away: it was this
look of Chriſt that reſtored St. Peter : ‘ They
‘ weep for their ſins,’ ſaith St. Ambroſe, ‘ whom
‘ Jeſus looks upon : St. Peter denies him once,
‘ and repents not, for Jeſus looked not back upon
‘ him ; he denies him the ſecond time, and yet he
‘ weeps not, for yet the Lord looked not back ; he
‘ denies him the third time, and Jeſus looks upon
‘ him and then he weeps bitterly*.’ Before I come to
make uſe of this, it will not be altogether impertinent to ſay ſomething unto ſome queries that here
ariſe concerning the condition of St. Peter, and in
him of all the elect of God, whilſt they are in a
ſtate of ſin unrepented of; for, as for St. Peter's
faith, which ſome make doubt of, there can, as I
conceive, no queſtion be made. It is not to be
thought that St. Peter had reverſed with himſelf
the confeſſion that he had formerly made of Chriſt,
or that he thought, doubtleſs I have erred, this is
not the perſon whom I took him to be : indeed,
through fear and cowardice he durſt not confeſs
that with his mouth unto ſalvation, which in his
heart he believed unto righteouſneſs: any thing
further than this, that ſpeech of our Saviour takes
away, wherein he tells him beforehand, ‘ I have

---

* Quos reſpicit Jeſus, plorant delictum : Negavit primo
Petrus, et non flevit ; quia non reſpexerat Dominus : negavit
ſecundo, non flevit, quia adhuc non reſpexerat Dominus : negavit tertio, et reſpexit Jeſus, et ille amariſſime flevit. Ad
Lucam x. c. 89.

' prayed that thy faith might not fail.' Luke xxii.
32. But since, our age hath had experience of
some, who, because the election of God standeth
sure, and Christ's sheep none can take out of his
hands, conclude therefore, that for the elect of
God there is no falling from grace, that to David
and Peter no ill could happen, no though (for so
they have given it out) that they had died in the
very act of their sin : to meet with such disputants, I will briefly lay down what I conceive is to
be thought in the point. Wherefore prepare thy
mouth for bread, as St. Bernard speaks *; hitherto I have given you milk, provide your stomachs
now for harder meat, and such as befits strong men
in Christ. Peter and Judas (for I will couple them
both together in my discourse, whilst they are
both joined together in sin) Peter, I say, and Judas, in regard of their own persons, were both,
more or less, in the same case, both fallen from
grace, both in a state of sin and damnation, till
the repentance of St. Peter altered the case on his
part. But the grace of God signifies two things :
either the purpose of God's election, the grace
and favour inherent in the person of God, which
he still casts upon those that are his, notwithstanding their manifold backslidings; or else it signifies
the habit of sanctifying qualities, inherent in the
regenerate man, those good graces of God, by
which he walks holy and unblameable. Again, the

* Parate fauces pani.

ſtate of damnation ſignifies likewiſe two things; either the purpoſe of God's reprobation, or elſe the habit of damnable qualities in the ſinful man. From the ſtate of grace, as it ſignifies the purpoſe of God to ſave, the elect can never fall; in the ſtate of damnation, as it ſignifies ſomething inherent in us, every man by nature is, and the elect of God, even after their calling many times fall into it: that is, they may and do many times fall into thoſe ſins, yea, for a time continue in them too, (David did ſo for a whole year's ſpace) which, except they be done away by repentance, inevitably bring forth eternal death; for the ſtate of mortal ſin, unrepented of, is truly and indeed the ſtate of death; yea the whole and ſole reaſon of the condemnation of every one that periſhes, for Chriſt hath ſaid it, ' Except ye repent, ye ſhall all ' periſh.' Luke xiii. 3. So then you ſee, that into the ſtate of damnation, as it ſignifies ſomething inherent in us, a man may fall, and yet not fall from the ſtate of grace, as it ſignifies God's purpoſe of election: for both theſe are compatible for a time. If then we look upon the perſons of Peter and Judas, both of them are in the ſtate of mortal ſin unrepented of, and therefore both in ſtate of damnation: but if we look back unto God, we ſhall ſee a hand reached out unto St. Peter, pulling him back as he is now running down the hill, which hand we do not ſee reached out unto Judas. Chriſt had a look in ſtore for St. Peter, which if it had

pleafed him to have lent unto Judas, Judas would
have done that which St. Peter did. When then
we pronounce St. Peter, and in him any of the
elect of God, as they are in St. Peter's cafe, to be
fallen from grace, we fpeak not with relation to
any purpofe of God; but we mean only, that
they have not that meafure of fanctification which
ought to be in every child which fhall be an heir
to life: and what hinders to pronounce that man
fallen from grace, whom we muft needs acknowledge to be in that ftate, in which if he continue,
there is no way open but to death? What then
may fome men fay, had St. Peter loft the fpirit of
adoption? had he not thofe fanctifying qualities
of faith, hope, and charity, which are proper to
the faints, and are given them by divine infpirati-
on in the moment of their converfion? was that
immortal feed of the word quite killed? No verily; How then? having all thefe, may he not yet
be called the child of death? I anfwer, he may,
and is indeed fo; for thefe do not make him, that
at no time he can be fo; but, that finally he fhall
not be fo, for they are not armour of proof to
keep out all darts, neither do they make our fouls
invulnerable, as the poets feign the body of Cyc-
nus or Achilles to have been; but they are precious balms evermore ready at hand to cure the
wound when it is given: they are not of force to
hinder mortal fin, (for then every foul in whom
they are, were pure, undefiled, neither were it

poffible, that the elect of God, after their converfion, fhould fall) but they are of force to work repentance, which makes all our wounds remedi-
able. He that is mortally fick and dies, and he that
is likewife mortally fick, and through help of re-
ftoring phyfic recovers, in this both agree, that
they are mortally fick, notwithftanding the recovery of one party. The wound of St. Peter and of
Judas was mortal, and in both feftred unto death;
but there was balm in Gilead for St. Peter, for
Judas there was none. The fting of the fiery fcorpion in the wildernefs was deadly, and all that
looked not on the brazen ferpent died: the brazen ferpent altered not the quality of the fcorpion's fting, it only hindered the working of the
poifon. The fting of fin in St. Peter and in Judas
was deadly, but he that was lift up on mount
Calvary, as the brazen ferpent was in the wildernefs, at him did St. Peter look and live; Judas did
not look, and therefore died. How comes it a-
bout, Beloved, that God every where in fcripture
threatens death, without exception, to all that repent not, if the ftate of fin unrepented of, in
whomfoever it is, be not indeed the ftate of death?
When David was intending to ftay in Keilah, and
fufpecting the inhabitants of that city, afks of God,
whether the men of Keilah would deliver him o-
ver into the hand of Saul?' 1 Sam. xxiii. 11. God
tells him, they would: and therefore certainly had
he ftaid there, he had been betrayed unto Saul.

To urge that St. Peter, becaufe of God's purpofe to fave him, could not have finally mifcarried, though he had died without repentance, (as fome have not ftuck to give out) is nothing elfe in effect, but to maintain againft God, that David, had he ftaid in Keilah, had not fallen into Saul's hands, becaufe we know it was God's purpofe to preferve David from the violence of Saul: all the determinations of God are of equal certainty: it was no more poffible for Saul to feize on David, than it is for the devil to pull one of God's elect out of his hand; as therefore the determinate purpofe of God to free David from the malice of Saul, took not away that fuppofition, If David go to Keilah, he fhall fall into the hands of Saul; fo neither doth the decree of God to fave his elect, deftroy the fuppofition, if they repent not, they die eternally; for the purpofes of God, though impoffible to be defeated, yet lay not upon things any violent neceffity, they exempt not from the ufe of ordinary means, they infringe not our liberty, they ftand very well with common cafualty; yea, thefe things are the very means by which his decrees are brought about.

I may not ftand longer upon this; I will draw but one fhort admonition, and fo to an end: Let no man prefume to look into the third heaven, to open the books of life and death, to pronounce over peremptorily of God's purpofe concerning himfelf, or any other man. Let every man look

into himſelf, and try whether he be in the faith or
no ? The fureſt means to try this, is to take an
impartial view of all our actions. Many deceive
themſelves, whilſt they argue from their faith to
their works, whereas they ought out of their
works to conclude their faith ; whilſt preſuming
they have faith, and the gifts of ſanctification,
they think all their actions warrantable : whereas
we ought firſt thoroughly to ſift all our actions,
to examine them at the touch of God's commandments, and if indeed we find them current, then
to conclude that they come from the ſanctifying
graces of the Holy Spirit. It is faith indeed that
gives the tincture, the die, the reliſh unto our actions ; yet, the only means to examine our faith,
is by our works. It is the nature of the tree that
gives the goodneſs, the favour, and pleaſantneſs to
the fruit ; yet, the fruit is the only means to us,
to know whether the tree be good ; ' By their
' fruit ye ſhall know them,' ſaith Chriſt. Matth.
vii. 16. It is a rule not only to know others, but
ourſelves too. To reaſon thus, I am of the elect,
I therefore have ſaving faith, and the reſt of the
ſanctifying qualities, therefore that which I do is
good ; thus, I ſay, to reaſon is very prepoſterous :
we muſt go a quite contrary courſe, and thus reaſon ; My life is good, and through the mercies of
God in Jeſus Chriſt, ſhall ſtand with God's juſtice : I therefore have the gifts of ſanctification,
and therefore am of God's elect : for St. Peter to

have faid with himfelf, I am of the elect, this fin therefore cannot endanger me, had been great prefumption; but, thus to have reafoned, My fin is deadly, therefore except I repent, I am not of the number of God's elect; this reafoning had well befitted St. Peter, and becomes every Chriftian man, whom common frailty drives into the like diftrefs.

I made my entrance into my fermon with the confideration of the wifdom of God, in permitting his chiefeft fervants to fall dangeroufly: I have largely exemplified it in the perfon of St. Peter: give me leave to make this further beneficial unto you, by drawing fome ufes from it; for great profit hath redounded to the church through the fall of thefe men. St. Ambrofe faith of this fall of St. Peter, 'His fin hath more availed us, than the righ- ' teoufnefs of many others *;' for wherefoever it pleafes the Holy Spirit of God to work effectually (I fpeak cauteloufly, becaufe I would give no place to prefumption) in him he makes excellent ufe oftimes, even of fin and evil. *Firft* of all, it is a tried cafe, that many times, through negligence and carelefnefs, we fuffer ourfelves to lie open to many advantages: in fuch a cafe as this, a blow given us, ferves us for a remembrance to call our wits about us, to ftir up the grace of God that is In us, which many times lies covered like fire un-

* Felicius ille cecidit quam caeteri fteterunt.   Ad Luc. x. c. 84.

der afhes; for as a fkilful wreftler, having fuffered
his adverfary to take advantage upon fome over-
fight, recollects himfelf, and comes forward with
greater ftrength and warinefs: fhame of the fall,
and impatience of difgrace, adds ftrength unto
him, and kindles him *: fo oft-times is it with the
faints of God; the fhame of having fallen, makes
them fummon up their forces, to look better about
them, to fulfil their duty in larger fort, than if they
had not flipt at all. Hence it is, that we fee that
of the bitterest enemies of the church have been
made the beft converts; of this we have a notable
example in St. Paul; how eager was he in the
quarrel of the Jews againft Chrift? None a more
mifchievous enemy to the Chriftians than he; yet,
when it pleafed God to fhew him his error, he
proved one of the moft excellent inftruments of
Chrift's glory that ever was on earth; and fo accordingly he gives himfelf a moft true teftimony,
' I have laboured more abundantly,' not than one
or two of them, but, ' than they all, 1 Cor. xv. 10.
his writings being as much in quantity as of them
all; and St. Luke's ftory being nothing elfe almoft but a regifter of the acts of St. Paul: the
fenfe and confcience, I doubt not, of that infinite
wrong done to the church, provoked him to meafure back to the utmoft of his power, his pains
and labour in making up the breach he had for-

* Tum pudor incendit vires et confcia virtus. Virg. Aeneid.
lib. v.

merly made. Here then is a notable leſſon for us, teaching us to make our former ſins and impieties admonitioners unto us, to know our own ſtrength, and by Chriſtian care and watchfulneſs to prevent all advantages, which the devil may take by our rechleſſneſs and negligence: for, Beloved, it is not ſo much our impotency and weakneſs, as our ſloth and careleſſneſs, againſt which the common enemy doth prevail; for through the grace of him that doth enable us, we are ſtronger than he: and the policy of Chriſtian warfare hath as many means to beat back and defend, as the deepeſt reach of Satan hath to give the onſet. The envious man in the goſpel ruſhed not into the field in deſpite of the huſbandman and the ſervants, but came and ſowed his tares ' whilſt men ſlept,' ſaith the text, Matth. xiii. 25. our neglect and careleſſneſs is the ſleep that he takes advantage of: when David was ſo ſtrangely overtaken, the ſcripture tells us ' he roſe from his bed, to walk on the top of his palace;' 2 Sam. xi. 2. from his bed indeed he aroſe, but not from his ſleep; for mark, I beſeech you, David had ſpent much of his time about the court, he had been abroad, and ſeen and ranſacked many cities, and doubtleſs he had ſeen many women as fair as the wife of Uriah, and that in his younger days, when he was more apt to kindle; why then now commits he ſo great an overſight? Look on him a while as now he is; he is now at reſt in his palace, at eaſe on his bed, and to ſolace himfelf, he muft rife and walk at the top of his houfe, and idly gaze upon a naked dame; of this his idlenefs the devil takes advantage ; this is the fleep in which he comes and fows tares in David's heart, even all manner of luft: fo that David fell as Adam did in paradife, not as a man that falls before an enemy ftronger than himfelf. The greateft part of the fins which we commit are in this rank with David's fin: 'He is faithful,' faith the apoftle, 'and fuffers no man to be tempted above 'his ftrength.' 1 Cor. x. 13. Many creatures, if they knew their ftrength, would never fuffer themfelves to be awed by man as they are. Beloved, we are become like horfe and mule, without underftanding, we know not our ftrength, we are more blind than the fervant of Elifha, and fee not that 'they that are with us are more, and more 'mighty, than they that are againft us :' 2 Kings vi. 16. The angels are miniftering fpirits, fent out of purpofe to guard us, and doubtlefs do many and great fervices for us, though we perceive not; we have the army of God, 'where are a 'thoufand bucklers, and all the weapons of the 'mighty;' Canticl. iv. 4. The helmet of falvation, the fword of the fpirit, the fhield of faith, to quench all the fiery darts of fin: only let us not neglect to buckle it on, and make ufe of it. We have to ftrive with an enemy, fuch a one as Hannibal reported Marcellus to be; 'A reftlefs enemy 'that is never quiet, howfoever the world goes;

' if he conquer us, he infolently infults upon us;
' if we foil him, he ftill bethinks himfelf how to
' fet upon us afrefh *.'   Let us not therefore fuppofe that the conqueft will be gotten by fitting
ftill, and wifhing all were well †.   We oft maintain againft the church of Rome, that our natural
abilities, whilft we live, ferve us not to fulfil the
law of God.   What boots it thus to difpute? fhall
the confeffion of our unablenefs to do what we
ought, excufe us at all, if we do not that which
we are able?   St. Auftin was of opinion, how
juftly I will not difpute, but of that opinion he
was, and it was the occafion of his book, *De fpi-*
ritu et litera, ad Marcellinum ; that it was poffible for us, even in this natural life, feconded by
the grace of God, perfectly to accomplifh what the
law requires at our hands.   Let the truth of this
be as it may be, certainly that is moft true which
the fame Father adds;   That let our ftrength be
what it will, yet, if we know not our duty, we
fhall do it no more, than the traveller, found of
body or limb, can go that way aright, of which he
is utterly ignorant: yea, let our ability be perfect, and let our knowledge be alfo abfolute, yet
if we have no mind, if we want a love unto our
duty, if · we· fuffer ourfelves to be overfwayed by

* Qui nec bonam, nec malam ferre fortunam poteft; feu
vicit, ferociter inftat victis; feu victus eft, inftaurat cum vic-
toribus certamen.   Liv. lib 17. c. 19.

† Sedendo et votis debellari poffe.   Liv. lib. 22. c. 14.

affection to other things, yet shall we not do our duty: for which of us, being at liberty, will do that which he hath no love unto? Beloved, as for our knowledge, God hath left unto us scripture, the perfect register of all our duty, the absolute itinerary and map of all the course which in this life we are to run; and as for love, he plentifully sheds it in the hearts of all those that by faithful prayer beg it of him: if we shall search the scripture to improve our knowledge, if we shall earnestly beg at his hands to inflame our love; let our natural possibilities be what they will; he that now doth little amongst us shall do much, and he that doth much shall do much more: and the promises made unto the Jews concerning their carnal enemies, shall be made good on us concerning our spiritual and ghostly enemies, ' one of us shall ' chase a thousand,' Deut. xxxii. 30. and ' if they ' come out against us one way, they shall flee be- ' fore us seven ways.' Deut. xxvii. 27. And thus much for the first use.

There is a *second* benefit of great weight and moment, which we reap out of the consideration of the errors of these excellent ministers of God ; namely, a lesson teaching us to beware of spiritual pride. Of all the vices which our nature is subject unto, this is the most dangerous, and of which we had need be most cautelous: for whereas all other vices proceed from some ill in us, from some sinful imbecillity of our nature, this alone arises out of

our good parts: other fins draw their being from
that original corruption which we drew from our
parents, but this may feem to be the mother of
that; as by which even natures unftained, and in
their primitive purity, may moft eafily fall. And
therefore, not without fome probability, is it concluded in the fchools, That no other crime could
throw the angels down from heaven but this.
That which one leaves for a memorial to great
men, that in dangerous times, ' it was a matter
' of like danger to have a great name, as an ill * ; '
that may I pronounce of a Chriftian man, the danger of his innocency is not much lefs than of his
faults. For this devil, when he cannot drive us to
defpair by reafon of our fin, takes another courfe,
to fee if he can make us prefume upon conceit of
our righteoufnefs : for, when by the preventing
grace of God, we keep ourfelves from greater offences, if we find ourfelves to have a love unto the
word of God, and the true profeffors of it, to be
rich in alms-deeds, to have a part in other acts of
righteoufnefs, he makes us firft take notice of thefe
good things in us ; notice taken, draws us to love
and admire them in us; felf-love draws us on to
compare ourfelves with others, then to prefer ourfelves before others, and thirdly to difdain others
in refpect of ourfelves. Here now is a gap laid o-
pen to a thoufand inconveniences : and hence it

* Non minus periculum ex magna fama quam ex mala,
Tacit. vit. Agricolae. c. 5.

is that we see divers times men, otherwise of life and reputation pure and unblameable, upon conceit and inconsiderateness, by a secret judgment of God, to fall upon extremes no less fearful, than are the issues of open profaneness and impiety. To cut off therefore all way that may be opened to let in spiritual pride, it hath pleased God to make use of this as of a sovereign remedy, namely, to permit, even in his most chosen vessels, evermore secret and hidden infirmities, and some times gross and open scapes, which may serve, when they look into themselves, to abate all overweening conceit of their own righteousness, and when they shall look into the errors of others, may be secret admonitioners unto them, not rashly to condemn them, considering their own weakness. I will therefore shut up this place with the saying of St. Ambrose; ' The fall of the saints is a very ' profitable thing; it hurts not me that St. Peter ' denied Christ, and the example of his amend- ' ment is very beneficial unto me*.' And so I come unto the preparative unto St. Peter's repentance, in these words, ' and he went forth.'

The wisdom of God hath taught the church sometime by express message delivered by words of mouth, sometime by dumb signs and actions.

* Etiam lapsus sanctorum utilis est ; ecce nihil nobis apostolus nocuit quod negavit, et plurimum profuit quod emendavit. Ambrof. serm. 46. *The Benedictins ascribe this piece to Maximus not to Ambrose.*

When Jeremy walked up and down the city with a yoke of wood about his neck, when Ezekiel lay upon his side, besieged a slate with the draught of Jerusalem upon it, and, like a banished man, carried his stuff upon his shoulders from place to place; they did no less prophesy the captivity, desolation, famine, and woe, which was to fall upon Jerusalem, than when they denounced it by direct word and speech: yea, many of the ordinary actions of the patriarchs, which seem to participate of chance, and to be in the same rank with those of other men, themselves (as a learned divine of our age, Mercerus, observes) not intending or understanding any such thing, contained by the dispensation of the Holy Ghost, especial lessons and instructions for us. That speech of Sarah, ' Cast ' out the bond woman and her son,' Gen. xxi. 10. seemed to Abraham only a speech of a cursed heart, and she herself perceives not herself to speak by direction from God, but moved with impatience of Ismael's petulant behaviour toward her son: yet, the Holy Ghost himself hath taught us, that this act of her prefigured a great mystery. Many disputations there are concerning the cause of this action of St. Peter's going forth: whether it were out of the common infirmity that is in most men, namely, a greater shame to repent than to offend? or, whether it were out of modesty and good nature, that he could not endure the sight of Christ, whom he had so grievously offend-

ed? Howſoever it were, we ſhall do this ſcripture no wrong, if we think it to contain an act
in outward ſhew caſual, and like unto the actions of other men, but inwardly indeed an eſpecial action of a perſon great in the ſight of God;
and therefore comprehending ſome eſpecial inſtruction. And, to ſpeak plainly, this abandoning
the place wherein he fell, the company for fear of
whom he fell, and thoſe things that were occaſioners of his ſin, doth not obſcurely point out unto us an eſpecial duty of ſpeedy relinquiſhing and
leaving of all, either friends, or place, or means,
or whatſoever elſe, though dearer unto us than
our right hand, than our right eye, if once they
become unto us inducements to ſin. In former
days, before the fulneſs of time came, the calling
of the elect of God was not by any one act more
often prefigured, than by this action of going
forth; when the purpoſe of God was to ſelect unto himſelf a church, and to begin it in Abraham,
' Come forth,' ſaith he unto him, ' out of thy
' country, and from thy kindred, and from thy
' father's houſe:' Gen. xii. 1. when Iſrael being
in Egypt, it pleaſed God to appoint them a ſet
form and manner of ſerving him, before this could
be done, they and all theirs muſt ' come forth of
' Egypt, they muſt not leave a hoof behind them.'
Exod. x. 26. When the time of the goſpel was come,
our Saviour holds the ſame courſe; none muſt be
of his company, but ſuch as come forth, ' leave all

and ' follow him:' Mark x. 21. and therefore the
apoſtle, putting the Hebrews in mind of their duty, expreſſes it in this very term, ' Let us go forth
' therefore unto him,' ſaith he, 'without the camp,
' bearing his reproach.' Heb. xiii. 13. And in
the original language of the New Teſtament, the
church hath her name from this thing, from being called forth; ſo that without a going forth
there is no church, no Chriſtianity, no ſervice to
God: the reaſon of all which is this, we are all by
nature in the high prieſt's court, as St. Peter was,
where we all deny and forſwear our Maſter, as
St. Peter did: neither is there any place for repentance, till, with St. Peter, we go forth and
weep.

For our further light, we are to diſtinguiſh the
practice of this our going forth, according to the
diverſity of the times of the church. In the firſt
ages, when Chriſtianity was like unto Chriſt, and
had no place to hide its head, no entertainment but
what perſecution, and oppreſſion, and fire, and
ſword could yield it; there was then required at
the hands of Chriſtians, an actual going forth, a
real leaving of riches, and friends, and lands, and
life, for the profeſſion of the goſpel. Afterward,
when the tempeſts of perſecutions were ſomewhat
allayed, and the ſky began to clear up, the neceſſity of actual relinquiſhing of all things ceaſed,
Chriſtians might then ſecurely hold life and lands,
and whatſoever was their own; yet, that it might

appear unto the world, that the refolution of Chriftian men was the fame as in times of diftrefs and want, fo likewife in time of peace and fecurity, it pleafed God to raife up many excellent men, as well of the laity as of the clergy, who, without conftraint, voluntarily and of themfelves, made liberal diftribution of all they had; left their means and their friends, and betook themfelves to deferts and folitary places, wholly giving themfelves over to meditation, to prayer, to fafting, to all feverity and rigidnefs of life : what opinion our times hath of thefe, I cannot eafily pronounce ; thus much I know fafely may be faid, that when this cuftom was in its primitive purity, there was no one thing more behoveful to the church; it was the feminary and nurfery of the fathers, and of all the famous ornaments of the church : thofe two things which afterwards, in the decay and ruin of this difcipline, the church fought to eftablifh by decrees and conftitutions, namely, to eftrange her priefts from the world, and bind them to a fingle life, were the neceffary effects of this manner of living ; for when from their childhood they had utterly fequeftered themfelves from the world, and long practifed the contempt of it ; when, by chaftifing their body, and keeping it under with long fafting, they had killed the heat of youth, it was not ambition, nor defire of wealth, nor beauty of women, that could withdraw them, or fway their affections.

That which afterwards was crept into the church, and bare the name of monkery, had indeed nothing of it but the name; under the pretence of poverty they seized into their possession the wealth and riches of the world, they removed themselves from barren soils into the fattest places of the land, from solitary desarts into the most frequented cities; they turned their poor cottages into stately palaces, their true fasting into formalizing and partial abstinence: so that instead of going forth, they took the next course to come into the world; they left not the world for Christ, but under pretence of Christ they gained the world, as Nazianzen speaks *: one of their own, St. Jerom by name, long ago complained of it; ' Some there ' are, more opulent as monks than they were ' while laics, and clergy who, under the indigent ' Jesus, possess wealth which under the deceitful ' evil spirit of riches they did not possess: in so ' much that the church mourns for the opulence ' of her children, who being yet children of this ' world, were poor †.'

But I forbear, and come to commend unto you another kind of going forth, necessary for all per-

---

* Ὡσπερ ἐκ ἀρετῆς τύπον, ἀλλ' ἀφορμὴν τῦ βίῳ τὴν τάξιν ταύτην εἶναι νομίζοντες.

† Nonnulli sunt ditiores monachi, quam fuerant seculares; et clerici qui possideant opes sub paupere Christo, quas sub fallaci et locuplete diabolo non habuerant; ut suspiret eos ecclesia divites, quos tenuit mundus ante mendicos. Lib. ii. Epist. ad Nepotianum.

fons, and for all times: there is a going forth in
act and execution, requisite only at some times,
and upon some occasions; there is a going forth
in will and affections; this, let the persons be of
what calling soever, and let the times be never so
favourable, God requires at the hands of every
one of us. We usually indeed distinguish the times
of the church into times of peace, and times of
persecution : the truth is, to a true Christian man
the times are always the same: ' There is a martyr-
' dom, saith one, even in time of peace * ;' for the
practice of a Christian man, in the calmest times,
in readiness and resolution, must nothing differ
from times of rage and fire. Josephus, writing of
the military exercises practised amongst the Romans, reports, that for seriousness they differed
from a true battle only in this, ' The battle was a
' bloody exercise, their exercise a bloodless battle†;'
like unto this must be the Christian exercise in
times of peace, neither must there be any difference betwixt those days of persecution, and these
of ours, but only this, those yielded martyrs with
blood, ours without. Let therefore every man
thoroughly examine his own heart, whether, upon suppolal of times of trial and persecution, he
can say with David, ' My heart is ready:' Psal.

* Habet etiam pax suos martyres.

† Καὶ ὑκ ἄν ἁμάρτοι τὶς ἐιπὼν, τὰς μὲν μελίτας αὐτῶν χωρὶς αἵματος παραλάξεις τὰς παρατάξεις δὶ, μεθ᾽ αἵματος μελίτας.
De Bell. Judaic. lib. iii. c. 5. §. 1.

cviii. 1. [old tranflation] whether he can fay of
his deareft pledges, 'All thefe have I counted dung
' for Chrift's fake?' Philip. iii. 8. whether he find
in himfelf that he can, if need be, even lay down
his life for his profeffion? He that cannot do thus,
what differs his faith from a temporary faith, or
from hypocrify? Mark, I befeech you, what I fay;
I will not affirm, I will only leave it to your Chriftian difcretion: a temporary faith, that is, a faith
refembled to the feed in the gofpel, which being
fown on the ftony ground, withered as foon as the
fun arofe, a faith that fails as foon as it feels the
heat of perfecution, can fave no man. May we not
with fome reafon think, that the faith of many a
one, who in time of peace feems to us, yea, and
to himfelf too peradventure, to die poffeffed of it,
is yet, notwithftanding, no better than a temporary faith, and therefore comes not fo far as to
fave him that hath it? Rufus, a certain philofopher, whenfoever any fcholars were brought unto
him to receive education under him, was wont to
ufe all poffible force of argument to diffuade them
from it; if nothing could prevail with them, but
needs they will be his hearers, this their pertinacy
he took for a fure token of a mind throughly fettled, and led, as it were by inftinct, to their ftudies. If God fhould ufe this method to try who
are his, and bring on us thofe temptations which
would make the man of a temporary faith to
fhrink, think we that all thofe who, in thefe times

of peace, have born the name of Chrift unto their
graves, would have born unto the rack, unto the
fword, unto the fire? Indeed to man, who knows
not the thoughts of his friend, fome trials fome
times are very neceffary; but he that knew and
foretold David what the refolution of the men of
Keilah would be, if Saul came to them, knows
likewife what the refolution of every one of us
would be, if a fiery trial fhould appear. Who
knows, therefore, whether God hath numbered
out the crowns of life, according to the number
of their fouls, who he foreknew would, in the
midft of all temptations and trials, continue unto
the end? For what difference is there betwixt the
faith that fails upon occafion, or that would fail if
occafion were offered? for the actual failing of faith
is not that that makes it temporary, it is only that
which detects it, which bewrays it unto us to be fo.
The faith therefore of that man which would have
funk as faft as St. Peter did, if tempefts had ari-
fen, notwithftanding that through the peace of the
church he dies poffeffed of, is no better than a
temporary, and cometh fhort of a faving faith. It
is a hard fpeech, fome man may fay; but let him
that thinks thus recount with himfelf, that it is a
hard way that leads to life. Beloved, deceive not
yourfelves; heaven never was, nor will be gotten
without martyrdom: In a word, my brethren,
try therefore yourfelves, whether you have in you
true refolution: fummon up your thoughts, fur-

vey every path in wich your affections were wont
to tread; fee whether you are prepared to leave
all for Chrift: if you find in yourfelves but one
affection looking back to Sodom, to the things of
this life, ' remember Lot's wife,' Luke xvii. 32.
her cafe is yours ; your are not yet fufficiently
provided for the day of battle.

CHRISTIAN

OMNIPOTENCY.

Philip. iv. 13.

I can do all things through Chrift, [that enableth, or] *that ftrengtheneth me.*

FROM henceforth let all complaint concerning the frailty and weaknefs of man's nature for ever ceafe: for behold our weaknefs fwallowed up of ftrength, and man is become omnipotent; ' I can do all things,' faith my Apoftle. The ftrongeft reafon, which the fubtileft above all the beafts of the field could invent, to draw our firft parents from their allegeance, was this, ' Ye fhall ' be like gods.' Gen iii. 5. Our Saviour, who is infinitely wifer to recall us, than our adverfary was to feduce us, takes the fame way to reftore, as *he* did to deftroy, and ufes that for phyfic, which the devil gave for poifon: Is this it, faith he unto us, that hath drawn you from me, that ye would be like unto Gods? why, then return again, and **ye** fhall be like gods, by imparting unto you fuch excellencies as are proper unto myfelf: as I myfelf do all things, fo fhall **you** likewife be enabled to do all things through me. It was the obfervation of the Heathen historian, ' That it is an error in ' men, thus to complain of the infirmities and weak- ' nefs of their nature*;' for man indeed is a crea- ture of great ftrength, and if at any time he find himfelf weak, it is through his fault, not through his nature: but he that fhall take into confidera- tion thefe words of my text, fhall far better than any natural man be able to perceive, that man hath no caufe to complain of his weaknefs. It was a tale that paffed among fome of the Heathen, that Vulcan, offended with the men of Athens, told them that they fhould be but fools; but Pallas, that favoured them, told them they fhould be fools indeed, but folly fhould never hurt them †. Beloved, our cafe is like to that of the men of A- thens; Vulcan, the devil, hath made us fools and weak, and fo we are indeed of ourfelves; but the Son of God, the true Pallas, the Wifdom of the Father, hath given us this gift, that our weaknefs fhall never hurt us: for, look what ftrength we loft in Adam, that, with infinite advantage, is fup- plied in Chrift. It was the parable of Iphicrates, that an army of harts, with a lion to their captain, would be able to vanquifh an army of lions, if

---

* Falfo queritur de natura fua genus humanum, quod im- becilla fit.   Salluft. Bell. Jugurth. c. 1.

† —— φασὶ γὰρ δυσϚυλίαν

Τῆδε τῇ πόλει προσεῖναι· ταῦτα μίν τοι τὺς Ϛεὺς,

Ἄττ' ἂν ὑμᾶς ἐξαμάρτητ', ἐπὶ τὸ βίλτιον τρίπειν.

Ariftophan. Νιφιλ. v. 588. et ib. fchol.

P 4

their captain were but a hart. Beloved, were mankind indeed but an army of harts, were we like
unto the fearful hind upon the mountains, that
ſtarts at every leaf that ſhakes; yet through Chriſt
that ſtrengtheneth us, having the Lion of the tribe
of Judah for our captain and leader, we ſhall be
able to vanquiſh all that force, which the lion that
goeth up and down, ſeeking whom he may devour, is able to bring againſt us. Indeed we do
many times ſadly bemoan our caſe, and much rue
the loſs, which, through the rechleſſneſs of our
firſt parents, hath befallen us; yet let us chear up
ourſelves, our fear is greater than our hurt. As
Elkanah ſpeaks unto Hannah, in the firſt of Samuel i. 8. ' Why weepeſt thou? am not I better
' unto thee than ten ſons?' So will we comfort
ourſelves in the like manner; let us ſorrow no
more for our loſs in Adam; for is not Chriſt ten-
fold better unto us, than all the good of paradiſe?
' The mulberry-tree indeed is broken down, but
' it is built up again with cedar.' Iſaiah ix. 10.
The loſs of that portion of ſtrength, wherewith
our nature was originally endued, is made up with
fulneſs of power in Chriſt; it is paſt that concluſion of Zeba and Zalmunna unto Gideon, in the
book of Judges viii. 21. ' As the man is, ſo is his
' ſtrength;' for now, Beloved, as God is, ſo is
our ſtrength. Wherefore, as St. Ambroſe ſpake
of St. Peter's fall, ' It hurt not me that Peter de-
' nied his Lord, but it hath profited me that Pe-

' ter repented *.'   So we may fpeak of the fall of
our firft parents, it hurts not us that Adam fell ;
nay, our ftrength and glory is much improved,
that by Chrift we are redeemed.   Our natural
weaknefs, be it never fo great, with this fupply
from Chrift, is far above all ftrength of which our.
nature, in its greateft perfection, was capable.   If
we furvey the particulars of that weaknefs, which
we drew from the loins of our firft parents, we
fhall find the chiefeft part of it to be in the lofs of
immortality.   For as for the lofs of that pleafant
place, the blindnefs of underftanding, and per-
verfenefs of will, being fuppofed to betide us immediately upon the fall, thefe feem weakneffes far
inferior to our mortality,   For God, forbidding us
the fruit of the tree of knowledge, and fetting
down the penalty that fhould enfue, making choice
(as it is moft likely) of the fearfulleft judgment,
and what he faw in his wifdom was moft likely to
awe us, threatens neither blindnefs of underftanding, nor crookednefs of nature, but tells us, ' What
' day ye eat of it, ye fhall die.' Gen. ii. 17.   Ye
fee, Beloved, with how great ftrength this mortal
weaknefs is repaired : for thus to be able to.en-
counter with death, the fearfulleft of all God's
curfes, and through Chrift overcome it, as all true

* Non mihi obfuit quod negavit Petrus, immo profuit,
quod emendavit. Serm. 46.   *The author quotes from memory.*

Chriſtians do, to turn the greateſt curſe into the greateſt bleſſing, is more than immortality.

Had not man been thus weak, he had never been thus ſtrong *. Again, on the contrary, let us conceive unto the utmoſt, what our ſtrength might be in our firſt eſtate, let us raiſe our conceit unto the higheſt note we can reach, yet ſhall we never find it to be greater than what here is expreſt in my text. For greater ability, than power to do all things, is not imaginable, ' I can do all things.' Beloved, theſe words are Anakims, they beſeem not the mouth of a man of ordinary ſtrength; he that hath right unto them muſt be one of the race of the giants at leaſt; for he ſaith not ſimply, ' I can,' though peradventure with ſome difficulty, hardly, with much labour and pains; but he ſaith, ' I can with eaſe,' I have valour and ſtrength to do them †. I aſk then, *firſt*, as the eunuch doth in the Acts, of whom ſpeaks our apoſtle this, of himſelf, or of ſome other man? I anſwer, both of himſelf, and all other Chriſtians; for every Chriſtian man, by reading it as he ought, makes it his own, for in reading it as he ought, he reads it with the ſame ſpirit with which St. Paul wrote it. Wherefore as St. Paul ſomewhere records of himſelf, that he was not found inferior to the chief apoſtles, ſo is it true, that the meaneſt Chriſtian that hears me this day, in all that is contained in

* Si non erraſſet, fecerat ille minus.   Martial.

† Not πώτα δύναμαι, but πάντα ἰσχύω.

my text, is parallelled, is nothing inferior unto
St. Paul, unto the chief apostles. What a comfort
then is this unto the brother of low degree, when
he considers with himself, that how mean soever
he may seem to be, either in the church or com-
monweal, yet notwithstanding, in so great a privilege as is this omnipotent power of doing all
things, he is equal unto St. Peter, unto St. Paul,
the greatest peers of the church? If then the
weakness of Christians be so strong, as to deserve
the name of almightiness, what name, what title,
doth the strength of a Christian deserve to bear?

Secondly, I ask what meaning hath this word
ἰχύω, this ' can do' in my text? I answer, very
large: *first*, though it be rendered by this word
doing, yet it comprehends sufferings too: for I
can, is as well to suffer as to do; and that our
blessed apostle, amongst other things, so meant it,
is apparent by the words foregoing my text. And
here is the first part of a Christian's omnipotency:
his patience is infinite, it suffers all things. Never
any contumely, never any loss, never any smart
so great, as could weary out Christian patience.
' Such examples,' saith Tertullian, ' such precepts,
' have we of Christian patience, as that with infi-
' dels they seem incredible, and call in question
' the truth of our profession; but with us they
' are the ground and foundation of faith *.' God

* Talia tantaque documenta, quorum magnitudo penes na-

himfelf did never yet try the utmoft of a Chriftian's patience; neither hath he created any objeét
that is able to equal it : yet he seems, for our in-
ftruétion, to have gone about to try what might
have been done: he commanded Abraham to facrifice his dear and only fon; ' So heavy,' faith
Tertullian, ' was the command, that God himfelf
' liked not it fhould be aéted; yet Abraham heard
' it patiently, and had fulfilled it, if God would
' have given him leave *.'· What fhould I fpeak of
poverty, of difeafe, of the fword, of fire, of death
itfelf. ' Oh! at what a lofs I am,' faith Gordius
the martyr in St. Bafil, ' that I can die but once
' for my Saviour † ?' Take the greateft inftance of
God's fury and wrath, even the pains laid up in hell
for the finner, and we fhall find that there have
been Chriftians, who, for the glory of God, would
gladly have endured them; St. Paul is the man
amongft all the faints of God, the greateft and
worthieft example of this wonderful ftrength, of
this omnipotency of a Chriftian man; what evil is
imaginable, which he did not either indeed, or at

tiones detraétatio fidei eft, penes nos vero, ratio, et ftruétio.
De Patientia. c. 3.

* Tam grave praeceptum, quod nec Deo perfici placebat,
patienter et audivit, et fi Deus voluiffet, impleffet.   De Patientia. c. 6.

† Οἷα ζημιῶμαι μὴ δυνάμινος ὑπὲρ Χριϛοῦ πολλάκις ἀποθανῶν.
Hom. in Gordium. §. 4.

leaſt in will and affection, undergo * ? ' I am on
' fire,' ſaith St. Chryſoſtom, ' when I ſpeak of St.
' Paul † :' and indeed, whom would it not inflame,
to read that admirable ſynopſis and brief of his
ſufferings, regiſtered in the ſecond of the Corinthians? xi. 23. ' In labours more abundant, in ſtripes
' above meaſure, in priſons more frequent, in deaths
' oft;' and could he do more? yes, he could; hitherto he reports hiſtorically what was done, and as
if that were not enough, he tells us what he would
have done ‡, and that his patience was able even
gladly to have encountered hell itſelf; I have prayed, ſaith he in the ninth of the Romans, I have prayed unto God, I have begged it at his hands, as a
favour, that, for the increaſe of his glory, through
the ſalvation of Iſrael, my kinſmen according to
the fleſh, I might become a caſt-away, and endure
the pains of eternal fire. Tertullian, conſidering
the wonderful patience of our Saviour upon his
croſs, thinks, that if there had been no other argument to prove him to be God, yet this alone
had been ſufficient. Hence eſpecially, ye Phariſees, ought ye to have acknowledged the Lord,
ſuch patience it was impoſſible for man to diſ-

---

* Omnem patientiae ſpeciem adverſus omnem diaboli vim
expunxit.   Tertull. de Patientia. c. 3.

† Ἐκκαίομαι γὰρ εἰς τὸν τῦ ἀνδρὸς πόθον, καὶ διὰ τῦτο συνε-
χῶς αὐτὸν περιςρέφων οὐ παυόμαι.   In cap. i. Geneſ. Homil. xi.
§. 5.

‡ Sed ubi hiſtoriam praeſtare non potuit, votum attulit.

play *. In like manner, may we truly say, were there no other argument to prove that Christ doth dwell in us, doth mightily strengthen and enable us, yet this wonderful measure of patience in so finite a creature, could never subsist, if God were not in us of a truth.

Again, ἰχνύω, this word of *doing* here in my text, signifies not only sufferings and patience, this were to make a Christian but a kind of stone: a Christian hath not only a buckler to resist, but he must have a sword to strike. Wherefore this word of *doing* must signify yet further some action and life, and so indeed it doth; for it notes unto us the most glorious and eminent kind of Christian action, victory and conquest; and when my apostle here saith, ' I can do all things,' his meaning is, I can overcome and conquer all things. And here is the second and most glorious part of Christian omnipotency; never was any true Christian overcome, or can be; for look how much he yields unto his enemy, so much he fails of his profession and title. David complains of Joab and his brethren, ' These sons of Zeruiah are too strong ' for me.' 2 Sam. xix. 22. But, Beloved, a Christian man finds none of these sons of Zeruiah, whom he needs to fear, or of whom he needs to complain. For as Aristotle tells us, that a magna-

* Hinc vel maxime, Pharisaei Dominum agnoscere debuistis; patientiam hujusmodi nemo hominum perpetraret. De Patientia. c. 3.

nimous man is he, ' who thinks nothing great *,'
but conceits all things as inferior to himfelf; fo
may we define a true Chriftian to be fuch a one,
as to whom nothing is dreadful, in whofe eye nothing under God carries any fhew of greatnefs.
St. Paul hath left us a catalogue, in the end of
the eighth to the Roman, of all the forces, outward and inward, bodily and ghoftly, that can be
muftered againft us ; ' Life, death, angels, prin-
' cipalities, powers, things prefent, things to come,
' heighth, depth, any creature' imaginable, and
pronounces of them, that in all thefe ' we are con-
' querors;' *conquerors* is too mean a word, we are
' more than conquerors †.' Rom. viii. 37. ' We
' conquer them,' faith St. Chryfoftom, ' with eafe,
' without any pains or fweat ‡.' We fhall not need
to bring forth againft them all our forces, a fmall
part of them will be fufficient to gain the day § ;
and not only to overcome them, but turn them to
our benefit and behoof. For fin is like unto Sampfon's lion, it comes upon us with open mouth to
devour us, but when we have flain it, we fhall
find honey in the belly of it. Wonderful therefore is the power of a Chriftian, who not only o-

---

* Ὦ ὐδὲν μέγα. Ethic. Nicom. lib. iv. c. 3.

† Ὑπερνικῶμεν.

‡ Μετ᾽ εὐκολίας ἁπάσης, χωρὶς πόνων ϗ ἱδρώτων. Hom. xv.
in epift. ad Roman.

§ ———— Paucas victoria dextras
Exigit.

vercomes, and conquers, and kills the viper, but,
like the fkilful apothecary, makes antidote and
treacle of him. Indeed our adverfaries feem to be
very great; St. Paul calls them by wonderful
names, as if he meant to affright us; ' Powers,
' principalities, depths;' Rom. viii. 39. ' the prince
' that ruleth in the air, the God of this world,'
Ephef. ii. 2. and what not? Yet notwithftanding,
as one fpeaks in Livy of the Macedonian war, as I
remember, ' We muft not think there will be any
' doubt of the victory, becaufe it is a war of great
' name and noife*;' for me-thinks I difcover in our
apoftle, when he ufes thefe ftrange aftonifhing
words, a fpiritual ftratagem, by which to ftir us
up, and make us ftand upon our guard, he makes
the largeft report of our enemies forces. We read
that one of the Roman captains, perceiving his foldiers unneceffarily to faint, draws out letters before them, and reads the news of that which never was, of I know not what kings with armies
and multitudes coming forthwith againft them ;
which art of his did much avail him to gain the
victory, becaufe it made the foldiers to recollect
themfelves, and fight with all their might. Beloved, I may not think that the apoftle, in making
this report of our enemies forces, relates that
which is not; but this, I think, I may fafely fay,
that he makes the moft of that which is: for it

* Non quam magni nominis bellum eft, tam difficilem exi-
ftimaveritis victoriam.

can never hurt us to take our enemy to be as
ftrong as he is, or peradventure ftronger, for this
is a very profitable error, it makes us more wary,
and provide ourfelves the better. But to flight
and contemn our enemy, to err on the contrary
fide, and think him to be weaker than he is, this
hath caufed many an overthrow. It is a rule
which Vegetius gives us; ' It is an hard matter
' to overcome him that truly knoweth his own
' ftrength, and the ftrength of his adverfary *.'
And here, Beloved, is the error of moft Chriftians, we do not know of what ftrength we are;
we look upon this body of ours, and fuppofe that
in fo weak and faint a fubject there cannot fub-
fift fo great ftrength, as we fpeak of; as if a man
fhould prize the liquor by the bafenefs of the veffel in which it is. As divers landlords have treafures hidden in their fields, which they know not
of, fo many of us have this treafure of omnipotency in us, but we care not to difcover it, and to
know it; did we but perfectly know our own
ftrength, and would we but compare it with the
ftrength of our enemies, we fhould plainly difcover, that we have fuch infinite advantage above
them, that our conqueft may feem not to be fo
great as is pretended: for the greater the advantages are, the glory of the victory is the lefs; and
that which makes a conqueft great, is not fo much

* Difficilè vincitur, qui de fuis, et adverfarii copiis vere
poteft judicare.   Lib. iii. c. 26.

the greatnefs of him that conquers, as the ftrength
and greatnefs of him that is overthrown. Now
what proportion is there betwixt the ftrength of
God himfelf dwelling in us, and all the ftrength of
heaven, earth, and hell befides? How then can
we count this fpiritual war fo fearful, which is wa-
ged upon fo unequal terms; in which, if we but give
the onfet, we are fure to gain the victory? To refift is to conquer*; for fo faith the apoftle, 'Refift
' the devil, and he fhall flee from you.' Jam. iv. 7.
There was never yet any Chriftian conquered,
that would not; and in this war not to yield the
victory, is to get it. As therefore one fpake of
Alexander's expedition into India, ' The matter
' was not much which he did, the greateft thing
' in it was, that he durft do it †:' fo confidering
our ftrength, and the weaknefs of our adverfaries, we may, without prejudice, fpeak even of the
worthieft foldiers that ever fought thefe fpiritual
battles, the greateft thing that we can admire in
them, is, that they durft do it. Would we but a
little examine the forces of our adverfaries, we
fhould quickly find it to be as I have faid. When
Alcibiades, a young gentleman of Athens, was a-
fraid to fpeak before the multitude, Socrates, to
put him in heart, afks him, Fear you, faith he,
fuch a one? and names one of the multitude to

* In quo fi modo congreffus cum hofte fis, viceris; refti-
tiffe viciffe eft.

† Bene aufus eft vana contemnere.

him; No, faith Alcibiades, he is but a tradefman:
Fear you fuch a one? faith he, and names a fecond; No, for he is but a peafant: or fuch a one?
and names a third: No, for he is but an ordinary
gentleman: Now, faith he, of fuch as thefe doth
the whole multitude confift: and by this device
he encouraged Alcibiades to fpeak. He that fhall
fear to encounter the multitude, and army of fpiritual adverfaries which are ready to fet themfelves
againft him, let him do by himfelf as Socrates did
by Alcibiades; let him fit down and confider with
himfelf his enemies one by one, and he fhall quickly difcover their weaknefs. It is a faying, ' That
' the firft thing that is overcome in a foldier is his
' eye*,' while he judges of his enemy by his multitude and provifion, rather than by his ftrength.
Beloved, if we judge not of our adverfary in grofs,
and as it were by the eye, we fhall eafily fee, that we
fhall not need to do as the king in the gofpel doth,
fend to his enemy with conditions of peace; for
there is no treaty of peace to be had with thefe.
' Had Zimri peace that flew his mafter,' faith the
fcripture, 2 Kings ix. 3 1. and, ' there is no peace
' unto the wicked, faith my God.' Ifaiah xlviii. 2 2.
Not only Zimri, and the wicked, but no Chriftian
hath, or can have peace, he muft be always as
fighting, and always conquering. Let us fingle
out fome one of this army, and let us examine his

* Primi in praeliis vincuntur oculi. Tacit. de moribus
German. c. 43.

ftrength. Is it Sin doth fo much affright us? I make
choice of it, becaufe it is the dreadfulleft enemy
that a Chriftian hath : let us a little confider its
ftrength, and we fhall quickly fee there is no fuch
need to fear it : fins are of two forts, either great
and capital, or fmall and ordinary fins : I know it
were a paradox in nature to tell you, that the
greateft and mightieft things are of leaft force; yet
this is true in the cafe we fpeak of, the greateft
things are the weakeft. Your own experience tells.
you, that rapes and murthers, parricide, poifon-
ing, treafon, and the reft of that rabble of arch-
fins, are the fins of the feweft, and that they have
no ftrength at all but upon the weakeft men; for
doubtlefs if they were the ftrongeft, they would
reign with greateft latitude, they would be the
commoneft, they would be the fins of the moft :
but wandering thoughts, idle words, petty lufts,
inconfiderate wrath, immoderate love to the things
of the world, and the reft of that fwarm of ordinary fins, thefe are they that have largeft extent
and dominion, and fome of thefe, or all of thefe,
more or lefs, prevail with every man. As the magicians in Exodus, when they faw not the power
of God in the ferpents, in the blood, in the frogs,
at the coming of the plague of the lice, prefently
cried, ' This is the finger of God :' Exod. viii. 19.
fo I know not how it comes to pafs, though we
fee and confefs that in thofe great and heinous
crimes, the devil hath leaft power; yet at the com-

ing of lice, of the rout of fmaller and ordinary
fins, we prefently yield ourfelves captives, and cry
out, the ftrength of the devil is in thefe; as if we
were like unto that fabulous rock in Pliny, which
if a man thruft at with his whole body, he could
not move it, yet a man might fhake it with one of
his fingers *. Now what an error is it in us Chriftians, when we fee the principal and captain fins
fo eafily vanquifhed, to think the common foldier
or leffer fort invincible? For certainly, if the
greateft fins be the weakeft, the leffer cannot be
very ftrong.

Secondly, is it original corruption that doth fo
much affright us? Let us confider this a little, and
fee what great caufe we have to fear it. And firft,
Beloved, let us take heed that we feem not to combat a fhadow, to fight with our own fancy, and
not fo much to find, as to feign an enemy. Miftake me not, I befeech you, I fpeak not this as
doubting that we drew any natural infection from
the loins of our parents: but granting this, I take
it to be impoffible to judge of what ftrength it is,
and deny that it is any fuch caufe why we fhould
take it to be fo ftrong, as that we fhould ftand in
fear to encounter it, and overcome it; for we can
never come to difcover how far our nature is neceffarily weak; for whilft we are in our infancy,

* Juxta Harpafa oppidum Afiae caùtes ftat horrenda, uno
digito mobilis; eadem fi toto corpore impellatur, refiftens.
Nat. Hift. lib. ii. c. 98.

and as yet not altered from that which God and
nature made us, none of us underſtand ourſelves;
and ere we can come to be of years to be able to
diſcover it, or define any thing concerning the nature of it, cuſtom or education, either good, hath
much abated, or evil hath much improved the
force of it; ſo that, for any thing we know, the
ſtrength of it may be much leſs than we ſuppoſe,
and that it is but a fear that makes it ſeem ſo
great. ' It is,' ſaith St. Chryſoſtom, ' the nature
' of timerous and fearful men evermore to be
' framing to themſelves cauſeleſs fears*.' I confeſs, it is a ſtrange thing, and it hath many times
much amazed me, to ſee how ripe to ſin many
children are, in their young and tender years;
and, ere they underſtand what the name of ſin and
evil means, they are unexpectedly, and no man
knows by what means, wonderfully prompt and
witty to villany and wickedneſs, as if they had
gone to ſchool to it in their mothers womb. I
know not to what cauſe to impute this thing, but
I verily ſuppoſe I might quit original ſin from the
guilt of it : for it is a ruled caſe, and concluded
by the general conſent of the ſchools, that original
ſin is alike in all: and St. Paul ſeems to me to
ſpeak to that purpoſe, when he ſaith, that ' God
' hath alike concluded all under ſin,' Galat. iii. 22.
and that ' all are alike deprived of the glory of

* Αἱ δειλαι φύσεις πλείονα τῶν ὄντων ἀναπλάτίην δύνανίαι.

' God.' Rom. iii. 23. Were therefore original sin
the cause of this strange exorbitancy in some young
children, they should all be so; a thing which our
own experience teaches us to be false; for we see
many times even in young children many good
and gracious things, which being followed with
good education, must needs come to excellent effect: ' In children,' saith Quintilian, ' many times
' an hope of excellent things appears, which in ri-
' per age, for want of cherishing, fades and wi-
' thers away; a certain sign that nature is not so
' weak, as parents and tutors are negligent * :'
whence then comes this difference? certainly not
from our nature, which is one in all, but from
some other cause. As for original sin, of what
strength it is I will not discuss: only thus much I
will say, there is none of us all but is much more
wicked than the strength of any primitive corruption can constrain. Again, let us take heed that
we abuse not ourselves, that we use not the names
of original weakness as a stale and stalking horse,
as a pretence to choke and cover somewhat else:
For oftentimes when evil education, wicked examples, long custom, and continuance in sin hath
bred in us an habit and necessity of sinning, presently original sin, and the weakness of man's nature, bear the blame. ' When through sloth and

* In pueris elucet spes plurimorum, quae cum emoritur
aetate, manifestum est, non naturam defecisse sed curam. Inst.
Orat. lib. i. c. 1.

' idleness, luxury and diftemper, our time is loft,
' our bodies decayed, our wits dulled, we caft all
' the fault on the weaknefs of our nature †;' that
' law of fin in our members,' of which St. Paul
fpake, Rom. vii. 23. and which fome take to be
original corruption; St. Auftin once pronounced
of it (whether he meant to ftand to it I know not,
but fo he once pronounced of it) ' That the law
' of fin, that carries us againft our wills to fin, is
' nothing elfe but the force and violence of long
' cuftom and continuance in fin ‡.' I know that,
by the error of our firft parents, the devil hath
blinded and bound us more than ever the Philiftines did Samfon; yet this needs not to make us
thus ftand in fear of original weaknefs; for blind
and bound as we are, let the devil build never fo
ftrong, yet if our hair be grown, if Chrift do
ftrengthen us, we fhall be able, Samfon-like, to
bear his ftrongeft pillars, and pull down his houfe
about his ears.

Thirdly, Is it the devil that we think fo ftrong
an adverfary? Let us a little confider his ftrength:
he may be confidered either as an inward enemy,
fuggefting unto us finful thoughts; or as an outward enemy, lying in wait to afflict us in body, in
goods, or the like. Firft, againft us inwardly, he

† Ubi per fecordiam, vires, tempus, ingenium, defluxere,
naturae infirmitas accufatur.   Salluft. Bell. Jugurth. c. 1.

‡ Lex peccati eft violentia confuetudinis.   Confef. lib. viii.
c. 5.

hath no force of his own; from ourselves it is that
he borrows this ftrength to overthrow us. In paradife he borrowed the ferpent to abufe us, but
now every man is that ferpent by which himfelf is
abufed. For as Hannibal having overthrown the
Romans, took their armour, and fought againft
them with their own weapons; fo the devil arms
himfelf againft us with our own ftrength, our fenfes, our will, our appetite; with thefe weapons he
fights againft us, and ufes us againft ourfelves;
let us but recover our own again, and the devil
will be difarmed: Think you that the devil is an
immediate ftickler in every fin that is committed?
I know you do: but take heed, left this be but
an excufe to unload your faults upon the devil, and
to build them upon his back; for St. Chryfoftom
thought otherwife; ' The devil's hand,' faith he,
' is not in every fault, many are done merely by
' our own careleffnefs*.' A negligent carelefs perfon fins, though the devil never tempt him †. Let
the truth of this lie where it will, I think I may
fafely fpeak thus much, that if we would but fhut
up our wills, and ufe that grace of God which is

---

* Οὐ γὰρ δὲ πάντα, αὐτὸς κατασκευάζει, ἀλλὰ πολλὰ, καὶ
ἀπὸ μόνης γίνεται τῆς νωθείας τῆς ἡμετέρας.

† Ὁ ἀσθενὴς κἂν μὴ διάβολος ᾖ, βλάπτεται.

I have not found this paffage in St. Chryfoftom, but the
fame thing is faid in words not much unlike. Ὁ ἀσθενὴς—
ὃ διαβόλου ἐκ ὄντος καταπίπλει. De Diab. Tentatore Homil. ii.
§. 2.

offered, I doubt not but a great part of this fuggefting power of his would fall to nothing. As
for that other force of his, by which he lies in
wait to annoy us outwardly, why fhould we fo
dread that? Are there not more with us both in
multitude and ftrength to preferve us? ' The an-
' gel of the Lord (faith the Pfalmift) pitches his
' tents round about thofe that fear him, to de-
' liver them;' Pf. xxxiv. 7. and the apoftle affures us, that ' the angels are miniftering fpirits,
' fent forth for thofe that fhall be heirs of falvation:'
Heb. i. 14. fhall we think that the ftrength of thofe
to preferve, is lefs than that of the evil angels to
deftroy? One Garcaeus, writing upon the meteors,
told me long fince, that whereas many times before great tempefts, there is wont to be heard, in
the air above us, great noife and rufhing, the caufe
of this was, the banding of good and evil angels,
the one ftriving to annoy us with tempefts, the o-
ther ftriving to preferve us from the danger of it.
And I doubt not, but as about Mofes's body, fo
about every faithful perfon, thefe do contend, the
one to hazard, the other to deliver. Yea, but the
devil infpires into us evil thoughts : well, and
cannot good angels infpire good? They are all,
for any thing appears, by the law of their creati-
on equal, and fhall we think that God did give
unto the devil an infpiring faculty to entangle,
which he denied to his good angels to free us
from? Though good angels could not infpire

good thoughts, yet God both can and doth: so that, for any thing yet appears, we have no such cause to stand in fear of the strength of the devil, either inwardly or outwardly. Thus have I examined the force of three of our principal enemies; I could proceed to examine other particulars of this army of our adversaries, the world, the flesh, persecutions, and the rest, and make the like question of them, as I have done of these, and so conclude as Socrates did to Alcibiades. If you have just cause to fear none of these, why should you fear them all, since that of such as these the whole knot of them consists? But I must proceed to search out yet another meaning of this word *doing* in my text; and that briefly.

Thirdly, Therefore we may take this word of doing in its largest sense: as if the apostle had meant literally, that indeed a Christian can do all things, that he had such a power and command over the creature, as that he could do with it what he list. In which sense it is likewise true, though with some limitation; and here is the third degree of our Christian omnipotency. In the former parts the omnipotency of a Christian suffered no restraint, it was illimited, unconfined. He is absolutely omnipotent in his patience, and can suffer all things: he is likewise absolutely omnipotent in battle, and can conquer all his enemies. But in this third signification, his power seems to be streightened: for how many things are there which no Chriſtian man can do ? yet he is ſo ſtreightened, as that his omnipotency ſuffers not. We are taught in the ſchools, though God be omnipotent, yet many things may be named which he cannot do: he cannot deny himſelf, he cannot lie, he cannot ſin, he cannot die. Yet may we not conclude, that therefore God is not omnipotent; for therefore is he the more omnipotent, becauſe he cannot do theſe things: for ability to do theſe things, is imperfection and weakneſs; but in God we muſt conceive nothing but what argues perfection and ſtrength. In ſome degree we may apply this unto ourſelves, in things that tend to Chriſtian perfection, every Chriſtian is omnipotent, he cannot raiſe the dead, turn water into wine, ſpeak with tongues: true, but if he could, had he for this any further degree of perfection above other Chriſtians ? our Saviour ſeems to deny it. ' For many ' (ſaith he) at that day ſhall come and ſay, Have ' we not caſt out devils, and wrought miracles in ' thy name ? And he will anſwer them, Away, I ' know you not.' Matth. vii. 22. Beloved, our Saviour loves not to ſlight any part of Chriſtian perfection: yet my meaning is not to deny unto a Chriſtian the power of doing miracles, for every Chriſtian man doth every day greater miracles than yet I have ſpoken of. But, Beloved, in this matter of miracles, we do much abuſe ourſelves; for why ſeems it unto us a greater miracle, that our Saviour once turned a little water into wine, than every

year in fo many vine-trees to turn that into wine
in the branches, which being received at the root
was mere water? Or why was it more wonderful for him once to feed five thoufand with five
loaves, than every year to feed the whole world,
by the ftrange multiplication of a few feeds caft
into the ground? After the fame manner do we
by the daily actions of Chriftian men. For why is
it a greater miracle to raife the dead, than for every man to raife himfelf from the death of fin to
the life of righteoufnefs? Why feems it more miraculous to open the eyes of him that was born
blind, than for every one of us to open the eyes
of his underftanding, which by reafon of original
corruption was born blind? For by the fame finger, by the fame power of God, by which the a-
poftles wrought thefe miracles, doth every Chriftian man do this: and without this finger, it is as
impoffible for us to do this, as for the apoftles to do
the miracles they did, without the affiftance of the
extraordinary power of Chrift. So that hitherto
in nothing are we found inferior unto the chief
apoftles: what if there be fome things we cannot
do? fhall this prejudice our power? It is a faying
in Quintilian, ' It muft not impeach the learning
' of a good Grammarian to be ignorant of fome
' things * : ' for there are many unneceffary quil-
lets and quirks in grammar, of which to purchafe

* Mihi inter virtutes Grammatici habebitur, aliqua nefcire.
Inft. Orat. lib. i. c. 9.

the knowledge, were but lofs of labour and time. Beloved, in the like manner may we fpeak of our-felves, it muft not difparage the power of a Chri-ftian, that he cannot do fome things. For in re-gard of the height and excellency of his profeffi-on, thefe inferior things which he cannot do, they are nought elfe but grammar quirks, and to be ambitious to do them, were but a nice, minute, and over-fuperftitious diligence. And yet a Chri-ftian, if he lift, may challenge this power, that he ' can do all things;' yea, even fuch things as he cannot do. St. Auftin anfwering a queftion made unto him, why the gift of tongues was ceafed in the church, and no man fpake with that variety of languages, which divers had in the primitive times, wittily tells us, ' That every one may juftly claim ' unto himfelf that miraculous gift of tongues.' For fince the church, which is the body of Chrift, of which we are but members, is far and wide difperfed over the earth, and is in fundry nations, which ufe fundry languages, every one of us may well be faid to fpeak with divers tongues; becaufe in that which is done by the whole, or by any part of it, every part may claim his fhare *. Be-

---

* *The paffage is in Fulgentius. Homil. de fancto die Pente-coftes.* Proinde fi quifquam dixerit alicui noftrûm; accepifti Spiritum Sanctum, quare non linguis omnibus loqueris? re-fpondere debet: loquor fane omnibus linguis, quia in eo fum Chrifti corpore, hoc eft, in ecclefia, quae loquitur omnibus linguis.

loved, how much more, by this reafon, may every one of us lay a far directer claim to an abfolute
power of doing all things, even in its largeft extent, fince I fay not fome inferior member, but
Chrift, who is our head, hath this power truly re-
fident in him. Howfoever therefore in each member it feems to be but partial, yet in our head it is
at full; and every one of us may affume to ourfelves this power of doing all things, becaufe we
are fubordinate members unto that head which
can do all things. But I muft leave this, and go
on to the remainder of my text.

Hitherto I have fpoken, firft of the perfon, *I.*
Secondly, of his power, *can do.* I fhould, by order of the words, proceed, in the third place, unto the fubject or object of this power pointed out
unto us in this word πάντα, *all things.* But the
fubject of this Chriftian power hath been fo neceffarily wrapped up, and tied together with the
power, that for the opening of it, I have been
conftrained to exemplify at large, both what this
all things is, and how far it doth extend: fo that
to enter upon it anew, were but to trouble you
with repetition of what is already fufficiently o-
pened. I will go on therefore unto the *fecond* general of my text. For here me-thinks that queftion
might be afked, which Dalilah afked of Samfon,
' Tell me, I pray thee, wherein this great ftrength
' lieth?' Judg, xvi. 6. Behold, Beloved, it is ex-

preffed in the laft words, ' through Chrift that
' ftrengtheneth.'

This is, as I told you, that hair wherein that
admirable ftrength of a Chriftian doth refide. I
confefs, I have hitherto fpoken of wonderful
things, and hardly to be credited; wherefore, left
the ftrangenefs of the argument call my credit into
queftion*, lo here I prefent unto you the ground
of all this: a fmall matter fometimes feems wonderful, till the caufe of it be difcovered, but as
foon as we know the caufe, we ceafe to marvel:
how ftrange foever my difcourfe of Chriftian omnipotency may feem, yet look but upon this caufe,
and now nothing fhall feem incredible. For to
doubt of the omnipotency of a Chriftian, is to
queftion the power of Chrift himfelf. As the
queen of Sheba told king Solomon, that fhe had
heard great things of him in her own country, but
now fhe faw truth did go beyond report: fo, Beloved, he that travels in the firft part of my text,
and wonders at the ftrange report of a Chriftian
man's power, let him come to the fecond part, to
our Solomon, to him that is greater than Solomon,
to Chrift, and he fhall find that the truth is greater than the fame of it; for if he that was poffeffed of the evil fpirit in the gofpel, was fo ftrong,
that being bound with chains and fetters, he brake
them all: of what ftrength muft he be then, whom

* Μὴ τὸ παράδοξον ὑποσχίσεως ἀπίσον δοκῇ.

it pleaſeth Chriſt to enable? or what chains or
fetters ſhall be put upon him, which he will not
break? From this doctrine therefore that Chriſt
is he that doth thus enable us, we learn two leſſons, which are, as it were, two props to keep us
upright, that we lean not either to the right hand
or to the left.

Firſt, Not to be dejected or diſmayed, by reaſon of this outward weakneſs and baſeneſs in which
we ſeem to be. Secondly, Not to be puft up upon opinion and conceit of that ſtrength and glory
which is within us and unſeen. For the firſt, for
our own outward weakneſs, be it what it will, we
cannot be more weak, more frail than Gideon's
pitchers: now, as in them their frailty was their
ſtrength, and by being broken, they put to flight
the army of the Midianites; ſo where it pleaſeth
Chriſt to work, that which ſeems weakneſs ſhall
become ſtrength, and turn to flight the ſtrongeſt
adverſary. ' Publius Decius is army enough, and
' while we have him, our enemies can never be
' too numerous *,' ſaid one in Livy; we may apply this unto ourſelves: be we never ſo weak, yet
Chriſt alone is army and forces enough, and with
him we can never have too many enemies. The
fleſh indeed is weak, for ſo our Saviour tells us,
Matth. xxvi. 41. yet this weakneſs of the fleſh is
no prejudice at all to the ſtrength of a Chriſtian;

* Satis ſibi copiarum cum Publio Decio, et nunquam nimium hoſtium fore.

for though the flesh be weak, yet the spirit is
strong, and so much our Saviour tells us too : and
why then do we not follow the stronger part?'
' If,' saith Tertullian, ' the spirit be stronger than
' the flesh, what madness is it in us to make choice
' of, and follow the weaker side * ? ' Which of
you is so improvident, as, in a faction, to make
choice of that side which he sees to be the weak-
est, and which he knows must fall †.

Again, this weakness of a Christian is only outward, within what he is, the words of my text do
sufficiently shew. Socrates outwardly was a man
of deformed shape, but he was one of an excellent
spirit; and therefore Alcibiades in Plato compares
him to an apothecary's box, which without had
painted upon it an ape, or a satyre, or some deformed thing; but within was full of sweet and
precious ointment. Thus, Beloved, it is with a
Christian, whatsoever outward deformity he seems
to have, howsoever he seems to be nothing but
rags without, yet he is ' all glorious within : '
Psal. xlv. 13. I have said ' ye are gods,' saith the
scripture, Psal. lxxx. 6. the magistrate is wont
to ingross and impropriate this scripture to himself; because sitting in place of authority, for execution of justice, he carries some resemblance

---

* Si spiritus carne fortior, quia generosior, nostra culpa in-
firmiora sectamur.   Ad Uxorem. lib i. 4.

† Nulla fides unquam miseros elegit amicos.   Lucan.
lib. viii. v. 535.

of God: but to whom can this scripture better belong than to the Christian man? For the magistrate indeed carries some shew of God without, but many times within is full of corruption and weakness; the Christian carries a shew of weakness without, but within is full of God and Christ.

The second thing which I told you we learned, was a lesson teaching us not to be puft up with opinion and conceit of our own outward strength and glory: for if any man, because of this, shall begin to think of himself above what he ought, let him know that he may say of his exceeding strength, no otherwise than the man in the book of Kings spake, when his ax was fallen into the water, ' Alas, master, it was but lent!' 2 Kings vi. 5. Those that build houses make antics which seem to hold up the beams, whereas indeed, as St. Paul tells the olive-branch, ' Thou bearest not ' the root, but the root thee:' Rom. xi. 18. so is it true in them, they bear not up the house, the house bears up them. Beloved, seem we never so strong, yet we are but antics; the strength by which the house of Christ doth stand, it is not ours, it is Christ's, who by that power, ' by which ' he is able to subdue all things to himself,' Philip. iii. 21. doth sustain both himself and us.

THE

DUTY

OF

CONSTANT PRAYER.

Luke xviii. 1.

And he fpake a parable unto them, to this end, that men ought always to pray, and not to faint.

MY text is like the temple of Jerufalem, it is the houfe of prayer, wherein we may learn many fpecial points of the fkill and practice of it. Now as that temple had two parts; Firft, the fore-front, the porch, the walk before it; and fe-condly, the temple itfelf: fo have thefe words like-wife two parts; Firft, there are words which ftand before like a porch or walk, and they are thefe, ' And he fpake a parable unto them:' Secondly, here are words like unto the temple itfelf, ' that ' men ought always to pray, and not to faint.'

If you pleafe, before we enter into the temple, or fpeak of thefe words, ' That men ought always ' to pray,' let us ftay and entertain ourfelves a

little in the porch, and fee what matter of meditation it will yield. ' And he fpake a parable unto
' them.' To inftruct and teach the ignorant, no
' method, no way, fo fpeedy and effectual as by
parables and fables ; Strabo gives the reafon of
it, ' For man is a creature naturally defirous to
' know * ; ' but it is according to the proverb, as
the cat defires fifh, loath to touch the water, loath
to take the pains to learn : knowledge is indeed a
thing very pleafant, but to learn is a thing harfh
and tedious above all the things in the world. The
book which St. John eats in the tenth of the Apo-
calypfe, was in his mouth fweet as honey, but bitter in his belly : Beloved, thofe ftudents that, like
St. John, eat up whole volumes, thefe find the
contrary ; for in the mouth, in the perufal, their
books are harfh and unpleafant ; but in the ftomach, when they are underftood and digefted,
then are they delightful and pleafurable. Yet one
thing, by the providence of God, our nature hath,
which makes this rough way to learn, more plain
and eafy ; it is fond of tales ; common experience
fhews we are all very defirous to hear narrations
and reports, either pleafant or ftrange ; wife men
therefore, and God himfelf, which is wifer than
men, being to train up mankind, a fubject dull of
hearing, and hardly drawn to learn, have from
time to time wrought upon this humour, upon

* Φιλειδήμων γὰρ ὁ ἄνθρωπος προοίμιον δὲ τύτυ τὸ φιλόμυθον.
Ccogr. lib. i. pag. 19. Edit. Cafaub.

R 3

this part of our difposition, and mitigated, fugar-
ed, as it were, the unpleafantnefs of a difficult and
hard leffon, with the fweetnefs of fome delightful
parable or fable: and St. Chryfoftom tells us of a
phyfician, who finding his patient to abhor phyfic, but infinitely long for wine, heating an earth-
en cup in the fire, and quenching it in wine, put
his potion therein, that fo the fick perfon being
deceived with the fmell of wine, might unawares
drink of the phyfic: or, that I may better draw
my comparifon from fcripture, as when Jacob
meant to be welcome to his father Ifaac, he put on
his brother Efau's apparel, and fo got accefs: So,
Beloved, wife men, when they meant either to inftruct the ignorant, or to reprove offenders, to
procure their welcome, and make their way more
paffable, have been wont for the moft part, as it
were, to clothe their leffon or reproof in a parable,
or to ferve it in a difh favouring of wine, that fo
Jacob might be admitted under Efau's coat, that
the fmell of the pleafantnefs of wine might draw
down the wholefomenefs of phyfic. Great and
fingular have been thofe effects, which this kind
of teaching by parables hath wrought in men; by
informing their ignorance, reproving their error,
working patience of reproof, opening the underftanding, moving the affections, and other fovereign commodities. And for this caufe not only
our poets and profane authors, but whole cities,
and men which gave laws to commonwealths, have

made especial choice of this course*: yea, our Saviour Christ himself hath filled the gospels with parables, made them like a divine and Christian Esop's Fables, because he found it to be exceeding profitable. For, first of all, it is the plainest and most familiar way, and, above all other, stoops to the capacity of the learner, as being drawn either from trees, or beasts, or from some ordinary, common, and known actions of men; as from a shepherd attending his flock, from an husbandman sowing corn in his field, from a fisher casting his net into the sea, from a woman putting leaven into her dough, or the like. So that in this respect a parable is like Moses's tabernacle, which outwardly was nothing but goats skins, or some ordinary stuff, but within it was silk, and purple, and gold. And indeed, since those we teach are either children, or ignorant persons who are but children, for every man in what he is ignorant, is no better than a child †, that manner of information fits best, which is most easy and familiar. Again, a parable is a kind of pattern and example, expressing unto us what we hear; now nothing doth more illustrate and explain than instance and example; in a parable, as it were upon a stage, the

* Τὺς μύθυς ἀνεδίξανίο ὐχ οἱ ποιηταὶ μόνον, ἀλλὰ ῥ αἱ πόλεις πολὺ πρότερον, ῥ οἱ νομοθέται, τῦ χρησίμυ χάριν. Strabo. Geogr. lib. i. p. 19.

† 'Ιδιώτης γὰρ πᾶς καὶ ἀπαίδευτος τρόπον τινὰ παῖς ἐςί. Strabo. Geogr. lib. i. p. 19.

thing that we are taught is in a manner acted, and set forth before our eyes.

Secondly, Parables do not only by their plainnefs open the underftanding, but they work upon the affections, and breed delight of hearing, by reafon of that facetenefs and wittinefs which is many times found in them, by reafon of which they infinuate themfelves, and creep into us, and, ere we are aware, work that end for which they were delivered. Who is not much moved with that parable of Jotham in the book of Judges, ix. 8. that ‘ the trees went forth to chufe a king;’ or that of Menenius Agrippa in Livy, that the parts of the body confpired againft the belly; by which the one fhewed the wickednefs of the men of Shechem againft the fons of Gideon; the other, the folly of the common people, in confpiring against the fenators and noblemen? And no marvel, Beloved, if this facetenefs of parables doth thus work with men, fince it feems to have had wonderful force with God himfelf: for when the Canaanitifh woman, in the gofpel, had long importuned our Saviour in the behalf of her daughter, and our Saviour had anfwered her with that fhort, cutting, and reproachful parable, ‘ It is not ‘ meet to take the children’s bread, and caft it un- ‘ to dogs;’ Matth. xv. 26. fhe facetely and wittily retorts and turns upon our Saviour his own parable; ‘ Truth, Lord,’ faith fhe, ‘ yet dogs do eat ‘ the crums that fall from their mafter’s table;’

be it that I am but a dog, I require no more than is due to a dog, even the crums that fall from your table: with which fpeech our Saviour was fo far taken, as that he feems to have been ftricken into a wonderment; for he prefently cries out, ' O wo- ' man, great is thy faith.'

Thirdly, There is one thing that this way of inftruction by parable hath above all other kinds of teaching; it ferves excellently for reproof; for man is a proud creature, impatient of plain and open check and reprehenfion; many times no way of dealing with him, when he hath offended, but by deceiving him with wilinefs and craft; he that comes rudely and plainly to reprehend, doth many times more hurt than good *. I fpeak not this on-ly in regard of minifterial reprehenfion, ufed by the preacher of the word, but of all other: for to reprove offenders is a common duty, and be-longs to every private man as well as to the mini-fter. St. Auftin, in his book *de Civitate Dei*, handling the queftion, Why in common calami-ties the good do bear a part as well as the evil, a-mongft many other reafons, gives this as a fpecial one, That good men are not careful enough in reproving the errors of their offending brethren, but, by connivency and filence, in a manner par-take in their fins, and, as it were by confent, make

* Πολλάκις ἀπατῆσαι δέον· ὁ γὰρ ἐξ εὐθείας προσενεχθεὶς κακὰ μιγάλα τὸν ὐκ ἀπατηθέντα ἀργάσατο.

them their own *. It fhall not be amifs therefore,
even for you of the laity, to hear fomething concerning this art of reprehenfion, as a duty concerning you as well as the preacher. For the wifdom and gentlenefs of a Chriftian is never better
feen than in reproving: now one common error
of reprehenders is their over-blunt and plain manner of rebuking; whilft they reprove the vice as
if they hated the perfon, and upbraid rather than
reprehend †; by this our importunity, we deftroy
more finners than we fave. It is an excellent obfervation in St. Chryfoftom, ' He who is violently
' urged to fhame, becomes infenfible of fhame ‡.'
Unfeafonable and importunate reprehenders make
offending perfons to fteel their forehead, and to
fet a good face upon their fact, as the phrafe of
the world is, and to feek out excufes and apologies for their fin. Tully tells us, that Antony the
orator, being to defend a perfon who was accufed of faction and fedition, bent his wits to maintain fedition was good, and not to be objected as
a fault §. That we force not our offending brethren unto this degree of impudency, let us confult with our charity, and know the quality and
nature of the offender. Hufbandmen tell us, that

* De Civit. Dei, lib. i. c. 9.

† Dum fic objurgent, quafi oderint.

‡ Ψυχὴ γάρ ἱκαδὰν ἀπιρυθριάσαι βιασθῇ, ἄς ἀναλγησίαν ἐκ-
πίπτη.

§ De Orat. lib. ii. §. 199.

the young and tender branches of a vine are not to be pruned away with a knife, but gently pulled away by hand. Beloved, before we reprove, let us know the condition of our brother, whether he be not like the young vine, foft and tender, and fo to be cured rather with the hand than with the knife: and if he be grown fo hard that he fhall need the knife, we muft not rafhly adventure of it, but know there is a fkill likewife in ufing the knife: as Ehud, in the book of Judges, when he went to kill Eglon, carries not his dagger in his hand, but comes unto him with a prefent, and had his dagger girt privily under his garment: or as a fkilful phyfician of whom we read, being to heal an impofthume, and finding the fick perfon to be afraid of lancing, privily wrapped up his knife in a fpunge, with which whilft he gently fmoothed the place, he lanced it: fo, Beloved, when we encounter our offending brother, we muft not openly carry the dagger in our hand, for this were to defy our brother; but we muft wrap our knife in our fpunge, and lance him whilft we fmooth him, and with all fweetnefs and gentlenefs of behaviour cure him; as Ifaiah the prophet cured Hezekias, by laying a plaifter of figs upon the fore. Men when they have offended are like unto fire, we muft take heed how we come too near them; and therefore as the Cherubims in the book of Ifaiah's prophecy takes a coal from the altar with the tongs: fo when the prophets dealt with them, they did not rudely handle them with their hands, but they came upon them warily under parables, as it were with the Cherubim tongs. How could Nathan have come so near unto king David, and drawn from him an acknowledgment of his sin, had he not come with the Cherubims tongs, and deceived him with a parable? Or how should the prophet have made king Ahab see his error in letting go king Benhadad, if he had not, as it were, put a trick upon the king, and disguised both himself and his speech, and masked his errand with the parable of him who let go the prisoner that was committed to his charge? So that in this respect, if we would define a parable, we must pronounce it to be a civil or spiritual stratagem, by which persons, who need instruction, are honestly and piously beguiled for their own profit. No marvel therefore, if our Saviour Christ in his preaching doth every where drive upon parables. For being to deliver to us so many lessons, so strange, so uncouth, so hard to learn, it was meet he should make choice of that method of teaching which hath most likelihood to prevail and commend them unto us. The doctrine which our Saviour in my text labours to beat into us, is the continuing and perpetuating of our prayer and religious meditation : a lesson hard to be attained, and therefore thrice he commends it unto us; once by example, twice by parable, both of them very effectual means to teach : by example of that im-

portunate Canaanitiſh woman, in the xv. of St.
Matthew: by a parable, firſt, in the xi.of St. Luke,
of him that lying warm in his bed, and loath to
riſe, yet at his friends importunity gets up, and
lends him bread; and ſecondly, by the parable of
the unjuſt judge here in my text.

But all this while I muſt not forget that I am
but in the porch and entrance into the temple,
where to walk too long, were, if not to loſe, yet
to abuſe my time. Let us now therefore enter
into the temple itſelf, and conſider the main words
of my text : ' That men ought always to pray,
' and not to faint:' which words have a double
meaning. Firſt, there is a ſenſe which the words
themſelves yield as they lie: Secondly, the ſenſe
and meaning in which the Holy Ghoſt intended
and ſpake them. If we look upon the ſenſe which
the words themſelves do give, it ſeems we are adviſed by them to be like Anna the propheteſs in
Luke ii. 11. ' who departed not from the temple,
' but ſerved God with faſting and prayer night
' and day.' In all places, at all times, in ſeaſon,
out of ſeaſon, upon occaſion, upon no occaſion,
perpetually without intermiſſion to pray; for thus
the words do run, ' that we ought always to pray,
' and not to faint.' But if we look upon the ſenſe
in which the Holy Ghoſt ſpake theſe words, and
conſider what was his intent when he wrote them,
we ſhall find that the leſſon which we are hence to
learn, is, That we be like unto Jacob in the book

of Genesis, wreftle with God, and tell him to his
face, that we will not let him go till he hath given
us his blessing: Gen. xxxii, 26. That we become
like bold-faced suitors, or impudent beggars, that
will not be put by with a denial: but when we
have poured out our supplications unto God, and
find his ear locked up against us, yet to commence
them again and again, and the third time; yea,
without any fainting, or giving over, till, by a
kind. of importunate and unmannerly devotion,
we have constrained God to let a blessing fall: and
that this was the intent of the Holy Ghost in this
place, it appears upon the very reading of the parable.

I will briefly speak unto you of both these senses in their order; and first of the sense which the
words do give, That we always ought without intermission to pray.

Devotion in ordinary persons is a thing easily
raised, and easily allayed: every strange event, e-
very fear, every little calamity or distress is enough
to put us into a strain of religious meditation; but
on the contrary side, a small matter doth again as
quickly kill it. It seems to be like a quotidian
ague, it comes by fits, every day it takes us, and
every day it leaves us: or like flax, or straw, or
such light and dry stuff, which easily kindles, and
as soon goes out. Indeed it is a good thing when
we find our hearts thus tender, and upon every
occasion ready to melt into devotion: for as to be

quick of fenfe is a fign of life, and the pureſt and
beſt complexions are quickeſt of fenfe; ſo it is a
great argument of ſpiritual life in us, and of purity of ſoul, when we are ſo eaſily apt to fall upon
devout meditation. But our Saviour requires yet
another quality in our devotion, it muſt be as laſting as it is quick. Quintilian adviſes his orator to
beware how he ſtand too long upon a place of
paſſion, becauſe that paſſion is not laſting, ' and
' men cannot long weep *.' But, Beloved, our
Saviour gives other precepts of Chriſtian oratory ;
he wills, if we will prevail with God, to inſiſt and
dwell long upon a place of religious paſſion, and
provide that our tears may be perpetual and never dry : an hard thing you will take it to be, yet
certainly it is very poſſible. There is a queſtion
raiſed among the great maſters of natural learning,
Whether or no there may be a lamp ſo provided,
that it may burn for ever ? And they think it may
be done. Beloved, our Saviour here teaches to
practiſe that in ſpirituals, which hath been but a
matter of ſpeculation in naturals, even ſo to kindle
and dreſs our lamps, as that they ſhall never go
out ; but be like unto the good houſewife's candle
in the Proverbs, that goes not out by night, or rather like the ſun which ſhines for evermore. Daniel is ſaid to have kindled this lamp, and to have
made his prayer thrice a day, David ſeven times a

* Nihil facilius quam lacrymas inareſcere.   Inſt. Orat.
lib. vi. c. 1.

day, but this is not enough; for in that the one is noted to have prayed seven times a day, the other thrice, it is likely at other times they did not pray; but God is not contented with this intermittent prayer; for if we look upon my text, we shall see that there must be no instant free from prayer: we must not measure our prayers by number. Number is a discrete quantity, as we call it, the parts of it are not connext, are not tied together, there is a separation, a distance betwixt them. That that measures out our prayer must be line and length, some continued quantity, whose parts have no separation, no intermission: for so saith my text, ' men ought always to pray.' *Always*, the whole life of a man ought to be but one continual prayer.

But let us a little consider how possible this is, and see if there be any thing that doth necessarily enforce intermission of prayer. And *first*, that wonderful lamp of which I but now told you great scholars had spoken, is not yet made, because they are not agreed of what matter to make it. And indeed in the world, things either are not at all, or being, do at length cease to be, either because there is no fit matter whence they may be framed, or else the matter of which they are made, vanishes and dies. But, Beloved, prayer is a strange thing, it can never want matter: it will be made out of any matter, upon any occasion whatsoever; whatsoever you do, where-

foever you are, doth minifter occafion of fome
kind of prayer; either of thankfgiving unto God
for his goodnefs; or of praifing and admiring his
greatnefs; or of petitioning to him in cafe of
want or diftrefs; or bewailing fome fin, or neglect
committed. Is it the confideration of God's benefits that will move us to thankfulnefs? Then certainly our thankfulnefs ought to be perpetual;
there is no perfon fo mean, no foul fo poor, and
diftreffed, and miferable, but if he fearch narrowly, he fhall find fome bleffing for which he owes
thankfulnefs unto God; if nothing elfe, yet his
very mifery and diftrefs is a fingular bleffing, if he
ufe it to that end for which it was fent. Is it the
confideration of diftrefs and affliction, and fome
degree of the curfe of God upon us, that will ftir
our devotion? Indeed this is it with moft men
that kindles the fire of prayer in our hearts: men
for the moft part are like unto the unflaked lime,
which never heats till you throw water upon it;
fo they never grow warm in devotion, till fomewhat contrary to their wifhes and difpofition begins to afflict them: then certainly our petitions
to God ought never to ceafe; for never was there
man in any moment of his life entirely happy, either in body, goods, or good name, every man
hath fome part of affliction. Bleffing and curfing,
though they feem to be enemies, and contrary one
to another, yet are never fevered, but go hand in

hand together. Some men have more of one, some of another, but there is no man but hath some part of both; wherefore as it seems not only prayer in general, but all kind, all sort of prayer ought to be continual. Prayer must not be, as it were, of one thread, we must blend and temper together all kind of prayer, our praise or thanks, our sorrow, and make our prayer like Joseph's party coloured coat, like a beautiful garment of sundry colours. So then, as fire goes not out so long as it hath matter to feed on, so what shall be able to interrupt our devotion, which hath so great and everlasting store of matter to continue it?

Secondly, many things in the world are necessarily intermitted, because they are tied to place or times; all places, all times are not convenient for them: but in case of prayer it is otherwise, it seeks no place, it attends no time; it is not necessary we should come to the church, or expect a Sabbath, or an holiday; for prayer indeed especially was the Sabbath ordained, yet prayer itself is Sabbathless, and admits no rest, no intermission at all: if our hands be clean, we must, as our apostle commands us, lift them up every where, at all times, and make every place a church, every day a Sabbath, every hour canonical. As you go to the market, as you stand in the streets, as you walk in the fields, in all these places you may pray

as well, and with as good acceptance, as in the
church *; for you yourselves are temples of the
Holy Ghost, if the grace of God be in you, more
precious than any of those which are made with
hands. The church of Rome hath made a part of
her Breviary, or Common-prayer-book, which she
calls ' The Itinerary of the Clergy,' and it is a set
form of prayer, which clergymen ought to use
when they set out on a journey, and are upon
their way; why she calls it the Itinerary of the
clergy, and impropriates it unto the clergy, I know
not; she might, for ought I see, have called it the
Itinerary of the Laity, since it is a duty belonging
unto them as well as to the minister: yet thus much
the example of that church teaches, that no place,
no occasion excludes prayer. We read in our
books, that one of the Ethnic emperors was much
taken, when he saw a woman going in the streets
with a vessel of water on her head, her child at
her girdle, her spindle in her hand twisting her
thread as she went; he thought it a wonderful
portion of diligence thus to employ all places and
times indifferently. Beloved, if it be thus with
bodily labour, how much more should it be so
with the labour of the soul, which is far more easy,
and needs not the help of any bodily instrument to
act it? And how welcome a spectacle will it be,

* "Εξιςι ὃ ἀνθρωπον εἰς ἀγοράν ἰμβάλλοντα, ὃ καθ' ἑαυτὸν βα-
δίζοντα εὐχάς ποιῆσθαι ἰκτινῶς. Chrysost. de Anna. serm. iv.
§. 6.

think you, unto the great King of heaven and
earth, when he fhall fee that no time, no occafion,
is able to interrupt the labour of our devotion? Is
it the time of feafting and jollity which feems to
prefcribe againft prayer? Indeed prayer is a grave
and fober action, and feems not to ftand with fport
and merriment; yet notwithftanding it is of fo
pliable a nature, that it will accommodate and fit
itfelf even to feafts and fportings. We read in the
book of Daniel, that when Belfhazzar made his
great and laft feaft to his princes and lords, that
they were merry, and drank wine in bowls, and
' praifed the gods of gold and filver, of brafs, and
' of iron, of wood, and of ftone.' Dan. v. 4. Beloved, fhall Ethnic feafts find room for their idolatrous worfhip, and praife of their golden, brazen,
wooden gods, and fhall not our Chriftian feafts
yield fome place for the praife of the true God of
heaven and earth? Laft of all, is it time of fleep
that feems to give a vacation and furceafe to
prayer? Beloved, fleep is no part of our life, we
are not accountable for things done or not done
then; Tertullian tells us, ' that an unclean dream
' fhall no more condemn us, than a dream of mar-
' tyrdom fhall crown us *; ' and the cafuifts do
teach, that loofe dreams in the night fhall never be
laid to our charge, if they be not occafioned by
lewd thoughts in the day; for they are not

* Non magis enim ob ftupri vifionem damnabimur, quam
ob martyrii coronabimur. De Anima. c. 45.

thoughts fpringing out, but caft into our hearts by
the devil, upon his fcore fhall they go, and we
fhall not reckon for them: fo then, though fleep
partake not of our devotion, yet this hinders not
the continualnefs of it. Ariftotle tells us, that men
who fleep perceive not any part of time to have
paffed, becaufe they tie the laft moment of their
watching with the firft moment of their awaking,
as having no fenfe of what paft betwixt, and fo
account of it as one continued time. Beloved, if
we do with our devotion as we do with our time,
if we fhut up the laft inftant of our watching with
a prayer, and refume that prayer at the firft inftant
of our waking, we have made it one continued
prayer without interruption.

Thirdly, and laft of all, the greateft reafon why
many bufineffes of the world cannot be acted perpetually, is, becaufe they muft give room to others.
The actions of the world are many times like unto quarrelfome birds, two of them cannot peaceably dwell in one bufh *. But prayer hath that
property which Ariftotle gives unto fubftance, it
is at peace, and holds good terms with all our cares
of the world. No bufinefs fo great, or that fo
much takes up the time and mind of a man, as
that it needs exclude prayer: it is of a foft and
fociable nature, and it can incorporate and fink
into our bufinefs like water into afhes, and never

---

* Unicum arbuftum non alit duos erithacos.

Μία λόχμη ὺ τρίφει δύο ἐριθάκυς.

increase the bulk of them; it can mix and inter-
weave itself with all our cares, without any hin-
derance unto them; nay, it is a great strength and
improvement unto them. ' For, saith St. Chry-
' sostom, as they that build houses of clay, must
' every where place studs and pieces of timber and
' wood so to strengthen the building; so all our
' cares of this life, which are no better than build-
' ings of dirt and clay, we must strengthen and
' compact together with frequent and often prayer,
' as with bonds and props of timber *.' Let no
man therefore think, that it is too much to require at the hands of men, at one and the self-
same instant, both to attend their vocation and
their prayer: for the mind of a man is a very agile
and nimble substance, and it is a wonderful thing
to see how many things it will at one moment apply itself unto without any confusion or let. Look
but upon the musician while he is in his practice,
he tunes his voice, fingers his instrument, reads
his dittay, marks the note, observes the time, all
these things, at one and the same instant, without

---

* Μιμώμιθα τὰς οἰκοδόμυς. ὃ γὰρ ἰκᾶνοι πλίνθυς μέλλονⁱες οἰκο-
δομεῖν, διὰ τὸ τῆς ὕλης σαθρὸν ξύλοις μακροῖς ἀποσφίγγυσι τὴν οἰ-
κοδομὴν, καὶ ὑδὲ διὰ πολλῦ τῦτο ποιῦσι τῦ διαςήμαⁱος, ἀλλὰ δι'
ὀλίγυ. ἵνα τῇ πυκνότηⁱι τῶν ξύλων τύτων ἀσφαλεςέραν τὴν συνθήκην
τῶν πλίνθων ἐργάσωνⁱαι τῦτο ὃ σὺ ποίησον, ὃ τὰς βιωτικὰς πράξεις
ἀπάσας καθάπερ ἱμαντώσεσί ξύλων, τῇ συνεχέᾳ τῶν εὐχῶν δια-
λαμβάνων πάντοθέν συ περίφραζον τὴν ζωήν. De Anna. serm. iv.
§. 5.

any diſtraction or impediment: thus ſhould men
do in caſe of devotion, and in the common acts of
our vocation, let prayer bear a part; for prayer
added unto diligent labour is like a ſweet voice to
a well-tuned inſtrument, and makes a pleaſing harmony in the ears of God. ' The good houſewiſe,'
ſaith St. Chryſoſtom, ' as ſhe ſits at her diſtaff,
' and reaches out her hand to the flax, may e-
' ven then lift up, if not her eyes, yet her mind un-
' to heaven, and conſecrate and hallow her work
' with earneſt prayer unto God *.' ' The huſ-
' bandman,' ſaith St. Jerom, ' at the plough-tail
' may ſing an hallelujah, the ſweating harveſt-man
' may refreſh himſelf with a pſalm, the gardener,
' whilſt he prunes his vines and arbours, may re-
' cord ſome one of David's ſonnets †.' The reaſon of this pliable nature of prayer is, becauſe it
is a thing of another condition than the acts of
the world are: it requires no outward labour of
the body, no outward faſhion and manner of doing, but is internally acted in the ſoul itſelf, and
leaves the outward members of our bodies free to
perform thoſe offices which require their help.
Our legal buſineſs in the world muſt be done in

---

* Ἔξεςι ᾖ γυναῖκα ἡλακάτην κατέχυσαν ᾖ ἱσυργῦσαν ἀναϹλίψαι
εἰς τὸν ὑρανὸν τῇ διανοίᾳ καὶ καλίσαι μιτὰ θερμότητος τὸν Θεόν.
De Anna. ſerm. iv. §. 6.

† Arator ſtivam tenens, hallelujah ſecantat, ſudans meſſor
pſalmis ſeſe evocat, et curva attondens falce vites vinitor aliquid Davidicum canit. Epiſt. lib. ii. ad Marcellum.

certain forms of breves and writs, and I know not
what variety of outward ceremony, or elſe it is
not warrantable: but prayer, Beloved, is not like
an obligation or indenture, it requires no outward
ſolemnity of words and ceremony. Quaint, witty,
and ſet forms of prayer proceed many times from
oſtentation more than devotion; for any thing I
know, it requires not ſo much as the moving of
the lips or tongue: nay, one thing I know more,
that the moſt forcible prayer tranſcends and far
exceeds all power of words. For St. Paul ſpeaking unto us concerning the moſt effectual kind of
prayer, calls it ' ſighs and groans that cannot be
' expreſſed *.' Rom. viii. 26. Nothing does cry ſo
loud in the ears of God as the ſighing of a contrite
and earneſt heart. We read in the xiv. of Exodus,
that God ſpeaks unto Moſes, ' Why crieſt thou
' unto me? command the children of Iſrael that
' they go forward;' yet there appears not in the
text any prayer that Moſes made, or word that he
ſpake. It was the earneſtneſs of Moſes's heart that
was ſo high-voiced, that did ſo ſound in the ears
of the Lord †. Wherefore true prayer hath no
commerce with the outward members of the body; for it requires not the voice, but the mind;

* Στενάγμαλα ἀλάληλα.

† This is taken from St. Baſil. Hom. in Pſ. cxiv. §. 2.
Ἡ ὐκ ἀκύεις ὅτι Μωϋσῆς μηδὲν φθιγγομένος, ἀλλὰ τοῖς ἀλαλήτοις
ἑαυτῦ ςεναγμοῖς ἐντυγχάνων τῷ Κυρίῳ, ἠκύετο, παρὰ τῦ Κυρίν
λίγονίος, τὶ βοᾷς πρὸς μὲ.

not the stretching of the hands, but the intention of the soul; not any outward shape or carriage of body, but the inward behaviour of the understanding *. How then can it slacken your worldly business and occasions, to mix with them sighs and groans, which are the most effectual kinds of prayer?

And let this suffice concerning the first meaning of the words. I will briefly speak concerning the second meaning, which I told you was the sense intended by the Holy Ghost when he wrote, and it is an exhortation to a religous importunity in our prayers, not to let our suits fall because they are not presently granted, but never to leave solliciting till we have prevailed, and so take the blessings of God by violence: this force, this violence is a thing most welcome unto God; for if the importunity of Esau's false, feigned, and malicious tears drew a blessing from his father Isaac, who yet had no greater store of blessings, as it seems; how much more shall the true religious importunity of zealous prayer pull a blessing out of the hands of God, who is rich in blessings above the sands of the sea in multitude? It is the courtiers rule, That over-modest suitors seldom speed: Beloved, we must follow the same rule in the court of heaven; intempestive bashfulness gets

* Οὐδὲ γὰρ ὕτω φωνῆς χρεία, ὡς διανοίας, ὑδὲ ἐκτάσεως χειρῶν, ὡς συντεταμίνης ψυχῆς, ὑδὲ σχήματος, ἀλλὰ φρωνήματος. Chryf. Hom. xix. de Abraam. id. Hom. de Chananaea.

nothing there. Faint asking does invite a denial *.
Will you know the true name of the behaviour
which prevails with God? St. Luke calls it importunity. xi. 8. and St. Chrysostom, speaking of
the behaviour of the Canaanitish woman in the xv.
of St. Matthew, tells us, ' She was importunate
' with a becoming assurance†;' impropriety, importunity, impudency, these be the names of that person and behaviour which you must put on, if you
mean to prevail in your suits with God. And indeed, if we consider that habit and manner that God
is wont to put on, when his children do become
suitors unto him, how he puts on a rigid, rough,
and untractable carriage, even towards his dearest
children, even then when he means them most
good, we shall plainly see, we must use such kind
of behaviour, if we will prevail with him: for
the more effectually to express this demeanour of
God towards his children, and to assure us it is so,
and to teach us importunity, our Saviour Christ,
that great master of requests, may seem to have
done himself some wrong; first, by drawing in a
manner odious comparisons, and likening the behaviour of God in these cases to a slothful friend, that
is loth to leave his warm bed to do his friend a
pleasure; and here in my text to an unjust judge,

* Qui timidè rogat, docet negare.

† Καλὴν ἀπηναισχύντεσι τὴν ἀναισχυντίαν. Hom. liii.
The learned reader will perceive that this expression does not
admit of a literal interpretation.

that fears neither God nor man: and secondly, by his own behaviour toward the Canaanitish woman. It is strange to observe, how though he were the meekest person that ever was upon earth, yet here he strives, as it were, to unnaturalize himself, and lay by his natural sweetness of disposition, almost to forget common humanity, and puts on a kind of sullen and surly person of purpose to deter her: you shall not find our Saviour in all the New Testament in such a mood, so bent to contemn and vilify a poor suitor. St. Austin, comparing together St. Matthew and St. Mark, who both of them record the same story, and gathering together the circumstances out of them both, tells us, that first she follows our Saviour in the street, and that our Saviour takes house, as it were, to shelter himself from her; but she comes after, and throws herself at his feet; and he, as offended with her importunity, again quits the house to be rid of her, and all this while deigns her not a word*. If any behaviour could have dashed a suit, and broken the heart of a poor suitor, this had been enough: but here is not all, we have a civil precept, that if we be not disposed to pleasure a suitor, yet to give him good words, and shape him a gentle answer; it is hard if we cannot afford a suitor a gentle word. We read of Titus the Emperor, that he would never suffer any man to go sad and discontented from him; yet

* De consensu Evangelist. lib. ii. c. 49.

our Saviour seems to have forgot this part of ci-
vility, being importuned to answer her, gives her
an answer worse than silence, and speaks words
like the piercing of a sword, as Solomon speaks,
'I may not take the childrens bread, and cast it
'unto dogs:' Matth. xv. 26. and yet after all this
strange copy of countenance, he fully subscribes to
her request. Beloved, God hath not only expressed thus much in parables, and practised these
strange delays upon Canaanitish women, but he
hath acted it indeed, and that upon his dearest
saints. David, one of the worthiest of his saints,
yet how passionately doth he cry out, 'How long,
'Lord, wilt thou forget me? how long shall I
'seek counsel in my soul, and be so vexed in my
'heart?' Pf. xiii. 1, 2. Not only the saints on
earth, but even those in heaven do seem to partake
in this demeanour of God: we read in the book
of the Revelation, that when the souls of the martyrs under the altar cried out, 'How long, Lord,
'just and holy, dost thou not avenge our blood
'from off the earth?' they received this answer,
'Have patience yet a little while.' Rev. vi. 10, 11.
It is storied of Diogenes, that he was wont to sup-
plicate to the statues, and to hold out his hands
and beg of them, that so he might learn to brook
and devour denial and tediousness of suit. Beloved, let us but meditate upon these examples,
which I have related, and we shall not need to
practise any of the Cynic's art. For if the saints

and blessed martyrs have their suits so long depending in the courts of heaven, then good reason
that we should learn to brook delays, and arm
ourselves with patience and expectation, when we
find the ears of God not so open to our requests.
When Joseph's brethren came down to buy corn,
he gave them but a coarse welcome, he spake
roughly unto them, he laid them in prison; yet
the text tells us, that his bowels melted upon
them, and at length he opened himself, and gave
them courteous entertainment. Beloved, when we
come unto God, as it were to buy corn, to beg at
his hands such blessings as we need, though he
speak roughly, though he deal more roughly with
us, yet let us know he hath still Joseph's bowels,
that his heart melts towards us, and at length he
will open himself, and entertain us lovingly: and be
it peradventure that we gain not what we look for,
yet our labour of prayer is not lost. The blessed
souls under the altar, of which I spake but now,
though their petition was not granted, yet ' had
' they long white garments given them.' Rev. vi.
11. Even so, Beloved, if the wisdom of God shall
not think it fit to perform our requests, yet he will
give us the long white garment, something which
shall be in lieu of a suit; though nothing else, yet
patience and contentment, which are the greatest
blessings upon earth.

CHRIST'S KINGDOM

NOT OF

THIS WORLD.

John xviii. 36.

*Jefus anfwered, My kingdom is not of this world:
if my kingdom were of this world, then would
my fervants fight, that I fhould not be delivered
to the Jews.*

AS in the kingdoms of the world there is an
art of courtfhip, a fkill and myftery teaching to manage them: fo in the fpiritual kingdom
of God and of Chrift, there is an holy policy,
there is an art of fpiritual courtfhip, which teaches
every fubject there how to demean and bear himfelf. But, as betwixt their kingdoms, fo betwixt
their arts and courtfhip, betwixt the courtier of
the one, and the courtier of the other, there is, as
Abraham tells the rich man in St. Luke, a mighty
gulf, a great diftance, a great difference, and not
only one, but many. Sundry of them I fhall have
occafion to touch in the procefs of my difcourfe ;
mean while I will fingle out one, which I will ufe

as a prologue and way unto my text. In the kingdoms of earthly princes, every subject is not fit to
make a courtier ; yea, were all fit, this were an
honour to be communicated only unto some. There
is a necessity of disproportion and inequality between men and men; and were all persons equal
the world could not consist. Of men of ordinary
fashion and parts, some must to the plough, some
to their merchandize, some to their books, some
to one trade, some to another: only, as Aristotle
calls them, men of more than common wit and
ability, active, choice, picked out of a thousand*,
such must they be that bear honours, attend on
princes persons, and serve in their courts. The
scripture tells us, that when king Solomon saw
that Jeroboam was an active, able, and industrious
young man, he took him and made him ruler over
all the charge of the house of Joseph. Again,
when David invited old Barzillai to the court, the
good old man excuses himself: ' I am,' saith he,
' fourscore years of age, and can thy servant taste
' what I eat, or what I drink? can I hear any
' more the voice of singing men and singing wo-
' men ? Lo here my son Chimham, he shall go
' with my lord the king, and do with him as shall
' seem good in thine eyes.' 2 Sam. xix. 35. Jeroboam and Chimham, strong, and able, and active persons, such are they that dwell in kings

* Οἱ χαρίεντες ᾗ πρακτικοί. Ethic. Nicom. lib. i. c. 3.

houses: of the rest, some are too old, some too young, some too dull, some too rude, or by some means or other unfit for such an end. Thus fares it with the honours of the world, they seem to participate of envy, or melancholy, and are of a solitary disposition; they are brightest when they are alone, or but in few; make them common, and they lose their grace; like lamps they may give light unto few, or to some one room, but no farther. But the honours in the court of the great King of heaven are of another nature, they rejoice in being communicated, and their glory is in the multitude of those that do partake in them. They are like unto the sun that rises, not to this or that man, but to all the world: in the court of God, no difference between Jeroboam and Barzillai; none too old, none too young; no indisposition, no imperfection makes you incapable of honours there; be but of his kingdom, and you are necessarily of his court: every man who is a subject there, is a courtier, yea, more than a courtier, he is a peer, he is a king, and hath an army of angels at his service, to pitch their tents about him, to deliver him; a guard of ministering spirits sent out to attend him for his safety. It shall not therefore be unseasonable for the meanest person that hears me this day, to hear as it were a lecture of spiritual policy and courtship; for no auditory can be unfit for such a lesson. Aristotle was wont to divide his lectures and readings into

acroamatical and exoterical : some of them contained only choice matter, and they were read privately to a select auditory; others contained but
ordinary stuff, and were promiscuously and in public exposed to the hearing of all that would : Beloved, we read no acroamatic lectures, the secrets
of the court of heaven (as far as it hath pleased
the King of heaven to reveal them) lie open alike
to all. Every man is alike of his court, alike of
his council; and the meanest among Christians
must not take it to be a thing without his sphere,
above his reach, but must make account of himself
as a fit hearer of a lesson in spiritual and saving
policy; since if he be a subject in the kingdom of
Christ, he can be no less than a courtier.

Now the first and main lesson to be learned by
a courtier, is, how to discover and know the disposition and nature of the lord whom he is to
serve, and the quality of that commonwealth in
which he bears a place *. That therefore our heavenly courtier may not mistake himself, but be
able to fit himself to the place he bears, I have
made choice of these few words, which but now I
read; words spoken by the king of that commonwealth, of which I am to treat, unto such as mean
to be his liege-men there : words which sufficiently open unto the Christian politician the state and

* Ad consilium de republica dandum caput est nosse rem-
publicam.   Cicero. de Orat. lib. ii. c. 82.

quality of that court in which he is to serve: ' My
' kingdom is not of this world, for if it were, then
' would my fervants fight;' which words feem
like the Parthian horfemen, whofe manner was to
ride one way, but to fhoot another way, they feem
to go apace towards Pilate, but they aim and fhoot
at another mark; or rather like unto the fpeaker
of them, unto our Saviour himfelf, when he was
in one of the villages of Samaria, Luke ix. 51.
where the text notes, that though he were in Samaria, ' yet his face was fet towards Jerufalem:'
fo, Beloved, though thefe words be fpoken to a
Samaritan, to an infidel, to Pilate, yet their face is
toward Jerufalem ; they are a leffon directed to
the fubjects of his fpiritual kingdom, of that Jerufalem which is from above, and is the mother of
us all.

In them we may confider two general parts.
First, a denuntiation and meffage unto us; and
fecondly, a fign to confirm the truth of it. For it
is the manner and method, as it were, which God
doth ufe, when he difpatches a meffage, to annex
a fign unto it, by which it may be known: when
he fent Mofes to the Ifraelites in Egypt, and Mofes required a fign, he gave him a fign in his
hand, in his rod ; when he fent Gideon againft
Midian, he gave him a fign in the fleece of wool
which was upon the floor ; when he fent the prophet to Jeroboam, to prophefy againft the altar in

Bethel, he gave him a sign, that the altar should rend, and the ashes fall out; when he sent Isaiah with a message to king Ahaz, he gave him a sign, ' Behold, a virgin shall conceive.' So, Beloved, in these words, there is a message, there is a sign : The first words are the message, ' My kingdom is ' not of this world;' the next words, ' For if it ' were, then would my servants fight.' These are Moses's rod, and Gideon's fleece; they are the sign which confirm the message.

The first part is a general proposition or maxim: the second is an example and particular instance of it: for in the first, our Saviour distinguishes his kingdom from the kingdoms of the world, and from all the fashions of them; in the second, a- mongst many other, he chuses one instance, where- in particularly he notes, that his kingdom is un- like to earthly kingdoms; for the kingdoms of the world are purchased and maintained by vio- lence and blood, but so is not his. The reason why our Saviour fastens upon this reason of diffi- militude and unlikeness, is, because in gaining and upholding temporal kingdoms, nothing so usual as the sword and war: no kingdom of the world but by the sword is either gotten, or held, or both. The sword in a secular commonwealth is like the rod in a school; remove that away, and men will take their liberty. It is the plea which the Tar- quins used to king Porsenna in Livy; ' The taste ' of liberty is so sweet, that except kings maintain

T 2

' their authority with as great violence, as the
' people affect their liberty, all things will run
' to confusion ; and kingdoms, which are the
' goodlieft things in the world, will quickly go to
' wreck * : when God gave a temporal kingdom
unto his own people, he fent Mofes and Jofhua before them to purchafe it with their fword ; when
they were poffeffed of this kingdom, he fends then
Gideon, and Samfon, and David, and many wor-
thies more, to maintain it by the fword: but now
being to open unto the world another kind of
kingdom, of rule and government, than hitherto
it had been acquainted with; he tells us, that he
is a king of a kingdom, which is erected and maintained, not by Jofhua and David, but by St. Peter and St. Paul ; not by the fword, but by the
Spirit ; not by violence, but by love ; not by
ftriving, but by yielding; not by fighting, but by
dying. Pilate had heard that he was a king: it
was the accufation which was framed againft him,
that he bare himfelf as king of the Jews; but becaufe he faw no pomp, no train, no guard about
him, he took it but as an idle report: to put him
therefore out of doubt, our Saviour affures him,
that he is a king, but of fuch a kingdom as he
could not fkill of : ' My kingdom is not of this

* Satis libertatem ipfam habere dulcedinis, nifi quantâ vi
civitates eam expetant, tantâ regna reges defendant, aequare
fumma infimis, adeffe finem regnis rei inter deos hominefque
pulcherrimae. Lib. ii. c. 9.

'world: if my kingdom were of this world, then
'would my fervants fight, that I fhould not be
'delivered to the Jews.' For the better unfold-
ing of which words; Firft, we will confider what
the meaning of this word *kingdom* is, for there lies
an ambiguity in it. Secondly, we will confider
what leffons for our inftruction the next words
will yield, ' Not of this world.'

Firft, Of this word *kingdom*. Our Saviour is
a king three manner of ways, and fo correlatively
hath three diftinct feveral kingdoms. He is firft
king in the largeft extent and meaning which can
poffibly be imagined, and that is, as he is Creator
and abfolute Lord of all creatures. Of this kingdom, heaven, earth, and hell are three large provinces: angels, men, and devils, his very enemies,
every creature, vifible and invifible, are fubjects
of this kingdom. The glory and ftrength of this
kingdom confifts leaft of all in men, and man is
the weakeft part of it; for there is fcarcely a creature in the world, by whom he hath not been conquered. When Alexander the Great had travelled
through India, and over-ran many large provinces, and conquered many popular cities; when
tidings came, that his foldiers in Greece had taken
fome fmall towns there, he fcorned the news, and
in contempt, Me-thinks (faid he) I hear of the
battle of Frogs and Mice. Beloved, if we look
upon thefe huge armies of creatures, and confider
of what wonderful ftrength they are, when the

Lord fummons them to battle; all the armies of men, and famous battles, of which we have fo large hiftories, in the comparifon of thefe, what are they, but Homer's tale, a Battle of Frogs and Mice ? Infinite legions of angels attend him in heaven, and every angel is an army : one angel, in the book of Kings, is fent out againft the army of the Affyrians, and in one night fourfcore thoufand perfons die for it. Bafe and contemptible creatures, when God calls for them, are of ftrength to conquer whole countries: he over-runs Egypt with his armies of frogs, and flies, and lice; and before his own people with an army of hornets chafes the Canaanites out of the land. Nay, the dull and fenfelefs elements are up in arms when God fummons them : he fhoots his hail-fhot; with his hail-ftones from heaven he deftroys more of the Canaanites, than the Ifraelites can with their fwords. As for his armies of fire and water, what power is able to withftand them ? Every creature, when God calls, is a foldier. How great then is the glory of this kingdom, of which the meaneft parts are invincible !

Secondly, again our Saviour is a king in a more reftrained and confined fenfe, as he is in heaven attended on by angels, and archangels, powers, principalities, and all the heavenly hoft. For though he be omniprefent, and fills every place both in heaven and earth, yet heaven is the palace and throne of this kingdom ; there is he better

feen and known, there with more ftate and honour ferved, and therefore more properly is his
kingdom faid to be there: and this is called his
kingdom of glory: the rules, and laws, and admirable orders of which kingdom, could we come
to fee and difcover, it would be with us as it
was with the queen of Sheba, when fhe came
to vifit Solomon, of whom the fcripture notes,
that when fhe heard his wifdom, and had feen
the order of his fervants, the attendance that was
given him, and the manner of his table, ' there
' was no more fpirit left in her.' 1 Kings x. 5.
Beloved, whilft this fpirit is in us, we cannot poffibly come to difcern the laws and orders of this
kingdom, and therefore I am conftrained to be filent.

Thirdly, our Saviour is a King in a fenfe yet
more impropriated. For as he took our nature
upon him, as he came into the world to redeem
mankind, and to conquer hell and death, fo is
there a kingdom annext unto him; a kingdom,
the purchafe whereof coft him much fweat and
blood, of which neither angels nor any other creature are a part, only that remnant of mankind,
that number of bleffed fouls, which, like a brand
out of the fire, by his death and paffion he hath
recovered out of the power of fin; and all thefe
alone are the fubjects of that kingdom. And this
is that which is called his kingdom of grace, and
which himfelf in fcripture every where calls his

T 4

church, his fpoufe, his body, his flock; and this
is that kingdom, which in this place is fpoken of,
and of which our Saviour tells Pilate, that it is not
of this world; — ' My kingdom is not of this
' world.'

Which words, at the firft reading, may feem
to favour of a little imperfection; for they are nothing elfe but a negation or denial. Now our
books teach us, that a negative makes nothing
known; for we know things by difcovering, not
what they are not, but what they are: yet when we
have well examined them, we fhall find that there
could not have been a fpeech delivered more effectual for the opening the nature of the church,
and the difcovery of men's errors in that refpect.
For I know no error fo common, fo frequent, fo
hardly to be rooted out, fo much hindering the
knowledge of the true nature of the church, as
this, that men do take the church to be like unto
the world. Tully tells us of a mufician, that being afked what the foul was, anfwered, that it
was harmony; ' He knew not (faith he) how to
' leave the principles of his own art *.' Again,
Plato's fcholars had been altogether bred up in
arithmetic, and the knowledge of numbers, and
hence it came, that when afterward they diverted
their ftudies to the knowledge of nature, or moral
philofophy, wherefoever they walked, they ftill
feigned to themfelves fomewhat like unto num-

* Et is à principiis artis fuae non receffit.

bers: the world they fuppofed was framed out of numbers; cities, and kingdoms, and commonwealths they thought ftood by numbers; number with them was fole principle and creator of every thing. Beloved, when we come to learn the quality and ftate of Chrift's kingdom, it fares much with us as it does with Tully's mufician, or Plato's fcholars; hardly can we forfake thofe principles in which we have been brought up. In the world we are born, in it we are bred, the world is the greateft part of our ftudy, to the true knowledge of God and of Chrift ftill we fancy unto us fomething of the world. It may feem but a light thing that I fhall fay, yet becaufe it feems fitly to open my meaning, I will not refrain to fpeak it: Lucian, when Priam's young fon was taken up into heaven, brings him in calling for milk and cheefe, and fuch country cates as he was wont to eat on earth *. Beloved, when we firft come to the table of God, to heavenly manna and angels food, it is much with us as it was with Priam's young fon, when he came firft into heaven, we cannot forget the milk and cheefe, and the grofs diet of the world. Our Saviour and his blefled apoftles had great and often experience of this error in men: when our Saviour preached to Nicodemus the doctrine of regeneration, and new birth, how doth he ftill harp upon a grofs conceit of a re-entry to be made into his mother's womb?

* The author feems to allude to Dial. Deor. iv.

When° he preached unto the Samaritan woman concerning the water of life, how hardly is she driven from thinking of a material elementary water, such as was in Jacob's well? When Simon Magus, in the Acts, saw, that by laying on of hands the apostles gave the Holy Ghost, he offers them money to purchase himself the like power: he had been trafficking and merchandizing in the world, and saw what authority, what a kingdom money had amongst men; he therefore presently conceited, that God, and heaven, and all would be had for money. To teach therefore the young courtier in the court of heaven, that he commit no such solecisms, that hereafter he speak the true language and dialect of God, our Saviour sets down this as a principal rule in our spiritual grammar, that his court is not of this world. Nay, Beloved, not only the young courtier, but many of the old servants in the court of Christ, are stained with this error. It is storied of Leonides, which was schoolmaster to Alexander the Great, that he infected his non-age with some vices, which followed him then when he was at man's estate*: Beloved, the world hath been a long time a schoolmaster unto us, and hath stained our non-age with some of these spots which appear in us, even then when we are strong men in Christ. When our

* Quae robustum quoque et jam maximum regem ab illa institutione pueriii sunt profecuta. Quint. Inst. Orat. lib. i. c. 2.

Saviour, in the Acts, after his refurrection, was difcourfing to his difciples concerning the kingdom of God, they prefently brake forth into this queftion, ' Wilt thou now reftore the kingdom un-' to Ifrael ?' Acts i. 6. Certainly this queftion betrays their ignorance, their thoughts ftill ran upon a kingdom like unto the kingdoms of the world, notwithftanding they had fo long, and fo often heard our Saviour to the contrary : our Saviour therefore fhortly takes them up; ' it is not yours,' your queftion is nothing to the purpofe ; the kingdom that I have fpoken of is another manner of kingdom than you conceive. Sixteen hundred years and more hath the gofpel been preached unto the world, and is this ftain fpunged out yet ? I doubt it. Whence arife thofe novel and late difputes of the notes and vifibility of the church ? Is it not from hence they of Rome take the world and the church to be like Mercury and Sofia in Plautus his comedies, fo like one another, that one of them muft wear a toy in his cap, that fo the fpectators may diftinguifh them ? whence comes it that they ftand fo much upon ftate and ceremony in the church ? Is it not from hence, that they think the church muft come in like Agrippa and Berenice in the Acts, as St. Luke fpeaks, Acts xxv. 23. with a great deal of pomp, and train, and fhew, and vanity; and that the fervice of God doth necefﬁarily require this noife and tumult of outward ftate and ceremony ? Whence comes it,

that we are at our wits ends, when we fee perfecution, and fword, and fire to rage againft the true
profeffors of the gofpel? Is it not becaufe, as thefe
bring ruin and defolation upon the kingdoms of
the world, fo we fuppofe they work no other effect in the kingdom of Chrift? All thefe conceits,
and many more of the like nature, fpring out of
no other fountain, than that old inveterate error,
which is fo hardly wiped out of our hearts, That
the ftate of the church and kingdom of Chrift
doth hold fome proportion, fome likenefs with the
ftate and managing of temporal kingdoms: wherefore to pluck out of our hearts a conceit fo antient, fo deeply rooted in us, our Saviour fpake moft
excellently, moft pertinently, and moft fully, when
he tells us, that his church, that ' his kingdom is
' not of this world.'

In which words of his there is contained the
true art of difcovering and knowing the true nature and effence of the church. For as they which
make ftatues, cut and pare away all fuperfluities of
the matter upon which they work; fo our Saviour, to fhew us the true proportion and feature of
the church, prunes away the world and all fuperfluous excrefcencies, and fends her to be feen, as
he did our firft parents in paradife, ftark naked:
as thofe elders in the apocryphal ftory of Sufanna,
when they would fee her beauty, commanded to
take off her mafk; fo he that longs to fee the
beauty of the church, muft pull off that mafk of

the world and outward shew. For as Judah in the book of Genesis, when Thamar sat veiled by the way-side, knew not his daughter from an whore: so whilst the church, the daughter and spouse of Christ, sits veiled with the world, and pomp, and shew, it will be an hard matter to discern her from an harlot. But yet further, to make the difference betwixt these kingdoms the more plainly to appear, and the better to fix it in your memories, I will briefly touch some of these heads in which they are most notoriously differenced.

The first head wherein the difference is seen, are the persons and subjects of this kingdom; for as the kingdom of Christ is not of this world, so the subjects of this kingdom are men of another world, and not of this. Every one of us bears a double person, and accordingly is the subject of a double kingdom: the Holy Ghost, by the Psalmist, divides heaven and earth betwixt God and man, and tells us, as for God, ' he is in heaven, ' but the earth hath he given to the children of ' men:' Ps. cxv. 16. so hath the same Spirit, by the apostle St. Paul, divided every one of our persons into heaven and earth, into an outward and earthly man, and into an inward and heavenly man: 1 Cor. xv. 44. this earth, that is this body of clay, hath he given to the sons of men, to the princes under whose government we live; but heaven, that is the inward and spiritual man, hath he reserved unto himself; they can restrain the out-

ward man, and moderate our outward actions, by
edicts and laws they can tie our hands and our
tongues; thus far they can go, and when they are
gone thus far, they can go no farther *: but to
rule the inward man in our hearts and fouls, to fet
up an imperial throne in our underſtandings and
wills, this part of our government belongs to God
and to Chriſt: thefe are the fubjects, this the government of his kingdom; men may be kings of
earth and bodies, but Chriſt alone is the king of
fpirits and fouls. Yet this inward government hath
influence upon our outward actions; for the authority of kings over our outward man is not fo
abfolute, but that it fuffers a great reſtraint ; it
muſt ſtretch no farther than the prince of our inward man pleafes : for if fecular princes ſtretch
out the ſkirts of their authority to command ought
by which our fouls are prejudiced, the king of
fouls hath in this cafe given us a greater command, ' That we rather obey God than men.' Acts
v. 29.

The fecond head wherein the difference betwixt thefe kingdoms is feen, is in their laws; for
as the kingdoms and the lawgivers, fo are their
laws very different : firſt, in their authors. The
laws by which the commonwealth of Rome was
antiently governed, were the works of many hands;
fome of them were the acts of the people; others

* ——Illa fe jactet in aula

Aeolus.   Virg. Aeneid.

were the decrees of the senate; others, the verdict of their judges; others, the opinions of wise men in cases of doubt; others, the rescripts and answers of their emperors, when they were consulted with *: but in the kingdom of Christ there are no acts of the people or decrees of the senate, no people, no senate, nor wise men, nor judges, had any hand in the laws by which it is governed; only the rescripts and writs of our king run here, these alone are the laws to which the subjects of this kingdom owe obedience. Again, the laws of both these kingdoms differ in regard of their quality and nature; for the laws of the kingdom of Christ are eternal, substantial, indispensible; but laws made by human authority are but light, superficial, and temporary; for all the human authority in the world can never enact one eternal and fundamental law. Let all the laws which men have made be laid together, and you shall see that they were made but upon occasion and circumstance either of time, or place, or persons in matters of themselves indifferent, and therefore either by discontinuance they either fell or ceased of themselves, or by reason of alteration of occasion and circumstance were necessarily revoked: those main fundamental laws upon which all the kingdoms of the world do stand, against theft, against murther, against adultery, dishonouring of parents, or the

* Plebiscita; senatus consulta; edicta praetorum; responsa prudentum; rescripta imperatorum.

like; they were never brought forth by man, neither were they the effects of any parliamentary feffions; they were written in our fouls from the beginning, long before there was any authority regal extant among men: the intent of him who firft enacted them was not to found a temporal, but to bring men to an eternal kingdom; and fo far forth as they are ufed for the maintaining of outward ftate they are ufurped, or at the beft but borrowed: fo that in this work of fettling even the kingdoms of this world, if we compare the laws of God with the laws of men, we fhall find, that God hath, as it were, founded the palaces and caftles, and ftrength of them; but men have, like little children, built houfes of clay and dirt, which every blaft of wind overturns.

The third head by which they may be feen, is in the notes and marks by which they may be known: for the kingdoms of the world are confined, their place is known, their fubjects are difcernable, they have badges, and tokens, and arms by which they are difcovered: but the church hath no fuch notes and marks, no herald hath as yet been found that could blazon the arms of that kingdom. Aefchylus the poet, defcribing the captains that came either for the fiege or defence of the city of Thebes in Beotia, brings them in, in their order, every one with their fhield, and upon his fhield fome device, and over that device a motto or word, according to the ufual fancies of men in that kind; but when he comes to Amphiaraus, he notes of him, that he had no device in his shield, no impress or word; and he gives the reason of it, ' Because he affected not shew, but to be that ' which others profest*.' But to carry marks, and notes, and devices, may well beseem the world which is led by fancy and shew; but the church is like Amphiaraus, she hath no device, no word in her shield, mark and essence with her are all one, and she hath no other note but to be: and, but that learned men must have something to busy their wits withal, these large discourses of the notes and marks by which we may know the church, might very well lie by, as containing nothing else but laborious vanities, and learned impertinences. For the church is not a thing that can be pointed out: the devil could shew our Saviour Christ all the kingdoms of the earth, and the glory of them, I hope the church was none of these; it is the glory of it not to be seen, and the note of it to be invisible; when we call any visible company of professors a church, it is but a word of courtesy: out of charity we hope men to be that which they do profess, and therefore we so speak as if they were that indeed whose name they bear; where, and who they are that make up this kingdom is a question unfit for any man to move:

* ——— Σῆμα δ' ἐκ ἐπῆν κύκλῳ.

Οὐ γὰρ δοχεῖν ἄριστος, ἀλλ' ἐῖναι Σέλει.

Aeschyl. Ἐπτὰ ἐπὶ Θήζαις. v. 597.

for the Lord only knoweth who are his. It is but
Popifh madnefs to fend men up and down the
world to find the church; it is like unto the children of the prophets, in the fecond of Kings ii. 17.
that would needs feek Elijah, or like the nobles in
Jerufalem, that would needs go feek Jeremiah the
prophet, but could not find him, becaufe the
Lord had hid him. Jerem. xxxvi. 26. For in regard of the profeffion, the church (as our Saviour
fpeaks) is like ' a city fet upon a hill,' Matth. v.
14. you may quickly fee and know what true
Chriftianity is; but in regard of the perfons the
kingdom of heaven is, as our Saviour again tells
us, ' like a treafure hidden in a field :' Matth. xiii.
44. except the place of their abode and their perfons were difcernible, who can tell, when we go
thus to feek them, whether we do not like falfe
hounds hunt counter (as the hunters phrafe is)
and fo go from the game. When Saul went to
feek his father's affes, he found a kingdom; let us
take heed left the contrary befall us, left while we
feek our Father's kingdom thus, we find but affes. Will you know where to find the kingdom of
Chrift ? Our Saviour directs you in the gofpel,
' The kingdom of heaven,' faith he, ' cometh not
' by obfervation, neither fhall ye fay, Lo here, or,
' lo there; but the kingdom of heaven is within
' you.' Luke xvii. 20, 21. Let every man therefore retire into himfelf, and fee if he can find this
kingdom in his heart; for if he find it not there,

in vain fhall he find it in all the world befides.

The fourth head wherein the difference of thefe kingdoms is feen, is outward ftate and ceremony; for outward pomp and fhew is one of the greateft ftays of the kingdom of this world: fome thing there muft be to amaze the people, and ftrike them into wonderment, or elfe majefty would quickly be contemned. The fcripture recounting unto us king Solomon's royalty, tells us of his magnificent buildings, of his royal throne, of his fervants, and his attendants, of his cup-bearers, of his meats, and thefe were the things which purchafed unto him the reputation of majefty, above all the kings of the earth. Beloved, the kingdom of Chrift is not like unto Solomon in his royalty, it is like unto David when he had put off all his royalty, and in a linen ephod, danced before the ark : and this plain and natural fimplicity of it is like unto the lilies of the field, more glorious than Solomon in all his royalty. The idolatrous fuperftitions of Paganifm ftood in great need of fuch pompous fo-lemnities; ' for,' as Tertullian tells us, ' being no-' thing of themfelves, they were to gain reputati-' on of being fomething by concealment, and by ' outward ftate make fhew of fomething anfwer-' able to the expectation they had raifed*.' The cafe of the kingdoms of the world is the fame;

---

* Ut opinionem fufpendio cognitionis aedificent, atque ita tantam majeftatem exhibere videantur, quantam praeftruxe-runt cupiditatem. Adv. Valentin. c. 1.

for all this ftate and magnificence ufed in the managing of them is nothing elfe but fecular idolatry, ufed to gain veneration and reverence unto
that, which, in comparifon of the kingdom we
fpeak of, is mere vanity. But the fceptre of the
kingdom of Chrift is a right fceptre, and to add
unto it outward ftate, and riches, and pomp, is
nothing elfe but to make a Centaur, marry and
join the kingdom of Chrift with the kingdom of
the world, which Chrift exprefly here in my text
hath divorced and put afunder. A thing which I
do the rather note, becaufe that the long continuance of fome ceremonies in the church have occafioned many, efpecially of the church of Rome, to
think that there is no religion, no fervice without
thefe ceremonies. Our books tell us of a poor
Spartan, that travelling in another country, and
feeing the beams and pofts of houfes fquared and
carved, afked, ' If the trees grew fo in thofe coun-
' tries?' Beloved, many men that have been long
acquainted with a form of worfhip, fquared and
carved, tricked and fet out with fhew and ceremony, fall upon this Spartan's conceit, think the
trees grow fo, and think that there is no natural
fhape and face of God's fervice but that. I confefs the fervice of God hath evermore fome ceremony attending it, and to our fathers, before
Chrift, may feem to have been neceffary, becaufe
God commanded it : but let us not deceive ourfelves, for neither is ceremony now, neither was

sacrifice then esteemed necessary, neither was the
command of God concerning it, by those to whom
it was given, ever taken to be peremptory: I will
begin the warrant of what I have said out of St.
Chrysostom; for in his comments upon the x. to
the Hebrews, he denies that ever God from the
beginning required, or that it was his will to ordain such an outward form of worship; and asking therefore of himself, ' How then seems he to
' have commanded it?' he answers, ' by conde-
' scending only, and submitting himself unto hu-
' man infirmity*;' now this condescending of
God, wherein it consisted, Oecumenius opens;
for because that men had a conceit, that it was
convenient to offer up some part of their substance
unto God, and so strongly were they possessed with
this conceit, that if they offered it not up to him,
they would offer it up to idols: God, saith he,
rather than they should offer unto idols, required
them to offer unto him. And thus was God understood by the holy men themselves, who lived
under the shadow of those ceremonies: for David, when he had made his peace with God, after that great sin of his, opens this mystery; ' For
' thou requirest not sacrifice,' saith he, ' else would
' I have given it thee; but thou delightest not in

---

* Καὶ τί θαυμάζεις, ἡ νῦν ὁ θελημά ἐςι τῦ θεῦ, ὅπωγε μηδὲ
ἐξαρχῆς θέλημα ἦν, τίς γὰρ ἐξιζήτησε ταῦτα, φησιν, ἐκ τῶν
χειρῶν ὑμῶν; πῶς ἂν αὐτὸς ἐπέταξε; συγκαταβαίνων. Chrysost.
ad Hebraeos. Hom. 18. §. 1.

' burnt offerings: the sacrifice of God is a broken
' spirit: a troubled and a contrite heart, O God,
' dost thou not despise.' Pf. li. 16, 17. After the
revolt of Jeroboam and the ten tribes from the
house of David, there were many devout and religious persons in Israel, and yet we find not that
they used the outward form of worship which was
commanded. Elias and Elisha, two great prophets
in Israel, did they ever go up to Jerusalem to
worship? Obadiah, a great courtier in king A-
hab's court, and one that feared the Lord exceedingly; the seven thousands which bowed not their
knees to Baal, when came they up to the temple
to offer? a thing which doubtless they would
have done, if they had understood the command-
ment of God in that behalf, to have been absolute.
Indeed, if we live in places where true religious
persons do resort, and assemble for the service of
God, it were a sin to neglect it. But otherwise it
is sufficient, if we keep us from the pollutions of
that place to which we are restrained. Why measure we God by ourselves, and because we are led
with gay shews, and goodly things, think it is so
with God *? Seneca reports, that a panto-mimus,
a puppet-player and dancer in Rome, because he
pleased the people well, was wont to go up every
day into the Capitol, and practised his art, and
dance before Jupiter, and thought he did the god

* Quid juvat hoc nostros templis admittere mores?

Perf. Sat. ii. v. 62.

a great pleasure *. Beloved, in many things we
are like unto this puppet-player, and do much
measure God by the people, by the world.

* Doctus Archimimus, senex jam decrepitus, quotidie in
Capitolio mimum agebat, quasi dii libenter spectarent quem
homines desierant.   Seneca apud Augustin. de Civitate Dei.
lib. vi. c. 10.

U 4

OF A

TENDER CONSCIENCE.

1 Sam. xxiv. 5.

And it came to pass afterward, that David's heart smote him, because he had cut off Saul's skirt.

TEmptation is the greatest occasioner of a Christian's honour: indeed, like an enemy, it threatens and endeavours his ruin; but in the conquest of it consists his crown and triumph. Were it possible for us to be at league and truce with this enemy, or to be without danger of gunshot, out of its reach, like the candle in the gospel, that is put under a bushel, the brightest part of our glory were quite obscured. As Maximus Tyrius spake of Hercules, ' If you take from him ' the savage beasts that he slew, and the tyrants ' whom he supprest, his journies and labours, you ' lop and cut off the manifest arms and limbs of ' Hercules's renown *:' so, take from a Christian his temptations, his persecutions, his contentions,

---

* Ἐὰν ἀφίλης αὐτῦ τὰ θηρία ᾗ τὺς δυνάςας ᾗ τὰς ἄνω ᾗ κάτω ὁδὺς, ᾗ τὰ δεινὰ ἐκῶνα πάντα, ἠκρωτηρίασας τὴν ἀρετὴν τῦ Ἡρακλίνς. Dissert. xxxv.

remove him from the devil, from the world, you deprive him of the chief matter and subject of his glory. Take Job from the dunghill; David from Saul; Daniel from the lions; the blessed martyrs from the rack, from the fire, from the sword; and what are they more than other men? As Samson tells Dalilah in the book of Judges, xvi. 17. ' If ' my hair be cut, then my strength will go from ' me, and I shall become weak, and like unto ano-' ther man;' so, Beloved, these things are, as it were, the hair wherein their strength lay; shave that away, and they shall presently become weak, and like unto other men. But temptations are of two sorts, some are like professed and open enemies, which proclaim open war against us, like Goliath, they publicly come forth and challenge us; and such are the outward evils that befall us, loss of goods, sickness, disease, dishonour, infamy, persecutions, and the like: others there are of a more secret, close, and retired nature, like unto traitors, that bear the behaviour and countenance of friends; that espy out their advantage, and set privily upon us; the most troublesome kind of enemies, with whom we can have neither peace nor war, and against whom we can neither be pro-vided nor secure*; these are our own corrupt thoughts and imaginations, which secretly lie in

* Per quos neutrum licet. nec tanquam in bello paratum esse, nec tanquam in pace securum. Seneca de Tranquil. Anim. c. 1.

our hearts, and watch their times to set on us, as
the Philistines did in Dalilah's chamber to surprize
Samson. For let a man but descend into himself, examine his own soul, take as it were an inventory of
the passions, affections, thoughts of his own heart,
look but what the number of them is, and let him
make account of so many enemies *; a sort of e-
nemies by so much the more dangerous, because
that all those outward enemies, of which I but
now spake, cannot come so near as to rase our
skin, or endanger one hair of our head, if these
give them not way: from these, as the asp borrows
poison from the viper †, do those other temptations borrow all their power and strength to hurt us.
For let us take a survey of all the outward afflic-
tions, miseries and calamities, which have befallen
all the saints of God in holy scripture, and let us
suppose them to be all set and bent against some
one alone, yet notwithstanding, as the three children in Daniel walked in the midst of the fire untouched, or as our Saviour Christ passed away
through the midst of the people, that were ga-

* Magnum de medico malum scorpium terra suppurat.
tot venena, quot ingenia; tot pernicies quot et species, tot do-
lores, quot colores; (as Tertullian rimes it.) Adv. Gnosticos.
c. 1. It is impossible to give a literal translation of this passage; it implys that each kind of serpents in Africa had its
own peculiar virulence.

† It would seem that the author here alludes to Tertullian.
adversf. Marcionem. lib. iii. c. 8.

thered together to mifchief him, and throw him
down the hill; fo fhall he be able to pafs from
them all, without any hurt or harm, if fome dif-
contented, or diftruftful, or defpairing, or proud,
or angry, or impure and luftful thought do not
betray him unto them, and as it were open a door,
and let them in. David, who is here the fubjeft of
my text, had very much ado with both forts of
enemies, and by his own experience found, that
this latter rank of fecret and privy enemies, in
ftrength far furpaffed the former. For whom neither the lion, nor the bear, nor Goliath, nor Saul,
nor the Philiftines could ever faften upon, or drive
to any inconvenience, one luftful thought forced
to adultery and murder, one proud conceit ftirred
up to number the people, and drew from God
great inconveniences and plagues both upon himfelf and his kingdom. How careful then ought we
to be, and to ftand on our gaurd, and keep a perpetual watch over our hearts, diligently to try
and examine our thoughts? Nor while we live
fhall we be able perfeftly to mafter, or fecurely to
triumph over them: the only way to fupprefs and
keep them down, is, to have a perpetual and careful jealoufy of them*. Now of this religious care
and watchfulnefs over our own thoughts, hath
the Holy Ghoft recorded for our ufe a notable example in thefe words, which but now I read, 'And

* Nunquam fecuro triumphantur otio, fed tantum follicito
premuntur imperio. Auguft.

' it came to pass afterward, that David's heart
' smote him, because he had cut off Saul's skirt.'

To relate unto you at large the occasion of
these words, and the story from whence they depend, were but to wrong you; for I cannot think
so meanly of your knowledge in scripture, as that
any of you can be ignorant of so famous a passage.
Yet thus much for the better opening of my way
unto such doctrines as I shall draw from this text,
I will call back unto your memories, that Saul
hunting after David to kill him, unwittingly stept
into a cave where David was; David having now
his enemy in his hand, and opportunity to revenge
himself, lets slip all thought of revenging, and only cuts off privily the lap of his garment. For this
deed, so harmless, so innocent, the scripture tells
us that his heart smote him, that he suffered great
anguish and remorse in conscience for it. That
which I will require you to note, is the tenderness
of conscience, and strange scrupulousness in David
for so small an action; for it will yield us a great
lesson. I say it appeareth not by scripture, that
David intended any mischief or treason to Saul, or
that he harboured in heart any disloyal thought
against him. This purpose of cutting off the lap
of Saul's garment, was no other than to purchase
to himself a harmless and honourable testimony of
his innocency, and to prove unto Saul, that there
was no likelihood that *he* sought his blood, whom
he spared, having him at so great an advantage.

Yet notwithſtanding, as if the rending of Saul's garment had been the wounding of Saul's body, or the ſhedding of his blood, David ſtands amazed, and is affrighted at ſo honourable, ſo innocent a thought. ' His heart ſmote him,' ſaith the ſcripture. As men that have been at ſea, and indangered through the raging of winds, and tempeſts, and floods, when afterward the weather is cleared up, the winds allayed, the ſea ſmoothed, and all calm, yet ſcarcely dare they ſet ſail again, and truſt to ſo uncertain, ſo fickle an element : ſo ſeems it to have fared with David in this place ; he was a man ſubject to the ſame paſſions with other men, and doubtleſs, through the raging of unruly and miſorderly affections, he had many times been in danger of ſpiritual ſhipwrack ; wherefore, and though now he could diſcover no tempeſt in his heart, though the face of his thoughts were as ſmooth as glaſs ; yet when he looks upon ſuch fair and calm affections, his heart miſgives him, and he dares not truſt them. This plain contains mighty mountains, this tranquillity is a tempeſt *. The care he hath over his own heart fills him with ſuſpicions, and ſtill he thinks ſomething, he knows not what, may be amiſs. But I muſt come unto the words. ' And it came to paſs afterward, that

---

* Licet in morem ſtagni fuſum aequor arrideat ; magnos hic campus montes habet ; tranquillitas iſta tempeſtas eſt. Hieron. Epiſt. lib. ii. ad Heliodorum.

' David's heart fmote him, becaufe he had cut off
' Saul's fkirt.'

In thefe words we will confider thefe three
things.

1. The perfon, David, ' And David's heart
' fmote him.'

2. David's follicitoufnefs, his care and jealoufy,
very fignificantly expreffed in the next words, ' his
' heart fmote him.'

3. The caufe of this his care and anxiety of
mind, in the laft words, ' becaufe he had cut off
' Saul's fkirt.'

In the *firft* point, that is, in the perfon, we
may confider his greatnefs, he was a king in expectation, and already anointed. A circumftance
by fo much the more confiderable, becaufe that
greatnefs is commonly taken to be a privilege to fin:
to be over careful and confcientious of our cour-
fes and actions are accounted virtues for private
perfons, kings have greater bufineffes than to examine every thought that comes into their hearts.
It is the anfwer of Julia, Auguftus the emperor's
daughter, when fhe was taxed for her too wanton
and licentious living, and counfelled to conform
herfelf to the fobriety and gravity of her father ;
' My father,' faith fhe, ' forgets himfelf to be Cae-
' far the emperor ; but I remember myfelf to be
' Caefar's daughter*. It was the fpeech of Ennius

---

* Pater meus oblivifcitur fe effe Caefarem ; ego vero memini me Caefaris filiam.

the poet, ' Private men in this have a privilege a-
' bove princes; private men may bemoan them-
' felves, but thus to do becomes not princes ∗: '
and if at any time thefe fad and heavy-hearted
thoughts do furprize them, they fhall never want
comforters to difpel them. When Ahab was for
fullennefs fallen down upon his bed, becaufe Na-
both would not yield him his vineyard, Jezebel is
prefently at hand, and asks him, ' Art thou this
' day king of Ifrael ?' 1 Kings xxi. 7. When Am-
mon pined away in the inceftuous love of his fifter
Thamar, Jonadab his companion comes unto him,
and asks him, ' Why is the king's fon fad every
' day ?' 2 Sam. xiii. 4. So that, as it feems, great
perfons can never be much or long fad. Yet David forgets his greatnefs, forgets his many occafions, gives no ear to his companions about him,
but gives himfelf over to a fcrupulous and ferious
confideration of an action in fhew and countenance
but light.

Secondly, As the perfon is great, fo is the care
and remorfe conceived upon the confideration of
his action exceeding great, which is our fecond
part: and therefore the Holy Ghoft expreffes it in
very fignificant terms: ' His heart fmote him;' a
phrafe in fcripture ufed by the Holy Ghoft, when
men begin to be fenfible, and repent them of fome
fin. When David had committed that great fin

∗ Plebs in hoc regi ante-ftat loco;
   Licet lachrimari plebi, regi honeftè non licet.

of numbering the people, and began to be apprehenfive of it, the fcripture tells us, that ' David's
' heart fmote him, when he had commanded Joab
' to number the people.' 1 Kings xxiv. 1 o. Wherefore by this fmiting we may not here underftand
fome light touch of confcience, like a grain of
powder, prefently kindled, and prefently gone :
for the moft hard and flinty hearts many times
yield fuch fparks as thefe. He that is moft flefhed
in fin, commits it not without fome remorfe ; for
fin evermore leaves fome fcruple, fome fting, fome
loathfomenefs in the hearts of thofe that are moft
inamoured of it. But as Simeon tells the bleffed
virgin in St. Luke's gofpel, ii, 3 5. A fword fhall
pierce through thine heart ; fo it feems to have been
with David. It was not fome light touch to rafe
only the furface and skin of the heart, but like a
fword it pierced deep into him : to teach us one
leffon, that actions fpotted, though but with the
leaft fufpicion of fin, ought not carelefsly to be
paffed by, or flightly glanced at, but we ought to
be deeply apprehenfive of them, and beftow greateft care and confideration upon them.

The *third* part of our text containeth the caufe
of David's remorfe, in the laft words, ' becaufe
' he cut off Saul's skirt.' In the two former parts
we had to do with greatnefs : there was 1. a great
perfon, and 2. great remorfe ; can we in this
third part find out any great caufe or reafon of
this, fo to make all parts proportionable ? Cer-

tainly he that fhall attentively read and weigh
thefe firft words of my text, and know the ftory,
might think that David had committed fome notable error, as fome great oppreffion, or fome cruel
flaughter, or fome fuch royal fin, which none but
kings and great men can commit. But, Beloved,
this my text feems to be like the windows in Solomon's temple, broad within, but narrow without: or like a pyramid, large and fpacious at
the bafis and ground of it, but fmall and fharp
at the top. The perfon and remorfe, which are
the ground and fubject of my text, both are great
and large; but the caufe, which is the very crown
and top of all, that is very fmall, yea peradventure none at all. For whether it be that myfelf, ac-
cuftomed to greater fins, and now grown old in
them, have loft all fenfe of fmall and petty errors,
or whether indeed there be no error at all in this
action of David, but only fome fancy, fome jealoufy arifing out of that godly and careful watch
he kept over all his ways; or whatfoever elfe it
was that caufed this fcruple or remorfe in David,
it is a very hard matter to difcover, and yet notwithftanding, that we may make more open pafs
unto fuch doctrines as I fhall raife out of thefe
words, let us a little fcan and confider what it was
in this action that made David thus ftrangely fcrupulous.

And firft of all, was it for that he had touched
and taken that which was none of his own, and

therefore might feem to fall within the compafs of the law againft injury and purloining? This feems not probable: for when afterward, in the like cafe, he came upon Saul as he was fleeping in the camp, and took from him the fpear and the pot of water which ftood at his head, we do not read that his head, that his heart fmote him, and yet he took what was none of his

Or, 2ly, was it that he did wrong and difho-nour Saul in mangling his garment? Indeed the Jews have a tradition, that this was the fin of which David was here fo fenfible. And therefore fay they, whereas we read in the firft of Kings, that when David grew old, they covered him with cloaths, but he gat no heat, this was the punifh-ment of his fin committed againft Saul: God fo providing, that garments fhould not be ferviceable to him, who had offended in wronging Saul's gar-ments. But this I muft let go as a fable.

Or, 3ly, was it that he had unadvifedly given way to fome difloyal thought, and at firft refolved to revenge himfelf on Saul, having him at the ad-vantage, though afterward he repented? Indeed St. Chryfoftom thinks fo; and therefore on thofe words at the latter end of the verfe next before my text, 'And David arofe,' he notes, 'See you ' not, faith he, what a tempeft of rage and anger ' begins to rife in him *;' for he fuppofeth him

* Εἶδις πᾶς ἠγίρθη τῆς ὀργῆς ὁ χειμών.   Hom. de Davide et Saule. i. §. 4.

to arife in heat and fury, with a refolution for
blood; but it pleafed God, in the way, to make
him relent, and change the purpofe of revenge into the action of cutting off his fkirt; and that
this fmiting of David's heart was nothing elfe but
his repenting himfelf for giving over-hafty entertainment to fuch a rebellious thought. But, Beloved, 'who fhall lay any thing to the charge of
' God's elect?' Rom. viii. 33. David's thoughts
were only known to God and himfelf. Since therefore God gives not this as a reafon of David's remorfe, but another thing; far be it from me, that
I fhould wrong David fo far, as to burden him
with that, with which none but God can charge
him. I rather chufe to follow St. Bafil's rule,
' Let the fcriptures be underftood as they lie *.'
The fcripture tells us, David's heart fmote him,
becaufe he cut off the fkirt of Saul's garment, and
not becaufe he had conceived againft Saul any
thought of blood. But what caufe then fhall we
give of David's remorfe? none other, Beloved,
but that religious and careful jealoufy which ftill
he had over his own thoughts, which made him
to fufpect all things, be they never fo fafe †, and
never to think himfelf fecure from the contagion

---

* Νοείσθω ὡς γέγραπlαι.——A good rule, which the fathers,
and particularly St. Bafil himfelf, would have done well to
have obferved. See his commentary upon Pf. xxviii. in our
tranflation Pf xxix.

† Pietatis affectu etiam quae tuta funt formidare. Hier.

of fin. It was with David, as it was wont to be
with men that are often troubled with ficknesses
and difeafes; they difquiet themfelves with every
little alteration in their bodies, repair to the phyfician when they are well, and think every heat
to be an ague-fit: thefe men are not fick; but
they do no know what it is to be in health *. In
the fame ftate is David, he had been often infected
with fpiritual weaknefs and difeafe, and therefore
he fufpects every motion of his heart, and takes
every thought to be a temptation; his foul was
not fick of any fin, but he did not know what it
was to be in fpiritual health.

For us, and for our ufe, hath the Holy Ghoft
regiftered this example of fcruple and tendernefs
of confcience. Let us return to ourfelves, and fee
what leffons we may learn hence for our behoof.
Men ufually are either grown old in fin, and therefore their eye-fight is decayed, they cannot eafily
fee and difcern fmaller fins: or elfe as Hagar, in
the book of Genefis xxi. 1 6. laid Ifmael afar off
from her, that fhe might not be grieved with the
fight of him; fo we labour to lay our fins far out
of ken, that the memory and fight of them might

---

* Qui ex longa et gravi valetudine expliciti, motiunculis,
levibufque interim offenfis perftringuntur, et cum reliquias effugerint, fufpicionibus tamen inquietantur, medicifque jam
fani manum porrigunt, et omnem calorem corporis fui calumniantur; horum non parum fanum eft corpus, fed fanitati parum affuevit. Seneca de tranquil. anim. c. 2.

not exafperate and trouble us. For the cure of both thefe infirmities, I have borrowed out of the Lord's treafury an optic glafs, which, if we ufe it, will reftore our decayed eye-fight, and quicken and make us read our fins in the fmalleft print; and let them lie never fo far from us, yet will it prefent them unto us in their true quantity and greatnefs. Towards the better ufe of which fpiritual glafs, one leffon would I efpecially commend unto you; to be perpetually jealous and fufpicious of your thoughts, and to be quick-fcented, eafily to trace the footing of fin, to be eafily fenfible of it, when we think ourfelves to have done amifs: a leffon naturally arifing, as I take it, out of David's example, commended unto us in this place. Now how abfolutely behooveful it is for us to hold a perpetual watch over our hearts, and be jealous of fuch thoughts as fpring out of them, it will appear by thefe reafons.

Firft, becaufe that fin is of fuch a fly infinuating nature, that it will privily creep in, and clofely cleave to our thoughts and intents, though we perceive it not. For as waters, though of themfelves moft pure, will relifh and favour of the earth and foil through which they pafs: fo thoughts in themfelves good, paffing through the corrupt and evil ground of our hearts, cannot but receive fome tincture, fome dye, fome relifh from them. When David had an intent to build God an houfe, he doubtlefs conceived no otherwife of

X 3

this his intent, than of a religious and honourable
purpose, and, in outward appearance, there was no
cause why he should doubt of God's acceptance;
yet we see this purpose of his misliked by God,
and rejected, and the reason given, ' because thou
' art a man of blood.' 1 Chron. xxii. 8. How
shall we then secure ourselves of any thought, if
such an intent as this, so favouring of zeal, of
sanctification, of love unto the glory of God, have
such a flaw in it as makes it unprofitable? and
how necessary is it, that we bring all our imaginations and intents to the fire and to the refining pot,
so throughly to try them, and bring them to their
highest point of purity and perfection? Be it, peradventure, that the action be in itself good; if it
be liable to any suspicion of evil, it is enough to
blast it. It is the Holy Ghost's rule, given by the
blessed apostle, that we ' abstain from all shew and
' appearance of evil,' 1 Thes. v. 22. that we refrain
as much as possible from all such actions as are capable of misconstruction. What is more lawful,
than for the labourer to have his hire? than for
those that labour in the gospel, to live by the gospel? Yet we see St. Paul refused this liberty, and
chose rather to work with his own hands; only
for this reason, because he would not give occasion to any, that would misinterpret his action, to
live at others cost, and feed on the sweat of others
brows. What befalls princes many times, and
great persons that have abused their authority, the

people rife and fupprefs them, deface their ftatues, forbid their coin, put away all things that bear any memory of them : fo feems our bleffed apoftle to deal here : look what actions they be which bear any infcription, any image and title, any fhew or fpot of fin, thefe hath he thought good even to banifh and quite prohibit. Our prophane ftories tell us, that when Julius Caefar had divorced his wife, being asked why he did fo, fince nothing was brought againft her to prove her difhoneft, his anfwer was, ' That fhe that will be wife of ' Caefar muft not only be free from difhonefty, ' but from all fufpicion of it * :' Beloved, St. Paul tells the Corinthians, that he had ' efpoufed them ' unto one hufband, that he might deliver them as ' a chafte virgin unto Chrift;' 2 Cor. xi. 2. and God every where in fcripture compares his church unto an efpoufed wife, and himfelf unto an hufband, a hufband far more jealous than ever Caefar was : How careful then muft that foul be, that intends to marry itfelf to fuch a jealous hufband, to abftain not only from all pollution of fin, but from all fufpicion of it ? Laft of all, it is Tertullian's fpeech, ' How much more will he dread to ' commit what is evil, who ftands in awe of doing ' what is lawful †.' It is wifdom fometimes to

* Meos tam fufpicione quam crimine judico carere oportere. Suet. Jul. Caef. c. 74.

† Quanto facilius illicita timebit, qui etiam licita verebitur. De cultu foeminarum. c. 10.

suspect and shun things that are lawful; for there are many actions in themselves good, which yet to many men become occasions of sin and scandal: for it is with our actions as it is with our meats and drinks; as divers meats fit not to divers constitutions of body, so all actions accord not well with all tempers of mind: as therefore what dish it is we easily surfeit of, though it be otherwise good, it is wisdom totally to abstain from; so look what actions they be in which we find ourselves prone to sin, it is good spiritual physic to use abstinence, and quite to leave them. For if our Saviour commands us to pluck out our eyes, and pare off our hands, if once they become unto us cause of sin, how much more then must we prune away all inward thoughts, all outward circumstances, which become occasion of offence unto us?

A second reason, why I would persuade you to entertain a jealousy of all your thoughts and actions, is a natural over-charitable affection, which I see to be in most men unto their own ways; and which is strange, the worse they are, the more are we naturally inclined to favour them: the reason is, because the worse they are, the more they are our own. When question was sometime made, Why good herbs grow so sparingly, and with great labour and pains, whereas weeds grow apace without any culture and tilling? it was answered, That the earth was a natural mother to

the one, to the other fhe was a ftep-mother; the
one fhe brought forth of herfelf, to the other fhe
was conftrained. Beloved, it is with our hearts
as it is with the earth, the natural fruit of them
is weeds and evil thoughts, unto them our hearts
are as mothers, they fpring up in us of themfelves,
without any care or manuring: but as for good
thoughts, if they be found in our hearts, they are
not natural, they are fet there by a high hand,
they are there by a kind of fpiritual inoculation
and grafting, as men graft apples and kind fruits
upon thorns and crabs: no marvel then, if like
choice herbs and fruits, they grow fo tenderly,
and need fo much care and cherifhing. As therefore parents, though their own children be very
deformed, yet love them more than others, though
more beautiful: fo corrupt and evil thoughts are
naturally dearer unto us than good, becaufe we
are as mothers unto them, to the reft we are but
ftep-dames.

Two notable fruits there are of this over-chari-
tablenefs to our own actions. Firft, a willingnefs
that we have to flatter, to deceive, and abufe our
own felves by pretences and excufes. There is a
plain, a downright, and as it were a country reprobate, one that fees his fin, and cares not much
to excufe it, and is content to go on, and as it
were in fimplicity to caft himfelf away: there is a
more witty, more refined, and, as it were, a more
gentleman-like reprobate, one that ftrives to fmooth

and gild over his fin, to deceive others and himfelf with excufes and apologies ; ' to take great
pains,' as St. Bafil fpeaks, 'and with the expence of
' a great deal of wit and art to damn himfelf *.'
When Saul, being fent againft Amalek, had fpared Agag and the beft and fatteft of the prey, at
Samuel's coming to vifit him, how doth he wipe
his mouth, as if all had been well, and trimly com-
pofes himfelf to entertain him, ' Bleffed art thou
' of the Lord, I have performed the command-
' ment of the Lord ?' 1 Sam. xv. 1 3. And when
Samuel had fhewed him his error, how quickly
hath he his excufe at his fingers ends, ' We have
' fpared the beft of the fheep and of the oxen to
' facrifice unto the Lord ?' ver. 1 6. ' He thinks,'
as Tertulliau fpeaks, ' to gull almighty God with
' fair and flattering pretences, and becomes a bawd
' to his own vice † ;' it is the common error of us
all, and in moft of our actions we do as Saul did,
endeavour to put tricks upon ourfelves: Beloved,
were we not partial, but rigid cenfurers of our own
thoughts, this corrupt fruit would quickly rot
and fall away.

Again, there is a fecond fruit fpringing out of
this favour and dotage in our own actions, an error as common, though not fo dangerous, for we
are content many times to acknowledge that fome-

---

* Μετὰ πλείονος τίχνης, ὁ παρασκιυῆς, ὁ πραγματείας ἀπο-
λίσθαι.

† Et Deo adulatur, et fibi lenocinatus.

thing is amifs in our actions, we will confefs them
to be fins, but we account of them as little fins,
fins of a leffer fize, not fo fearful, eafily pardonable. There is a finner, who by committing fome
great and heinous crime, as Tertullian calls it,
' fuch a fin as with open mouth devours falvati-
' on *,' doth, as it were, with one ftep leap into
hell, and of this kind of finners the number is
fewer: but abundance there are, who avoiding
great and heinous fins, by committing leffer fins,
as they think, can be content to go by degrees,
and as it were ftep by ftep into hell. Beloved, let
us a little put on the optic glafs I but now fpake
of, that we may fee whether any fin be fo fmall as
we take it: I know there is difference of fins ;
our Saviour tells us, that there is a beam, and
there is a mote: but withal this I know, that the
beft way to keep us from fin, is to loath even the
leaft, as if it were the greateft †; if we look
through this glafs, it will make us think every mote
a beam. Sins in themfelves are unequal, but in regard of us, and of our endeavour to avoid them,
they are all equal. ' Fly from evil,' faith the Pfalmift, Pf. xxxvii. 27. [old tranflation] he tells us
not, that there is one greater evil from which we
muft fly, and another lefs, from which it is e-
nough if we do but go: but he bids us fly, and to

* Crimen devoratorium falutis. De Idolatr. c. 1.

† Minima pro maximis cavere. Hieron. Epift. lib. ii.
ad Celantiam.

make hafte alike from all. To think that a fin is
lefs than it is, may be dangerous, for it makes us
the lefs careful to avoid it: but to miftake on the
other hand, and think a fin greater than it is,
this is a very profitable error. Would to God we
did always thus err; for befides that there is no
danger in it, it makes us more fearful to commit
fin. Our Saviour reprehends the Pharifees in the
gofpel, becaufe they could ' ftrain at gnats, but
' fwallow camels;' Matth. xxiii. 24. but yet it is
true, that men learn at length to fwallow camels,
by fwallowing gnats at firft: no finner fo hardy
as to fet upon the greateft fins at firft *. The way
by which men train up themfelves to the committing grofs and heinous fins, is by not being
at firft confcientious of leffer fins; ' and indeed,'
faith Paulinus in St. Jerom, ' who dares call any
' fin little, that is committed againft God † ? '
Small contempts againft great princes are accounted great overfights ; for what is wanting in the
thing, is made up in the worth of the perfon.
How great a fin then is the fmalleft contempt that
is done againft God? It is the beft wifdom for
us, not fo much to confider what is commanded,
as who it is that commanded it; to confider, I

* Nemo repente fuit turpiffimus. Juvenal.

† Et fane nefcio, an poffimus leve aliquod peccatum dicere quod in Dei contemptum admittitur. Lib. ii. Epift. ad Celantiam. *This epiftle is fuppofed to be by Paulinus, although in-
ferted in the works of Jerom.*

fay, not the fmallnefs of the law, but the greatnefs of the lawgiver *. Sins comparatively may be
counted greater or leffer, but abfolutely none can
be counted fmall. To conclude then this point,
' Charity fufpecteth no harm,' faith St. Paul,
1 Cor. xiii. 6. true, but we muft note, that fome
virtues in us concern ourfelves, as faith, hope,
temperance, and the like: fome virtues concern
not ourfelves, but others; but fuch an one is charity. Charity that wills Chriftians to think well
of all others, can have little room upon ourfelves:
let us then make ufe of this charity towards our
neighbours; hope the beft of all their actions;
but let us take heed how we be over-charitably
minded to ourfelves. Caefar profeffed, that he
would rather die, than fufpect his friends ; and
he fped accordingly, for he died by the treachery
of thofe friends whom he fufpected not. Let us
take heed how we he over-kind unto our own
thoughts, how we think it an error to be too fufpicious of them: ' and thou too my fon†;' peradventure thofe fons of our own hearts, whom we
leaft fufpect, will in the end prove thofe who fhall
betray us.

But I come to a third reafon. A third reafon

---

* Prudentiffimus ille eft, qui non tam confiderat quid juf-
tum fit, quam illum, qui jufferit ; nec quantitatem imperii,
fed imperantis cogitat dignitatem. Ibid.

† Καὶ σὺ τίκνον. —— The words of Caefar to Decimus
Brutus.

why I shall advise you to this jealousy over your own thoughts, is the difficulty of discovering them betime, and discerning of what spirit they are. For our heart is like that field in the gospel, in which the husbandman sows good corn, and the enemy sows tares. Matth. xiii. 25. God infuseth good thoughts, and the devil ill. Now as weeds many times at their first budding are hardly known from good herbs; so, at the first springing and budding of our thoughts, a hard matter it is to know the weed from the good herb, the corn from the tare. As Judah, in the book of Genesis, knew not Tamar, till the fruit of his sin committed with her began to shew itself: so, till the fruits of our thoughts and purposes begin to appear, except we search very narrowly, we can scarcely discover of what rank they are. 'Then the iron that lay in 'the bottom, will swim at the top of the water, 'and among the pleasant palm-trees will be found 'the bitterness of myrrh*.' We read in the second of Samuel, vi. 7. that when the ark was brought from Kirjath-jearim, the oxen that drew the cart shook it, and Uzzah reaching out his hand

* It is probable that this passage will seem obscure to many readers. The author alludes to the complaint which Jerom makes of the avarice of some monks in his age. 'Vi-'dimus nuper et planximus Croesi opes unius morte depre-'hensas, urbisque stipes, quasi in usus pauperum congregatas, 'stirpi et posteris derelictas. *Tunc ferrum quod latebat in pro-'fundo supernatavit aquae, et inter palmarum arbores myrrhae*

to save it from falling, for his good service was
laid dead in the place. Doubtless Uzzah his accompanying the ark was a sign of his love unto it;
his love unto it begat in him a fear to see it in
danger; his fear to see it in danger bred in him a
desire to keep it from danger. See, Beloved, what
a number of golden thoughts are here; yet, as
we read in the book of Job, when ' the servants of
' God came and stood before him, Satan also came
' and stood amongst them;' Job i. 6. So in this
chorus and quire of these angelical thoughts, the
devil finds a place to rest himself in: for this desire of Uzzah to save the ark from danger, made
him forget what was written, that none should
touch the ark, save only the priests; Numb. iii. 38.
the breach of which precept brought that fearful judgment upon him. You see, Beloved, that
though the course of our thoughts be like Jacob's
ladder, and God himself be at one end of them,
yet Satan, if he can, will be at the other. Let
us learn, by this example of Uzzah, betimes to
discover our thoughts, and not to suffer them to
grow till their fruit betray them. Indeed our Saviour hath given us a rule, ' You shall know them
' by their fruits;' Matth. vii. 16. but we must

' amaritudo monstrata est.' He compares selfishness and rapa-
city, among those of the monastic profession, to the bitter waters of Marah, near the palm-trees of Elim, Exod. xv. 23. 27.
and the discovery of such secret enormities to ' the iron that
' did swim.' 2 Kings vi. 6.

take heed that we extend not this rule too far:
Uzzah felt the fruit of his thoughts to his own
coft. It is never good trying conclufions there,
where the chaftifement inftantly follows the offence. Let us learn to decipher our thoughts
then, when we may do it without danger, whilft
they are in the feed, whilft they are yet but budding and peeping above ground, whilft yet there
is only need of the weed-hook, and not of the
hatchet *.

A *fourth* reafon yet there is, for which I would
counfel you to hold a ftrict hand over your
thoughts, and it is, becaufe that from outward
fins we can better preferve ourfelves, than from
our fins in thought. Beloved, there is a tranfient
fin, and there is an immanent fin; there is a fin
that is outwardly acted by the fervice of the body, there is a fin that requires not the help of
the body, but is committed inwardly in the very
thought and foul, a fpeculative or an intellectual
fin. Outward fins are many ways paffed by, means
may be wanting, company may hinder, time and
place may be inconvenient; but for fpeculative fins,
or fins in thought, all times, all occafions, all places, are alike. ' A man,' faith St. Bafil, ' of great
' gravity and countenance fits in the midft of the
' market-place, with many hundreds about him,
' and looking upon him, yet notwithftanding this
' man, even this man, in the midft of all the compa-

* Donec farculo tantum opus eft, non fecuri.

' ny, fancies to himself what he desires, and in
' his imaginations goes unto the place of sin, or
' rather retires into his own heart, and there he
' finds place and means to commit a sin that hath
' no witness but God*. If we retire to our private chambers, these sins will follow us thither, and
as Baanah and Rechab did by Ish-bosheth Saul's
son, they will find us out upon our beds, and slay
us there. If we go to the church, they will find us
out there, and as Adrammelech and Sharezer slew
Sennacherib, whilst he was worshipping his god;
they will set upon us even in the midst of our ho-
liest meditations and prayers: neither chamber
no church, no place so private, none so holy, that
can give us sanctuary, or shelter us from them.
St. Jerom confesses thus much of himself, that
when he had forsaken the world, all outward occasions of sin, and gone into the desert, and shut
himself up in a poor cell, and macerated his body
with watchings, with fastings, and perpetual prayers
and religious exercise †, yet could he not be se-

---

* Καὶ πῦ τὶς τῶν σοβαρῶν ἢ καλωφρυωμένων ἐπὶ σεμνότηι, πλάσμα
σωφροσύνης ἔξωθεν περικείμενος, ἐν μέσαις καθιζόμενος πολλάκις ταῖς
ἐπ' ἀρετῇ αὐτὸν μακαρίζουσιν, ἀπέδραμα τῇ διανοίᾳ πρὸς τὸν τῆς ἁμαρ-
τίας τόπον ἐν τῷ ἀφανεῖ τῆς καρδίας κινήματι. Ἴδε τῇ φαντασίᾳ καὶ
σκιαδαζόμενος, ἀνετυπώσατο τινὰ ὁμιλίαν οὐκ εὐπρεπῆ, καὶ ὅλως ἐν τῷ
κρυφαίῳ τῆς καρδίας ἐργαστηρίῳ, ἐναργῶς ἐν ἑαυτῷ τὴν ἡδονὴν ζωγρα-
φήσας, ἁμάρτυρον ἴσω τὴν ἁμαρτίαν εἰργάσατο, ἀγνοῶτος πᾶσιν,
ἕως ἂν ἔλθῃ ὁ ἀποκαλύπτων τὰ κρυπτὰ τοῦ σκότους, ἢ φανερῶν τὰς
βουλὰς τῶν καρδιῶν. ‖Homil. ad illud, Attende tibi ipsi.

† In the former editions, ~~some corrupted~~ Greek ~~words~~,

Y

cure from them; ' his body was now grown pale,
' and meagre, and cold, but yet his heart burnt with
' unlawful desires*.'. Again, they are sins of quick
and easy dispatch; they are done, as St. Basil
notes, in a moment of time, without labour of
body, without care of mind †: one wanton look
makes us guilty of adultery, one angry conceit
guilty of murder, one covetous conceit guilty of
robbery. Whatsoever is outwardly committed, either with difficulty of circumstance, or labour of
body, or danger of law, *that* is inwardly committed in the soul without any trouble at all. Fifthly,
consider but the strength of your thoughts, and
you will see there is great reason to keep them
low; for there was no man yet that ever was foil-
ed but by them, and not by the outward acting
of sin. For the outward action is but the bark of
the sin; but the very body and substance of sin is
the wicked thought. ' Beware of men,' saith our
Saviour, Matth. x. 17. when he gave his apostles
counsel how to provide for their safety in times of
outward danger: but if you will provide against

particularly καμκνίαις, are here quoted: it is probable that the
author meant to allude to Gr. Nazianzen. de vita sua. vol. 2.
Rig. edit. Morel.

Εὐχαῖς, στιναγμοῖς, δάκρυσι, χαμιυνίαις. This last word,
which signifies ' lying on the ground,' the translator of Nazianzen renders thus, *chameunia.*

* Pallebant ora jejuniis, et mens desideriis aestuabat in fri-
gido corpore.   Ad Eustoch. de custod. virginitatis.

† Αχρόνως, ἀκόπως, ἀπραγματιύτως.

inward dangers, we shall not need to beware of
men, or of any outward force whatsoever. Let
every man beware of himself, for in this case, every man is his own greatest enemy.

To draw then to a conclusion : That sins of
thoughts prevail not against us, our way is, by a
jealous care, first, to prevent them ; and to this
hath the greatest part of my discourse hitherto
tended. Secondly, if we have suffered them to
gain a little ground upon us, let us betimes take
the reins into our own hands, and pull them back
again, and cast out our adversary whilst he is yet
weak. ' Such,' saith St. Chrysostom, ' are the souls
' of holy men; their recovery is so quick, that
' they may seem to have risen before they fell *.'
It is a great sign of spiritual life in us, to be quickly sensible of the first track and footing of sin.
For as bodies of the best and purest complexion
have their senses quickest, so that soul which soon-
est perceives the first scent of sin, is of the divinest
temper. Our books tell us, that Dionysius the
Tyrant was grown so gross and fat, that though
men thrust bodkins into him, he could not feel
it †. Beloved, there is a sinner like unto this Dionysius ; David tells us of him, when he describes
unto us a sinner ' whose heart is fat as brawn.'
Pf. cxix. 70. [old translation.] That we fall not
therefore into that like stupidity and senselessness,

* Τοιαῦται γὰρ τῶν ἁγίων αἱ ψυχαὶ, πρὶν ἔπεσον ἀνίσανται.
† Aelian. var. Hist. lib. ix. c. 13.

our way is to catch thofe young foxes, and ftrangle them in the neft. . ' Suffer not your thoughts,' faith St. Jerom, ' to increafe and gather ftrength ' upon you *.' For as the man that touches only at hot iron, and ftays not on it, burns not his hand, fo the firft glances of evil thoughts harm us not; the harm is, if by confent, though never fo little, you ftay upon them. To be free from all onfet of evil thoughts is a matter impoffible, whilft we have thefe hearts of flefh. That man is praife-worthy, who affoon as any unclean thought, any child of Babylon is born in his heart, ftraightway ftrangles it in the birth, and dafhes it againft the rock, which rock is Chrift †.

---

* Nolo finas cogitationes crefcere.　Ad Euftoch. de Cuftod. Virginitatis.

† Ille laudatur, ille praedicatur beatus, qui ut coeperit co-gitare fordida, ftatim interficit cogitatus, et allidit ad petram, petra autem eft Chriftus.　Hieron. ibid.

THE END OF THE SECOND VOLUME.